LANGUAGE ISSUES IN COMPARATIVE EDUCATION

COMPARATIVE AND INTERNATIONAL EDUCATION:
A DIVERSITY OF VOICES
Volume 24

Scope

Comparative and International Education: A Diversity of Voices aims to provide a comprehensive range of titles, making available to readers work from across the comparative and international education research community. Authors will represent as broad a range of voices as possible, from geographic, cultural and ideological standpoints. The editors are making a conscious effort to disseminate the work of newer scholars as well as that of well-established writers. The series includes authored books and edited works focusing upon current issues and controversies in a field that is undergoing changes as profound as the geopolitical and economic forces that are reshaping our worlds. The series aims to provide books which present new work, in which the range of methodologies associated with comparative education and international education are both exemplified and opened up for debate. As the series develops, it is intended that new writers from settings and locations not frequently part of the English language discourse will find a place in the list.

Language Issues in Comparative Education

Inclusive Teaching and Learning in Non-Dominant
Languages and Cultures

Edited by

Carol Benson
Stockholm University, Stockholm, Sweden

and

Kimmo Kosonen
Payap University & SIL International, Chiang Mai, Thailand

SENSE PUBLISHERS
ROTTERDAM / BOSTON / TAIPEI

A C.I.P. record for this book is available from the Library of Congress.

ISBN 978-94-6209-216-7 (paperback)
ISBN 978-94-6209-217-4 (hardback)
ISBN 978-94-6209-218-1 (e-book)

Published by: Sense Publishers,
P.O. Box 21858, 3001 AW Rotterdam, The Netherlands
https://www.sensepublishers.com/

Printed on acid-free paper

DEDICATION

This book is dedicated with love and respect to the memory of

Dr. Neville Alexander
22 October 1936–27 August 2012

proponent of a multilingual, multicultural South Africa
and world

"*Serious, solid, convincing, interesting, lots of new data. All educational decision makers need this book – so do teachers and politicians. If research can change people's monolingual mindset and give non-dominant language speakers (and, with them, all of us) a chance, this is the book.*"
– **Tove Skutnabb-Kangas**, Emerita, Åbo Akademi University, Finland

"*This book moves education toward liberation of students and educators, while liberating readers from unquestioned assumptions in the language and education field. Drawing on cases from minoritized communities in Asia, Africa, and the Americas, the book takes the local perspective of non-dominant language communities in arguing for a multilingual habitus in educational development. Beyond the volume's comprehensiveness and comparative focus, Benson and Kosonen masterfully extend theories and clarify terminology that is inclusive of the non-dominant contexts that are here included.*"
– **Ofelia García**, City University of New York, USA

"*Language Issues in Comparative Education is an important contribution to our understanding of the complex interplay between language policies and practices in education and the broader socio-political and economic forces that shape society as a whole. A richly textured collection, it offers a powerful vision of the possible, now and in the future.*"
– **Alamin Mazrui**, Rutgers State University of New Jersey, USA

"*Careful attention to the language part of multilingual education, and the intimate connection of language and culture, makes this book essential reading for researchers and practitioners alike. Different contexts, different issues, different foci distinguish the chapters, but the imperative to incorporate learners' languages in their educational experience unites them.*"
– **Carolyn Temple Adger,** Center for Applied Linguistics, Washington DC, USA

TABLE OF CONTENTS

FOREWORD

SHELDON SHAEFFER

I'm a glass half-empty kind of person, inclined to a pessimistic view of the present and even more of the future. From this point of view, the world's "now" is becoming ever less inclusive and its "then" ever less likely to be sustainable.

Many countries of the world have achieved or are in the process of achieving many of the Millennium Development Goals (MDGs) and Education for All (EFA) targets set for the world in 2000 and due to be achieved by 2015. This is the good, glass half-full picture. But many of these achievements have been the result of increases in nationally aggregated averages (e.g. in school enrolment, child survival etc.) which have masked what are often sharply increased disparities *within* nations (glass half-empty!) by gender, ability, location (urban-rural-remote), socio-economic status (upper versus lower quintile) and ethnic/linguistic status (majority/dominant versus minority/non-dominant). Thus, the world is becoming both less inclusive, with the marginalized and disempowered becoming more so, and less sustainable, as many demographic, social, economic, and environmental trends appear to be going in the wrong direction. It is therefore essential to address the reasons for these trends and examine what can be done to fill the glass.

This volume, "Language Issues in Comparative Education: Inclusive Teaching and Learning in Non-dominant Languages and Cultures," addresses these trends in two critical ways. First, the authors explore the role of languages and cultures in education systems in transforming and liberating the potential of learners from ethnolinguistic communities usually excluded from access to quality basic education. The logic is persuasive: (1) hundreds of millions of children around the world are forced to study in a language they barely understand; and (2) children become most easily literate in their mother tongue, their language of daily use, and the skills they gain in this process can be applied subsequently to gain literacy in national and international languages. Bringing their languages and cultures into the classroom is thus an important way to make education more inclusive and equitable.

Some of the authors explore opposition to this logic in terms of practical obstacles (too many languages, no orthographies, no teachers, no texts, no funds) – obstacles usually able to be resolved by well-planned mother tongue-based programs – and, more profoundly, a deeply embedded ideology of national unity (one people, one language, one nation) and a consequent fear of doing anything to empower groups likely to threaten this ideology. They also explore how ethnolinguistic minorities or even majorities are kept out of the mainstream of their nation's social, economic, and political life and institutions, and how these excluded people are let into that mainstream life – if at all – only once they leave behind their ethnic and linguistic identity and take on the language and culture of the dominant society, a society usually larger in numbers, richer, and more politically powerful.

The contributions of this volume should also be seen in light of the broader issue – beyond education but able to be prevented by education – of the absolute loss of languages and the cultures that carry them in the context of a globalizing and modernizing world. Languages are living things; they need to develop, thrive, and be used effectively, including in education – and many need to be revitalized and even saved from an early death – in order for all people of the world, especially those most excluded and disadvantaged, to benefit from development. A dynamic, living language, in other words, is essential to the well-being and sustainability of any human society. But linguistic diversity, as with cultural diversity and biological diversity, is under serious threat around the world, with a large percentage of the several thousand languages currently spoken likely to die by the end of the century; ironically, education is one of the most significant perpetrators of this trend.

In the current and post-2015 development agenda, the discourse revolves around economic, social and, above all, environmental sustainability (especially, most visibly, climate change) – with culture and language, it seems, relegated to a place of much less importance. This volume brings these important themes back into the spotlight, offering comparative views of what linguistically and culturally relevant education means for learners and their communities. Though most of the authors discuss the challenges faced by non-dominant communities, many also describe successes in countries such as Bangladesh, Cambodia, the Philippines and Thailand in Asia as well as Cameroon, Eritrea, and Kenya in Africa. Others use ethnography to give voice to members of non-dominant community members as diverse as Indigenous Mexican mothers and Navajo elders in the United States and Pulaar school directors in Senegal.

If readers take these messages to heart, this volume may make a significant difference to the discourse around language and culture in education: firstly at the school level, by helping to empower ethnolinguistic minorities to speak, read, and further develop their own language and culture and to learn better in the process; and secondly, in the global debate around any future development agenda(s), in order to ensure a role for linguistic and cultural diversity in filling the glass, guaranteeing for all of us a sustainable future.

Sheldon Shaeffer
Consultant and Former Director
UNESCO Asia-Pacific Regional Bureau for Education
Bangkok

KIMMO KOSONEN & CAROL BENSON

INTRODUCTION

*Inclusive Teaching and Learning through the Use of Non-Dominant
Languages and Cultures*

LANGUAGE ISSUES IN COMPARATIVE EDUCATION

This book explores current issues of language(s), culture(s) and power in education. Each chapter expands on a paper presented at the 55th Annual Conference of the Comparative and International Education Society (CIES) held in Montreal, Quebec in May 2011 with the theme *L'éducation c'est ce qui libère/Education is that which liberates*. It is fitting that we came together in officially bilingual, actually multilingual and multicultural Montreal. We as authors and editors were inspired both by the theme of liberation and by the relevance of comparative research and analysis to the exploration of linguistic and cultural issues in education. Taken as a whole, our chapters draw linkages between the experiences of Indigenous people of the Americas, multilingual Africans and ethnolinguistic minority people in Asia in discussing efforts to bring learners' own non-dominant languages and cultures into the educational systems that purport to serve them.

For an education system to be truly liberatory, it must deal with issues of domination, and must attempt to right some wrongs (Ghosh, 2011). We the editors both have as a central research focus the mismatch between the languages people speak and the languages that are privileged by the school and other institutions of power. Some time ago we began using the term *non-dominant languages* (abbreviated as NDLs) to refer to the languages or language varieties spoken in a given state that are not considered the most prominent in terms of number, prestige or official use by the government and/or the education system (Kosonen, 2010). In contrast, the term *dominant language* (DL) refers to the/a language that has official status and high prestige and is spoken by dominant group members (Benson & Kosonen, 2012). These language-related terms have been extended to cultures and social groups in this volume, as they have been adopted by many of our contributors to highlight the power differentials involved in the quest for more equitable educational approaches.

It has been estimated that there are nearly 7000 languages spoken in the world today (Lewis, 2009), yet only a few hundred of them are used as languages of education, and most of these are dominant languages (see table in Walter and

C. Benson and K. Kosonen (eds.), Language Issues in Comparative Education, 1–16.
© *2013 Sense Publishers. All rights reserved.*

Benson, 2012: 283). Despite the fact that most countries and indeed their societies are multilingual, their educational systems tend to function in only one or two languages, due in part to the long-standing fallacy that national unity is built around a single language. Against this fallacy we would argue that using one language and excluding many others actually creates divisions, inequalities and inequities, because it means that hundreds of millions of people worldwide are forced to learn – or teach – through a language in which they are not proficient.

Lack of proficiency in the language of instruction, when viewed from a dominant and monolingual perspective, is generally seen as a deficiency, and learners from non-dominant groups are thus perceived as deficient even before they begin their school careers. It is common to hear that there is a "language barrier." Learners are not seen for what they already know and can do, which would be consistent with constructivist theory and learner-centered approaches (e.g. Vygotsky, 1978); instead they are identified by what they are missing. Ruiz (1984) would call this a "language as problem" orientation. Gogolin (2002; see also Bourdieu, 1991) gets to the root of this orientation by showing how a monolingual habitus, or set of unquestioned assumptions concerning the desirability of a single dominant language, governs a great deal of decision-making in education worldwide. As a result, bi- or multilingualism is often rendered either invisible or undesirable.

We can thus ask this question: Is the school designed for the learner, or is it trying to impose on that learner a single dominant language, culture and way of life? Further, if we adopt the complementary views that the process of education can be liberated and liberating (e.g. Freire, 1970) and that a habitus can change as the result of new experiences (e.g. Bourdieu, 1991), we must ask a follow-up question: How can people's eyes be opened to the alternatives?

Most of the chapters in this book are concerned with appropriate and participatory design of educational services for members of non-dominant groups. Reflecting an important area of research and practice in comparative and international education, many authors examine the roles played by national ministries of education and international development agencies. Underlying our discussions is an underlying critique of long-standing "best practices" where planners replicate dominant models of schooling nationally and internationally, often reproducing inequities and limiting people's opportunities for further learning and employment. The promotion of dominant languages in education maintains and even widens the gap between dominant and non-dominant groups. This has long been true in low-income "Southern" countries, where languages imposed by colonial and/or local elites have been privileged as national and/or official languages. The North is no exception; more serious consideration of educational language issues is clearly needed when it comes to serving regional and minority groups as well as new multilingual and multicultural communities created by internal and international migration.[i]

Since the 1990s, the concept of Education for All and subsequent establishment of the Millennium Development Goals (e.g. UNESCO, 2012; United Nations, 2012) have driven rapid expansion of educational systems around the world. In recent years increasing attention has been paid to the *quality* of mass education and the degree to which it is *inclusive* of all learners. Due to improved availability of educational statistics disaggregated by gender, ethnicity and language (e.g. EFA GMR, 2011), disparities in educational achievement which were previously hidden have come to light, and issues of language and culture are being re-examined. These issues are not new; over sixty years ago UNESCO made a clear statement of the necessity of the learner's home language ("mother tongue") in basic education (UNESCO, 1953). What is new is that there is greater and wider recognition by education ministries, development agencies and even stakeholders regarding the cross-cutting nature of language(s) and culture(s) in education. This means more programs and policies where learners' own languages are used for some part of instruction, and where learners' cultures are better represented in curricula and materials (see Heugh & Skutnabb-Kangas, 2012 for some recent examples). High-level discussions between researchers, development agencies and politicians are taking place, such as a landmark international conference organized in Bangkok in November of 2010 by a group of development partners that explicitly linked achievement of the MDGs to using learners' own languages for instruction (UNESCO, 2010, 2012). Highlighted speakers who described the importance of first languages in education at the conference included the Prime Minister of Thailand and the former First Lady of East Timor (Royal Thai Embassy, 2010; SEAMEO, 2010). Recent years have also seen the expansion of international and regional networks by donors, cooperation agencies and NGOs, practitioners, academics and others involved in language, education and development issues.

This new or renewed attention being paid to language of instruction issues has brought in new partners, and new challenges. One challenge appears to be getting specialists in different fields to speak with and listen to each other. A current example is the USA-led push for early grade reading assessment (EGRA) and the much-needed attention to early literacy it has brought about in low-income multilingual countries. As shown by some contributions to this volume, many aspects of the EGRA assessment and resulting promotion of certain teaching and learning approaches are based on research and practice in the North, specifically in monolingual English-speaking contexts, and need to be better informed by research on multilingual, multicultural education. Fortunately, CIES has provided an important forum for exchanges between specialists, with contributions from some of the networks already mentioned, and with this collection of chapters we aim to carry the discussions forward.

This volume thus brings together some of the latest thinking and research on language in comparative education, with a timely focus on how non-dominant languages and cultures can contribute to the liberation of learners as well as education systems through inclusive educational approaches. Though the issues are quite universal, they are manifested in different ways in different contexts, and we have been able to capture some of that diversity by including both low- and high-income country cases and by exploring a wide range of approaches from pre-primary to higher education, including adult basic education and teacher professionalization. Throughout the book we link development efforts with longstanding research on and principles of multilingual, multicultural education. It is our aim to promote more organized, collaborative progress toward incorporating learners' languages and cultures into education for quality, equity and liberation.

DISCUSSING LANGUAGES AND CULTURES IN COMPARATIVE EDUCATION: KEY TERMS AND CONCEPTS

Like the field of comparative and international education and CIES as an organization, the chapters of this volume approach the theme from a variety of academic disciplines and perspectives. Some of the authors are teachers or teacher trainers; some are anthropologists or linguists; some are development practitioners and some language policy specialists; and all are educational researchers. We represent the diversity of backgrounds one finds working in educational development, where terms, concepts and contexts can be quite distinct.

For this volume to provide a useful and coherent comparative analysis of individual contexts and world regions, we as editors asked the contributors to make use of key terms and concepts in the same ways we understood them, or to make any unconventional uses or diverging views explicit. Diversity in terminology is understandable given the different realities experienced by stakeholders in different countries and regions, as well as the constant need to find ways to contest standard terms, particularly in calling attention to oppressive power relations. We have thus shared definitions across chapters and developed our thinking throughout the process. This book now represents our collective efforts to consolidate some of the latest – and in our opinion the most relevant – terminology being used in the study of language issues in comparative education. We hope it will be useful to fellow researchers as well as to those with whom we work, including local practitioners and specialists, policymakers and international colleagues who are as yet unfamiliar with concepts in multilingual, multicultural education.

Terms Related to Non-Dominant Communities

We use the term ethnolinguistic community or group to refer to a group of people who share a culture, ethnicity and/or language that distinguishes them from other communities (Kosonen, 2005, 2010). All people are members of one or more ethnolinguistic communities, whether they are non-dominant or dominant in the society or country in which they live.[ii] We use ethnolinguistic minority in reference to an ethnolinguistic community which is either fewer in terms of number or less prestigious in terms of power and economic status than the predominant group(s) in the given state (ibid.).

In different parts of the world, terms such as "ethnic minorities," "tribals," "hill tribes," "natives" or "indigenous peoples" are used to discuss ethnolinguistic minority communities. Though these terms are used even by official sources, they are contested, may be derogatory, and are understood differently in different contexts. Because they make cross-national comparison difficult, they are rarely used in this volume, and exceptions are duly noted.

"Indigenous Peoples," which is a problematic term in some parts of the world, is widely used in the Americas and in contexts where the legal rights of original peoples are being supported, e.g. for the Saami of northern Europe or certain groups in Southeast Asian countries.[iii] The United Nations, for example, has developed international legal instruments to recognize and promote the rights of Indigenous Peoples (United Nations, 2008; Skutnabb-Kangas & Dunbar, 2010), though the definitions provided are very broad in an attempt to cover many different situations. Other examples would be Aboriginal Australia and Aotearoa/New Zealand, cases not covered in this volume but well represented elsewhere. Ball and McIvor (Chapter 1 in this volume) provide some guidance, defining Indigenous Peoples as "the first peoples of a colonized land." In the Canadian context they are specifically referring to three types of Indigenous groups: First Nations, Métis, and Inuit.

With this guidance, we use the term *Indigenous* with a capital *I* to privilege the peoples or life ways that originate from the geographical place in question as opposed to coming from outside. In this book, *Indigenous* is applied most often to Original Peoples of the Americas, where they can also be considered ethnolinguistic minorities with distinct cultures. Many speak non-dominant languages – but not all, due to past and present-day oppression, as is the case of Navajo in the USA and minority groups of Coastal Nicaragua (White, Chapter 12) along with Indigenous Mexicans living in the USA (Menchaca Bishop & Kelly, Chapter 5).[iv] Interestingly, we rarely use the term Indigenous in African or Asian countries, where nearly everyone is indigenous to the continent.[v]

The term *ethnolinguistic minority* is applied most often in Southeast Asia and the Pacific (Kosonen, Chapter 2; Stone, Chapter 9). It should be noted that not all ethnolinguistic minorities are Indigenous Peoples, nor are they always numerical minorities:

> [T]he term 'minority' is often ambiguous and may be interpreted differently in distinct contexts because it may have both numerical and social or political dimensions. In some cases it may be simply used as a euphemism for non-elite or subordinate groups, whether they constitute a numerical majority or minority in relation to some other group that is politically and socially dominant. (UNESCO, 2003: 13)

In many Asian countries there are non-dominant ethnolinguistic communities that are in the majority, or at least are more numerous than dominant groups (Lewis, 2009), e.g. speakers of Western Punjabi in Pakistan and Javanese in Indonesia, both of which are the largest ethnolinguistic communities in their countries. Neither is discussed in this volume, but their cases are comparable to those of large Indigenous groups like Quechua/Quichua speakers in Bolivia and Peru, or to ethnolinguistic groups in multilingual African countries, where relative dominance or non-dominance is due to historical, political or other power-related factors but not directly to population size.

Terms Related to Languages in Education

We have adopted the term non-dominant languages (NDLs) in part to avoid the more ambiguous terms "minority language" or "indigenous language," and in part to highlight the oppressed status of these languages relative to dominant languages (DLs) of power, which is useful when discussing education policy and school use of learners' home languages. However, as already mentioned, the NDL-DL distinction may not always be clear; for example, some so-called mother tongue-based multilingual education programs are not using each learner's home language but rather a "dominant NDL" of the region, or a dominant (standard) variety of the local NDL. Neither case is necessarily bad; a more widely spoken NDL is likely to be "closer" linguistically and/or culturally to learners' actual first languages than the DL would be, and use of a "dominant NDL" may possibly be more feasible economically (see e.g. Benson's 2003 example from Guinea-Bissau, and Brock-Utne's arguments regarding Kiswahili in Tanzania, Chapter 4 in this volume). However, for pedagogical purposes it is important to differentiate between types of NDLs, and that necessitates additional terms.

In this book we consider a *local language* (also called vernacular[vi] or Indigenous language by some) to be one spoken in a relatively restricted geographical area, and one not commonly learned as a second language by people outside the community (Kosonen, 2005). Local languages are almost exclusively autochthonous, i.e. they originate from the place where they are spoken, and nearly always NDLs. They tend to: (a) lack written form; (b) be in the early stages of linguistic development (i.e. not yet standardized); and/or (c) be considered unsuitable for use in education due to low status relative to the DL and/or small number of speakers (ibid.). While it can be argued that local languages should be used in education, it is rarely possible through official means.

The term *first language* or *L1* refers to a language a person speaks as a *mother tongue, vernacular, native language*, or *home language*. It should be noted that bi- or multilingual people may consider *several* languages their home or first languages. For L1 we use the range of definitions of mother tongue by Skutnabb-Kangas (2000) as a language that one (a) has learnt first; (b) identifies with; (c) knows best; and/or (d) uses most (see also UNESCO, 2003). We propose making the term plural (an option that Skutnabb-Kangas herself supports) and adding (e) speaks and understands competently enough to learn academic content at the appropriate age level (Benson & Kosonen, 2012). Benson (chapter 15, this volume) notes that for educational purposes it is important to assess which languages individual learners speak proficiently, particularly when they enter school. According to language learning theory and principles of bilingual education (e.g. Cummins, 2009; Thomas and Collier, 2002), having two or more strong NDLs in one's repertoire should be an asset to the learning of additional languages (both NDLs and DLs) as well as academic content.

With regard to *standard* or *non-standard varieties* (also known as "dialects") of NDLs, or DLs for that matter, the field lacks well-defined terminology. As already mentioned, we avoid the term "dialect" because of its inaccurate use, particularly in post-colonial countries, to imply that NDLs are not fully developed "languages." "Dialect" has also been used with slightly more accuracy to refer to pidgins and creoles that developed as a result of historic contact between DLs and NDLs, but the pejorative connotation remains, despite the fact that they are fully developed languages that tend to serve as lingua francae (see below) and have been successfully used in education (see e.g. the work of Siegel, 1997, 2008).

The somewhat fuzzy distinction between *language* and *variety* (or *dialect* in the linguistic sense) involves mutual intelligibility; i.e. when speakers of different varieties understand each other sufficiently and can communicate without great difficulty they can be said to speak varieties or dialects of the same language (Kosonen, 2005). Mutual intelligibility can be defined in lexical terms, e.g. two varieties share a high percentage of the same vocabulary, or in attitudinal terms, but not all linguists agree on the criteria to differentiate between a language and a dialect (see Lewis, 2009, for widely accepted criteria). There are at least two problems with the variety issue from our point of view. The first problem is that they may represent a monolingual habitus; multilingual speakers of Bantu languages, for example, are metalinguistically aware enough to be able to adapt their own languages to understand their neighbors but not necessarily those living further away, leading specialists to refer to the Bantu languages as a continuum (e.g. Prah, 2008). In terms of educational language use, this would suggest that "dominant NDLs" could be used for education in certain regions, rather than attempting to use each local language. However, the second problem with the variety issue is that mutual intelligibility is judged by adult speakers, not by school-aged children. It cannot be expected that young children who are just beginning their school careers have had exposure to a standard variety of their local NDL or other languages spoken in the area.

A *language of wider communication (LWC)* – also called a *lingua franca, regional language* or *trade language* – is a language that speakers of different local languages use to communicate with each other (Kosonen, 2005), and which is spoken more widely than a local or home language; examples are creoles (as mentioned above) or widely spoken regional languages like Wolof in Senegal (see Sarr, chapter 6 in this volume), used by various ethnolinguistic communities to communicate with each other. As dominant NDLs, they may be useful in education, but as mentioned above they may not be so widely spoken among young children.

A *second language (L2)* is seen broadly as a language that is not the learner's first language, but one that she or he is required to study or use. It may be an LWC, i.e. spoken in the immediate environment of the learner, or it may be a foreign language, i.e. not heard in the learner's environment (Kosonen, 2005). For speakers of NDLs, the L2 is often a DL, usually a national or official language, used in formal domains like schools, clinics and government. The main problem with the concept of L2 in education is that the pedagogical strategies should be different depending on whether the L2 is an LWC or a foreign language. Benson (Chapter 15 in this volume) proposes an elaboration of the L2 concept to distinguish between the two, using $L2_{env}$ for a language to which the learner is exposed in her/his environment and L2$_{sch}$ for a language to which the learner is exposed only at school.

According to Crystal (1999: 227), a *national language* is "a language that is considered to be the chief language of a nation state," whereas an *official language* is a language that is "used in such public domains as the law courts, government, and broadcasting. In many countries, there is no difference between the national and official language" (Crystal, ibid.). It should be noted, however, that in some post-colonial contexts, particularly African ones, *national languages* refer to non-dominant languages spoken within the "nation"; further, some countries like Nigeria and Guinea use the term *national languages* to endow certain larger or more widely used NDLs with a special status that is below *official* but above other NDLs.

A final term that is used in this volume is *international language,* referring most often to European ex-colonial (or exogenous) languages. In post-colonial countries these may also be official languages, particularly in Latin America and many parts of Africa, though less so in Asia.

Terms in Bi- and Multilingual Education

"*Bilingualism* or *multilingualism* is the use of more than one language in daily life" (UNESCO, 2003: 12), but it is also the purposeful use of two or more languages in educational policy and practice. Terms in this domain often refer to issues in language policy and/or to certain models or methodologies that are put in place to make education more equitable and inclusive. They are in opposition to terms like *submersion* education, which refers to the instructional use of a language that learners do not understand or speak well. Submersion, which connotes drowning, occurs when children who speak NDLs are put into DL-medium classrooms without any provision for accommodating or alleviating the disadvantages created by lack of understanding (Skutnabb-Kangas, 2000: 582-587).

Language policy in this volume means legislation on and de facto practices pertaining to the use of languages in a society, whereas *language-in-education policy* means legislation on and practices pertaining to languages or media of instruction and languages of literacy used in basic education (Kosonen & Young, 2009). A *language of instruction* is a language through which the contents of the curriculum in a given educational system or a part of it are taught and learned, whereas a *language of literacy* is a language through which reading and writing are initially learned, for example, both through printed written materials and oral language development (Kosonen, 2005; Kosonen & Young, 2009).

There are two common terms related to individual language proficiencies and/or to the goals of a bi- or multilingual program: *multilingual/multilingualism* and *plurilingual/ plurilingualism*. These terms, which tend to be used interchangeably in English-based international discourse, can refer to societies as well as to individuals. However, in Europe (and in Bahry's Chapter 3 in this volume), a distinction is made, where *multilingual* refers to societies and *plurilingual* to individuals (e.g. Council of Europe, 2006). We find this an interesting distinction which remains to be explored.

Bilingual/multilingual education (MLE) means the systematic use of more than one language for instruction and literacy learning, and *biliteracy* refers to the use of more than one language for reading and writing. *Mother tongue-based, L1-based or first language first MLE* (which is increasingly being abbreviated MTBMLE in the literature) refers to a system of multilingual education which begins with or is based on learners' first language or mother tongue (see Benson, Chapter 15 in this volume). This term is used to distinguish MLE based on learners' own languages from programs that employ several languages but exclude learners' own. It also excludes programs that use the L1 *orally* as an *auxiliary language* to facilitate understanding of the curricular content and textbooks written in DLs (Kosonen & Young, 2009).[vii] Oral use of a language can be officially endorsed, but it is more often informal based on the decisions at the school level or even in individual classrooms. We don't consider oral use of a language – even if it is addition to the official language of instruction – making an education system bi-/multilingual.

As the term *mother tongue* is problematic when taken literally – which happens when second-language speakers use the term in any language, e.g. the United Nations' 'Mother Language Day' – we prefer to use *first language-based* or *L1-based MLE*. We are aware that this term also requires further development, which we hope will be sparked by this volume.

A final aspect of MLE that is central to the discussions in this volume is the *intercultural* aspect of bi- and multilingual programs. *Bilingual intercultural education (EIB/BIE),* from the Spanish *educación intercultural bilingüe* as practiced in countries like Bolivia and Guatemala, refers to the very important cultural components of inclusive education for Indigenous learners. In its Latin American conceptualization, EIB/BIE is meant to integrate local cultural values and lifeways into L1 instruction and to teach about the dominant culture while teaching the dominant language as an L2 or foreign language. In other parts of the world, local culture has been brought into the classroom in the name of *curricular relevance*, i.e. to help learners understand curricular content, whether or not the L1 is used as a medium of instruction. A relatively recent incarnation of this approach has been to add a separate *local curriculum* component to primary curricula. As Ruiz de Forsberg and Borges Månsson describe in the case of Mozambique (Chapter 11, this volume), operationalizing the local curriculum component involves the support of community members, who are called on to share local skills (also called *Indigenous knowledges*; see e.g. Sarr in Chapter 6, this volume) using the NDL that they share with learners. Recent work in Latin America (López, 2009 in Benson, Chapter 15, this volume) uses the concept of *interculturalism* to empower learners to address the power differentials between dominant cultures and their own.

Terms Related to Development of NDLs for Educational Use

Language development in the context of language planning is commonly seen as consisting of three parts: status planning, corpus planning, and acquisition planning (Cooper, 1989). *Status planning* refers to decisions about which languages are used for official and educational purposes, i.e. language policy. *Acquisition planning* has to do with the methods by which people should be taught and learn particular languages. Finally, *corpus planning* encompasses linguistic activities related to development of languages themselves, including the creation and improvement of writing systems and standardization of language use in written form. Non-dominant languages are frequently in need of development in written form for domains like education in which they have traditionally been underutilized. In this volume, discussions of language or linguistic development of NDLs refer mainly to corpus planning to enable acquisition planning, i.e. use of these NDLs in education.

Some contributors to this volume discuss the need to create or improve the *orthography* of an NDL, which is a standard system for writing that includes spelling and punctuation rules (Crystal, 1999). A closely related term is *script,* which is "the graphic form of the units of a writing system (e.g. the Roman vs. the Cyrillic alphabet)" (Crystal, 1999: 299). Some languages use an *alphabet,* or set of symbols (letters) that represent the sounds of the language; others (e.g. Mandarin) use *pictographs* or other visual representations of meaningful units of speech.

ORGANIZATION OF THE BOOK

This volume comprises 15 chapters in addition to this Introduction that take a strategic comparative perspective on education systems, regions of the world, and ethnolinguistic groups. Among the authors are researchers who are well established in the field as well as new scholars whose research is recent and relevant. Individually and together, we examine the liberatory potential of using non-dominant languages and cultures in education. The chapters are divided into four broad themes: 1) language-in-education policy issues, 2) community and parent voices, 3) classroom practices and teacher voices, and 4) researcher voices. In this section we provide a brief summary of each theme and chapter.

Before our detailed description of the contents, we would like to call attention to the form in which they are presented, which we feel is consistent with the intent of this volume. Each chapter begins with an abstract written in a non-dominant or lesser-known language, which serves to expose readers to these languages, to demonstrate that they can be used to express academic concepts, and to exhibit the wealth of linguistic resources that are available to us all. Each language is identified by a three-letter code which, according to an international linguistic standard, indicates the exact variety used (see Lewis, 2009, for more information on this system).

Part I begins with overarching issues of language policy in education. There are four chapters with examples from three continents: Africa, Asia and North

America. In *Chapter 1*, Jessica Ball and Onowa McIvor start off the discussion with a highly critical review of the situation of Indigenous languages and cultures in education in Canada, setting the stage for other contributors to address issues of power and domination. They explore community-driven heritage language teaching as a small but positive step toward respecting Indigenous learners, and outline a revitalization program that would go well beyond formal education to involve non-dominant group members in their own liberatory processes.

With *Chapter 2*, Kimmo Kosonen moves the discussion to Southeast Asia and a comparison and contrast of recent language-in-education policy developments in Cambodia, Thailand and Vietnam. His critical analysis demonstrates how written policies in Cambodia and Thailand appear to be working in parallel with regional trends to provide more latitude for NDLs in education, while Vietnam appears to be going against the trend by weakening official written policy support for NDLs. Interestingly, in Vietnam the expansion of some provincial level initiatives is underway, which may actually facilitate implementation of NDL-based MLE.

Stephen Bahry's *Chapter 3* makes a highly significant contribution to the literature on Afghanistan with his discussion of the potential role of language in educational reform and societal reconstruction. Pulling together the scant available information about the country's linguistic and societal diversity and about current language-in-education policies and practices, he demonstrates that for education reform to succeed, policy makers – along with the international organizations supporting them – must take learners' own languages into account.

In *Chapter 4*, Birgit Brock-Utne wraps up the first part of this volume by extending her impressive body of work on language and education issues in Eastern Africa to the examples of Sri Lanka and Malaysia to call attention to the importance of teaching technical subjects in learners' first languages. Using these and other examples, she critiques the 2006 decision by Zanzibar to reintroduce DL English as the language of instruction for mathematics and the sciences beginning at grade five, which is both disempowering and unnecessary given that NDL Kiswahili is the first language of all learners in Zanzibar.

Part II of the volume moves us from the big picture to more local perspectives with two studies that give voice to NDL community members regarding how their languages and cultures should or should not be a part of their children's educations. The first study comes in *Chapter 5*, by Laura Menchaca Bishop and Prema Kelley, who explore the informal language policies and practices implemented at home by Indigenous Mexican families living in New York. Their interviews demonstrate that parents are acutely aware that their NDLs are doubly dominated, both by Mexican Spanish and by American English. Lacking support from educators or from society, parents may sacrifice their languages and cultures in an effort to spare their children the discrimination they have experienced themselves.

The second study, by Karla Giuliano Sarr in *Chapter 6*, turns our attention to Indigenous knowledge and education in southeastern Senegal. Using an innovative classroom game along with interview data, she explores the views of children, teachers, and community members regarding Indigenous and Western forms of knowledge. Due to tension between these forms of knowledge, people develop a sense of inadequacy and a negative view of their own culture that is only exacerbated by use of DL French as a language of instruction. The study demonstrates that the non-dominant language and culture must be respected by the school for education to be liberatory.

Part III directs our attention to classroom practices and the perspectives of teachers, representing another range of contexts from Africa, Asia and the Americas. Beginning with *Chapter 7*, Gowri Vijayakumar, Elizabeth Pearce and Meherun Nahar collaborate to evaluate a bilingual, bicultural preschool program for Adivasi children in Bangladesh. Their data show that children from this program outperform their peers in language development and cultural awareness, as well as being more engaged in learning. Meanwhile, however, issues of dominance mean that community members and teachers are conflicted about local language use in education beyond the informal preschool level.

In *Chapter 8*, Janelle Johnson explores teacher attitudes toward their potential role as agents of change in programs for Indigenous learners in Guatemala and Mexico. Having participated in a transnational professional development program, these teachers find themselves struggling to decolonize their own minds as well as the minds of others, and to support learners who are marginalized in economic as well as linguistic and cultural ways. Teachers' own words are used to highlight the challenges they face in implementing bilingual intercultural pedagogy in the classroom, with implications for field support of bilingual teachers.

Teachers are also the focus of Rebecca Stone's *Chapter 9*, this time in the context of an L1-based MLE program in rural Philippines. She examines the effects of specific training activities on Indigenous first grade teachers' attitudes towards implementing L1-based pedagogy. Her findings – that they need time to learn about their own languages, create their own L1 materials and reflect on their own experiences as learners – have implications for other programs where teachers are being "converted" from L2-based to L1-based teaching.

In *Chapter 10*, Pauline Rea-Dickins and Guoxing Yu expand on Brock-Utne's earlier observations about the medium of instruction in Zanzibar, this time using empirical studies to explore student performance in mathematics and the sciences according to different modes of assessment – English only, Kiswahili only, or both languages. Their findings identify specific challenges that learners face when trying to demonstrate their knowledge through an unfamiliar language, yet paradoxically show how learners aspire to use the dominant language at school despite lack of exposure to that language in their daily lives.

Chapter 11 by Nuzzly Ruiz de Forsberg and Alícia Borges Månsson moves the focus to operationalizing the local curriculum component of the educational reform in Mozambican primary schools to include local cultural inputs by community members. Their study raises the question of how communities can be empowered to participate in formal educational processes if decision-making is still done in a top-down manner, but they remain hopeful that the local curriculum will bring community values and languages into the classroom.

Kerry White takes us back to the Americas in *Chapter 12* with her comparison of community-based education in two Indigenous contexts: the autonomous regions of Nicaragua and the Navajo Nation in the USA. While the two communities have different aims – the former working to accommodate diverse languages and cultures, and the latter working to revitalize their heritage language and culture – both have found that success comes from being connected with their histories, respecting deep-seated cultural values, and going beyond the school to make the community the center of activity. This chapter, like the others in this section, offers specific implications for policy and practice.

Part IV concludes this volume with a collection of researcher perspectives, all drawing on the authors' diverse yet complementary experiences in multilingual and intercultural education to highlight current research and practice – and important future directions. To begin with, Leila Schroeder demonstrates in *Chapter 13* that the assessment of early grade reading skills in multilingual African countries is not a matter of simply transposing Western, monolingual English-based assumptions about literacy onto multilingual, multicultural learners. She challenges the applicability of particular theories to reading pedagogy in most African linguistic systems, arguing that literacy and development professionals should exercise much more care in developing appropriate methods and materials.

In *Chapter 14*, Stephen Walter expands on the theme of reading assessment in multilingual contexts, using data from a range of low-income countries to call into question the use of Western standards for reading rate, reading accuracy, and comprehension to track reading progress in basic education. He finds evidence that language of instruction is the most significant factor in the widely observed "deficit" in reading skill development in low-income countries relative to high-income, which suggests that much more attention should be paid to NDLs in early and developing literacy and learning.

Carol Benson concludes the section and the volume with her *Chapter 15* calling for the adoption of a multilingual rather than a monolingual habitus in educational development. Providing evidence of Northern, English-language biases in theoretical perspectives, she argues that existing research and practice require adaptation to the multilingual, multicultural realities of many low-income contexts – from which the North could learn a great deal. She concludes by pointing out that no learner's needs are met by education in a single dominant language; rather, learners should be helped to develop the bi-/multilingual skills needed to have healthy, productive lives with meaningful interaction at the home and family, community, regional, national and global levels. A multilingual habitus in education would thus be liberatory for all.

NOTES

[i] See Benson (forthcoming) for a cross-regional analysis of lessons learned in Northern and Southern contexts.

[ii] We recognize that use of the dominant/non-dominant labels could create false dichotomies, and that among non-dominant groups some dominate relative to others; similarly, groups that are dominant in one context (e.g. Khmer speakers in Cambodia) may be non-dominant in another (e.g. Khmer speakers in Vietnam). It is the relative nature of the terms that gives them their value in discussing how more equitable education can be designed.

iii In Cambodia, for example, certain groups considered Indigenous have been given the right to bilingual education, while other non-dominant groups are denied this right, leading to controversy over longevity in the region instead of focusing on language rights in education (Benson & Kosonen, 2012; Kosonen, Chapter 2 in this volume).

iv In these cases, a term that is often applied is *heritage language*, signaling that even if people no longer speak the language, they identify with the culture and language associated with their grandparents or earlier ancestors.

v One exception is the term *indigenous language*, which is used to distinguish between e.g. African and European colonial languages; however, even this distinction can be complicated due to indigenized varieties of colonial languages, e.g. Mozambican Portuguese or Nigerian English. Another is *indigenous knowledge*, as discussed by Sarr (Chapter 6) in the case of Senegal.

vi By actual definition the term "vernacular" is not problematic; however, like the term "dialect," it is often used in post-colonial contexts, particularly in French or Portuguese, to imply that NDLs do not merit recognition as "languages."

vii While this practice is certainly better than nothing, and is even called "bilingual education" in some contexts, specialists do NOT consider it first language-based MLE.

REFERENCES

Benson, Carol (2003). Possibilities for educational language choice in multilingual Guinea-Bissau. In Leena Huss, Antoinette Camilleri, & Kendall King (Eds.), *Transcending monolingualism: Family, school and society* (pp. 67-87). Lisse, Netherlands: Swets and Zeitlinger.

Benson, Carol (forthcoming). Adopting a multilingual habitus: What North and South can learn from each other regarding the essential role of non-dominant languages in education. In Victoria Zenotz, Jasone Cenoz, & Durk Gorter (Eds.), *Minority languages and multilingual education*. London: Springer.

Benson, Carol, & Kosonen, Kimmo (2012). A critical comparison of language-in-education policy and practice in four Southeast Asian countries and Ethiopia. In Kathleen Heugh & Tove Skutnabb-Kangas (Eds.), *Multilingual education and sustainable diversity work: From periphery to centre* (pp. 111-137). New York: Routledge.

Bourdieu, Pierre (1991). *Language and symbolic power*. Cambridge: Cambridge University Press.

Council of Europe (Feb. 2006). *Plurilingual education in Europe. 50 years of international cooperation*. Strasbourg, France: Council of Europe, Language Policy Division. (http://www.coe.int/t/dg4/linguistic/Source/PlurinlingalEducation_En.pdf)

Cooper, Robert L. (1989). *Language planning and social change*. Cambridge: Cambridge University Press.

Cummins, Jim (2009). Fundamental psycholinguistic and sociological principles underlying educational success for linguistic minority students. In Tove Skutnabb-Kangas, Robert Phillipson, Ajit K. Mohanty & Minati Panda (Eds.), *Social justice through multilingual education* (pp. 19-35). Clevedon: Multilingual Matters.

Crystal, David (1999). *The Penguin dictionary of language*, 2nd Edition. London: Penguin.

EFA GMR (2011). *Education for All global monitoring report. The hidden crisis: Armed conflict and education*. Paris: UNESCO Publishing.

Freire, Paulo (1970). *Pedagogy of the oppressed*. London: Penguin Books.

Ghosh, Ratna (Spring 2011). The liberating potential of multiculturalism in Canada: Ideals and realities. In Ratna Ghosh & Kevin McDonough (Eds.), *Canadian issues/Thèmes canadiens*, Special edition: 55th Annual Conference of the Comparative and International Education Society/Édition spéciale dans le cadre du 55e congrès annuel de la Société d'Éducation Comparée et Internationale. Montréal: Association for Canadian Studies/Association d'études canadiennes.

Gogolin, Ingrid (2002). Linguistic and cultural diversity in Europe: A challenge for educational research and practice. ECER Keynote. *European Educational Research Journal, 1*(1), 123-138.

Heugh, Kathleen, & Skutnabb-Kangas, Tove (Eds.) (2012). *Multilingual education and sustainable diversity work: From periphery to centre*. New York: Routledge.

Kosonen, Kimmo (2005). Education in local languages: Policy and practice in South-East Asia. In *First language first: Community-based literacy programmes for minority language context in Asia* (pp. 96-134). Bangkok: UNESCO.

Kosonen, Kimmo (2009). Language-in-education policies in Southeast Asia: An overview. In Kimmo Kosonen & Catherine Young (Eds.), *Mother tongue as bridge language of instruction: Policies and experiences in Southeast Asia* (pp. 22-43). Bangkok: Southeast Asian Ministers of Education Organization (SEAMEO).

Kosonen, Kimmo (2010). Ethnolinguistic minorities and non-dominant languages in mainland Southeast Asian language-in-education policies. In A. M. Geo JaJa & Suzanne Majhanovich (Eds.), *Education, language, and economics: Growing national and global dilemmas* (pp. 73-88). Rotterdam/Boston/Taipei: Sense Publishers.

Kosonen, Kimmo & Young, Catherene (Eds.) (2009). *Mother tongue as bridge language of instruction: Policies and experiences in Southeast Asia*. Bangkok: Southeast Asian Ministers of Education Organization (SEAMEO).

Lewis, M. Paul (Ed.) (2009). *Ethnologue: Languages of the world*, Sixteenth edition. Dallas, TX: SIL International. (http://www.ethnologue.com/)

Prah, Kwesi K. (2008). Language, literacy and knowledge production in Africa. In Brian Street & Nancy Hornberger (Eds.), *Encyclopedia of language and education* (2nd ed.), Vol. 2: *Literacy* (pp. 29-39). New York: Springer.

Royal Thai Embassy (2010). Opening speech by Mr. Abhisit Vejjajiva, Prime Minister of the Kingdom of Thailand, at the International Conference on Language, Education and the Millennium Development Goals. 9 Nov. 2010, Twin Towers Hotel, Bangkok.
(http://www.seameo.org/LanguageMDGConference2010/doc/speech/LD2010_PM-Speech.pdf)

Ruiz, Richard (1984). Orientations in language planning. *Journal of the National Association of Bilingual Education*, *8*, 15-34.

SEAMEO (2010). The role of MLE in early childhood care and development programmes and in the successful transition to Primary School. Keynote speech by Ms. Kirsty Sword Gusmão (Chair of Timor-Leste National Commission for UNESCO, Chair of National Education Commission, Chair of Alola Foundation, Goodwill Ambassador for Education, Democratic Republic of Timor-Leste) at the International Conference on Language, Education and the Millennium Development Goals. 9 Nov. 2010, Twin Towers Hotel, Bangkok.
(http://www.seameo.org/LanguageMDGConference2010/doc/presentations/day1/KirstySwordGusm ao-sn.pdf)

Siegel, Jeff (1997). Formal vs. non-formal vernacular education: The education reform in Papua New Guinea. *Journal of Multilingual and Multicultural Development*, *18*(3), 206-222.

Siegel, Jeff (2008). *The emergence of Pidgin and Creole languages*. Oxford/ New York: Oxford University Press.

Skutnabb-Kangas, Tove (2000). *Linguistic genocide in education – Or worldwide diversity and human rights?* Mahwah, NJ: Lawrence Erlbaum Associates.

Skutnabb-Kangas, Tove, & Dunbar, Robert (2010). Indigenous children's education as linguistic genocide and a crime against humanity? A global view. Gáldu Čála. Journal of Indigenous Peoples' Rights no. 1. Guovdageaidnu/Kautokeino: Galdu, Resource Centre for the Rights of Indigenous Peoples. (http://www.e-pages.dk/grusweb/55/)

Thomas, Wayne, & Collier, Virginia (2002). *A national of school effectiveness for language minority students' long-term academic achievement*. Santa Cruz CA: Center for Research on Education, Diversity and Excellence. (http://www.crede.ucsc.edu/research/llaa/1.1_final.html)

UNESCO (1953). *The use of vernacular languages in education*. Report of the UNESCO Meeting of Specialists (1951). Monographs on Fundamental Education III. Paris: UNESCO.

UNESCO (2003). *Education in a multilingual world.* UNESCO Education Position Paper. Paris: UNESCO. (http://unesdoc.unesco.org/images/0012/001297/129728e.pdf)

UNESCO (2010). *International Conference on Language, Education and the Millennium Development Goals (MDGs).* November 9-11, 2010, Bangkok.
(http://www.seameo.org/LanguageMDGConference2010/)

UNESCO (2012). *Why language matters for the millennium development goals.* Bangkok: UNESCO Bangkok. (http://unesdoc.unesco.org/images/0021/002152/215296E.pdf)

United Nations (March 2008). United Nations Declaration on the Rights of Indigenous Peoples. New York: United Nations. (http://www.un.org/esa/socdev/unpfii/documents/DRIPS_en.pdf)

United Nations (2012). The Millennium Development Goals Report 2012. New York: United Nations. (http://www.un.org/millenniumgoals/pdf/MDG%20Report%202012.pdf)

Vygotsky, Lev (1978). *Mind in society. The development of higher psychological processes.* Cambridge, MA: Harvard University Press.

Walter, Steve, & Benson, Carol (2012). Language policy and medium of instruction in formal education. In Bernard Spolsky (Ed.), *The Cambridge handbook of language policy* (pp. 278-300). Cambridge: Cambridge University Press.

Kimmo Kosonen
SIL International & Payap University, Thailand

Carol Benson
International Consultant in Educational Language Issues

PART I:

LANGUAGE-IN-EDUCATION POLICY ISSUES

JESSICA BALL & ONOWA MCIVOR

1. CANADA'S BIG CHILL

Indigenous Languages in Education

ABSTRACT

wihtaskamihk kîkâc kahkiyaw nîhîyaw pîkiskwîwina î namatîpayiwa wiya môniyâw onîkânîwak kayâs kâkiy sihcikîcik ka nakinahkwâw nîhiyaw osihcikîwina. atawiya anohc kanâta askiy kâpimipayihtâcik î tipahamok nîhiyaw awâsisak kakisinâmâkosicik mîna apisis î tipahamok mîna ta kakwiy miciminamâ nîhiyawîwin. namoya mâka mitoni tapwîy kontayiwâk î nîsohkamâkawinaw ka miciminamâ nipîkiskwîwinân. pako kwayas ka sihcikiy kîspin tâpwiy kâ kakwiy miciminamâ nîhîyawîwin îkwa tapwiy kwayas ka kiskinâhamowâyâ kicowâsim'sinân. ôma masinayikanis îwihcikâtîw tânihki kîkâc kâ namatîpayicik nipîkiskwîwinân îkwa takahki sihcikîwina mîna misowiy kâ apicihtâcik ka pasikwînahkwâw nîhiyawîwin nanântawisi. (*Translated into Nîhîyawîwin (Northern Cree) [crk], a language of Canada, by Art Napoleon*)

Canada's Indigenous languages are at risk of extinction because of government policies that have actively opposed or neglected them. A few positive steps by government include investments in Aboriginal Head Start, a culturally based early childhood program, as well as a federal Aboriginal Languages Initiative. Overall, however, government and public schools have yet to demonstrate serious support for Indigenous language revitalization. Language-in-education policies must address the historically and legislatively created needs of Indigenous Peoples to increase the number of Indigenous language speakers and honor the right of Indigenous children to be educated in their language and according to their heritage, with culturally meaningful curricula, cultural safety, and dignity. This chapter describes how Canada arrived at a state of Indigenous language devastation, then explores some promising developments in community-driven heritage language teaching, and finally presents an ecologically comprehensive strategy for Indigenous language revitalization that draws on and goes beyond the roles of formal schooling.

C. Benson and K. Kosonen (eds.), Language Issues in Comparative Education, 19–38.

It's been a cold 130 years for Canada's first languages, and the thaw is still awaited. (Fettes & Norton, 2000: 29)

INTRODUCTION

A basic Canadian value is that regardless of where children live, programs for promoting their optimal development should be accessible, available, and linguistically and culturally appropriate to them (Canadian Centre for Justice, 2001). Yet despite being party to innumerable universal declarations and policy documents enshrining the rights of Indigenous Peoples to practice and perpetuate their cultures and languages, including children's right to both learn and be educated in their mother tongue (United Nations, 2008), government efforts to implement these commitments have moved at glacial speed. Less than one-fifth of Aboriginal[i] children in Canada are learning their ancestral languages, and this number is dwindling (Statistics Canada, 2006). The forecast for preserving and revitalizing Canada's Indigenous languages is gloomy (Norris, 2007): All are at risk of extinction within this century because of government policies that have actively opposed or neglected them.

This chapter describes how Canada has arrived at the current state of Indigenous language devastation and how schooling has been used to pursue a national policy that recognizes only two colonial languages – English and French – to the detriment of Indigenous language maintenance and of Indigenous children's school success. Language-in-education policies and a host of other threats undermine Indigenous languages. Immediate threats include the (unofficial) promotion of monolingualism through a lack of state support for a multilingual society and the global expansion of English. Another set of risk factors is the plethora of other competing and urgent concerns facing Indigenous[ii] communities due to past and present effects of colonization. These include: poverty, addictions, mental and physical health issues, protracted treaty negotiations, (re)building self-governance, and conflicts between Indigenous communities and various levels of government over rights to natural resources and protection of traditional Indigenous lands.

We begin with an overview of the current status of Indigenous language-in-education developments in Canada, describing both challenges and early indicators of promise. Next we outline the multiple levels of intervention needed to support the survival of Indigenous languages and examine the roles that non-formal and formal education could play to promote Indigenous learners' language retention and school success. We encourage a view of language as not only a medium of instruction, but as "the life blood of a people," with the capacity to carry "the spirit of the past to the children of the present" (Aboriginal Head Start Association of British Columbia, 2011: 1). Language is widely understood by Indigenous Peoples as the vehicle for the intergenerational transmission of knowledge, culture, spirituality and identity.

OVERVIEW OF INDIGENOUS LANGUAGE LEARNING IN CANADA

Current Conditions

Among the approximately 7,000 languages presently spoken in the world, up to 90% are predicted to disappear within the next century (Lewis, 2009). This pattern holds in Canada, which has 11 Indigenous language families comprised of 50 or more Indigenous languages (Norris, 2007). Language death occurs when one group is colonized and assimilated by another and adopts its language (Crystal, 1997), either forcibly or by choice. Over the past 400 years, Indigenous Peoples in Canada have experienced a succession of colonial government incursions, including genocide, forced relocation of villages, linguistic imperialism, prohibition of Indigenous economic, social, and political systems, and enforced enrolment of children in Indian residential schools (McCarty, 2003). These processes have already obliterated ten Indigenous languages (Norris, 2007) and nearly extinguished all others; only Nîhîyaw (Cree), Anishnaabe (Ojibway), and Inuttitut (Inuit), due to their large population bases, are expected to survive the current century (ibid.).

Tremendous diversity exists among Indigenous Peoples in Canada on dimensions that affect the survival of their languages, including population size, oral and written language use, number of dialects, level of language documentation, cultures, histories, political organization, social and health conditions, and geographic location. Further, Indigenous language communities vary with regard to their engagement in policy creation and motivation towards sustaining their languages in or outside formal schooling (Task Force on Aboriginal Languages and Cultures, 2005; Fettes & Norton, 2000). Although each group has had different experiences, some commonalities exist, and these are outlined below. The authors have been involved in Indigenous language revitalization in various ways for the past 10 years ranging from language nest (early childhood immersion) to adult Indigenous language learning, with focus on the speech and language development of Indigenous children and on the impacts of language in education policies in Canada.

Declining Intergenerational Transmission of Indigenous Languages

The number of children who are learning a certain language is arguably the best indicator of its health and longevity (Barrena et al., 2007). The most recent Canadian census data indicate that only 12.4% of Indigenous children aged 0-4 are learning an Indigenous language at home; another 5% are acquiring one as an additional language (Norris, 2006). About two-thirds of these children are Inuit living in Canada's northernmost regions; one-third are First Nation[iii] children living on reserves.[iv] Over 60% of Indigenous children are growing up in urban and peri-urban settings off reserves. Few of these children are learning an Indigenous language, mainly as a result of language loss among parents and grandparents who were forced to attend English-only residential schools, but also due to ongoing monolingual education policies. Children whose home or preschool supports them in learning an Indigenous language almost invariably are required to start primary school (i.e., Kindergarten and Grade 1) in English or French. This lack of language support is of grave concern, as expressed by the Assembly of First Nations (2000), First Nation scholars (e.g. Battiste, 2000), linguists (e.g. Phillipson, 1992) and others. Some researchers warn that mainstreaming young speakers of Indigenous languages into English- or French-medium schooling is a form of linguistic genocide (Day, 1985); they predict that English and French will continue to replace Indigenous languages until no native speakers remain.

Mismatched Languages and Learning Goals at School Entry

With most Indigenous children in Canada now speaking English or French as their first language, one might assume they would not experience difficulties attributable to language mismatches at school. However, language and culture-based challenges figure prominently among factors that may account for high rates of learning difficulties and early attrition. First, there are still communities where a majority of children speak their Indigenous language but are forced to start school in English or French, with no support for transferring skills from the more familiar language to the newly introduced language. In Labrador, 35% of Innu children never attend school, a trend that is partly due to an unfamiliar language environment (English) and school culture that is seen by Innu children and their parents as "foreign, devoid of culturally relevant curriculum, and having little or no relevance to their lives" (Philpott, 2006: 373). Second, many children, especially in rural and remote communities, speak a non-standard variety of English that creates communication difficulties for children and their teachers. Several Canadian investigators have reported unique difficulties confronting children who start kindergarten speaking an Indigenous language or a non-standard variety of English or French that is different from the language of instruction (Ball & Bernhardt, 2008; Crago, 1990; Wright, Taylor, & Macarthur, 2000). Third, the pragmatics of communication in some Indigenous families and communities may be at odds with the discourse expectations of non-Indigenous professionals in institutions of the dominant culture, including public schools. For example, Indigenous children may have been socialized not to answer questions to which they know an older person already knows the answer (e.g., rhetorical questions such as "What colour is the sky today?") (Ball & Bernhardt, 2008). The forms of oral narratives that are recognized in their home communities as constituting a 'good story' may be seen by non-Indigenous teachers as lacking in the necessary elements of story-telling (e.g., context setting, linear time line) (Peltier, 2011). They may have a propensity to want to learn by watching and doing rather than by listening and following explicit instructions. Failure by teachers or non-Indigenous peers to recognize, value or encourage these forms of learning readiness can cause low self-esteem, cultural identity confusion and conflict, difficulties for parents wanting to accompany their children in their journeys through formal education, and overall lack of engagement in formal education. Altogether, the situation nationwide raises serious doubts about whether Canadian public schools are willing or able to support the social inclusion, linguistic rights and educational success of Indigenous children.

Many Indigenous parents, Elders,[v] and leaders argue that linguistically and culturally inappropriate teaching methods, curricula, and learning assessment procedures frequently result in serious negative consequences for their children (Canadian Centre for Justice, 2001; Royal Commission on Aboriginal Peoples, 1996). For example, many Indigenous children have social and environmental literacies that are valued and adaptive within the context of their everyday lives, but that are not valued or even recognized by mainstream teachers focused almost exclusively on text-based literacy. They may speak a variety of English that is the norm in their home communities but that is not readily accepted or understood by non-Indigenous teachers (Ball & Bernhardt, 2008). Consequences may include undermining Indigenous parents' goals for children; creating cultural alienation among young people; inhibiting development of school readiness skills; perceiving Indigenous children as socially reticent or resistant to instruction; and over-identifying developmental delays and disorders, especially in the speech-language domain (Hibel, Faircloth, & Farkas, 2008). While the nature and scope of misguided practice no doubt varies across schools and regions, overall Canada is failing to support the educational success of Indigenous children (Canadian Council on Learning, 2009). It is worth noting that while the number of Indigenous, professionally-accredited teachers is growing, there are few teaching in off-reserve schools and even fewer who are speakers of their Indigenous languages.

Cultural Learning through Language

Indigenous language speakers are concerned that, as fewer children learn their ancestral language, not only their languages but also their cultures will be lost (Royal Commission on Aboriginal People, 1996). Indigenous languages convey culturally based ways of interpreting the world and experiences within it (Battiste, 2000), and it is impossible to translate the deep meanings of words and concepts into the languages of other cultures. When children learn their Indigenous languages from infancy, they are able to consolidate a culturally cohesive identity with links to the land, to traditional knowledge, to Elders, and to their communities (Battiste, 2000; Crystal, 1997). According to a national task force, "the ability to speak one's own language helps people to understand who they are in relation to themselves, their families, and their communities, and to Creation itself" (Task Force on Aboriginal Languages and Cultures, 2005: iv). One of the few Indigenous speech and language pathologists in Canada, Sharla Peltier, explains:

> We're taught that our language comes from the Creator and that speaking it acknowledges our connection. We're taught that our voice is a sacred gift and that there is a lot of power in our words. When we speak, our words go around the world forever. (Ball, 2006: 1)

Given the importance of Indigenous languages for preserving Indigenous cultural identity, knowledge, social belonging, spiritual life, and existence on the political landscape, the potential for education to promote or hinder Indigenous children's opportunities to learn their mother tongues is of critical concern.

HISTORICAL EXPLOITATION OF SCHOOLING FOR LINGUISTIC ASSIMILATION

Links between language, education, and sovereignty were not lost on the early colonizers of the land called Canada, where using schools to strip Indigenous children of their culture and language is a long-standing tradition. Because the historical treatment of Indigenous Peoples has created enormous challenges for intergenerational transmission of Indigenous languages (and, arguably, Indigenous children's educational engagement), a brief history is provided here.

History of Indigenous Language Policy in Canada

The new country of Canada froze out Indigenous languages from the outset (Derwing & Munro, 2007). At confederation in 1867, policies supported by legislation and funding established the nation as bilingual in English and French (Gourd, 2007). A century later, heightened political tensions about the comparative status of the two languages led in 1963 to a Royal Commission mandated to study the country's "two founding races" and "other ethnic groups" (Innis, 1973, Foreword), but the latter were defined as those who had immigrated to Canada (Royal Commission on Bilingualism and Biculturalism, 1967). Indigenous Peoples, despite their efforts to be included and to have their language rights considered, were rendered invisible in policy and practice (Laurendeau & Dunton, 2006). From this foundation of cultural and linguistic imperialism, the Commission recommended an Official Languages Act, enacted in 1969, securing English and French as the official state languages (Burnaby, 1996). The Commission did assert Canada's responsibility to do "everything that is possible ... to help the native populations preserve their cultural heritage, which is an essential part of the patrimony of all Canadians" (Royal Commission on Bilingualism and Biculturalism, 1967, Vol 1: xxv). However, responsibility for language maintenance was left entirely in the hands of Indigenous people who had no resources to ensure creation of opportunities for young people to learn through and develop in their Indigenous languages. This failure to recognize Indigenous languages as official created, in effect, a policy of exclusion.

Variable Control of Language and Education

Over the past two decades, the Assembly of First Nations (1990, 1991, 1992, 2000) produced four reports calling for official recognition of Indigenous languages. Parliament recently passed the Aboriginal Languages of Canada Act (Senate of Canada, 2009), but this Act falls short of calling for legislative action to guarantee support for language preservation and revitalization efforts, including public schooling offered in Indigenous languages. Instead it recommends creating local bylaws to declare languages as "official" within a particular Indigenous community. This provision mirrors an earlier national policy allowing for local control of education of First Nation children who attend schools on reserves, and means that children may access education in an Indigenous language *if* they live on a reserve, *if* the reserve operates a school, and *if* that school has the community mandate and resources to offer education in the Indigenous language. Although rare, there are a few schools able to provide this kind of education (e.g. in Secwepemc territory in British Columbia and Mohawk territory in Quebec), but few or no resources are provided by the federal government.

Some bright spots in Canada's North give hope despite the country's gloomy language policy environment. The Official Languages Act of the Northwest Territories (1988), including the Yukon Territory, recognizes nine Indigenous languages in addition to English and French. The Nunavut Official Languages Act (Parliament of Canada, 2009) recognizes Inuttitut, Inuinnaqtun, English, and French. Education in Indigenous languages is more readily available throughout these northern regions, which are the traditional territory of the Inuit, approximately 70,000 people strong (Statistics Canada, 2006).

Against Time and against the Odds

Despite progress in some regions of the country and ongoing advocacy by national Indigenous organizations, barriers to Indigenous language preservation appear almost insurmountable. A contributing factor is the lack of support of the non-Indigenous population and, in some locations, of Indigenous people themselves. In the first case, non-Indigenous Canadians have never been educated about the rich language resources that are part of the country's heritage. Canadian mainstream media reinforce a construction of Canada as populated entirely by immigrants. Within a context of ongoing disinformation and social stigma surrounding Indigenous Peoples, their rights, and their roles in Canada's history, widespread apathy, if not overt negativity, exists about the importance of teaching Indigenous languages. Further, "a history of Canadian government suppression and oppression of the Native language has created an attitude of apathy and fatalism about the need and utility of Native languages" (Assembly of First Nations, 1992: 2). This makes it difficult for people to mobilize successfully on behalf of their languages and cultures. For Indigenous communities struggling with challenges to their very survival, including their right to live on traditional lands, language issues may be seen as secondary at best (Romaine, 2002).

Indian Residential Schools: Multigenerational Impacts

Around the world, language-in-education policies are often motivated by an explicit or hidden curriculum of assimilation (Ball, 2011; Milloy, 1999). Canada's overt intentions are among the worst, where successive governments historically legitimated the forced removal of Indigenous children from their families and communities to Indian residential schools and, later, to non-Indigenous adoptive and foster homes. In the late 1800s, the colonial government recognized that language is the main channel for culture and lifestyle, and anticipated that if children were prevented from speaking their mother tongue, their cultures would likely die out (Milloy, 1999). For a century, Indigenous children in Canada were forced through legislation to attend Indian residential schools, with a penalty of incarceration for parents who did not comply (Milloy, 1999). While the residential school era began winding down in Canada in the 1950s, the last school did not close until 1996 (Milloy, 1999). Canada has since offered an apology to those affected by the residential school era (Office of the Prime Minister, 2008), however, measures taken toward retribution and reconciliation remain controversial.

The degradation of children's languages and cultures in residential schools instilled a belief among many of today's Indigenous parents and grandparents that their language was inferior and their forms of social interaction and spiritual practice were unspeakably demonic (Wesley-Esquimaux & Smoleski, 2004). In most residential schools, children were forced to stop speaking their home language, to stop communicating with their siblings, to repudiate their cultures and to relinquish their Indian names (Miller, 1996). As a result, many of today's Indigenous parents and grandparents lost not only their capacity to speak their languages but also their confidence in using *any* language effectively (Lafrance & Collins, 2003). Even more fundamentally, many lost confidence in their capacity to engage in the kinds of care-giving social interactions that promote attachment in families (Chrisjohn, Young, & Maraun, 1997). As Hart and Risley (1995) have shown, everyday family interactions are the primary contexts for developing vocalization and speech communication. A rewarding experience of verbal communication within the context of caring relationships is critical to optimal oral language development during infancy and early childhood, which in turn is foundational for subsequent literacy. Indigenous scholar Lorna Williams has explained that when Indigenous people were told by colonial educators and Indian agents that their language was unclean, uncivilized and not useful for learning or for commerce, many parents developed a sense of shame about speaking the only language they knew, and the capacity and spirit for transmitting caring and knowledge through verbal interaction with their children was greatly attenuated (personal communication with Lorna Williams, 2006). Parents and grandparents who experienced poor parental modeling or abuse in residential schools or other settings may require extra support to learn how to engage in spontaneous, nurturing, language-mediated interchanges with their young ones (Wesley-Esquimaux & Smoleski, 2004). Policy makers and educators need to appreciate language development as an aspect of intergenerational family development that is relevant to a range of policy areas, including social justice, community development, education, literacy, and healing for Indian residential school survivors and the children of survivors.

Indigenous Language and Education Policy

In the 1970s, Indigenous organizations became increasingly vocal about their rights to raise and educate their own children and to practice their own cultures, languages, and forms of government, which included a growing sovereignty movement. Indigenous rights activists, scholars, and parents emphasized the loss of identity, cultural knowledge, personal well-being, and social belonging caused by language-in-education policies that have denied Indigenous children the right to be educated in their mother tongue. Initially, activists saw Indigenous language policy, support for language revitalization initiatives, and language-in-education policy as interconnected. In 1972 the National Indian Brotherhood published a pivotal paper – "Indian Control of Indian Education" – that led to swift government action in the devolution of responsibility for education to First Nations themselves followed by continued strides towards the goal of self-determined Indigenous education in Canada (Assembly of First Nations, 2003).

As noted by the Assembly for First Nations (1992: 2), "any strategy to increase the number of speakers of any language must necessarily involve the education system." However, over the past two decades, international movements for language revitalization and self-determination in education have become increasingly separate. This uncoupling of language and education policy is a common problem around the world that results in missed opportunities for language advocates and educators for mutually beneficial, coordinated efforts and avoiding working at cross purposes. Nevertheless, just as colonial governments have been instrumental in the demise of Indigenous languages and cultures by excluding Indigenous languages in policies and exploiting the power of the school system, the potential of schooling must now be harnessed as part of a multipronged approach to revive and maintain Indigenous languages and cultures.

STRATEGIES FOR INDIGENOUS LANGUAGE TEACHING IN
EDUCATION SETTINGS

Strengthening Capacity for Language Teaching

Training programs for Indigenous language teachers have been instituted at a few postsecondary institutions in Canada. For example, in 1999, the First Nations Education Steering Committee (FNESC) forged a partnership with the British Columbia College of Teachers to create an accredited Developmental Standard Teaching Certificate (First Nations Education Steering Committee, 2001). The program enables First Nation communities to partner with postsecondary institutions to offer community-based teacher training focused on Indigenous language revitalization. The University of Victoria partnered with an Indigenous education centre to co-create a university-accredited Certificate in Aboriginal Language Revitalization, which now transitions into a baccalaureate teaching degree. The University of Alberta annually delivers a Canadian Indigenous Languages and Literacy Development Institute (CILLDI) focusing on teaching Indigenous language teachers.

Indigenous Language as an Elective Subject of Study

A growing number of schools in Canada with a high enrolment of Indigenous students now offer classes in the Indigenous language that is most prevalent in their catchment area. Typically a language speaker from the local area is hired on a part-time basis to teach students – not all of whom are Indigenous – who elect to study the language. British Columbia's Ministry of Education has created a system whereby school districts can create curriculum in a language other than English or French and offer it as a second language from Grades 5-12.[vi] However, there is little support for these initiatives and little evidence that teaching an Indigenous language as a subject supports oral proficiency and literacy to the degree necessary for higher order cognitive skills or for linguistic transfer to acquiring other languages (Hinton, 2001). Except in the North (because of the activism mentioned earlier) and in some communities on reserve lands where it is feasible to make Indigenous language recovery a focus of community development work, youngsters typically have no opportunities to hear or interact in the language outside the classroom.

Immersion Schooling

Language revitalization scholars tend to agree that, in the absence of language immersion at home, immersion schooling programs stand the best chance of producing a new generation of proficient speakers (Grenoble & Whaley, 2006; McCarty, 2003). Several Indigenous immersion programs[vii] exist in Canada, but as Richards and Burnaby (2008) report, there has been no comprehensive study to date. Some have been documented; for example, Fulford (2007) identified the following Indigenous immersion programs as some of the most successful in Canada: the Eskasoni school in Nova Scotia, the Waskaganish schools in Quebec, and Chief Ahtam School near Adam's Lake, BC.

Bilingual Schooling

Beginning around 2001, a few completely bilingual community-controlled schools have been introduced in Canada, including a K-12 Cree-English school in Thompson, Manitoba (Fulford, 2007) and 14 K-3 Inuttitut-English schools in Nunavik (Louis & Taylor, 2001). Kahnawà:ke in Quebec has a school that started as a Mohawk-English program and has moved increasingly towards a full immersion approach, where more attention is placed on the Indigenous language, in this case Mohawk. In 1982, when the program was described as a partial immer-sion approach, two research teams explored outcomes for children in grades one and three. Both studies concluded that, compared to control subjects in English-only primary education, the Mohawk immersion students increased their ability to speak Mohawk, spoke Mohawk more often outside the classroom, scored equally well on tests of English acquisition, and performed equally well on academic tests (Hoover, 1992; Lambert et al., 1984). A study of Inuttitut-English bilingual primary schools in Nunavik indicates that their main impact has been on personal and collective self-esteem, because children and their parents have regained control over education, and because culturally based curriculum content came in when the Indigenous language became the medium for sharing and creating knowledge (Wright & Taylor, 1995). Guèvremont and Kohen (2010) report, based on the Aboriginal People's Survey results of 2006: "Children who spoke an Aboriginal language and learned it in school were more likely to be rated as doing very well in school" (ibid.: 13) and "Aboriginal language was associated with positive school outcomes for children if learned in school" (ibid.: 19). Unfortunately, while research from outside Canada shows that bilingual schools can make an important contribution to language revitalization, no controlled studies with carefully designed outcome measures have yet been done in Canada (Charron, 2010).

Language Initiatives in Early Childhood Programs

Although formal schooling would be the preferred site for supporting Indigenous language acquisition, it is not currently viable in Canada. However, there is gathering momentum in communities for promoting Indigenous language acquisition through community-driven programs at the pre-primary level. Initiatives include language nests for infants and toddlers, heritage-language-based and bilingual early childhood programs, and Aboriginal Head Start. These programs involve community members who have some degree of proficiency with the children's heritage language(s). Cross-cultural investigators have demonstrated the potential utility of collaborative, strengths-based approaches to language-in-education practices (Crago, 1992; van Kleek, 1994). Community members are uniquely positioned to identify core features of language socialization, to understand the contexts of child development and care in the community, and to offer insights to teachers about the conditions, needs, and goals of a family or community (Rogoff, 1990) However, a well-established principle in language research is that early childhood is not the best time for children in these contexts to begin learning a second language (Asher & Garcia, 1969; Snow & Hoefnagel-Hoehle, 1978), unless it is an everyday language spoken at home or in an alternative care environment such as daycare.

An Ecologically Comprehensive Strategy

A federal task force concluded that "language revitalization can occur through formal education but maintenance or retention of the Aboriginal language necessitates the interaction of multiple social spheres where the language can be accessed, expressed and transmitted" (Task Force on Aboriginal Languages and Cultures, 2005: 38). Figure 1 below portrays the interdependent ecological systems in which Indigenous young children and their families are nested. Supportive interventions could be introduced in any or all of these contexts to promote Indigenous language acquisition through education, either by using an Indigenous language as a medium of instruction, as in immersion and bilingual approaches, or at least by teaching it as a subject. This schema situates the family as the core – or heart – of language-mediated relationships between caregivers and young children. However, responsibility cannot rest solely with Indigenous families and communities to ensure that Indigenous languages do not die. Partners and allies are needed in government, non-government organizations, academe, schools, the media, and society as a whole.

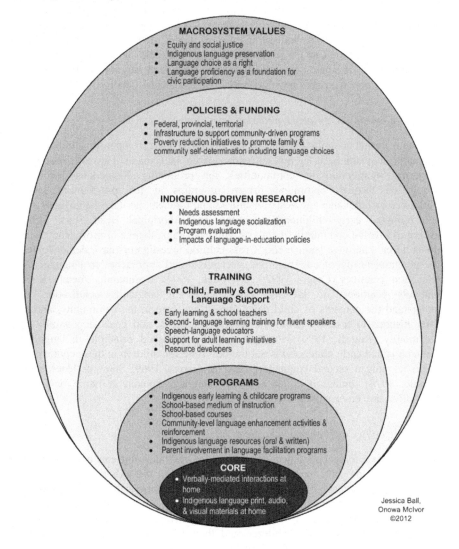

Figure 1. Systems of support for Indigenous language acquisition and maintenance in Canada

Investments in the areas identified in Figure 1 would yield new knowledge and a potentially effective system of supports driven by Indigenous community agendas and organizations. Partnerships across Indigenous organizations, postsecondary institutions, and health, education, and social development sectors could support new resources, capacity, and program strategies. Support for Indigenous language and literacy facilitation could be expected to:

– help retain endangered languages;
– promote cultural continuity and self-esteem;
– counteract prevalent misconstructions of cultural and language differences as communication and parenting deficits;
– reduce high rates of diversion of Indigenous children at school entry to special programs for learning support, with their attendant social stigma and exclusions; and
– increase social inclusion of Indigenous children within the fabric of Canadian society.

Policy reforms and interventions at only one or two of these levels – for example, Indigenous language immersion preschools without provisions for ongoing opportunities to learn in an Indigenous language, or early childhood immersion programs without support for parental pathways to language proficiency – are not likely to yield either measurable gains in Indigenous language maintenance or educational equity for Indigenous children. As already discussed, most Indigenous children and their parents in Canada learn English or French as a first language and acquire their heritage language, if at all, as a second language. A growing body of research shows that the process of second language learning is longer, harder, and more complex than previously believed (Lightbown, 2008). Children cannot develop proficiency through preschool immersion programs only, or through after-school language clubs; they require long-term instruction in their heritage language, as well as opportunities to use the language for learning and practice with increasingly complex forms of the language in functional settings (Collier, 1989). While learning more than one language has been associated with enhanced cognitive flexibility and metalinguistic awareness once children are fully bilingual (Bialystok, 1991; King & Mackey, 2007), there can be real risks to children's academic achievement if they are struggling to learn more than one language over an inadequate time period without adequate supports. Children need ongoing support for developing proficiency in their first language in order not to fall behind in content area learning, as well as ongoing opportunities to develop proficiency in their second language (Ball, 2011). For these reasons, piecemeal, bootstrapped approaches that depend solely upon community-initiated and sustained efforts are not likely to yield sought-after gains in Indigenous children's educational success and Indigenous language recovery.

FUTURE DIRECTIONS

In a colonial country like Canada, Indigenous language exists within "a historically charged and politically loaded landscape" (Aylward, 2010: 297). Political will is needed to support increasing numbers of Indigenous children entering schools to learn the language that is their birthright and to succeed academically. Political will must be followed by action taken by school administrators and teachers, informed by a program of research to generate knowledge about what kinds of innovations are likely to be effective and under what conditions (Ball, 2008).

Now that Canada has acknowledged responsibility for the debacle of the Indian residential schools (Office of the Prime Minister, 2008), it must take action. Payments to individual victims do nothing to bring back Indigenous languages and cultural knowledge that were beaten to the brink of extinction. One meaningful reparation the government could make is to create policies, backed by secure and sufficient resources to implement them, to support a multi-pronged, locally controlled strategy for ensuring that Indigenous children have opportunities to acquire their heritage languages. Investments are needed to design, deliver, document, and evaluate innovative language development programs that: (a) are culturally and linguistically appropriate; (b) assist Indigenous parents to play active roles in achieving their goals for their young children's language development; (c) avoid extensive reliance on professionally accredited teachers who almost invariably do not speak an Indigenous language and are likely to be unaware of the language socialization environments and expectations for Indigenous learners; and/or (d) create fast-track alternative post-secondary training to increase the number of Indigenous teachers while concurrently supporting them to develop proficiency in their languages.

The idea that children should be 'ready' for school is a popular one, but Canadian public schools have yet to demonstrate that they are ready for Indigenous children. Language-in-education policies must address the historically created needs and goals of Indigenous families, as well as their specific needs for ensuring that children have opportunities to learn an Indigenous language within the context of culturally meaningful teaching and curricula, cultural safety, and dignity (Canadian Council on Learning, 2007). Understanding cultural variations in language varieties, language socialization, and the pragmatics of verbal and written communication heightens awareness of the potential cultural biases in education programs. For example, Heath (1983) found that children whose home culture values listening, observing, and "doing" over "talking" – as is likely to be the case for most Indigenous families – are more likely to be marginalized in a mainstream school that values verbal explanations and oral participation. Even if schooling is provided only in the dominant language, educators can support Indigenous children by understanding how children's early language socialization is likely to influence their interests, attention, memory, story-telling, social interactions, and responses to pedagogical techniques.

The priority placed by Indigenous organizations on Indigenous-led programs suggests the need for programs that assist family members to promote children's Indigenous language acquisition in the home from birth. As children approach the age of school entry, language promotion strategies need to reinforce positive cultural identity and promote success in school through programs that bridge the gap from home to school. Scholars specializing in Indigenous language acquisition must be supported to work alongside community advocates, activists, speakers, and learners to maximize limited resources and time. An immediate need exists for methodologically sound research that examines outcomes of initiatives such as Nunavik's bilingual programs and immersion programs in Kahnawà:ke that have existed for over two decades. Research that has been done to date (e.g., Brittain, Dyck, Rose, & MacKenzie, 2006; Peter, Hirata-Edds, & Montgomery-Anderson, 2008; Zwanziger, Allen, & Genesee, 2006) represents a starting point. However, much more must be done to document innovative ways of promoting, reviving and continuing Indigenous languages.

The experiences of other non-dominant groups internationally suggest that the most promising approach to creating new speakers is through immersion, beginning with language nests (Wilson & Kamana, 2001) and followed by full-immersion schooling (Aguliera & LeCompte, 2007). Other approaches that have produced proficient Indigenous language speakers include the Accelerated Second Language Acquisition method (Strengthening Indigenous languages and Cultures, 2011; Sarkar & Metallic, 2009), and the Master-Apprentice Language Learning program (Hinton, 2001). Efforts must reach members of every generation within a community.

Given past and present policies governing the education of Indigenous children in Canada, there is reason to be discouraged about the survival of Indigenous languages and the cultural knowledges and identities they embody. Still, the Indigenous population is growing at twice the rate of the non-Indigenous population (Statistics Canada, 2006), and increasing numbers of Indigenous communities are becoming aware both of the urgency of saving their languages and of their children's rights to be supported in learning their heritage languages. If languages are indeed "the life blood of a people" (Aboriginal Head Start Association of British Columbia, 2011), allowing them to die can only be seen as a form of cultural genocide.

Within Canada's generally chilly climate for Indigenous languages and Indigenous language-in-education initiatives, a slight warming trend includes the federal government's Aboriginal Head Start, which funds over 500 locally operated early childhood programs, and the Aboriginal Languages Initiative (ALI), which provides $5 million (CAD) annually to be divided equally among provinces and territories (Andrews Miller, 2008). Much more must be done. Providing equitable resources and supports for Indigenous children to exercise their right to learn their mother tongue and to maximize their potential for bilingual learning throughout their school years is a critical component of a comprehensive strategy that could potentially restore Indigenous languages within one or two generations.

NOTES

[i] Aboriginal is a legal term meaning the First Nations, Métis, and Inuit people of Canada.
[ii] Indigenous is a contemporary term used globally with a capital 'I' to refer to the first peoples of a colonized land. It is used throughout this chapter to mean the three distinct Indigenous groups of Canada (First Nations, Métis, and Inuit).

iii First Nation is a political term created by the Indigenous leaders of Canada to assert their position as the first, organized communities of self-governing peoples in the land now called Canada.

iv Reservations, commonly known as reserves, are lands set aside by the federal government for the use and habitation of First Nation people.

v The word Elders is capitalized as a sign of respect for senior members of Indigenous communities who are not only elderly but also are carriers of the history and wisdom of their People.

vi The British Columbia Ministry of Education provincial language template application site describes this initiative: http://www.bced.gov.bc.ca/irp/template_developed.php.

vii Immersion in this context is used to mean language learning methods in which the target language, in this case Indigenous, is "the medium as well as the object of instruction" (Ellis, 2005: 217).

REFERENCES

Aboriginal Head Start Association of British Columbia (2011). *Resources.* (http://www.ahsabc.net/viewcategory/17)

Aguliera, Dorothy, & LeCompte, Margaret (2007). Resiliency in Native languages: The tale of three Indigenous communities' experiences with language immersion. *Journal of American Indian Education, 46*(3), 11-36.

Andrews Miller, Heather (2008). Mi'kmaq and Maliseet languages to be revitalized. *Windspeaker, 25*(12), 26.

Asher, James J., & Garcia, Ramiro (1969). The optimal age to learn a foreign language. *Modern Language Journal, 53,* 334-341.

Assembly of First Nations (1990). *Towards linguistic justice for First Nations.* Ottawa, ON: Author. Education Secretariat.

Assembly of First Nations (1991). *Report of the national conference on Aboriginal languages and literacy.* Ottawa, ON: Author.

Assembly of First Nations (1992). *Towards rebirth of First Nations languages.* Ottawa, ON: Author.

Assembly of First Nations (2000). *A time to listen and a time to act: National First Nations language strategy.* Ottawa, ON: Assembly of First Nations: Language Secretariat.

Assembly of First Nations (2003). *"Investing in the future": First Nations education in Canada.* Ottawa, ON: Assembly of First Nations.

Aylward, M. Lynn (2010). The role of Inuit languages in Nunavut schooling: Nunavut teachers talk about bilingual education. *Canadian Journal of Education, 33*(2), 295-328.

Ball, Jessica (2006). *Talking points: Exploring needs and concepts for Aboriginal early childhood language facilitation and supports.* Concept paper prepared for Public Health Agency of Canada – Aboriginal Head Start in Urban and Northern Communities, Ottawa.

Ball, Jessica (2008). Promoting equity and dignity for Aboriginal children in Canada. *IRPP Choices, 14*(7), 1-30.

Ball, Jessica (2011). *Enhancing learning of children from diverse language backgrounds: Mother tongue-based bilingual or multilingual education in early childhood and early primary school years.* Paris: UNESCO. (http://unesdoc.unesco.org/images/0021/002122/212270e.pdf)

Ball, Jessica, & Bernhardt, Barbara May (2008). First Nations English dialects in Canada: Implications for speech-language pathology practice. *Clinical Linguistics and Phonetics, 22*(8), 570-588.

Barrena, Andoni, Amorrortu, Esti, Ortega, Ane, Uranga, Belen, Izagirre, Esti, & Idiazabal, Itziar (2007). Does the number of speakers of a language determine its fate? *International Journal of the Sociology of Language, 186,* 125-139.

Battiste, Marie (2000). Maintaining Indigenous identity, language, and culture in modern society. In Marie Battiste (Ed.), *Reclaiming Indigenous voice and vision* (pp. 192-208). Vancouver, BC: UBC Press.

Bialystok, Ellen (Ed.) (1991). *Language processing in bilingual children.* Cambridge, MA: Cambridge University Press.

Brittain, Julie, Dyck, Carrie, Rose, Yvan, & MacKenzie, Marguerite (2006). *The Chiasibi Child Language Acquisition Study (CCLAS): A progress report.* Presentation at the 38th Algonquian Conference, University of British Columbia, Vancouver, BC, October 27-29, 2006.

Burnaby, Barbara (1996). Language policies in Canada. In Michael L. Herriman & Barbara Burnaby (Eds.), *Language policies in English dominant countries: Six case studies* (pp. 159-219). Clevedon, UK: Multilingual Matters.

Canadian Centre for Justice (2001). *Indigenous peoples in Canada.* Statistics Profile Series. Ottawa, ON: Minister of Industry.

Canadian Council on Learning (2007). *State of learning in Canada: No time for complacency.* Ottawa, ON: Author.

Canadian Council on Learning (2009). *The state of Aboriginal learning in Canada: A holistic approach to measuring success.* (http://www.ccl-cca.ca/sal2009)

Charron, Nadine (2010). *Exploring the links between Aboriginal-language-medium instruction and academic performance: A literature review in support of the PCH Aboriginal Languages Initiative.* Canada Heritage: Aboriginal Affairs Branch, Policy and Research Directorate.

Chrisjohn, Roland David, & Young, Sherri Lynn, with Maraun, Michael (1997). *The circle game: Shadows and substance in the Indian residential school experience in Canada.* Penticton, BC: Theytus.

Collier, Virginia P. (1989). How long? A synthesis of research on academic achievement in second language. *TESOL Quarterly, 23,* 509-531.

Crago, Martha (1990). Development of communicative competence in Inuit children: Implications for speech-language pathology. *Journal of Childhood Communication Disorders, 13,* 73-83.

Crago, Martha (1992). Ethnography and language socialization: A cross-cultural perspective. *Topics in Language Disorders, 12*(3), 28-39.

Crystal, David (1997). *English as a global language.* Cambridge, UK: Cambridge University Press.

Crystal, David (2000). *Language death.* Cambridge, UK: Cambridge University Press.

Day, Richard (1985). The ultimate inequality: Linguistic genocide. In Nessa Wolfson & Joan Manes (Eds.), *Language of inequality* (pp. 163-181). Berlin, Germany: Mouton de Gruyter.

Derwing, Tracey M., & Munro, Murray J. (2007). Canadian policies on immigrant language education. In Reva Joshee & Lauri Johnson (Eds.), *Multicultural education policies in Canada and the United States* (pp. 93-106). Vancouver, BC: UBC Press.

Ellis, Rod (2005). Principles of instructed language learning. *System, 33,* 209-224.

Fettes, Mark, & Norton, Ruth (2000). Voices of winter: Aboriginal languages and public policy in Canada. In Marlene Brant Castellano, Lynne Davis, & Louise Lahache (Eds.), *Aboriginal education* (pp. 29-54). Vancouver, BC: UBC Press.

First Nations Education Steering Committee (2001). Developmental standard term certificate (DSTC): Bulletin. *Aboriginal Languages Newsletter, 1,* 4.

Fulford, George (2007). *Sharing our success: More case studies in Aboriginal schooling.* Kelowna, BC: Society for the Advancement of Excellence in Education.

Gourd, Karen M. (2007). A critical examination of language policies and practices in Canada and the United States. In Reva Joshee & Lauri Johnson (Eds.), *Multicultural education policies in Canada and the United States* (pp. 120-128). Vancouver, BC: UBC Press.

Grenoble, Lenore A., & Whaley, Lindsay J. (2006). *Saving languages: An introduction to language revitalization.* Cambridge, UK: Cambridge University Press.

Guèvremont, Anne, & Kohen, Dafna (2010). *Knowledge of an Aboriginal language and school outcomes.* Ottawa, ON: Statistics Canada, Health Analysis Division.

Hart, Betty, & Risley, Todd R. (1995). *Meaningful differences in the everyday experience of young American children*. Baltimore, MD: Paul H. Brookes.

Heath, Shirley Brice (1983). *Ways with words: Language, life and work in communities and classrooms*. Cambridge, UK: Cambridge University Press.

Hibel, Jacob, Faircloth, Susan C., & Farkas, George (2008). Unpacking the placement of American Indian and Alaska native students. *Harvard Educational Review, 78*(3), 498-528.

Hinton, Leanne (2001). The master-apprentice language learning program. In Leanne Hinton & Kenneth Hale (Eds.), *The green book of language revitalization in practice* (pp. 217-226). San Diego, CA: Academic Press.

Hoover, Michael, & The Kanien'kehaka Raotitiohkwa Cultural Center (1992). The revival of the language in Kahnawake. *Canadian Journal of Native Studies, 12*(2), 269-287.

Innis, Hugh R. (1973). *Bilingualism and biculturalism: An abridged version of the Royal Commission report*. Toronto, ON: McClelland & Stewart with the Secretary of the State Dept. and Information Canada.

King, Kendall, & Mackey, Alison (2007). *The bilingual edge: Why, when, and how to teach your child a second language*. New York: Collins.

Lafrance, Jean, & Collins, Don (2003). Residential schools and Indigenous parenting: Voice of parents. *Native Social Work Journal, 4*, 104-125.

Lambert, Wallace E., Genesee, Fred, Holobow, Naomi, & McGilly, C. (1984). *An evaluation of a partial Mohawk immersion program in the Kahnawake Schools*. McGill University, Unpublished paper.

Laurendeau, Andre, & Dunton, Davidson (2006). *The CBC digital archives website*. (http://archives.cbc.ca/politics/language_culture/dossier/655/)

Lewis, M. Paul (Ed.) (2009). *Ethnologue: Languages of the world*, Sixteenth edition. Dallas, TX: SIL International. (http://www.ethnologue.com/)

Lightbown, Patsy M. (2008). Easy as pie? Children learning languages. Concordia Working Papers in *Applied Linguistics, 1*, 1-25.

Louis, Winnifred, & Taylor, Donald M. (2001). When the survival of a language is at stake: The future of Inuttitut in Arctic Québec. *Journal of Language and Social Psychology, 20*(1-2), 111-143.

McCarty, Teresa (2003). Revitalising Indigenous languages in homogenising times. *Comparative Education, 39*(2), 147-163.

Miller, James Rodger (1996).*Shingwauk's vision: A history of Native residential schools*. Toronto, ON: University of Toronto Press.

Milloy, John Sheridan (1999). *"A national crime": The Canadian government and the residential school system, 1879 to 1986*. Winnipeg, MB: University of Manitoba Press.

Norris, Mary Jane (2006). Aboriginal languages in Canada: Trends and perspectives on maintenance and revitalization. In Jerry P. White, Dan Beavon, & Susan Wingert (Eds.), *Indigenous policy research: Moving forward, making a difference*, Vol. 3 (pp. 197-228). Toronto, ON: Thompson Educational Publishing.

Norris, Mary Jane (2007). Aboriginal languages in Canada: Emerging trends and perspectives on second language acquisition. *Canadian Social Trends, 83*, 20-28.

Northwest Territories (1988). *Official languages act*. Yellowknife, NT: Government of the Northwest Territories.

Office of the Prime Minister (2008). *PM offers full apology on behalf of Canadians for the Indian residential schools system*. (http://pm.gc.ca/eng/media.asp?id=2146)

Parliament of Canada (2009). *Nunavut official languages act*. (http://www.parl.gc.ca)

Peltier, Sharla (2010). *Valuing children's story-telling from an Anishnaabe orality perspective*. Unpublished M.Ed. Thesis, Nipissing University, North Bay, Ontario.
(http://www.ecdip.org/docs/pdf/Sharla%27s%20Final%20Revision%20without%20signatures.pdf)

Peter, Lizette, Hirata-Edds, Tracy, & Montgomery-Anderson, Bradley (2008). Verb development by children in the Cherokee language immersion program, with implications for teaching. *International Journal of Applied Linguistics, 18*(2), 166-187.

Phillipson, Robert (1992). *Linguistic imperialism.* Oxford, UK: Oxford University Press.

Philpott, David F. (2006). Identifying the learning needs of Innu students: Creating a model of culturally appropriate assessment. *The Canadian Journal of Native Studies, 26*(2), 361-381.

Richards, Merle & Burnaby, Barbara (2008). Restoring Aboriginal languages: Immersion and intensive program models in Canada. In Tara Williams Fortune & Diane Tedick (Eds.), *Pathways to multilingualism: Evolving perspectives on immersion education* (pp. 221-241). Clevedon, UK: Multilingual Matters.

Rogoff, Barbara (1990). *Apprenticeship in thinking: Cognitive development in social context.* New York: Oxford.

Romaine, Suzanne (2002). The impact of language policy on endangered languages. *International Journal on Multicultural Societies, 4*(2), 194-212.

Royal Commission on Aboriginal Peoples(1996). *Gathering strength: Report of the Royal Commission on Aboriginal Peoples.* Ottawa, ON: Minister of Supply and Services.

Royal Commission on Bilingualism and Biculturalism (1967). *Report of the Royal Commission on bilingualism and biculturalism: General introduction and book 1, the official languages.* Ottawa, ON: Queen's Printer.

Sarkar, Mela, & Metallic, Mali A'n (2009). Indigenizing the structural syllabus: The challenge of revitalizing Mi'gmaq in Listuguj. *Canadian Modern Language Review, 66*(1), 49-71.

Senate of Canada (2009). *Bill S-237: An act for the advancement of the Aboriginal languages of Canada and to recognize and respect Aboriginal language rights.* Ottawa, ON: Publishing and Depository Services.

Snow, Catherine E., & Hoefnagel-Hoehle, M. (1978). The critical period for language acquisition: Evidence from second language learning. *Child Development, 49,* 1114-1118.

Statistics Canada (2006). *Aboriginal peoples of Canada: A demographic profile, 2006 Census.* Ottawa, ON: Author.

Strengthening Indigenous languages and cultures. (n.d.) (http://www.nsilc.org/index.htm)

Task Force on Aboriginal Languages and Cultures (2005). *Towards a new beginning: A foundational report for a strategy to revitalize First Nation, Inuit and Métis languages and cultures.* Ottawa, ON: Department of Canadian Heritage.

United Nations (2008). United Nations declaration on the rights of Indigenous Peoples. New York, NY: Author.

van Kleeck, Anne (1994). Potential cultural bias in training parents as conversational partners with their children who have delays in language development. *American Journal of Speech-Language Pathology, 3*(1), 67-78.

Wesley-Esquimaux, Cynthia C., & Smolewski, Magdalena. (2004). *Historic trauma and Aboriginal healing.* Ottawa, ON: Indigenous Healing Foundation.

Wilson, William H., & Kamana, Kauanoe (2001). "Mai loko mai O ka 'I'ini: Proceeding from a dream": The 'Aha Punana Leo connection in Hawaiian language revitalization. In Leanne Hinton & Kenneth Hale (Eds.), *The green book of language revitalization in practice* (pp. 147-176). San Diego, CA: Academic Press.

Wright, Stephen C., Taylor, Donald M., & Macarthur, Judy (2000). Subtractive bilingualism and the survival of the Inuit language: Heritage- versus second-language education. *Journal of Educational Psychology, 92*(1), 63-84.

Zwanziger, Elizabeth E., Allen, Shanley E. M., & Genesee, Fred (2006). Cross-linguistic influence in bilingual acquisition: Subject omission in learners of Inuktitut and English. *Journal of Child Language, 32,* 893-910.

Jessica Ball
School of Child and Youth Care
University of Victoria, Canada

Onowa McIvor
Indigenous Education
University of Victoria, Canada

KIMMO KOSONEN[i]

2. THE USE OF NON-DOMINANT LANGUAGES IN EDUCATION IN CAMBODIA, THAILAND AND VIETNAM

Two Steps Forward, One Step Back

ABSTRACT

Monikielisten maiden koulutusjärjestelmät ovat perinteisesti suosineet valtakieliä ja jättäneet vähemmistökielet vähemmälle huomiolle. Tämä on johtanut eriarvoisuuteen. Oppijoiden ensikieleen perustuva monikielinen opetus voi siksi olla vähemmistökielten puhujille hyvin vapauttavaa. Kambodzha, Thaimaa ja Vietnam ovat alkaneet kokeilla paikalliskielten käyttöä opetuksessa. Tämä artikkeli keskittyy seuraaviin kysymyksiin: 1) kieli- ja koulutuspolitiikan muutokset alueella, 2) Kambodzhan ja Thaimaan uusi kielipolitiikka, mikä tukee aiempaa enemmän paikalliskielten käyttöä, 3) "heikentyvä" lainsäädäntötuki paikalliskielille Vietnamissa ja 4) ensikieleen perustuvan monikielisen opetuksen toiminta ja vahvistuminen alueella. Artikkeli osoittaa, että koulutuksen kieliongelma on ratkaistavissa, jos koulutuspolitiikka sitoutuu paikalliskielten opetuskäyttöön ja monikielinen opetus johtaa vahvan ensikielisen lukutaidon omaksumiseen myös vähemmistökielillä luoden perustan kaikelle myöhemmälle oppimiselle. (*Translated into Finnish [fin], a language of Finland, by the author.*)

Education systems in multilingual nations have traditionally ignored non-dominant languages (NDL) in favor of the dominant languages, leading to gross inequalities. Therefore, for speakers of NDLs, multilingual education (MLE) based on their first language (L1) can be highly liberating. Cambodia, Thailand and Vietnam are experimenting with the use of NDLs as languages of instruction. This chapter discusses educational language issues in the region by focusing on: 1) the changing policy environment in Southeast Asia, 2) new Cambodian and Thai policies that provide more official support for NDLs, 3) Vietnam's "weakening" written policy support for NDLs, and 4) the functioning and strengthening of L1-based MLE programs in the region. The chapter concludes that addressing the language of instruction issue is possible when education policies support the use of NDLs, and when MLE programs provide strong literacy skills in learners' L1s – as the foundation for all further learning.

C. Benson and K. Kosonen (eds.), Language Issues in Comparative Education, 39–58.
© *2013 Sense Publishers. All rights reserved.*

INTRODUCTION

Primary education shall be compulsory and free of charge. In local primary schools, citizens of ethnic *minorities* shall *have the right to be educated in their own language.* (Vietnamese Constitution 1946: Article 15, emphasis added)

The idea of offering education in non-dominant languages (NDL) is not entirely new in Southeast Asia, as this quote from the first Constitution of the Democratic Republic of Vietnam shows. However, the idea has remained theoretical for decades; only recently have some countries in the region actually begun using NDLs in educational practice in areas where dominant national languages are not widely spoken. One reason for the change is that hitherto hidden disparities in educational achievement due to gender, ethnicity, disability and language have become more apparent. This is due firstly to advocacy by international and non-governmental organizations as well as some academics and activists, and secondly to the availability of more disaggregated statistics related to educational quality (see e.g. Benson, 2004; Kosonen & Young, 2009; UNESCO, 2007a, 2007b, 2008a; 2008b, 2012a, 2012b). Southeast Asian countries are not alone; education systems in many multilingual contexts invariably favor dominant languages (DL) over non-dominant ones. Since many speakers of NDLs have insufficient knowledge of the DLs used for instruction, they experience unequal access to education and inferior quality of education provided. Various approaches have been introduced to make education systems more accommodating to members of non-dominant ethnolinguistic communities, among them and perhaps most importantly first language-based education (e.g. Benson; Stone; Walter, all in this volume).

This chapter attempts to outline trends in language-in-education policy in three Southeast Asian countries: Cambodia, Thailand and Vietnam. The main focus is on policy documents[ii] (or parts of them) dealing with NDLs in education. Particular attention is paid to Vietnamese policy, which seems to be taking a different direction than the policies in Cambodia and Thailand, even though the practice may not be very different. Thus, policy developments in Vietnam are given an additional section after this introduction to establish the context for discussion. I also look briefly at the relationship between policy and actual practice regarding the use of NDLs in education. Finally, I attempt to determine similarities and differences in policies and practices in the three countries.

The chapter draws from research conducted over the past ten years on Southeast Asian language-in-education policies and practices (Kosonen, 2004, 2005, 2007, 2008, 2009a, 2009b, 2010; Benson & Kosonen, 2012; Kosonen & Person, 2013; Kosonen, Shaeffer, & Vu, 2010; Kosonen & Young, 2009; Kosonen, Young, & Malone, 2007). The English translations of quotes from various constitutions are from the "Constitution Finder" (2012), and in the case of older Vietnamese constitutions from "The Constitutions of Vietnam" (2003). In addition to policy documents, data sources include various project reports as well as informal interviews of practitioners and policy makers in the region. Because there is little published research on the chapter's theme, many arguments are based on my long-term observations on language-in-education developments in the region. I have worked as a consultant and researcher in all three countries discussed here, and I am also in regular contact with a network of trusted colleagues working in the region on language and education issues.

VIETNAM: A TRADITIONAL LEADER IN NDL POLICY SUPPORT?

I began this chapter with a quote from the quite progressive Vietnamese Constitution of 1946. It is important to note that this constitution was written during a particularly unstable time in the country's history. Ho Chi Minh had declared Vietnam independent after the Second World War, and although Japanese forces had departed, the French still considered the country a colony (Karnow, 1997; LePoer, 1989).

Consequently, two Indo-China wars broke out, and the first Vietnamese Constitution never had a real chance to be applied in practice, though it remained in effect in communist-controlled areas until 1954. Cima (1989: online source, no pages) claims that the purpose of this first constitution was "essentially to provide the communist regime with a democratic appearance." The idea that everyone had a right to education in his or her own language was apparently influenced by the constitution of the Soviet Union at the time and the fact that the Indo-Chinese communist party had many members and soldiers from a variety of ethnolinguistic communities. Nonetheless, it is worth noting that there may never have been an intention to carry out the various guarantees of rights such as freedom of speech, assembly and the press (ibid.).

All subsequent Vietnamese constitutions have been less explicit than the Constitution of 1946 about the use of non-dominant languages in education. The second Constitution of 1959 gave all nationalities[iii] "the right to use their spoken and written languages" (Article 3). The third Constitution of 1980 elaborated on this by stating that "all nationalities have the right to use their own spoken languages and scripts"[iv] (Article 5). The current Constitution of 1992 is almost identical, though the problematic term "script" has been replaced: "Every nationality has the right to use its own spoken language and system of writing" (Article 5).

These documents would seem to indicate that Vietnam has been a leader in the region in terms of NDL use in education. Currently, the right to educational use of non-dominant languages is still mentioned, but it is not clear what is actually meant by "use" in this context. Nonetheless, many other policy documents have appeared in Vietnam that discuss the role of NDLs in education in more detail, and some educational development projects have included NDLs (Bui & Bui, 2009; Kosonen, 2004, 2009a; Vu, 2008; World Bank, 2009).

Meanwhile, a trend of increasing written policy support for and the actual practice in the use of non-dominant languages in education has emerged across Asia (Benson & Kosonen, 2013; Kosonen, 2009b, 2010; Kosonen & Young, 2009; Multilingual Philippines, 2012; UNESCO, 2007a, 2007b, 2008b, 2012a, 2012b).

Practical implications of this trend can be seen in the three countries discussed in this chapter as well as in Bangladesh, India, Nepal, Pakistan, the Philippines and Timor-Leste (UNESCO, 2012a).

NATIONAL CONTEXTS

This section sets the stage for discussion of Southeast Asian language-in-education policies. It provides basic information on national-level linguistic situations and a general introduction to the language and education issues in each of the three countries.

Cambodia

In the Kingdom of Cambodia, the Khmer are the dominant ethnolinguistic group in terms of power and number, as they comprise approximately 90 percent of the population. Even though there are 21 other languages spoken by the remaining ten percent, Cambodia is among the least linguistically diverse nations in Asia (Kosonen, 2009b; Lewis, 2009). Most ethnolinguistic minority groups in the country are small in number, apart from the Cham, Chinese, and Vietnamese, whose populations are in the hundreds of thousands (Kosonen, 2007, 2009b, 2010; Leclerc, 2012; Lewis, 2009; Neou Sun, 2009).

The Constitution of 1993 establishes Khmer as the official language and gives the Khmer script[v] an official status (Constitution Finder, 2012). Until the late 1990s, Khmer was exclusively the language of instruction at all levels of education, though schools in some areas had also been teaching Chinese or Vietnamese as subjects of study. L1-based bilingual[vi] education programs in formal and nonformal education have been initiated by various international agencies and non-governmental organizations (NGOs) in close collaboration with provincial education authorities and local communities. Five non-dominant languages, namely Brao, Bunong, Kavet, Krung and Tampuan, have thus far been introduced as languages of instruction, and work is ongoing in three additional languages: Jarai, Kaco' and Kui (Benson, 2011; Benson & Kosonen, 2012; CARE International Cambodia, 2004; Kosonen, 2007, 2009b, 2010; Noorlander & Ven, 2008; Neou Sun, 2009; Thomas, 2002; UNESCO, 2007b, 2008, 2012a).

Thailand

In the Kingdom of Thailand, Standard Thai (based on Central Thai as spoken in the capital, Bangkok) is the de facto official and national language. An estimated 50% of Thai citizens speak Standard or Central Thai as their first language. Standard Thai is the dominant language of the country and widely spoken throughout the country as a second language, but there are no reliable data on the extent of people's bilingualism (Kosonen, 2007, 2008, 2010; Kosonen & Person, 2013). More than eighty languages are spoken in Thailand, and the populations of some ethnolinguistic communities, such as Lao-Isan, Kammeuang, Pak Tai, Pattani

Malay, and Northern Khmer, are in the millions. In addition, there are at least one hundred thousand speakers of Sgaw Karen, Kui, Phuthai, and some Chinese languages (Kosonen & Person, 2013; Leclerc, 2012; Lewis, 2009).

Standard Thai is the language of instruction at all levels of education, and has been so almost exclusively for about one hundred years (Kosonen & Person, 2013; Prapasapong, 2009). However, for approximately half of the population of Thailand – possibly more – this language is not their first, and many children have comprehension problems in early childhood education programs and the early grades of primary school (Kosonen, 2008; Kosonen & Person, 2013; Smalley, 1994). Consequently, the dominant use of Standard Thai as the LOI is a major obstacle to educational achievement in many parts of the country.

In line with regional trends, debates on language and education issues have increased in Thailand among educators and politicians as well as in the media. Recent policy decisions have provided more latitude for ethnolinguistic minority people to use their languages in various ways, and several NDLs are currently used in L1-based education pilot projects (Kosonen, 2007, 2008, 2010; Kosonen & Person, 2013).

Vietnam

In the Socialist Republic of Vietnam, the Vietnamese-speaking Kinh are the dominant ethnolinguistic group, accounting for about 86 percent of the population. The remaining 14 percent comprises a number of non-dominant ethnolinguistic communities, many of whom lack exposure to the Vietnamese language. Several minority groups have large populations, including the Tay, Thai, Muong, Hoa (i.e. Chinese) and Khmer with populations of more than one million each. Five more groups, the Nung, Hmong, Dao, Gia Rai, and Ede, have populations in the hundreds of thousands. Nearly thirty non-dominant languages already have writing systems, and language development is ongoing in others (Bui & Bui, 2009; Benson & Kosonen, 2012; Kosonen, 2004, 2006, 2009a, 2009b, 2010; Leclerc, 2012; Lewis, 2009; Vu, 2008; World Bank, 2009).

The Vietnamese government officially recognizes fifty-four ethnic groups, according to the official classification of "nationalities" by the state. According to unofficial estimates and linguistic surveys, approximately one hundred languages are spoken in the country (Leclerc, 2012; Lewis, 2009). Reasons for this apparent discrepancy are similar to other countries such as China, Laos and the former Soviet Union, as Soviet-influenced approaches to ethnolinguistic classification have not necessarily been based on the languages people speak but on political factors (Benson & Kosonen, 2012; Kosonen, 2009a; Stites, 1999; UN-HRC, 2011; World Bank, 2009).

This ethnolinguistic classification as imposed by the state can cause confusion regarding the educational performance of learners by nationality. Many members of larger and more urbanized ethnic groups such as the Hoa, Muong, and Tay, for example, speak Vietnamese competently, some being bilingual and some having altogether lost their heritage languages[vii] (Kosonen, 2004, 2009a). The educational success of people from these groups in Vietnamese-medium education has been used to argue against the need for first language-based education among other, less assimilated minority populations, seriously impairing their access to quality education.

LANGUAGE-IN-EDUCATION POLICIES

This section outlines the main language-in-education policy positions of the three countries based on the available policy documents, particularly on statements regarding the use of NDLs in education. Brief interpretations of the current policies are provided as well.

Cambodia

Until late 2007, no explicit written policy support existed in Cambodia for the use of NDLs in education. However, the positive results of several pilot projects in L1-based education, as mentioned above, seem to have positively influenced policy developments. The Education Law of 2007 gives authorities the right to choose the language(s) of instruction,[viii] by issuing special sub-decrees or decisions in areas where *Khmer Lue*[ix] or Indigenous languages[x] are spoken (Benson, 2011; Kosonen 2007, 2009b, 2010; Neou Sun, 2009; UNESCO, 2011). This represents the first time that a Cambodian law gives explicit attention to non-dominant languages in education.

Unfortunately, it is not clear whether the law also refers to the three largest NDLs, namely Cham, Chinese, and Vietnamese, which are commonly considered non-Indigenous (and the latter two being immigrant) languages. The Lao, with a larger population than many Khmer Lue groups, also fall into this category. The Cham are considered by many Khmer people as well as by the Cambodian state as *Khmer Islam*, i.e. Muslim Khmers (Bredenburg, 2010), though they have a distinct culture and language unrelated to Khmer (Lewis, 2009). Overall, like children from the smaller Indigenous communities covered by the law, children from these larger "non-Indigenous" ethnolinguistic communities often lack access to the Khmer language. Thus because of their classification, "non-Indigenous" children are not as yet given access to education in their own languages.

The community schools model (Neou Sun, 2009; Noorlander & Ven, 2008; Siren, 2009) developed and piloted by CARE International has provided the basis for the "Guidelines on implementation of bilingual education programs for indigenous children in highland provinces," which was signed by the Minister of Education, Youth and Sports in August 2010 and subsequently disseminated to the provinces involved. The Guidelines essentially concretize parts of the 2007 Education Law for the geographical areas where the majority speak NDLs. Although the Guidelines do not define what bilingual education exactly means in the Cambodian context, the document does describe how bilingual education will be implemented and expanded at the primary level by the Ministry and its partners in five highland provinces, namely Kratie, Mondulkiri, Preah Vihear, Ratanakiri and Stung Treng.

The Guidelines document provides a chart of a transitional two-language education model which stipulates the use of L1 (the home language) and L2 (Khmer) as follows: in Grade 1, 80% of curriculum is learned in the L1, in Grade 2, 60% in L1, and in Grade 3, 30% in L1. The dominant language, Khmer, is introduced gradually in the first three grades. From Grade 4 all instruction will be in Khmer, even in non-Khmer speaking areas. The Guidelines also support the use of NDLs and the gradual introduction of the dominant language to non-Khmer-speaking children in early childhood education, but no details are provided on implementation or the balance between L1 and L2 use.

Cambodia must be congratulated for putting L1-based bilingual education into official policy and practice. Neither Thailand nor Vietnam has such detailed policy documents on the use of NDLs in education. An evaluation report states that "[w]ith adoption of the Guidelines, the MoEYS has taken a very important step, from relatively small-scale piloting ... to expansion to ... [several] provinces with significant minority populations" (Benson, 2011: 17). It is easy to agree with this statement, but at the same time it is important to note that the current policy is not without problems. As Benson (ibid.) noted, the Guidelines support a fairly short duration of L1 use, i.e. an early-exit model of bilingual education, and a "transitional philosophy" is clearly evident. These issues were raised and briefly discussed at a national symposium in November 2011 (UNESCO, 2011), but even though both MoEYS officials and international agency representatives acknowledge the issues, to date no changes have been made to the early transition model.

In sum, despite the positive policy developments, several challenges still remain in the Cambodian language-in-education scene:

- Firstly, who counts as Indigenous in Cambodia and/or as eligible for multilingual education? What provision, if any, is provided for Cham and other "non-Indigenous" children who are not fluent speakers of Khmer?
- Secondly, what is the future of L1-based instruction in nonformal education? The non-formal (NFE) sector is not mentioned in the Guidelines, and the November 2011 symposium (ibid.), which actually focused on NFE, did not produce any tangible outcomes.
- Finally, is the use of the non-Khmer scripts allowed for writing NDLs – for example, in writing Jarai, which is a cross-border language using the Roman script in Vietnam? In addition, the draft orthography of Kui was rejected in April 2012 by the MoEYS, so Kui cannot be used in MLE as stipulated in the Guidelines. This case raises a question about the future of orthographies for previously unwritten NDLs, as there seems to be some reluctance on the part of MoEYS to actually expand multilingual education to new languages.

Thailand

The status of non-dominant languages in Thai society is still ambiguous. Different groups of people hold different views on the language issue. Various activities promoting NDLs – conducted mostly by language communities and other non-governmental actors – have preceded the actual written language policies in Thailand. Government authorities have allowed many ethnolinguistic communities and their partners, such as academics and NGOs, to work quite freely in the NFE sector. This has perhaps been due to the unthreatened dominance of Standard Thai along with a laissez-faire attitude among many civil servants.

Academics and organizations working broadly on language issues, including non-dominant languages, started discussing the need for an explicit written language policy in the early 2000s. It was eventually the Royal Institute of Thailand that coordinated the drafting of the Kingdom's first National Language Policy (NLP). In 2006 a special NLP drafting committee was appointed. The coordination role fell quite naturally to the Institute, as it is the official authority on the Thai language, and its members represent the highest levels of academic excellence in Thailand. More than a dozen public fora and academic meetings were organized to gather information on the current language situation, raise awareness on the language issues, and help pave the way for policy development (Kosonen & Person, 2013; Person, 2010).

The policy that emerged was signed by then-Prime Minister Abhisit Vejjajiva in 2010, and two years later by the current government head, PM Yingluck Shinawatra. While the NLP deals with a wide range of issues relating to languages, the key points relating to non-dominant languages, and their use in education, are:

– [V]arious ethnic groups ... have the *right to use their mother tongues* in their homes, in their communities, and in public places. This includes the *use* of their *mother tongue in the education system* for their young people. (NLP, 2010, Section 4, emphasis added)

[The NLP] ... support[s] the use of the *ethnic languages*, or the mother tongue, as the *first language of children in the education system*. (NLP, 2010, Section 4, emphasis added)

It is the policy of the government to promote bilingual or multilingual education for the youth of the ethnic groups whose mother tongue is different from the national language (Thai) ... in order to *strengthen the study of the Thai* language and to support the *cognitive development and education of children*. (NLP, 2010, Section 5, emphasis added)

It is clear that this policy supports the use of *all* languages spoken in Thailand as the basis for further learning. Furthermore, the policy promotes L1-based multilingual education for all who do not speak Standard Thai at home.

The rationales given by the NLP for L1 use are particularly interesting. Usually – at least in most of Asia – the main justification given for the use of NDLs is to teach the dominant language more effectively, which is also the first rationale of the Thai policy. However, the NLP also calls for the use of learners' first languages as the basis for *cognitive development*, which in a way respects NDLs in their own right. Few other Asian countries have policies as explicit as this about the benefits of L1-based education, or use the proven theoretical grounds to justify L1-based education in non-dominant languages.[xi]

While it is not yet clear how the new policy will be operationalized, the NLP does provide official government support for the use of NDLs as languages of instruction. The Royal Institute has also initiated a project to officially recognize NDL orthographies based on the Thai script. The Pattani Malay orthography was the first to go through an approval process, which represented the first time that a Thai government agency has granted formal recognition to NDL orthography (Kosonen & Person, 2013; Person 2010).

Even with the introduction of a quite progressive written language policy, Thailand is not without challenges, including the following:

– Firstly, will the outlined actions of the NLP actually be implemented, and by whom? Some stakeholders are quite skeptical about whether these good policy statements will ever be implemented by the Thai Ministry of Education.
– Secondly, as very few members of the Thai public, government officials or decision-makers understand the importance of L1-based education, how can awareness on language issues be raised?
– Thirdly, will it be possible to advocate for L1-based education for speakers of languages related to Standard Thai, as these languages are usually seen as dialects even though some are quite distinct?
– Finally, given the unstable political situation in recent years, how can policies supporting NDLs in education be protected so they will not be caught in political battles?

Vietnam

The national and official language in Vietnam is Vietnamese, and it functions as the language of wider communication throughout the country. As mentioned earlier, the use of non-dominant languages in society and education is supported by various policy documents, such as constitutions, laws, decrees and decisions (Bui & Bui, 2009; Kosonen, 2004, 2009a, 2009b; Kosonen, Shaeffer, & Vu, 2010; Vu, 2008; World Bank, 2009).

Despite support for NDLs in numerous policy documents, in practice Vietnamese has remained the main language of instruction at all levels of education, even in non-Vietnamese-speaking areas. There is confusion over conflicting statements in different documents and their relative weight. Interestingly, around 10 NDLs have been used in programs called "bilingual education" (Kosonen, 2004, 2006, 2009a; UNESCO, 2008b; Vu, 2008, 2010), which have taught NDLs only as subjects of study for a few hours per week. These programs are top-down government directed (Kosonen, 2009a; UN-HRC, 2011), with little if any contribution from the ethnolinguistic minority communities themselves, unlike in many other Asian countries.

There is a Department of Ethnic Minority Education at the Ministry of Education and Training (MoET) which could be expected to promote NDLs and cultures. Instead, its stated priorities are the extension of Vietnamese-medium preschool programs into ethnic minority areas, investment in boarding schools for younger ethnic minority learners, the improvement and "strengthening" of Vietnamese language learning at all levels, and the creation of a sixth primary year so that Vietnamese can be "mastered" (Benson & Kosonen, 2012; EMED, 2007; Vu, 2010). Since the mid-1990s, boarding schools that use Vietnamese almost exclusively have been extended to ethnic minority areas. State officials see this program as a strategy to provide "equal educational opportunities" for non-Kinh people in highland areas, but experiences from other countries show that such boarding schools are rarely anything more than an assimilation strategy (Benson & Kosonen, 2012; Kosonen 2004, 2009a; World Bank, 2009).

In order to understand the state's current position on the role of NDLs in education in Vietnam, the most current and important language-in-education policy documents must be analyzed. The following are citations from key articles of the 2005 Education Law, and Government Decree No 82/2010/ND-CP "on teaching and learning ethnic minority languages in general and continuing educational institutions":

> Vietnamese is the *official language to be used in schools* and other educational institutions ... The State shall enable ethnic minority people to *learn their* spoken and written *languages* in order to preserve and develop their ethnic cultural identity, helping pupils from ethnic minorities easily absorb knowledge. (Vietnamese Education Law, 2005: Article 7, emphasis added)

> Ethnic minority languages are taught *as a subject* in general and continuing education institutions. (Vietnamese Government Decree 82/2010/ND-CP: Article 6, emphasis added)

> The Decree regulates in detail the teaching and learning of ethnic minority languages including the conditions, content, *methods and forms of teaching and learning* ... All the previous *regulations which conflict* with the Decree will be *abrogated*. (Ibid.: Article 1 and 14, emphasis added)

The Law and the Decree are closely related, as the Decree attempts to provide practical guidelines for the implementation of the Law in terms of NDLs in basic education (formal and nonformal sectors), excluding early childhood education (ECE). It is worth noting that the Decree went through a development process of five years, and different drafts had slightly different foci, possibly reflecting the differing positions of different factions in the MoET and other state agencies. It seems as if there is an attempt with the Decree to represent the government's last word on NDLs in education. Even though the Decree probably intends to put some order to the confusion over conflicting statements of the past, it leaves us with many questions about the role of NDLs in education. Some remaining aspects are unclear:

- Does the Decree allow first language-based bi- or multilingual education in NDLs, e.g. the externally-funded pilot projects currently operating? Educationalists have reportedly interpreted the Decree as "a continuing restriction on the teaching of ethnic minority languages solely as separate language courses, not to be used as the medium of instruction" (UN-HRC, 2011: 14).
- If NDLs can only be used as subjects of study, what will happen to the pilots when their external funding runs out?
- What does Vietnamese as the official language of education mean in practice – must it be the sole or the main language of instruction?

NON-DOMINANT LANGUAGES IN EDUCATIONAL PRACTICE

This section describes current use of NDLs in education in the three countries, including pilot projects and research results. These examples reflect recent developments in the region, while demonstrating the "power" of effective practice in NDL use. Available space does not allow a thorough description of NDL practice, but the works cited can be consulted as they elaborate on these points.

Pilot Projects as Demonstrations of Effective Practice

In Cambodia and Thailand, successful pilot projects using NDLs have led to the review and ultimate rewriting of existing language-in-education policies. The Cambodian experience in using NDLs, initiated by International Cooperation Cambodia, CARE International and other partners, provides an excellent example. Students in Cambodian pilot programs in both formal and non-formal systems are learning to read in their first languages as well as Khmer and are using both languages for further learning. Community school language committees consisting of NDL community members have been integrally involved in language and curriculum development, the production of learning materials, and the identification of volunteer teachers. Important factors of success in the "CARE model" pilots, which are now being implemented more widely in the formal sector, include the active participation of communities through these committees, the hiring and training of local staff who speak the NDLs used as LOIs, and the adoption of an alternative school calendar that is suited to local farming conditions (AKP, 2012; Benson, 2011; Benson & Kosonen, 2012; CARE International Cambodia, 2004; Kosonen, 2007, 2010; Neou Sun, 2009; Noorlander & Ven, 2008; Thomas, 2002; UNESCO, 2007b, 2008b).

In Thailand, an action research project using a widely spoken NDL, Pattani Malay, as a language of instruction represents the first serious attempt to address educational language issues in Southern Thailand. The project, which is based on the principle of long-term use of the L1 for literacy and learning, was initiated by by Mahidol University and other non-governmental actors, and is supported the Thailand Research Fund and UNICEF, with technical support from SIL International (Aluyufri 2008; Premsrirat, 2008, 2009; Paramal, 2008; SEAMEO, 2009). Another promising project involving long-term L1 use is operating in the Kanchanaburi Province, using Mon and Standard Thai as languages of instruction (Tienmee, 2009). This initiative is a result of collaboration between a Thai NGO, the Foundation for Applied Linguistics (FAL) and the Ministry of Education (MOE), with technical support from Payap University and SIL International (ibid.). FAL and MOE are also involved in small-scale MLE programs in Northern Thailand, mostly in ECE and the early grades of primary, using four NDLs: Akha, Hmong, Lahu and Pwo Karen (Kosonen & Person, 2013; Tan, 2011; UNESCO, 2012a).

Finally, despite the gap between written policy and educational practice, some initiatives that use NDLs in education are operating in Vietnam. One project supported by Save the Children employs para-professional teaching assistants to promote oral classroom communication in the L1, though they stop short of using these languages for literacy (Benson & Kosonen, 2012; Kosonen, 2009a; Vu, 2010). An action research project by MoET and UNICEF takes a fully bilingual approach from preschool to the end of primary at grade 5, in clusters of schools in three provinces, representing three NDLs: Hmong, J'rai and Khmer. This program uses L1 literacy as a basis for learning additional languages and academic content, and has received technical support from many of us working in the region (Bui & Bui, 2009; Benson & Kosonen, 2012; Malone, 2010; Shaeffer, 2010; UNICEF, 2011).

NDLs have also been brought into primary education by other means. In some areas of Thailand, for example, "local curriculum" (up to 30% of learning time) is used for teaching at least six different NDLs (Prapasapong, 2009; UNESCO, 2012a). The local curriculum component is used less in Cambodia and Vietnam for teaching NDLs, but it is used in other countries (see Ruiz de Forsberg and Borges Månsson, Chapter 11 in this volume) and it could be a good platform for introducing new NDLs into the formal education system. However, it must be remembered that in the case of Vietnam, the teaching of NDLs as school subjects has not led to adoption of L1-based education.

Research on NDL Communities and Learners

Research on the conditions of NDL communities and learners has contributed to greater public awareness of language and education issues, which has in some cases led to the revision of practices and policies to better serve diverse populations. For example, as a result of recent research, the Thai MOE now acknowledges that many minority learners are prevented from performing up to their true potential if only Standard Thai is used as the LOI (Kosonen, 2008; Kosonen & Person, 2013). Prapasapong (2009) cites a MOE survey showing that in some areas there is a mismatch between teachers' NDLs and those of their students, meaning that they do not necessarily understand each other, making learning inefficient. Based on learning results from the Pattani Malay MLE pilot in Thailand, Walter (2011) has shown that speakers of the NDL studying in their L1 perform far better in all tested school subjects – including the DL, Standard Thai – than speakers of the NDL taught only in the DL.

In Vietnam, evidence from the pilot project on MLE mentioned earlier has been important in addressing the issue of "presumed obstacles" to NDL use in education. For years Vietnamese government officials have relied on common myths, e.g. that L1-based bilingual education is not feasible in "such a linguistically diverse context" (Bui & Bui, 2009; Kosonen, 2004, 2009a; Kosonen, Shaeffer, & Vu, 2010; Viet Nam News, 2011; World Bank, 2009). Another presumed obstacle is the lack of teachers who speak NDLs; however, recent yet-unpublished (Jim Owen, pers. comm. 2012) research regarding the linguistically diverse Lao Cai province – in which a L1-based education pilot is currently operating – shows that most schools comprise only one or two ethnolinguistic groups and that many teachers have some proficiency in local NDLs. The presumed heterogeneity is mostly in towns influenced by migration, which are not the target areas of L1-based programs. It is likely that the situation is similar or even more conducive to L1-based education in other provinces that are linguistically less diverse.

LATEST ISSUES AND TRENDS

When Cambodian, Thai and Vietnamese policies and practices with regard to NDLs are compared, some interesting commonalities and differences emerge. The biggest difference between these three countries is what I call "the philosophy of policies and practices" – the ideologies and principles guiding decision-making and action. Another key difference is the level of freedom or space in which NGOs and Civil Society Organizations (CSO) to function, and consequently be involved in L1-based education.

Vietnam has issued many supportive policy statements, but most could be considered rhetoric because few have been put to practice. In addition, as in other one-party states influenced by the Soviet Union, there has been very little latitude for local CSOs or community-based initiatives, and the work of international non-governmental organizations (INGOs) has been restricted more in Vietnam than in neighboring countries. Yet Vietnam has been relatively independent in its decision-making on language-in-education issues, as outside actors seem to have had less influence on policy formation than in Cambodia or Thailand – for better or for worse.

In terms of their philosophies of policies and practices, Cambodia and Thailand have been quite different, probably due to a certain extent to their different political systems. Until recently neither country has issued explicit policy statements on NDLs or their use in education. This may have been unintentional, as most decision-makers are members of dominant ethnolinguistic communities (as they also are in Vietnam) and may not be aware of the linguistic diversity existing in their countries, or of the need to address language-in-education issues. However, local CSOs, NGOs, academics as well as INGOs have been quite free to advocate for L1-based education and to initiate various projects at the local level. Consequently, some piloting and action research in L1-based education has been possible without official policy support. These conditions, which experienced South African language advocates might call "enabling" (Heugh, 1995), have allowed various actors in Cambodia and Thailand to work towards more inclusive educational approaches. Today it is clear that government agencies and official policy documents are aligning themselves with this trend by providing increased support for NDLs in education. These developments have not occurred in a vacuum, but reflect – and contribute to – the regional trend of increasing L1-based bi- and multilingual education.

Meanwhile, and somewhat inexplicably, Vietnam has gradually weakened its statements in official documents on the importance and use of NDLs in education. One possible explanation is that government officials no longer take for granted the policy statements that were adapted from – and sometimes even literal translations of – Soviet documents. Thus, documents may have been revised to better reflect the true intentions of the Vietnamese Communist Party and the State. Vietnam continues to be quite inward-looking, and few stakeholders are aware of international research, policy and practice in bilingual education. (This might explain why, as mentioned above, the teaching of NDLs as subjects at some grade levels could mistakenly be called "bilingual education.") In sum, statements in the most current and relevant Vietnamese policy documents are clearer but weaker than those of their neighbors in Cambodia and Thailand.

It is ironic that at the same time Vietnam has weakened policy support for NDLs in education, at least half a dozen other countries of Asia and the Pacific region are strengthening their use of NDLs. It is also surprising that the two Vietnamese pilot projects using NDLs in education – both sponsored by international agencies – are operating without major problems, and are in fact achieving positive results. Interestingly, some NDL communities and education officials in Lao Cai province have become so excited about the potential of L1-based education that the provincial education administration is using some of its regular budget to fund expansion of MLE initiatives (UN-HRC, 2011; UNICEF, 2011; Viet Nam News, 2011). One reason for the inconsistencies may be the fact that these projects began several years before Decree 82/2010/ND-CP was approved, and no new NDL projects have started since the Decree was passed. The real reasons for this apparent mismatch between words and deeds can only be guessed, but perhaps the Decree is not intended to be taken any more literally than the positive statements of the 1948 Constitution, making the lives of non-Vietnamese stakeholders ever more complicated.

It can be concluded that the approach chosen in Vietnam has been more top-down compared to the others. Of these three countries – and perhaps throughout Southeast and East Asia and the Pacific region – Vietnam has had the biggest gap between the rhetoric and reality in terms of latitude for NDLs in education. Most discouragingly, based on the assumption that learners' L1s are the best means for achieving high quality education, Vietnamese officials seem to be weakening the previously supportive policy statements to match their inaction and non-implementation of earlier "strong on the surface"-type policies.

Fortunately, Cambodia and Thailand are following the international trend of recognizing the importance of NDLs in education. Written policies are being introduced or strengthened on the basis of advocacy and/or demonstration of successful outcomes of L1-based education. Previously in both Cambodia and Thailand the use of NDLs in education was stronger in practice than in written policy. In order to reduce the gap between the policy and practice, the Cambodian and Thai governments have strengthened their written policies, not weakened them.

CONCLUSION

This chapter has shown that more supportive language-in-education policies and the increasing use of NDLs in education in Cambodia and Thailand are in line with a regional trend. In Vietnam the opposite is happening, i.e. weakening policy support for and potentially less use of NDLs in education. It can be concluded that what we are seeing in Mainland Southeast Asia is two steps forward and one step back in the policies designed to make education more appropriate and equitable for speakers of NDLs.

Despite their current advantages over Vietnam in terms of policy development, the situations in Cambodia and Thailand are far from ideal. All three countries could still greatly improve their language-in-education policies, and implementation of these policies, to establish a clear legal foundation for the development and use of all NDLs at all levels of education. Several important questions remain unanswered and require further investigation, including the following:

– Why are Vietnam's written policies going against the regional trend of increased use of NDLs, and even against local interests and practices in some areas of the country?

– Why have Cambodia and Thailand failed to support all languages in education, particularly the largest NDLs?

– Why are most NDL-based educational projects initiated by non-governmental organizations rather than by appropriate government agencies like education ministries?

– How can the roles of civil society and NGO actors be expanded, even in top-down Vietnam where all local organizations have links with the Party and the State, so that NDL-based education can be expanded and sustained?

As all three cases show, addressing language-in-education issues for ethnolinguistic minority learners is possible when 1) policies give sufficient latitude for use of non-dominant languages and 2) when MLE programs use and develop learners' L1s for sufficiently long periods for learners to achieve strong literacy and thinking skills. There is a great deal of evidence (e.g. Ball, 2010; Heugh & Skutnabb-Kangas, 2012; Ouane & Glanz, 2011; Walter & Benson, 2012) that "short-cuts" are rarely effective in providing a strong enough foundation in the

L1 for further learning, and such programs do not give learners the full benefits of L1-based MLE (see Benson; and Walter, both in this volume). The recommendation would thus be that the best support to speakers of NDLs would be educational programs that provide functional literacy in the L1, long-term use of the L1 as a LOI, and gradual introduction of dominant languages. Cambodia, Thailand and Vietnam could all be encouraged to expand their policies and practices further, in line with these recommendations, so that education can be more equitable for all, including the speakers of non-dominant languages.

NOTES

[i] I wish to acknowledge the very useful comments and suggestions by Carol Benson and Dennis Malone on this chapter.

[ii] No official English translations were available for any of these documents, thus unofficial ones have been cited. Using the official Thai version of the National Language Policy, I was able to confirm the English translation to be accurate, but as I am not proficient in Khmer or Vietnamese I must rely on the unofficial translations of Cambodian and Vietnamese documents made by NGOs or by the governments themselves. These are normally accurate enough for common usage.

[iii] "Nationality" in Vietnam – as well as in China and other countries influenced by the Soviet Union – is the government's category to identify different ethnolinguistic communities. Individual nationality is mostly based on real or assumed racial lineage, and often relates to the heritage language of the community. However, the government's ethnolinguistic classifications do not always reflect the linguistic or cultural realities of the communities themselves.

[iv] In Vietnam and other countries influenced by policies and ideology of the Soviet Union, the term *script* is often used in an unconventional manner, basically referring to orthography or writing system rather than a script per se, as discussed in the Introduction to this volume.

[v] The script provision is often interpreted to mean that NDL orthographies must be based on the Khmer script, even if a particular language has used a non-Khmer script historically or does so in other countries.

[vi] The term "bilingual education" is used in Cambodia to refer to programs that start in the L1 and teach additional languages; these are now called multilingual education (MLE) in most Asian countries.

[vii] Similar situations exist in Thailand and other Southeast Asian countries, particularly among ethnic Chinese and Central Thai-related groups, but these people are likely to be considered members of the dominant ethnolinguistic community. In Vietnam, the "stamp" of the official heritage nationality stays with a person (and is printed in one's official identification card) even if linguistic assimilation has occurred.

[viii] It is important to note that earlier drafts of the law gave stronger support to NDLs by stating that ethnic minorities have the right to L1 instruction in public schools, but over the years of refining the law the terms were weakened, possibly due to nationalistic political actors feeling that national unity would be endangered.

[ix] In Cambodia, "Khmer Lue" is often translated to English as "indigenous" or "indigenous people" (with no capital letter showing awareness of international rights issues).

[x] These are NDLs related to Khmer as well as Jarai, an unrelated Austronesian language.

[xi] One positive exception is recent LOI policy in the Philippines (see Multilingual Philippines, 2013; Stone, in this volume), where L1-based MLE in NDLs is justified on pedagogical, linguistic and cultural grounds.

REFERENCES

AKP (2012). *Cambodia recognised as role model in Asia-Pacific region for mother tongue-based bilingual education.* February 21, 2012. Phnom Penh: Agence Kampuchea Presse.

Aluyufri, Sabe Abdullah (2008). *The role of Patani Malay in Thailand's southern border provinces.* A paper presented at the International Conference on National Language Policy: Language Diversity for National Unity. Bangkok, 4-5 July 2008.

Ball, Jessica, (2010). *Enhancing learning of children from diverse language backgrounds: Mother tongue-based bilingual or multilingual education in the early years.* Paris: UNESCO.

Benson, Carol (2004). The importance of mother tongue-based schooling for educational quality. Background paper for EFA Global Monitoring Report 2005. In UNESCO, *Education for All: The quality imperative.* Paris: UNESCO.

Benson, Carol (2011). *Evaluation of the state of bilingual education in Cambodia.* Undertaken November 2010 to March 2011for MoEYS with UNICEF support. Unpublished.

Benson, Carol, & Kosonen, Kimmo (2012). A critical comparison of language-in-education policy and practice in four Southeast Asian countries and Ethiopia. In Kathleen Heugh & Tove Skutnabb-Kangas (Eds.), *Multilingual education and sustainable diversity work: From periphery to center* (pp. 111-137). New York: Routledge.

Bredenburg, Kurt (2010). *Assessment of Cham and migrant children's educational needs in Cambodia.* A paper presented at the International Conference on Language, Education and the Millennium Development Goals, November 9-11, 2010, Bangkok, Thailand. (http://www.seameo.org/LanguageMDGConference2010/doc/presentations/day1/KurtBredenberg-ppt.pdf)

Bui, Thi Ngoc Diep, & Bui, Van Thanh (2009). Language-in-education policies in Vietnam. In Kimmo Kosonen & Catherine Young (Eds.), *Mother tongue as bridge language of instruction: Policies and experiences in Southeast Asia* (pp. 109-116). Bangkok: Southeast Asian Ministers of Education Organization (SEAMEO).

CARE International Cambodia (2004). Cambodia: Highland Children's Education Project (HCEP), Ratanakiri Province. In Linda King & Sabine Schielmann (Eds.), *The challenge of Indigenous education: Practice and perspectives* (pp. 113-122). Paris: UNESCO.

Cima, Ronald J. (1989). Vietnam: Historical setting. In Ronald J. Cima (Ed.), *Vietnam: A country study.* Washington, DC: Library of Congress, Federal Research Division. (http://lcweb2.loc.gov/frd/cs/vntoc.html)

Constitution Finder (2012). University of Richmond, VA, USA. (http://confinder.richmond.edu/index.html)

EMED (2007). *Functions and responsibilities of the Ethnic Minority Education Department.* Hanoi: MOET, Ethnic Minority Education Department. Unpublished.

Heugh, Kathleen (1995). Disabling and enabling: Implications of language policy trends in South Africa. In Rajend Mesthrie (Ed.), *Language and social history. Studies in South African sociolinguistics* (pp. 329-348). Cape Town: David Philip.

Heugh, Kathleen, & Skutnabb-Kangas, Tove (Eds.) (2012). *Multilingual education and sustainable diversity work: From periphery to center.* New York: Routledge.

Karnow, Stanley (1997). *Vietnam: A history.* New York: Penguin Books.

Kosonen, Kimmo (2004). *Language in education policy and practice in Vietnam.* Commissioned study. September 2004. Hanoi: UNICEF.

Kosonen, Kimmo (2005). Education in local languages: Policy and practice in South-East Asia. In UNESCO, *First language first: Community-based literacy programmes for minority language context in Asia* (pp. 96-134). Bangkok: UNESCO.

Kosonen, Kimmo (2006). Multigrade teaching among ethnic minority children: The language issue. In Linley Cornish (Ed.), *Reaching EFA through multi-grade teaching: Issues, contexts and practices* (pp. 239-258). Armidale, NSW, Australia: Kardoorair Press.

Kosonen, Kimmo (2007). Vernaculars in literacy and basic education in Cambodia, Laos and Thailand. In Anthony J. Liddicoat (Ed.), *Issues in language planning and literacy* (pp. 122-142). Clevedon, UK: Multilingual Matters.

Kosonen, Kimmo (2008). Literacy in local languages in Thailand: Language maintenance in a globalised world. *International Journal of Bilingual Education and Bilingualism, 11*(2), 170-188.

Kosonen, Kimmo (2009a). Assessment of opportunities and challenges for the implementation of mother tongue based bi-lingual education (MTBBE) in Vietnam, Phase 1. Commissioned study. October 2009. Hanoi: UNESCO Hanoi. Unpublished report.

Kosonen, Kimmo (2009b). Language-in-education policies in Southeast Asia: An overview. In Kimmo Kosonen & Catherine Young (Eds.), *Mother tongue as bridge language of instruction: Policies and experiences in Southeast Asia* (pp. 22-43). Bangkok: Southeast Asian Ministers of Education Organization (SEAMEO).

Kosonen, Kimmo (2010). Ethnolinguistic minorities and non-dominant languages in mainland Southeast Asian language-in-education policies. In A. M. Geo-JaJa & S. Majhanovich (Eds.), *Education, language, and economics: Growing national and global dilemmas* (pp. 73-88). Rotterdam/Boston/Taipei: Sense Publishers.

Kosonen, Kimmo, & Young, Catherine (Eds.) (2009). *Mother tongue as bridge language of instruction: Policies and experiences in Southeast Asia.* Bangkok: Southeast Asian Ministers of Education Organization (SEAMEO).

Kosonen, Kimmo, & Person, Kirk R. (2013). Languages, identities and education in Thailand. In Peter Sercombe & Ruanni Tupas (Eds.), *Language, identities and education in Asia.* Palgrave Macmillan. Forthcoming.

Kosonen, Kimmo; Young, Catherine & Malone, Susan (2007). *Promoting Literacy in Multilingual Settings.* Bangkok: UNESCO.

Kosonen, Kimmo, Shaeffer, Sheldon, & Vu, Thi Thanh Huong (2010). *Strengthening Vietnamese language skills for ethnic minorities through mother tongue-based multi-lingual education.* Draft UN Policy Discussion Paper. Hanoi: UNESCO.

Leclerc, Jacques (2012). *L'aménagement linguistique dans le monde* [Language planning around the world]. Quebec: TLFQ, Université Laval. (http://www.tlfq.ulaval.ca/axl/index.html)

LePoer, Barbara L. (1989). Vietnam: Government and politics. In Ronald J. Cima (Ed.), *Vietnam: A country study.* Washington, DC: Library of Congress, Federal Research Division. (http://lcweb2.loc.gov/frd/cs/vntoc.html)

Lewis, M. Paul (Ed.) (2009). *Ethnologue: Languages of the world,* Sixteenth edition. Dallas, TX: SIL International.

Malone, Susan (2010). *Consultancy report: UNICEF and MOET action research on mother tongue based bilingual education in Viet Nam, September to December 2010.* Hanoi: UNICEF Viet Nam. Unpublished.

Multilingual Philippines (2013). *Multilingual Philippines do not leave your language alone.* (http://multilingualphilippines.com/)

Neou Sun (2009). Education policies for ethnic minorities in Cambodia. In Kimmo Kosonen & Catherine Young (Eds.), *Mother tongue as bridge language of instruction: Policies and experiences in Southeast Asia* (pp. 62-68). Bangkok: SEAMEO.

Noorlander, Jan, & Ven, Churk (2008). *Cambodia's highland community education program.* A paper presented at the Second International Conference on Language Development, Language Revitalization and Multilingual Education in Ethnolinguistic Communities. Bangkok, 1-3 July 2008.

Ouane, Adama, & Glanz, Christine (Eds.) (2011). *Optimising learning, education and publishing in Africa: The language factor. A review and analysis of theory and practice in mother-tongue and bilingual education in sub-Saharan Africa.* Hamburg, Germany: UNESCO Institute for Lifelong Learning (UIL), the Association for the Development of Education in Africa (ADEA)/African Development Bank.

Paramal, Waemaji (2008). *Success and challenges in developing a writing system for Patani Malay.* Paper presented at the International Conference on National Language Policy: Language Diversity for National Unity. Bangkok, 4-5 July 2008.

Person, Kirk R. (2010). Language policy in Thailand: Historical background and current work of the Royal Institute. In *Proceedings from the International Academic Conference on Language Policy in*

Commemoration of the 20ᵗʰ Anniversary of the National Institute of the Korean Language (pp. 151-172). Seoul: National Institute of the Korean Language.

Prapasapong, Busaba (2009). Language policy and development of education management in public schools in Thailand. In Kimmo Kosonen & Catherine Young (Eds.), *Mother tongue as bridge language of instruction: Policies and experiences in Southeast Asia* (pp. 102-108). Bangkok: SEAMEO.

Premsrirat, Suwilai (2008). Language for national reconciliation: Southern Thailand. *EENET – Enabling Education 12*, 16-17.

Premsrirat, Suwilai (2009). *Bilingual education for national reconciliation in Southern Thailand: A role for Patani Malay and Thai*. Paper presented at SEAMEO's regional meeting on the dissemination of project results and identification of good functioning models, "Project on Mother Tongue as Bridge Language of Instruction in Southeast Asian Countries: Policy, Strategies and Advocacy." Bangkok, 24-26 February 2009.

SEAMEO (2009). *Project on mother tongue as bridge language of instruction in Southeast Asian Countries: Policy, strategies and advocacy*. Proceedings of the regional meeting on the dissemination of project results and identification of good functioning models. Bangkok, 24-26 February 2009. Bangkok: Southeast Asian Ministers of Education Organization.

Shaeffer, Sheldon (2010). *Strengthening the Vietnamese competence of ethnic minorities through mother tongue-based multilingual education (MTB-MLE). Mission Report for UNESCO*. Hanoi, February 24-March 10, 2010.

Siren, Un (2009). The mother tongue as a bridge language of instruction in Cambodia. In Kimmo Kosonen & Catherine Young (Eds.), *Mother tongue as bridge language of instruction: Policies and experiences in Southeast Asia* (pp. 148-152). Bangkok: SEAMEO.

Smalley, William A. (1994). *Linguistic diversity and national unity: Language ecology in Thailand*. Chicago: University of Chicago Press.

Stites, Regie (1999). Writing cultural boundaries: National minority language policy, literacy planning, and bilingual education. In Gerard A. Postiglione (Ed.), *China's national minority education* (pp. 95-130). New York: Falmer.

Tan Hoong Yen (2011). *Using Hmong in pre-primary education in Thailand: An evaluation of the orthography acceptance, teacher training and reported outcomes in a pilot project*. Unpublished MA Thesis in Linguistics. Chiang Mai: Payap University.

The Constitutions of Vietnam (2003). *The constitutions of Vietnam 1946 – 1959 – 1980 – 1992*. Hanoi: Thế Giới Publishers.

Thomas, Anne (2002). Bilingual community-based education in the Cambodian highlands: A successful approach for enabling access to education by indigenous peoples. *Journal of Southeast Asian Education, 3*(1), 26-58.

Tienmee, Wanna (2009). *The Mon-Thai bilingual project, Wat Wang Wiwekaram School, Kanchanaburi province*. A paper presented at SEAMEO's Regional Meeting on the Dissemination of Project Results and Identification of Good Functioning Models, "Project on Mother Tongue as Bridge Language of Instruction in Southeast Asian Countries: Policy, Strategies and Advocacy." Bangkok, 24-26 February 2009.

UNESCO (2007a). *Advocacy kit for promoting multilingual education: Including the excluded*. Bangkok: UNESCO Asia and Pacific Regional Bureau for Education, 5 booklets.

UNESCO (2007b). *Mother tongue-based literacy programmes: Case studies of good practice in Asia*. Bangkok: UNESCO Asia and Pacific Regional Bureau for Education.

UNESCO (2008a). *Education for All global monitoring report 2008: Education for All by 2015: Will we make it?* Paris: UNESCO.

UNESCO (2008b). *Improving the quality of mother tongue-based literacy and learning. Case studies from Asia, Africa and South America*. Bangkok: UNESCO Asia and Pacific Regional Bureau for Education.

UNESCO (2011). *Workshop on Bilingual Education – Bilingual education: Creating Learner Friendly Environment for All.* Organized by Ministry of Education, Youth and Sports (MoEYS), International Cooperation Cambodia (ICC) and United Nations Educational, Scientific and Cultural Organization (UNESCO). Phnom Penh, Cambodia, November 17-18, 2011.

UNESCO (2012a). *MLE mapping data.* The Asia MLE Working Group. Bangkok: UNESCO Bangkok. (http://www.unescobkk.org/education/multilingual-education/mle-mapping-data/)

UNESCO (2012b). *Why languages matter for the Millennium Development Goals.* Bangkok: UNESCO Bangkok, Asia and Pacific Regional Bureau of Education.

UNICEF (2011). *Progamme brief. Action research on mother tongue-based bilingual education: Achieving quality, equitable education.* Hanoi: UNICEF Viet Nam.

UN-HRC (2011). *Report of the independent expert on minority issues, Gay McDougall, Mission to Viet Nam (5-15 July 2010).* Human Rights Council, Sixteenth session. New York: United Nations General Assembly.

Viet Nam News (2011). Mong children learn lessons in mother tongue. *Viet Nam News,* 24 May.

Vu, Thi Thanh Huong (2008). *Ethnic minority languages in Vietnam: Policy and implementation issues.* Paper presented at the Second International Conference on Language Development, Language Revitalization and Multilingual Education in Ethnolinguistic Communities. Bangkok, 1-3 July 2008.

Vu, Thi Thanh Huong (2010). *Enhancing education quality for ethnic minority children through the use of teaching assistants.* Hanoi: Save the Children. Unpublished report.

Walter, Steve (2011). *Analyzing MLE Data: A "Stream-of-consciousness."* Set of Heuristics. Unpublished manuscript.

Walter, Steve and Benson, Carol (2012). Language policy and medium of instruction in formal education. In Spolsky, Bernard (Ed.), *The Cambridge handbook of language policy* (pp. 278-300). Cambridge: Cambridge University Press.

World Bank (2009). *Country social analysis: Ethnicity and development in Vietnam.* Washington, DC: The International Bank for Reconstruction and Development/World Bank.

Kimmo Kosonen
SIL International & Payap University
Chiang Mai, Thailand

STEPHEN A. BAHRY[i]

3. LANGUAGE IN AFGHANISTAN'S EDUCATION REFORM: DOES IT PLAY A ROLE IN PEACE AND RECONCILIATION?

ABSTRACT

Ikim bob dar borai Afghonistona way paywastagii ziv at jam'iyat murakabiyaten and uf joi islohoti maorif, aznaw virextowi jami'iyat, osoixi, at tar yakdidaryatowi mardumeni Afghoniston bora andi naql kixt. Ilmi adabiyot dar borai ziven, jam'iyat, ma'orif, digarsawuch gap and kor dar sohai ziven, at ik-hozira imkoniyateni qonuni dar jodai ziven gunoguni at lapzivak ma'orif- andi yand undi tahlil sach. Ba'd az dai, ikim bob, Afghoniston at tashkiloteni bainalmilaliya uf uhdadoriyen bahs kixt. Khulosa ikididi yordam baroi lapzivi at lapzivak ma'orif ghalath sust. Id nowobasta ba vidowi yi shumor sozmoneni bainalmilali idi wath mod ziven peshrawi dar asosi ma'orifi thaw ziva chun yi qolib baroi bashand ta'lim at tarbiya Afghoniston sharoitandi tarafdori kinan. (*Translated into the Rushani variety of Rushani-Shughni [sgh], a language spoken in Afghanistan, China, Pakistan and Tajikistan, by Sarfaroz Niyozov.*)

This chapter focuses on Afghanistan's sociolinguistic complexity and its place in educational reform, societal reconstruction, peace and reconciliation. Literature is reviewed on languages, society and education, and on changing language policy and practice and current constitutional provisions regarding linguistic and social pluralism and multilingualism in education. The chapter then discusses implementation by Afghanistani and international organizations of these commitments, finding little international support for plurilingualism and multilingual education, despite a number of small international organizations that support the development of mother tongue-based bi-/multilingual education (MTBMLE) as a model for quality education in Afghanistan.

INTRODUCTION

While Afghanistan has been constantly in the international news for over thirty years, there has been little or no attention to language issues in the international research literature. A search by the author of several databases for English-language publications on language and education in Afghanistan found only one on this topic since 2000, while there were numerous publications identified on education and peace, conflict, equity and social reconstruction.

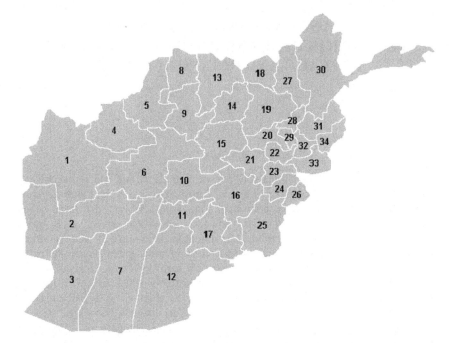

1 Herāt	7 Helmand	13 Balkh	19 Baghlān	25 Paktīkā	31 Nūrestān
2 Farāh	8 Jowzjān	14 Samangān	20 Parwān	26 Khowst	32 Laghmān
3 Nīmrūz	9 Sar-e-Pol	15 Bāmīān	21 Wardak	27 Takhār	33 Nangārhār
4 Bādghīs	10 Dāykondī	16 Ghaznī	22 Kābul	28 Panjshīr	34 Konar
5 Fāryāb	11 Orūzgān	17 Zābol	23 Lowgar	29 Kāpīsā	
6 Ghowr	12 Kandahār	18 Kondoz	24 Paktīā	30 Badakhshān	

Figure 1. Afghanistan and its provinces. (Source: Public domain basemap)

This seems to indicate that international scholars and international organizations supporting educational development do not see an important link between mutual understanding, equity of opportunities and the inclusion of home language and culture in school, or consider language and education as important in Afghanistan's educational reconstruction. Yet this is in great contrast to the prominent place given to language issues in national reconciliation and reconstruction within Afghanistan itself, where the new constitution commits the state to teaching in two languages, Dari and Pashto, on a national scale, and in three or more languages in regions where other languages are spoken.

This chapter is an exploratory review of current linguistic diversity in Afghanistan, of the historic role played by Afghanistan's languages in formal education, and of current policy towards multiple languages in education. In particular, the chapter will explore the challenges of development and implementation of language-in-education policies as well as the gap between the government's strong formal commitment to and its provision of education in multiple languages of Afghanistan. Further, the chapter will discuss the scant attention paid by international researchers and organizations to the research and development work necessary to implement multilingual education in Afghanistan.

LINGUISTIC DIVERSITY IN AFGHANISTAN

As a crossroads in Central Eurasia, it is no surprise that Afghanistan is characterized by considerable social and linguistic diversity. Table 1 displays information on most of the languages of Afghanistan by language family, branch and sub-branch, estimated number of speakers and language status according to the 1980 Constitution. The four status types in the table derive from Kieffer (1983) based on provisions of the 1980 Constitution for official and national languages, and based on estimated number of speakers and manner of use in local contexts.[ii] Afghanistan exhibits large-scale societal multilingualism, and considerable individual plurilingualism[iii] in West Iranian, East Iranian, Indic, Turkic, Mongolic, and Dravidian languages (Barfield, 2010; Bashir, 2006; Kieffer, 1983, 2006).

Nevertheless, most discussion focuses on two languages: Pashto (also known as Pashtu, Pakhto or Pakhtu), and Dari, the Afghanistan variety of Persian,[iv] perhaps because both function not only as primary languages of many speech communities, but also as languages of wider communication (LWC) for speakers of other languages. Furthermore, there is a tendency for Dari to more commonly act as LWC in cases of interaction among Dari and Pashto speakers than the converse. This kind of asymmetrical bilingualism is also found among regionally restricted languages of wider communication.[v] For instance, Rzehak (2009) reports that Brahui speakers are frequently bilingual in Balochi, a local LWC, while Balochi speakers generally do not learn Brahui.

Thus, to refer to Afghanistan as a multilingual society and many Afghanistani citizens as plurilinguals inadequately captures this sociolinguistic complexity. It is more fruitful to look at languages in Afghanistan using the lenses of language ecology (Hornberger, 2002), diglossia and bilingualism (Ferguson, 1959; Fishman, 1967), and language hierarchy (Dwyer, 2005). Based on descriptions of language use in the literature reviewed in this chapter, I have constructed an illustrative partial language hierarchy within Afghanistan's language ecology (see Figure 2).

Table 1. Languages of Afghanistan. Sources: Adapted from Lewis (2009), Kieffer (1983), and Owens (2007)

Language family	Branch	Sub-branch	Language	Estimated number of speakers[vi]	Status in 1980
Indo-Iranian	Iranian	Northwest	Baluchi	200,000 (1979)	National
			Pashto	8,000,000 (2000)	Official
		Northeast	Shugni / Roshani (Pamiri)	20,000 (1994)	Local
			Sanglechi / Eshkashemi (Pamiri)	1,000 (1900)	Local
			Munji (Pamiri)	3,770 (2000)	Local
			Wakhi (Pamiri)	9,570 (2000)	Local
		Southwest	Dari/Persian	5,600,000 (1996)	Official
		Southeast	Parachi	600	Residual
			Ormuri	50	Residual
	Indo-Aryan	Nurestani	Kati	15,000 (1994)	National
			Waygali	1,500 (2000)	Local
			Ashkun	1,200 (2000)	Local
			Prasun	1,000 (2000)	Local
		Dardic	Pashai	108,000 (1982)	National
			Gawar-bati	8,000	Local
			Tiro	n.a.	Residual
		Indian	Punjabi	n.a.	Local
			Sindhi	n.a.	Local
			Gojri	2,000 (1994)	Local
			Inku	n.a.	Local
Altaic	Turkic		Uzbek	1,400,000 (1991)	National
			Turkmen	500,000 (1995)	National
			Kyrgyz	750 (2000)	Local
			Uighur	3,000	Residual
	Mongolic		Mogoli	200	Residual
Semitic			Central Asian Arabic	5,000 (1967)	Residual
Dravidian			Brahui	200,000 (1980)	Local

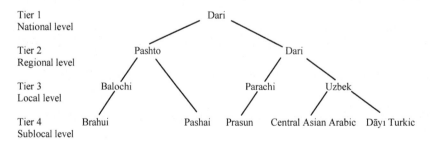

Figure 2. Selected illustration of national-regional-local language hierarchies within Afghanistan's language ecology. (Sources: Author's analysis and synthesis of Baldauf, 2007; Kieffer, 1983, 1997; Owens, 2007; Rzehak, 2009; Yun, 2003, 2008)

The 1980 Constitution gave equal official status to Pashto, the language of the Pashtun ethnic group, and Dari Persian, the language of several of Afghanistan's ethnic groups, which is also the most widely known LWC in Afghanistan. The 1980 Constitution designated as *national* languages those languages apart from the two official languages that could be used in publishing or broadcast media, or as languages of instruction (LOI) in schools. Kieffer (1983) uses the term *local* languages for languages that go constitutionally unrecognized despite being used by a sizable population in a particular context, and *residual* languages for those whose transmission is endangered.

Some of the complexity of this language ecology is the 21st-century remnant of 19th-century Pashtun nation-building, where intra-Pashtun rivalry led to some Pashtun groups being resettled in non-Pashtun-speaking areas, with the aim of weakening their power, and established a Pashtun presence in more regions of Afghanistan (Naby, 1984). Naby, who worked as a teacher in schools in Mazar-e-Sharif in the Uzbek-speaking northwest in the 1960s, observes:

> [T]he Pushtu (sic) language, although still an infrequently heard language in places like Mazar-i-Sharif and Kunduz, can nevertheless be used in government offices almost interchangeably with Persian because government appointees to these regions can count on being able to staff their offices with indigenous Pushtu speakers. In the same manner Kabul can justify its insistence on the instruction of Pushtu in northern schools not only because Pushtu is the national language of Afghanistan and one of its two official languages (with Dari/Persian), but also because a significant, if minor portion of the students come from Pushtun families. ... Afghan institutions such as public schools have acted to instill in graduates a certain sense of being Afghans, but the retention of Uzbek language and culture appears to affect the attitudes and activities of younger Uzbeks. (Naby, 1984: 12)

Clearly, Afghanistan's language ecology is much more complex than the relatively uncomplicated image presented in the media (Hakala, 2011; Nawid, 2011).

LANGUAGE POLICY AND PLANNING IN AFGHANISTAN

Historical Background

Official efforts at language policy and planning since the late 19th century have generally focused on languages other than Dari/Persian, at times attempting to raise the status of Pashto, the language of the politically dominant Pashtuns, for purposes of modernization and building a national Afghanistan civic identity. Indeed, many non-Pashtuns treat the term *Afghan* as synonymous with *Pashtun* rather than as a term of self-designation. Beginning in the 1870s, there has been a continuous program of centralized modernization and nation building based on the Pashtuns. At the same time, there have been intermittent efforts to raise the status of Pashto to supplement or replace Dari as a language of administration (Barfield,

2010; Black, Dupree, Endicott-West, & Naby, 1991; Kakar, 1971, in Olesen, 1995; Roberts, 2003; Shahrani, 1988).

Efforts to make Pashto a language of administration peaked in the 1950s. In order to support the requirement for the Pashtu language to perform high status official functions, a Pashto Academy was opened whose aim was "to purify the Pashtu language and stimulate the development and dissemination of its literature" (Newell, 1988: 113). This "purification" amounted to corpus development of Pashto, "i.e., the development of Pashto concepts to replace existing Farsi [Persian] words commonly used" (Olesen, 1995: 205).

However, a new constitution was promulgated in 1964, whose Article 3 stated that Pashto would continue as an official language, while Dari Persian would be reinstated as a parallel official language (Afghanistan, 2005). This constitution retained a formal commitment not only to the status development of Pashto but also to its corpus development, stating in Article 35 that "[i]t is the duty of the state to prepare and implement an effective program for the development and strengthening of the national language, Pashto" (ibid.: 226).

Although Pashtuns were dominant within military and political spheres of the Afghan state from an early period, state administration had mainly been conducted by Persian speakers. At the same time, modernization initiatives in education made Pashto a language of instruction. This combined with increased state support for education through provision of boarding schools in rural areas led to increasing rural-urban migration of educated Pashtuns, who demanded a role in urban and national life in their language (Olesen, 1995). Table 2 shows LOI practices in the provinces and regions of Afghanistan in 1967, revealing Dari-dominant and Pashto-dominant zones, along with a third zone where both were used as LOIs.

Table 2. Language of Instruction (LOI) by Province and Region in 1967. (Source: adapted by author from Ministry of Education, 1967, in Samady, 2001)

LOI Practices	West	North	Centre	South	East
Dari-medium only	Ghor Herat	Badakhshan Kunduz Takhar	Bamyan	–	–
Both	Badghis Farah	Baghlan Balkh Faryab Jawzjan Samangan	Kabul Kapisa Logar Parwan Wardak	Ghazni Nimroz Oruzan	–
Pashto-medium only	–	–	–	Helmand Kandahar Zabul	Kunar Laghman Nangarhar Paktia

In 1978, following Soviet-style language policy, the Khalqi faction of the Communist Party of Afghanistan announced a policy of greater use of the non-dominant languages of Afghanistan for official purposes. This included education and publication in Uzbek, Turkmen and Baluchi in addition to Dari and Pashto, and according to some reports it included languages of Nuristan as well (Naby, 1980; Newell, 1989). Thus, the anti-regional, anti-rural, anti-Pashto effect of de facto language policy in modern schools may in part explain the source of anti-Dari feelings that have arisen among unpersianized Pashtuns. During the Taliban's rule, for example, Pashto is said to have replaced Dari at Kabul University (Tohiri, 2002), while according to one Baluchi resident of Nimroz province:

> You could go to every office, if your language was Pashto. You could do everything. Nobody asked you where you were coming from and where you were going. If you spoke Persian or Baluchi they thought you were cursing at them. This is how they were. (Rzehak, 2009: 193)

Some argue that the Pashtun elite may have used Pashtun linguistic and cultural symbols as a means of maintaining hegemony over unpersianized Pashtuns (Hanifi, 2004). Seen in this light, anti-Dari actions can be understood as part of an intra-Pashtun dispute, between persianized and unpersianized Pashtuns.

Recent Changes in Language Policy

As noted above, the 2004 Constitution makes more particular statements about Afghanistan's languages than have any previous constitutions. Table 3 lists its detailed provisions regarding languages. Most significant perhaps is Article 17, which commits the state to whatever measures are necessary to promote education, which arguably means that in certain districts languages other than Pashto or Dari should be taught in schools, or ideally used as languages of instruction.

Table 3. Articles on languages and education in Afghanistan's 2004 Constitution. (Source: Afghanistan, 2004)

Art. **16**	– From amongst Pashto, Dari, Uzbeki, Turkmani, Baluchi, Pachaie, Nuristani, Pamiri, and other current languages in the country, Pashto and Dari shall be the official languages of the state. – In areas where the majority of the people speak in any one of Uzbeki, Turkmani, Pachaie, Nuristani, Baluchi or Pamiri languages, any of the aforementioned language, in addition to Pashto and Dari, shall be the third official language, the usage of which shall be regulated by law. – The state shall design and apply effective programs to foster and develop all languages of Afghanistan.
Art. **43**	– The state shall adopt necessary measures to foster education at all levels. – (1) Education is the right of all citizens of Afghanistan, which shall be provided up to the level of the B.A. (lisâns), free of charge by the state. – (2) The state is obliged to devise and implement effective programs for a balanced expansion of education all over Afghanistan, and to provide compulsory intermediate level education. – (3) The state is also required to provide the opportunity to teach native languages in the areas where they are spoken.

Indeed, the most recent draft of the national strategic plan for education for the years 2010-2014 does take the step of examining the implementation of bilingual Dari-Pashto education nationally and the provision of opportunity for speakers of non-dominant languages to learn their languages in school as well. For example, there is planning for the development of textbooks for grades 1 to 12 teaching in Turkmen, Uzbek, Pashai, Baluch, as well as Pamiri and Nurestani languages to be completed by 2014 (Afghanistan Ministry of Education, 2010).[vii]

Since Articles 16 and 43 of the Constitution lay out commitments both to the development of all languages and to quality education for all, certain tensions may arise from different notions of quality and its relationship to various language-in-education models. The commitment to quality basic education seems to require an emphasis on teaching in whatever language(s) children know best, while quality preparation for higher levels of education, which has been delivered largely in Dari, seems to suggest the need for some effective form of Dari learning. As we have seen above, Dari and Pashto have both been used as LOIs with the other language taught as a subject, and the *either-or* logic of presuming that only one can be chosen as LOI has precluded a bilingual approach in which two or more languages could be used as LOIs.

However, given what is known about the role of first language development in supporting second language development, and the superior results of enrichment bilingual education for non-dominant language minority learners (Cummins, 2001; May, 2008; Thomas & Collier, 2002), the most effective model for non-Dari speakers would be a strong form of bilingual education which includes long- term use and development of the first language. However, some specialists (e.g. Zholdoshalieva, 2010, citing the case of isolated nomadic populations such as the Kyrgyz of the Pamir Mountains) caution that beyond using community languages, the curriculum must be appropriately adapted to meet community needs.

Over the last hundred years, there has been at times constitutional silence on the official status of languages, leaving choice of use up to tradition and/or local contestation; at other times, status has been given to either Persian Dari, Pashto, or both as official languages prescribed by law. Thus, the current Constitution's concern for languages other than Dari and Pashto is unprecedented. This concern is the result of a political compromise negotiated between pro- and anti-Pashto forces. The first draft of the new Constitution conferred official status on Dari and Pashto alone, but among Pashtuns, identification of Pashto with the state was so strong that it was demanded that the Constitution specify that the national anthem is to be sung *only* in Pashto (Adeney, 2008). Non-tolerance of broader language rights led to a political impasse in negotiations over the draft:

The debates over language policy occurred late, and creation of the Constitution almost foundered on them. On January 1, 2004, 40% of the delegates boycotted the CLJ (Constitutional Loya Jirga). This boycott was predicated around several issues: the power of the presidency, the lack of effective powers for provincial legislatures (Uzbeks in particular), and the lack of language rights (especially for Tajiks, Uzbeks, and Hazaras). (Adeney, 2008: 553-554)

Adeney argues that the eventual granting of local official status to other languages commits the state to these languages and their communities, and may signal the state's intention to protect language rights within a multilingual Afghanistan with plurilingual citizens, perhaps fostering Afghanistan's de facto multiple identities:

> The recognition of provincial languages is unlikely to pose any significant threat to the unity of Afghanistan. This is largely so because the recognition of provincial languages will most likely promote dual identities, including a sense of loyalty to the center. After all, the recognition of poly-ethnic rights in terms of language policy has conferred a sense of perceived worth by the central government to Afghanistan's various "linguistic communities," as well as offering them access to power, especially at the local level. Indeed, the granting of these polyethnic rights could actually prove to be a powerful integrative force for post-Taliban Afghanistan. (Adeney, 2008: 554)

For more than a century of language policy oscillation, the element common to all policy options has been the absence of all languages other than Dari and Pashto from Afghanistan's multilingual language ecology. However, the question then arises how effective the corpus development and popularization of Afghanistan's other languages will be in the face of the country's historically limited ability to translate de jure Pashto official status into de facto official functions over the past hundred years. Clearly, considerable support is needed for de jure policy to actually be implemented. The question now becomes whether multilingual education policy represents a genuine commitment of the government which will receive necessary support, or whether these commitments will simply be part of the "politics of recognition" (Taylor, 1992) – i.e. lip service – in Afghanistani terms.

Language of Instruction in State Schools

The capital, Kabul, has long been a Dari-speaking centre; while other languages may be heard in the private sphere, in public Dari Persian is predominant. As a result, the political predominance of Pashtuns in Afghanistan has not translated into increased status of Pashto, since Pashtuns migrating to the capital generally have or develop bilingual Pashto-Dari proficiency, while Pashtun elite families long resident in Kabul have experienced language shift, becoming Dari-dominant or monolingual Dari speakers (Hyman, 2002).

In 1904 and 1927, two modern secondary schools staffed by Muslims from British India were opened in Kabul, along with a French-sponsored (1922) and German-sponsored (1924) school, followed by the establishment of Kabul University in 1932. These lycées feature Dari-Persian and either English, French or German as language of instruction (Ewans, 2002; Rubin, 1991). Thus, the developing elite has become highly centralized, oriented towards Dari and European languages, which has presented an entrance barrier for rural candidates, particularly native-speakers of languages besides Dari. Thus, among non-Dari speakers, state education has supported subtractive bilingualism at best, at worst, assimilation and language shift.

SUPPORT FOR BILINGUAL AND MULTILINGUAL EDUCATION AS PART OF EDUCATIONAL RECONSTRUCTION IN AFGHANISTAN

As mentioned above, support from the international research community for Afghanistan's commitments regarding bi- and multilingual education is in little evidence based on a search of English language literature published since 2004.

Large international organizations such as the World Bank (WB) are funding many education initiatives in Afghanistan, based (as in other countries) on strategic planning by the Ministry of Education. In several parts of the world, WB has made a commitment to support mother tongue-based bi-/multilingual education (MTBMLE) as a model for quality education of language minorities (Abadzi, 2006; Dutcher & Tucker, 1996; Bender et. al., 2005; World Bank, 1995). However, WB documents and materials on education in Afghanistan do not refer to a bilingual education option, not even to argue against it.[viii]

Moreover, one WB publication entitled, *A guide to government in Afghanistan* (Evans et al., 2004) fails to refer to national policies regarding official language status of Dari and/or Pashto; while it provides an English-Dari glossary for key government terminology, it makes no reference to Pashto as an administrative language. This silence on the status of Pashto can be seen either as an implicit pro-Dari stance, or simply as a realistic reflection of Dari's de facto pre-eminence in government, irrespective of policy; or it could be seen as a reflection of a language-blind orientation of WB educational planning in this region. Similarly, a major education project proposed by the Asian Development Bank (ADB, 2002) makes no reference to Afghanistan's linguistic diversity nor to the issue of language of instruction, despite an emphasis on community-based education.

When examined as a whole, the lack of explicit mention of the language-in-education issue in programs and publications of large international agencies seems to suggest disagreement with or ignorance of its importance, reticence to deal with the issue, tacit support for Dari-dominant approaches, or support for maintenance of the status quo, with Pashto and Dari as LOIs in their respective spheres of dominance. Similarly, in documents on Afghanistan's educational reconstruction there is no mention of Afghanistan's constitutional commitment to raising the status of Uzbek and other regional languages, or of the National Education Strategy of the Ministry of Education (MOE) to developing curriculum and textbooks and training teachers in languages other than the official ones.

UNESCO (2003) restates its long-standing international commitment to the use of non-dominant languages in education, maintaining the view that it is "axiomatic that the best medium for teaching a child is his (sic) mother tongue" (1953: 11; 2003). More recently, in the specific case of Afghanistan, UNESCO has stated that as part of the education reform process "there must also be consideration of the appropriate linguistic policy for use of mother tongue and other national languages in the study of various subjects" (UNESCO, 2002: 12); the same document recommends that an assessment be carried out to identify "which language(s) to use as the medium of instruction, and as a foreign language, in different locations, grades, and for different teaching subjects" (ibid.: 30). Save the Children is undertaking such an assessment in Afghanistan at the time of this writing (Save the Children Afghanistan, personal communication, Jan. 7, 2012). In the meantime, UNESCO (2002: 80) recommends to "[u]se and distribute rapidly the available teaching-learning materials in Pashto, Dari and other languages." Moreover, great emphasis is given in UNESCO's report to the weakness of technical knowledge available in Dari and Pashto, and the inability of most of Afghanistan's people to access information in foreign languages, without referring to any need for corpus development of Afghanistan's languages in order to do so; the authors argue that this situation necessitates strong support for foreign language instruction (ibid.: 66). Of course, this is contrary to Japan's successful approach, which emphasized corpus development of modern terminology by adapting existing language resources and translating foreign works *into* modernized Japanese, supplemented by teaching of foreign languages (Coulmas, 1989).

Another report on education and conflict (Smith, 2010) argues that monolingual language-in-education policies in multilingual societies may produce or exacerbate interethnic conflict, but it does not extend those arguments to the case of Afghanistan. At the same time, UNESCO recently awarded one of its annual prizes for literacy projects to a mother tongue literacy program for non-dominant languages in Afghanistan (UNESCO, 2009). This project, implemented by an NGO called SERVE Afghanistan, focuses on literacy in Pashto and in Pashai languages in rural eastern Afghanistan (Yun, 2003, 2008). Although many Pashai are bilingual in Pashto, virtually none were literate in L1 and few in Pashto or Dari before the establishment of an adult Pashto literacy project in 1999. In 2003, a Pashai script was introduced, and the development of Pashai-Pashto bilingual books and dictionaries was begun, to be followed later by trilingual Pashai-Pashto-English books and resources (Yun, 2003). Now both children in primary school and adults in literacy classes are experiencing bilingual education, learning in Pashai in addition to the regular Pashto-medium instruction. Furthermore, discussion is underway towards adding Dari to these programs, in effect creating multilingual education (Yun, 2008). Communities with Pashto-only instruction have noted that children with Pashai-Pashto instruction are faring better in school and have requested to participate in Pashai language lessons (SERVE, 2010).

LANGUAGE AND EDUCATION AMID CONTESTED SOCIETAL VISIONS

For over a century, various groups have been endeavoring to modernize Afghanistan, a process which has brought to the fore contested visions over the nature of the state and society and its relation to the various subgroups resident in Afghanistan. Thus, some see Afghanistan as based on one titular nationality, the Afghans (Pashtuns), which not only is, but should be, politically predominant.

This thinking, when allied with monolithic notions of the nation-state founded on one nationality and language, leads to promotion of a single language through state functions such as administration and schooling. Contrasted with this notion are more traditional approaches to language within Afghanistan, wherein formal education was largely the learning of traditional books in literary languages, classical Arabic and Persian/Dari, with supplementary oral instruction given by teachers in whatever languages they shared with their students. Pashto, for example, despite its traditionally lower status than Dari as a literary language in which higher knowledge would be written down, was used for recording oral literature and popularizing religious knowledge, and had considerable status as an oral language of wider communication (Hakala, 2011; Miran, 1977; Nawid, 2011).

Nevertheless, modernization has occurred with centralization of modern state functions including education in the capital city, Kabul, which has long been a Dari-dominant zone. This has led to several interesting tensions in language policy. Despite Dari speakers' lack of political dominance, the prestige of Dari in the spheres of culture, knowledge, education, and public administration has led to it being used not only by Tajiks, but by other language groups, including Pashtuns. Indeed, as already mentioned, educated Pashtun families serving the state and located in Kabul have generally been bilingual in Pashto and Dari, often undergoing eventual language shift to Dari. This prestige of Dari is a holdover from traditional education in Afghanistan.

The complex language ecology of Andkhoy in Northwestern Afghanistan's Faryab province, for example, includes classical literary Turkic taught in home-based schools, local spoken varieties of Uzbek and Turkmen and Dayī, a language sharing some features of both (Baldauf, 2007). These varieties co-exist with Dari and Pashto as well as the variety of Uzbek broadcast from Uzbekistan.

The question remains, however, whether the commitment of the government to education in multiple languages is strong enough for these provisions to be implemented. Recent interviews with Uzbek-speaking students in one school, for example, demonstrate a desire for instruction in their first language, but, nevertheless, no new Uzbek-language textbooks were observed in use in that school (Dryden-Peterson, 2010). It has similarly been estimated that on a national basis, 23.8% of the population of over 5 million has had no access to education in their first language (Pinnock, 2009: 51). Pinnock further identifies countries where ethnic and linguistic fractionalization and absence of instruction in the learner's L1 for non-dominant linguistic groups threatens the quality of education and poses a risk to stability of the state. On these grounds, Pinnock characterizes Afghanistan as a failed state, perhaps both from its sociolinguistic divisions and in part from inequitable access to education in the mother tongue.

CONCLUSION

A national report on achievement of Millennium Development Goals in Afghanistan (Afghanistan, 2008) notes that net enrolment in primary education has increased from a baseline value of 54% in 2002 to 60% in 2008, quite close to the planned MDG target of 100% primary enrolment by 2020. However, progress in primary education completion rates (at grade 5) is modest, showing a change from 25% in 2002 to 38% in 2005, well below the planned target for this date of 50-60%. Similarly, estimated literacy rates for youth aged 15-24 have showed only a slight change from 34% in 2002 to 36.5% in 2008, which is well below the targeted rate of over 50%. While noting substantial quantitative progress in enrolment, the report points out significant qualitative challenges in learning, particularly in terms of educational attainment and the development of literacy. Female school enrolment and attendance have been rising rapidly, but still remain well below the male rates (Afghanistan, 2008: 10). Judging by other experiences, in the case of rural girls who are speakers of non-dominant languages, lack of access to primary education in their first language may impede access and achievement (Benson, 2005).

However, while much attention is given to increasing the quality of education even in rural districts, and particularly among girls, the report (Afghanistan, 2008) does not refer at all to language of instruction or discuss in what languages literacy is being developed, nor does it make any reference to the constitutional provisions regarding instruction in children's first languages. The MOE does point out that development of materials to teach in languages other than Dari and Pashto is ongoing, but that there is a further need to develop staff trained to teach new curriculum in these languages (Afghanistan Ministry of Education, 2011).

Pinnock (2009) argues that attention to mother tongue-based instruction is a key element of quality education in low-income countries, particularly in fragile states with high linguistic diversity, and she critiques some international funders for paying inadequate attention to the role of language in quality education. MTBMLE as one element in conflict reduction and increased gender equity in education go virtually unmentioned by large international actors in Afghanistan's educational reconstruction or by English-language researchers, all of whom largely focus on peace and gender equity. There is thus a clear disconnect between Afghanistan's commitments to MTBMLE and the level of support for this among the research community and large international funders. Awareness of the importance of MTBMLE to educational quality and equity in Afghanistan is confined to general written support from some international agencies, and at least one program implemented on a local scale by an international NGO.

It is too soon to predict the consequences of this disconnect. Perhaps the MOE's program of linguistic diversification of the curriculum will proceed successfully without extensive international support. Or perhaps the relative indifference internationally to the development of a more pluralistic Afghanistan through MTBMLE will discourage stakeholders in Afghanistan from implementing this vision, and will constitute a case of "traveling international policy" (Bahry, 2005a).[ix]

Research on the perceptions of students, families and communities who are speakers of non-dominant languages in both Northern and Southern contexts has pointed out that school use of the community's language(s) and its culture(s) can play a key role in how people perceive educational quality and their own social empowerment and identity (Bahry, 2012; Cummins, 2001; Dryden-Peterson, 2010). Of course, the lack of serious theoretical discussion on what forms of bilingual and multicultural education are most suitable from the perspective of non-dominant communities can itself be disempowering (Cummins, 2000).

We could also question the effectiveness of teaching Dari and Pashto as second languages instead of instituting a strong form of bilingual/multilingual education where they are used as LOIs to teach some curriculum content. Such a model of education would seem ideal for realizing the goal of a plurilingual citizenry in a multilingual, multicultural Afghanistan (Baker, 2011; May, 2008; Thomas & Collier, 2002) – and it would appear to contribute significantly to the peace and reconciliation that is so sought-after at this time. But is the inclusion of multiple languages in education policy intended merely to provide token recognition for these languages, but not to foster a pluralistic education system and society?

As Giustozzi (2010) points out regarding nation-building in Afghanistan, there is a continued political and educational imbalance among Afghanistan's sociocultural groups. There has clearly been much contestation and debate regarding the place of various languages in public space and in the institutions of the state. This contestation is not simply a dispute over languages, but one over the nature of Afghanistan as a society and state. The same negotiations that demanded and achieved recognition for multiple languages also saw failed demands by Uzbek and Hazara representatives to recast Afghanistan as a federation of provinces, rather than a unitary centralized state (Adeney, 2008).

Of course, there is no guarantee that provinces of a federated Afghanistan would embrace multilingualism/plurilingualism. They might, as has happened in the newly independent states of Central Asia, promote one, not all, of the previously subordinate languages to the detriment of others[x]. The impasse of the linguistic status quo is reflective of contested visions of the nature of Afghanistan society and its state, and whether it is a project of all the peoples of Afghanistan, or of one titular group. This continuing paradox of Afghanistan can perhaps best be illustrated by the new national anthem, obligatorily sung in Pashto, which recognizes all of Afghanistan's peoples in only one of its languages:

> This land is Afghanistan – It is the pride of every Afghan
> The land of peace, the land of the sword – Its sons are all brave.
> This is the country of every tribe – Land of Baluch, and Uzbeks, Pashtoons,
> and Hazaras – Turkman and Tajiks with them,
> Arabs and Gojars, Pamirian, Nooristanis,
> Barahawi, and Qizilbash – Also Aimaq, and Pashaye
> This Land will shine for ever – Like the sun in the blue sky
> In the chest of Asia – It will remain as the heart for ever
> We will follow the one God –
> We all say, Allah is great, We all say, Allah is great[xi]

Clearly, reconstruction is not made less complex by ignoring Afghanistan's sociolinguistic reality. Inadequate attention towards language may exacerbate this complexity, potentially hampering efforts towards peace and reconciliation.

However, recent efforts towards embodying a pluralistic vision of Afghanistan society through programs such as mother tongue-based bi-/multilingual education may signal an important step towards including sociolinguistic reality in efforts at reconstruction and reconciliation.

NOTES

[i] The author wishes to acknowledge the assistance provided by Gelareh Keshavarz with Persian language materials. In addition, Spogmai Akseer and Sarfaroz Niyozov provided essential critical feedback on an earlier draft of this chapter.

[ii] Local languages have a relatively stable number of speakers, while so-called "residual" languages are those whose speakers are undergoing language shift, most frequently to Pashto or Dari.

[iii] Multilingualism here refers to the presence of multiple languages in a language ecology, and plurilingualism to individuals able to speak two or more languages, consistent with Council of Europe's terminology (see http://www.coe.int/t/dg4/linguistic/division_EN.asp).

[iv] In 1964, partly for political reasons, a decision was made to refer to the Afghanistan variety of Persian by the traditional term Dari to distinguish it from Iranian Persian (Dupree, 1978).

[v] Ferguson (1959) introduced the term diglossia to refer to situations where two very different varieties of a language are used for both high and low prestige purposes within one community, with not all members proficient in the high prestige variety. Fishman (1967) extended this concept to classify two types of diglossic situations: those with and without bilingualism (where the high prestige variety is a different language or dialect), and two types of bilingualism (those where diglossia is and is not present).

[vi] The last census in 1979-80 census was incomplete, providing imprecise and contested figures that can only be used as an approximation of numbers of languages and their speakers.

[vii] Pamiri languages are not LOIs in Tajikistan (Bahry, 2005b; Bahry, Niyozov, & Shamatov, 2008).

[viii] A search of the data and research section of World Bank's website for "bilingual education" yielded 46 hits, while "education" AND "Afghanistan" produced 115 hits, yet "bilingual education" AND "Afghanistan" produced no hits. In a recent World Bank publication (2009) on quality education in Afghanistan there is no mention of children's languages or school LOI as related to quality.

[ix] "Traveling policy" refers to policy imported into one context from a quite different context, which may then undergo radical reinterpretation. Bahry (2005a) showed that WB policy preferences for education reform in Tajikistan differed substantially from the analysis of the Ministry of Education, and argued that without sufficient dialogue and adaptation, the substantial weight of international actors has the potential to lead to adoption of educational policies not suited to the new context. Others have argued that traveling policy also occurs where a potentially beneficial external policy is adopted, but then "hijacked" for completely different purposes by the borrowers (Silova, 2005).

[x] See Bahry, Niyozov, and Shamatov (2008) for more on post-Soviet Central Asian language-in-education policies that are attempting to promote titular, republican languages in competition with Russian, while providing weak support for non-dominant local languages.

[xi] Source: http://www.afghan-web.com/anthem.

REFERENCES

Abadzi, Helen (2006). *Efficient learning for the poor: Insights from the frontier of cognitive neuroscience*. Washington, DC: World Bank.

ADB (2002). *Community-based gender sensitive education for the poor*. Project proposal. Japan Fund for Poverty Reduction JFPR: AFG 36484. Manila: Asian Development Bank.

Adeney, Katharine (2008). Constitutional design and the political salience of "Community" identity in Afghanistan: Prospects for the emergence of ethnic conflicts in the post-Taliban era. *Asian Survey*, 48(4), 535-557.

Afghanistan (2004). *Constitution of the Islamic Republic of Afghanistan*. (http://www.servat.unibe.ch/icl/af00000_.html)

Afghanistan (2005). Constitution of Afghanistan, October 1, 1964. Reprinted in Dari and English translation. In Nadjma Yassari (Ed.), *The Sharī'a in the constitutions of Afghanistan, Iran, and Egypt: Implications for private law* (pp. 209-259). Tübingen, Germany: Mohr Siebeck.

Afghanistan (2008). *Millenium development goals: Islamic Republic of Afghanistan.* Vision 2020. Annual Progress Report. Kabul, Afghanistan: Islamic Republic of Afghanistan.

Afghanistan Ministry of Education (2010). *Draft National Education Strategic Plan for Afghanistan (1389-1393/2010-2014).* Kabul, Afghanistan: Department of Planning and Evaluation.

Afghanistan Ministry of Education (2011). *Response to EFA Global Monitoring Report - 2011.* Kabul, Afghanistan: Ministry of Education. (http://english.moe.gov.af/index.php/policy-plan/72-reports/77-response-to-efa-global-monitoring-report-2011)

Bahry, Stephen (2005a). Travelling policy and local spaces in the Republic of Tajikistan: A comparison of the attitudes of Tajikistan and the World Bank towards textbook provision. *European Educational Research Journal, 4*(1), 60-78.

Bahry, Stephen (2005b). The potential of bilingual education in educational development of minority language children in Mountainous Badakhshan, Tajikistan. In H. Coleman, J. Gulyamova, & A. Thomas (Eds.), *Asia and beyond* (pp. 46-63). Tashkent, Uzbekistan: British Council.

Bahry, Stephen (2012). What constitutes quality in minority education? A multiple embedded case study of stakeholder perspectives on minority linguistic and cultural content in school-based curriculum in Sunan Yughur Autonomous County, Gansu. *Frontiers of Education in China, 7*(3), 376-416.

Bahry, Stephen, Niyozov, Sarfaroz, & Shamatov, Duishon (2008). Bilingual education in Central Asia. In Jim Cummins & Nancy H. Hornberger (Eds.), *Encyclopedia of language and education*, 2nd Edition, Volume 5: *Bilingual education* (pp. 205-221). New York: Springer Science + Business Media LLC.

Baker, Colin (2011). *Foundations of bilingual education and bilingualism* (5th ed.). Bristol, England: Multilingual Matters.

Baldauf, Ingeborg (2007). The Dāyı ~ Kārgıl of Andkhoy: Language, history and typical professions. Discourses on local identity. *Asien,* July, 135-152.

Barfield, Thomas J. (2010). *Afghanistan: A cultural and political history.* Princeton, NJ: Princeton University Press.

Bashir, Elena (2006). Indo-Iranian frontier languages. *Encyclopaedia Iranica,* Online Edition, November 15, 2006 (http://www.iranicaonline.org/articles/indo-iranian-frontier-languages-and-the-influence-of-persian)

Bender, Penelope; Dutcher, Nadine; Klaus, David; Shore, Jane, & Tesar, Charlie (2005). *In their own language, Education for All.* Education Notes. Washington, D.C.: The World Bank.

Benson, Carol (2005). *Girls, educational equity and mother tongue-based teaching.* Bangkok, Thailand: UNESCO Bangkok.

Black, Cyril E., Dupree, Louis, Endicott-West, Elizabeth, & Naby, Eden (1991). *The modernization of Inner Asia.* Armonk, New York: M. E. Sharpe.

Coulmas, Florian (1989). Language adaptation. In Coulmas, Florian (Ed.), *Language adaptation* (pp. 1-25). Cambridge, England: Cambridge University Press.

Cummins, Jim (2000). *Language, power and pedagogy: Bilingual children in the crossfire.* Clevedon, England: Multilingual Matters.

Cummins, Jim (2001). *Negotiating identities: Education for empowerment in a diverse society* (2nd ed.). Los Angeles: California Association for Bilingual Education.

Dryden-Peterson, Sarah (2010). *Barriers to accessing education in conflict-affected fragile states. Case Study: Afghanistan.* Save The Children.

Dupree, Louis (1978). Language and politics in Afghanistan. In Clarence Maloney (Ed.), *Language and civilization change in South Asia* (pp. 131-141). Leiden, Netherlands: E. J. Brill.

Dutcher, Nadine, & Tucker, G. Richard (1996). *The use of first and second languages in education.* Pacific Islands Discussion Paper, 1, East Asia and Pacific Region. Washington, DC: World Bank.

Dwyer, Arienne M. (2005). *The Xinjiang conflict: Uyghur identity, language policy, and political discourse.* Policy Studies 15. Washington, D.C.: East-West Center. (http://www.eastwestcenter.org/fileadmin/stored/pdfs/PS015.pdf)

Evans, Anne, Manning, Nick, Osmani, Yasin, Tully, Anne, & Wilder, Andrew (2004). *A guide to government in Afghanistan.* Washington, DC: World Bank.

Ewans, Martin (2002). *Afghanistan: A new history* (2nd ed.). London: RoutledgeCurzon.

Ferguson, Charles A. (1959). Diglossia. *Word, 15,* 325-340.

Fishman, Joshua A. (1967). Bilingualism with and without diglossia; diglossia with and without bilingualism. *Journal of Social Issues, 23*(2), 29-38.

Giustozzi, Antonio (2010). *Nation-building is not for all: The politics of education in Afghanistan.* Kabul, Afghanistan: Afghanistan Analysts Network. (http://aan-afghanistan.com/uploads/ AAN-Politics-of-Education.pdf)

Hakala, Walter N. (2011). Locating 'Pashto' in Afghanistan: A survey of secondary sources. In Harold F. Schiffman (Ed.), *Language policy and language conflict in Afghanistan and its neighbors* (pp. 53-88). Leiden, the Netherlands: Brill.

Hanifi, M. Jamil (2004). Editing the past: Colonial production of hegemony through the "Loya Jerga" in Afghanistan. *Iranian Studies, 37*(2), 295-322.

Hornberger, Nancy H. (2002). Multilingual language policies and the Continua of Biliteracy: An ecological approach. *Language Policy, 1,* 27-51.

Hyman, Anthony (2002). Nationalism in Afghanistan. *International Journal of Middle East Studies, 34*(2), 299-315.

Kieffer, Charles (1983). Afghanistan. V. Languages. *Encyclopedia Iranica, Vol. I,* Fasc. 5, 501-516.

Kieffer, Charles (2003). Hazāra. iv. Hazāragi dialect. *Encyclopaedia Iranica,* Online Edition, December 15, 2003. (http://www.iranicaonline.org/articles/hazara-4)

Lewis, M. Paul (Ed.) (2009). *Ethnologue: Languages of the world,* Sixteenth edition. Dallas, Texas: SIL International.

May, Stephen A. (2008). Bilingual/immersion education: What the research tells us. In Jim Cummins & Nancy H. Hornberger (Eds.), *Encyclopedia of language and education,* 2nd Edition, Volume 5: *Bilingual education* (pp. 19-34). New York: Springer Science + Business Media LLC.

Miran, M. Alam (1977). *The functions of national languages in Afghanistan.* New York: Afghanistan Council, Asia Society.

Naby, Eden (1980).The ethnic factor in Soviet-Afghan relations. *Asian Survey, 20*(3), 237-256.

Naby, Eden (1984). The Uzbeks in Afghanistan. *Central Asian Survey, 3*(1), 1-21.

Nawid, Senzil (2011). Language policy in Afghanistan: Linguistic diversity and national unity. In Harold F. Schiffman (Ed.), *Language policy and language conflict in Afghanistan and its neighbors* (pp. 31-52). Leiden, the Netherlands: Brill.

Newell, Richard S. (1988). The prospects for state-building in Afghanistan. In Ali Banuazizi & Myron Weiner (Eds.), *The state, religion, and ethnic politics: Afghanistan, Iran, and Pakistan* (pp. 104-124). Syracuse, New York: Syracuse University Press.

Newell, Richard S. (1989). Post-Soviet Afghanistan: The position of the minorities. *Asian Survey 29*(11): 1090-1108.

Olesen, Asta (1995). *Islam and politics in Afghanistan.* Richmond, England: Curzon Press.

Owens, Jonathan (2007). Endangered languages of the Middle East. In Matthias Brenzinger (Ed.), *Language diversity endangered* (pp. 263-277). Berlin, Germany: Walter de Gruyter.

Pinnock, Helen (2009). *Language and education: The missing link.* Reading/ London, England: CfBT Educational Trust and Save the Children UK.

Roberts, Jeffery J. (2003). *The origins of conflict in Afghanistan.* Westport, CT: Greenwood Publishing Group.

Rubin, Barnett R. (1991). The old regime in Afghanistan: Recruitment and training of a state élite. *Central Asian Survey, 10*(3), 73-100.

Rzehak, Lutz (2009). Remembering the Taliban. In Robert D. Crews & Amin Tarzi (Eds.), *The Taliban and the crisis of Afghanistan* (pp. 182-211). Cambridge, Massachusetts: Harvard University Press.

Samady, Saif R. (2001). *Education and Afghan society in the twentieth century*. Paris: UNESCO.

SERVE (2010). *SERVE Afghanistan: Annual Report 2010*. Kabul, Afghanistan. (http://www.serveafghanistan.org/storage/annual%20rpt%202010.pdf)

Shahrani, M. Nazif (1988). State building and social fragmentation in Afghanistan: A social perspective. In Ali Banuazizi & Myron Weiner (Eds.), *The state, religion, and ethnic politics: Afghanistan, Iran, and Pakistan* (pp. 23-74). Syracuse, New York: Syracuse University Press.

Silova, Iveta (2005). Traveling Policies: Hijacked in Central Asia. *European Educational Research Journal, 4*(1), 50-59.

Smith, Alan (2010). *The hidden crisis: Armed conflict and education: The influence of education on conflict and peace building*. Background paper prepared for the Education for All Global Monitoring Report 2011. UNESCO Report 2011/ED/EFA/MRT/PI/48.

Taylor, Charles (1992). The politics of recognition. In Amy Guttman (Ed.), *Multiculturalism and "The politics of recognition"* (pp. 25-73). Princeton, NJ: Princeton University Press.

Thomas, Wayne, & Collier, Victoria (2002). *A national study of school effectiveness for language minority students' long-term academic achievement*. University of California, Berkeley, California: Center for Research on Education, Diversity and Excellence.

Tohiri, S. (2002). *Bo suquti Tolibon dar Afghoniston zaboni Dari maqomi peshinai khudro kasb mekunad* [With the fall of the Taliban, the Dari language is regaining its previous status in Afghanistan]. January 26, 2002. Radio Ozodi Tajik language (http://www.ozodi.org/content/article/1122353.html)

UNESCO (1953). *The use of vernacular languages in education*. Monographs in Fundamental Education, VIII. Paris: UNESCO.

UNESCO (2002). *UNESCO education reconstruction programme for Afghanistan: Components and development projects*. Paris: UNESCO.

UNESCO (2003). *Education in a multilingual world*. UNESCO Education Position Paper. Paris: UNESCO.

UNESCO (2009). *Afghan minority language project succeeds against the odds*. August, 2009. UNESCO Education Sector Newsletter.

World Bank (1995). *Priorities and strategies for education*. Washington, DC: World Bank.

World Bank (2009). *Afghanistan education quality improvement project (EQUIP)*. Human Development Unit, South Asia Region. Report No: ICR00001263. Washington, D.C.: World Bank.

Yun, Ju-Hong (2003). *Pashai language development project: Promoting Pashai language, literacy and community development*. A paper presented at the Conference on Language Development, Language Revitalization, and Multilingual Education in Minority Communities in Asia. November 6-8, 2003, Bangkok, Thailand. (http://www.sil.org/asia/ldc/parallel_papers/ju-hong_yun.pdf)

Yun, Ju-Hong (2008). Afghanistan. Mother tongue and multilingual education in Afghanistan: The Pashai language development project. In UNESCO, *Improving the quality of mother tongue-based literacy and learning: Case studies from Asia, Africa and South America* (pp. 14-27). Bangkok, Thailand: UNESCO Bangkok.

Zholdoshalieva, Rakhat (2010). *Inclusion and exclusion of indigenous knowledge, culture and language: The Kyrgyz minority in Central and Inner Asia*. The 54th Comparative International Education Society Annual Conference, University of Chicago, Illinois, USA, March 1-5.

Stephen A. Bahry
Ontario Institute for Studies in Education
University of Toronto, Canada

BIRGIT BROCK-UTNE

4. LANGUAGE AND LIBERATION

Language of Instruction for Mathematics and Science:
A Comparison and Contrast of Practices Focusing on Tanzania

ABSTRACT

Sura hii inahusu lugha ya kufundishia kwenye nchi za Afrika (anglophone). Hasa inahusu ufundishaji wa sayansi na teknolojia. Nchi zilizoiwala Afrika zinatumia misaada kuimarisha lugha zao kama lugha za kufundishia katika shule za Afrika. Hakuna shule hata moja ya sekondari Afrika nzima inayotumia lugha ya kiafrika kama lugha ya kufundishia. Mifano kutoka Sri Lanka na Malaysia inaonyesha kwamba ni muhimu sana ufundishaji wa sayansi na teknolojia ukafanyika katika lugha ambayo wanafunzi wanaielewa, yaani lugha wanayotumia kila wakati. Mwaka 2006 Zanzibar ilitangaza kurudisha lugha ya kiingereza kama lugha ya kufundishia masomo ya hisabati na sayansi kuanzia darasa la tano, katika shule zote za serikali. Aidha kiswahili ni lugha ya kwanza kwa wakazi wengi wa Zanzibar. Kwenye sura hii ninajaribu kuchambua misukumo nyuma ya mwenendo huu na nani anafaidika nao. (*Translated to Kiswahili [swh], the lingua franca of Tanzania, by the author, with thanks to Jane Bakahwehmama for making a final check.*)

This chapter deals with the language of instruction (LOI) issues in so-called "Anglophone" African countries. It especially looks at the teaching of science and technology. The former colonial powers use large parts of their aid budgets to promote their own languages as languages of instruction in the schools in Africa. No secondary school in Africa has an African language as the LOI. Examples from Sri Lanka and Malaysia show that it is especially important that the teaching of science is done in a familiar language, the language children normally speak. Yet in 2006 Zanzibar reintroduced English as the language of instruction from grade five in mathematics and science subjects in all government primary schools – and that on an island where Kiswahili is the first language of the whole population. In my chapter I attempt to analyze the forces behind this move and who profits from it.

C. Benson and K. Kosonen (eds.), Language Issues in Comparative Education, 77–93.
© *2013 Sense Publishers. All rights reserved.*

INTRODUCTION:
ENGLISH AS THE LANGUAGE OF SCIENCE AND TECHNOLOGY

It is difficult to understand where the belief comes from that science is better learnt in English than in other languages and that "English is the language of science and technology." (Wedikkarage, 2009: 264)

In 2005 I spent several weeks sitting hour after hour in the back of a secondary school classroom in Tanzania (Brock-Utne, 2005). I observed that students did not understand what the teacher was saying when he spoke English, and often would ask the teacher to express himself in Kiswahili, a language they all speak and understand very well. My eyes fell especially on one gentle looking boy who was completely passive and obviously did not understand anything of what was going on. Once I heard him ask one of his classmates in Kiswahili what the teacher had said. When I spoke in Kiswahili to him during the break afterwards, and mentioned that I had noticed that he did not understand the language of instruction LOI, he admitted that my observation was correct. He did have great difficulties following the teacher, especially if the teacher did not switch to Kiswahili during the lesson. I asked him if it would not have been much better for him had the lesson been given in Kiswahili throughout. He admitted that it certainly would have been much easier. Then he would be able to understand what the teacher was saying. Yet when I then asked him if he thought there should be a change in the language of instruction, he said no, he did not think so, because English was the language of science and technology – the language of modernization and all technological development. Without knowing English, one could not get a good job. He had to learn English and could not see another way than having it as a language of instruction.

SCIENCE EDUCATION AND ENGLISH MEDIUM:
THE SRI LANKAN EXPERIENCE

The claim that "we need English as the language of technological development" is repeated several times in the report on the *Education System for the 21st Century in Tanzania* (URT, 1993). Yet the claim seems unfounded. As Rugemalira et al. maintained over two decades ago:

[If this is true] it should be demonstrated that countries such as Finland, Norway, China or Japan, which do not teach their children through the medium of an "international language," are isolated and have lost track of technological developments beyond their borders. (Rugemalira et al., 1990: 31)

Since Finland, Norway, China and Japan all do a reasonable job of teaching through their own languages, at least for their majority groups, the myth of English superiority can be seriously questioned.

In an article on Education for All (EFA) policy lessons, Mehrotra draws our attention to what he sees as the most important characteristic of those developing countries that really target the poor and have the highest percentage of the population with a completed basic education:

> The experience of the high-achievers has been unequivocal: the mother tongue was used as the medium of instruction at the primary level in all cases. (Mehrotra, 1998: 479)

One of the countries that Mehrotra looked at was Sri Lanka. The case of Sri Lanka offers more evidence that national languages, even in a developing country, are perfectly capable of expressing scientific concepts. Sri Lanka introduced its two major languages, Sinhala and Tamil, as languages of instruction in education, replacing English even before having obtained independence from Britain in 1948 (Wedikkarage, 2009). Steps were taken to introduce these languages as media of instruction in all primary schools in 1945, secondary schools in 1953 and at universities in 1960. According to Wedikkarage, local educators argued that the change of medium of instruction from English to the national languages, Sinhala and Tamil, enabled the vast majority of students to learn science subjects in the standard variety of their first languages,[i] which ran counter to the idea that studying these subjects in English would be an advantage.

Sri Lankan educators now say that using national languages in education in Sri Lanka has contributed remarkably to the development process of the country. Sri Lanka enjoys a literacy rate of 91%, the second highest in South Asia after the Maldives at 98%, and among the highest in mid- and low-income countries, and it can boast 100% participation in primary education (UNESCO, 2011). The former Director of Education at the Curriculum Development Center, Ministry of Education, Sri Lanka has written about the great advantages offered to the Sri Lankan population by introducing Sinhala and Tamil as languages of instruction – especially for the teaching of science and technology:

> The transition from English to the national languages as the medium of instruction in science helped to destroy the great barrier that existed between the privileged English educated classes; between the science educated elite and the non-science educated masses; between science itself and the people. It gave confidence to the common man [sic] that science is within his reach and to the teachers and pupils that a knowledge of English need not necessarily be a prerequisite for learning science. (Ranaweera, 1976: 423)

Ranaweera relates that the change of medium of instruction in science and mathematics lagged behind the other subjects because of special difficulties, like the absence of scientific and technical terms, textbooks, and proficient teachers. Yet he finds the greatest need to switch over to the national languages in the science subjects. He gives two reasons for this claim:

– First, science education was considered the main instrument through which national development goals and improvements in the quality of life of the masses could be achieved. Thus, there was a need to expand science education, which was constrained by the English medium.

– Second, in order to achieve the wider objectives of science education, such as inculcation of the methods and attitudes of science, old didactic approaches had to be replaced by activity- and inquiry-based approaches, requiring greater dialogue, discussion, and interaction (both pupil-teacher and pupil-pupil). "Such an approach makes a heavy demand on the language ability of the pupils and will be more successful if the medium of instruction is also the first language of the pupils" (Ranaweera, 1976: 417).

Despite these observations in the 1970s, Sri Lankan educational authorities reintroduced English in 2001 as a medium of instruction for science classes at grades 12 and 13 (also known as General Certificate of Education Advanced Level or GCE A-Level) in selected government schools. Wedikkarage (2009) critically analyzes the discourses that led to a reverse in language of instruction for A-Level science, finding that the objective was to improve English language competence. The idea that using English as a medium leads to improved English competence emerges as a central but totally unsubstantiated belief. Further, in Sri Lanka, a country where science teaching has taken place for nearly 40 years in Sinhala and Tamil, it has been difficult to find teachers who are willing and competent enough to teach science in English. Similarly, these schools were forced to relax selection criteria to fill English medium classes—and many of these students soon sought permission to return to national language medium classes, creating administrative problems. According to the students interviewed (Wedikkarage, 2006), most teachers in English-medium classes resorted to either Sinhala or Tamil when they could not properly explain their lessons in English. According to the same students, their teachers were far more effective presenting their subject matter when they taught in their first language

The failure to teach English effectively as a second language has been used as a pretence to reintroduce English medium into the public school system in Sri Lanka. However, the study by Wedikkarage effectively illustrates the difficulties both teachers and students face when using English as a medium of instruction, and suggests that what is required in the Sri Lankan context is not to go back to English medium but to help students learn English well as a foreign, yet important language. It is doubtful that private sector employers would demand job seekers to have studied in English-medium schools; what they might want is people with a good knowledge of English.

THE CASE OF MALAYSIA

Some of us have argued that without instruction in a language in which a learner is comfortable and proficient there is no future for African development (Prah & Brock-Utne, 2009). The experiences of post-colonial Asian and Western European countries point irrefutably to the inherent value in education based in a language the learners understand – or at least education in popular, widely spoken languages of wider communication. In our book (ibid.) we argue against the use of expressions like "mother tongue," "first language," "L1," and so on, since many Africans grow up with three or more languages and would not identify a single "first language" (e.g. Ouane, 2009; Kimizi, 2009; see also Kosonen & Benson's Introduction, and Benson, this volume). We have frequently argued that the prosperity and economic prowess of modern Asia is, in no small measure, attributable to the use of languages confidently understood, spoken and written by the overwhelming masses of the people. In Japan, Mongolia, South and North Korea just a small percentage of the population are not speakers of the official language (Lewis, 2009). In Cambodia, Vietnam and Bangladesh this is in the 10% range. Several authors in Kosonen and Young (2009), however, remind us that there are hundreds of millions of Asians who have to study through an alien language, which in many cases is not a colonial, but an Asian dominant language.

In Malaysia, a former British colony, the language of instruction was switched from English to Malay in 1957. In 2003, Prime Minister Mahathir Mohammad started a program to resume teaching math and science in English. Most other subjects were taught in Malay. The problems caused by this change of policy have now led Malaysia to reinstate the use of Malay for all subjects in national schools and the use of Chinese and Tamil in vernacular schools. According to Watson (2011), while urban elites did not like it, most people supported the change back to Malay, Tamil and Mandarin. In July 2009, for example, the Associated Press reported:

> Malaysia said Wednesday (8 July, 2009) that it would abandon the use of English to teach mathematics and science, bowing to protesters who demanded more use of the national Malay language. Malay will be reinstated in state-financed schools starting in 2012 because teaching in English caused academic results in those subjects to slip, Education Minister Muhyiddin Yassin said. There have been months of high-profile demonstrations by politicians and linguists, especially from the ethnic Malay majority, who say a six-year-old policy of using English undermines their struggle to modernize their mother tongue. English was once the medium of instruction in most schools in Malaysia, a former British colony. Nationalist leaders switched to Malay less than two decades after independence in 1957. In 2003, Prime Minister Mahathir Mohammad started a program to resume teaching math and science in English. Most other subjects are taught in Malay. (NYT, 2009)

As history has shown, Malaysia has undergone a trying journey to reach where it stands today on the issue of language of education. As the news report further clarifies and elaborates:

> Deputy premier Muhyiddin Yassin said that from 2012 the subjects will be taught in Bahasa Malaysia in national schools, or in Chinese and Tamil in vernacular schools. Critics of the six-year policy of using English to teach the subjects argue that it has dragged down students' performance and is particularly unfair on children who are not proficient in the language. "I wouldn't say it's a complete failure but it has not achieved the desired

objectives that it was supposed to achieve," Muhyiddin told a press conference. "The government is convinced that science and maths need to be taught in a language that will be easily understood by students, which is Bahasa Malaysia in national schools, Mandarin in Chinese schools and Tamil in Tamil schools." (AFP, 2009)

Interestingly, it would appear that whereas in some South and Southeast Asian countries people demonstrate in the streets in favor of the use of familiar languages as languages of instruction for science and technological education, in African contexts there is no such reaction. On the contrary, people have often followed the elites in support of the use of the colonial languages as languages of instruction, particularly in the so-called Anglophone countries like Tanzania.

Many Africans admire the visible success of contemporary Asia in all areas of the social and economic lives of Asians but are unable to easily see the connection between this scientific, technological and economic ascendancy of Asia and the wide use of dominant Asian languages as languages of instruction. If language is understood to be the central feature of culture and development is seen as ultimately a cultural phenomenon, it is not difficult to see the interconnections between language and development. In our introduction to a book on multilingualism in Africa (Prah and Brock-Utne, 2009), we are not suggesting that the use of one of the learner's most familiar languages as the language of instruction automatically leads to social development. We are suggesting that there are many factors which contribute to development, but development cannot occur in the post-colonial circumstances of Africa and other parts of the world without using people's languages as the central languages of instruction.

EXAMPLES FROM TANZANIA

One of my Tanzanian students recalls her own school days:

I can recall from my school days about my Chemistry teacher who every ten minutes or so he would ask us: "Any question students?" Nobody answered and he would conclude: "If there are no questions, then you have understood everything!" We did not understand him at all, not only because he taught in English only, he spoke American English! – he was a Peace Corps [volunteer teacher]. The issue was language, as it is in our contemporary schools. (Mwinsheikhe, 2002: 73-74)

Mwinsheikhe went on to study the effects of using English or Kiswahili as the language of instruction in secondary schools in Tanzania. For her PhD research, undertaken under the umbrella of the LOITASA[ii] project, Mwinsheikhe (2007) worked with Vuzo (2007) to ask Form I teachers to teach the same topic, first using English or code-switching between English and Kiswahili for one class, and then some days later using only Kiswahili for another class. Two different secondary schools were used, and six weeks spent in each of them, gathering both quantitative and qualitative data. Mwinsheikhe concentrated on biology lessons while Vuzo concentrated on lessons in geography. I spent three weeks with them in the first school and two weeks in the second school, both to increase the reliability of the findings and to get first-hand field experience in this context. My own data (Brock-Utne, 2007a) were all qualitative and related to the interaction between teacher and pupils according to whether the teacher taught in English or in Kiswahli. I found that when the teachers taught in Kiswahili, they smiled more, seemed happier, and even joked with the pupils. The pupils were attentive and very active, raising their hands frequently, sometimes entering into debates with the teacher and arguing against her arguments. They had a lot of knowledge about the topic discussed and liked sharing knowledge and debating. On the other hand, when teachers taught in English, they hardly smiled, and they punished pupils by having them stand for long periods of time next to their desks if they could not find the right answer in English. When teaching was conducted in English, the pupils looked down and were totally passive, afraid that they would be asked questions. Pupils were never punished when teachers taught in Kiswahili, a fact about which these teachers were not aware until we pointed this out to them, providing evidence from our observations.

After six weeks of teaching the same topic, once to a group taught in Kiswahli and another group taught in English, knowledge tests were administered in English to the group taught in English and in Kiswahili to the group taught in Kiswahili (see Table 1). A large standard deviation suggests a large amount of variability of scores around the mean, whereas a small standard deviation indicates little variability. Vuzo (2007) found that there was a much higher standard deviation in the group who had had English as the language of instruction compared to the groups taught in code-switching or in Kiswahili. The standard deviation for the group that had Kiswahili as the LOI was the smallest (sd=13.18) compared to that of the group whose teachers code-switched (sd=15.83) and that of the group which had English as the LOI (sd=18.01). This indicates that using Kiswahili as the LOI facilitates more equitable performance among students. The teachers had the same impression, noting that students did not differ much in performance when Kiswahili was the LOI. As Table 1 shows, there are immense differences in mean scores, the advantage going to the Kiswahili LOI group over the English LOI group, particularly in school Y.

Table 1. Mean scores for knowledge test 1 by language of instruction.
(Source: Vuzo, 2007: 259)

	Code-switching	Kiswahili	English
School X	57	63	52
School Y	56	64	46

Both Mwinsheikhe (2007) and Vuzo (2007) found that when the same teacher taught using different LOIs, students performed much better in Kiswahili. These examples show clearly that students learn new knowledge better when they can use a familiar language rather than a foreign one. Vuzo's results also show that use of English as LOI increases differences between students. The large spread of scores for English LOI shows how the use of English may contribute to social segregation, the opposite of poverty alleviation. Put another way, the use of an LOI which is unfamiliar to most students is a recipe for increased inequality. It may benefit a very small group of students who have well-to-do parents who take them to English-speaking countries, have English-speaking guests, buy them English books, videos and games, and/or pay for English tutors.

The use of an unfamiliar language of instruction is, then, an excellent way to keep people from advancing. Over a decade ago, the Ministry of Education and Culture (MoEC) in Tanzania issued a policy document in Kiswahili entitled Sera ya Utamaduni. Section 3.4 of this policy document gives a detailed account of why Kiswahili deserves to be the medium of instruction instead of English, including this statement:

> Kama tutaendelea kufundisha kwa lugha ya Kiingereza, sayansi na teknolojia ambayo tunahitaji sana kwa maendeleo ya taifa letu katika karne ya ishirini na moja itaendelea kuwa haki ya watu wachache wanaofahamu Kiingereza.
> [If we continue teaching in English, the science and technology that we highly need for the development of our nation in the 21st century will remain the right of few individuals who are proficient in English.] (MoEC, 1999: 19, my translation)

With this the government admits that the use of English in teaching hinders the development of education, science and technology in Tanzania.

UNDERSTANDING OF SCIENCE CONCEPTS

As part of the LOISA[iii] project, Langenhoven (2006, 2010) looked at the understanding of science concepts among grade 6 learners in the Western Cape Province of South Africa, some of whom had been taught in English (a language foreign to most) and some in isiXhosa (their home language). The test item, taken verbatim from the workbook used by teachers for teaching module 1 of grade 6 on "Ecosystems and environmental balance," was: "Describe TWO natural resources that have been exploited (damaged) by humans."

The item was chosen for coding and analysis because it lent itself to expressions of learning competence through writing. It was translated into isiXhosa for the group taught in isiXhosa and kept in English for the group taught in English. Results of the test are reflected in Table 2.

Table 2. Percentage of students able to describe damaged natural resources. (Source: Langenhoven, 2006: 262)

	Incorrect	One Example	Two Examples
isiXhosa	12	48	40
English	97	3	0

As seen in Table 2, 88% (22/25) of the pupils taught in isiXhosa were able to express themselves correctly in writing, giving one or two examples of natural resources that have been exploited (damaged) by humans. They wrote in isiXhosa, the language in which they are most proficient, in a manner that was understandable, and it was evident from their answers that the concept of damage to natural resources had been well understood. The pupils taught in English had great difficulty writing about this concept in English; 97% (30/31) gave incorrect answers. According to Langenhoven, "This result is shocking and raises many questions about education policy and its outcomes" (2006: 262). He gives some examples of the weak responses received when learners were forced to learn through and write in English:

Pupil 1: It say they bring death at our home but they don't.

Pupil 2: Sheep we damage them by killing them, after all we took them to the fire we make meat by them.

Pupil 3: Fungi and bacteria they stay in the bread. They damage in the bread, people do not eat the bread.

Pupil 4: The frog that we are the amphibian that are living organisms. This frog he live in a forest because is living thing. The frog that we have damages the forest. We have their damages of the frog that are. (Langenhoven, 2006: 262)

As the examples demonstrate, some pupils were unable to understand the question in English. They wrote about things that appear to have been learned by memory, the idea being that any English writing about science is worth a try. This writing ranges from personal experiences to snatches of classroom teaching and learning experiences. Their writing also reveals misunderstanding of animal characteristics and habitats.

Also in the Western Cape Province, a PhD research study undertaken by Nomlomo (2007) showed a positive correlation between the use of learners' first language (isiXhosa) as a medium of instruction and their understanding and academic performance in science. That is, Nomlomo found that learning through the home language (isiXhosa) enhanced understanding of science concepts, in contrast to learning through English, which in reality is a foreign language for children living in Khyalitsha, the township where the research was conducted. Nomlomo (2008) went on to explore the idea that science teachers need to possess both adequate subject matter knowledge and the ability to get this subject knowledge across to learners. Such communication is infinitely easier in a language in which both teachers and learners are proficient.

Other studies on the teaching of science in Africa show similar results when they contrast teaching through a familiar African language with teaching through a foreign European language. In a study done some years ago in Botswana (Prophet & Dow, 1994), a set of science concepts was taught to Form I secondary students: an experimental group in Setswana and a control group in English. The researchers tested understanding of concepts and found that students taught in Setswana had developed a significantly better understanding of the concepts than those taught in English.

In the 2003 TIMSS (Trends in International Mathematics and Science Study) mathematics test for grade eight, it was reported that Ghana finished number 44 out of the 45 countries that participated. Ghanaian students scored an average of 276 points, compared to the international average of 466. In two articles published in Ghana News, two mathematics teachers try to explain these low results in mathematics (Fredua-Kwarteng & Ahia, 2005a) and in science (Fredua-Kwarteng & Ahia, 2005b). They start by pointing out that a country whose national pedagogy is compatible with the test (i.e. where the test was developed) is likely to do better than other countries, and in Ghana "students simply memorize the algorithms and regurgitate them during tests or examinations" (ibid., 2005a). The main reason that students do not learn problem-solving and problem-posing skills is the use of a foreign medium of instruction:

> Since Ghanaian students took the test in English (the so-called official language of Ghana), those whose first language is non-English are at great disadvantage. We are not surprised that countries that top-performed in the mathematics test – Taiwan, Malaysia, Latvia, Russia – used their own language to teach and learn mathematics. (Fredua-Kwarteng & Ahia, 2005a)

The authors argue that a Ghanaian student would be likely to answer most of the questions correctly if the questions were translated into his or her first or home language, continuing:

> Some Ghanaians theorize that a person becomes increasingly proficient in a foreign language after using it … for a long time … [T]he unfortunate thing is that most of these students would psychologically drop out of mathematics before they attain English proficiency! … Some Ghanaians also argue that using English for instruction makes it possible for Ghanaians to "transport" their education to any of the English-speaking countries. But […] when Ghanaian students at the secondary level enroll in schools in Canada they are confronted with two main tasks. They have to find the meaning of mathematical concepts and also the words to communicate the meaning of those concepts. Asian students, on the other hand, have to find the words to express their understanding of mathematical concepts. This is because they have already learnt the meanings of mathematics concepts in their own

language. So whose education is more portable? (Fredua-Kwarteng & Ahia 2005a)

The authors further criticize the mathematics and science tests for being rooted in a Western, especially American environment, using unfamiliar concepts like a "parking lot." From their professional experience, students are more likely to solve mathematical problems if they can relate to the cultural context of the problem.

Mammino (2010), an Italian professor of chemistry, presents a collection of interesting reflections based on over 20 years of experience teaching general chemistry and physical chemistry courses in Zambia, Lesotho and South Africa. Since 1997 she has worked in South Africa at the University of Venda (UNIVEN), an historically Black university (HBU) that serves students from poor rural backgrounds. The HBUs were universities "for blacks only" during the apartheid period, which, according to the political criteria of those times, implied both poor resources and poor educational approaches, aimed at ensuring that black students would not have a chance to excel. Mammino notes that the country-wide scarcity of qualified secondary school science teachers affects rural areas more extensively, resulting in the serious under-preparedness of most students who enter UNIVEN. She provides extensive documentation of the impact of using a language different from the home language to approach chemistry. She analyzes the difficulties encountered by tertiary level chemistry students in second-language disadvantaged contexts. The results demonstrate the importance of utilizing languages learners understand to approach chemistry. Mammino stresses that the language of science is not just terminology. Communication or thought generation requires much more than technical terms; the technical terms must be linked by words to build meanings, and these words (verbs, adjectives, prepositions, logical connectives, etc.) pertain to the language utilized. Technical terms are thus immersed in a sea of common words that constitute the backbone of communication:

> Knowing the meaning and roles of these common words, being able to understand what they communicate (on reading or listening) and to use them so as to communicate a wanted meaning (on speaking or writing) become essential instruments to ensure correctness and clarity in any form of communication. In particular, rigorous wording usage by the teacher enhances the quality of explanations and helps prevent confusion and misconceptions. The inevitable general inference is that language mastering is the key to science learning as well as to creativity in the sciences. This, together with the acknowledgment of the paramount internalization depth of word-concept and expression-concept correspondences within the mother tongue, points to the essential role of the mother tongue as the natural ground to develop language mastering up to the highest sophistication levels and, in particular, up to the levels that are needed for science communication and science learning. (Mammino, 2010: 8)

According to Mammino, chemistry and chemistry education are particularly sensitive to language-related aspects in teaching and learning, due to the use of descriptions through language and through mathematics at two intertwining description levels (macroscopic and microscopic), the use of a symbols system that is probably the most extensive and articulated in the sciences, and the continuous interplay between observation and interpretation, all of which demand substantial language mastery.

In an experiment Mammino (1995) conducted at the National University of Lesotho, students who had written incorrect or meaningless statements in their chemistry examinations were asked to explain their views on the given issues through their first language, which was then translated into English by a non-chemist to ensure that there would be no automatic improvement of the explanations. In several cases, the translated answer corresponded to reasonable chemistry, demonstrating that students had understood the chemistry but had not been able to express their ideas. Mammino also found that absurd or meaningless answers were often related to grammar and sentence construction, as well as the selection and combination of words.

WHAT IS ZANZIBAR UP TO?

Zanzibar, a large semi-autonomous island state which is administratively part of Tanzania, provides an interesting case study regarding the LOI of mathematics and science. In connection with a World Bank loan to the education sector and a consultancy report (MEVT/UoB, 2005) showing that English competence was very low among primary school pupils, even among those given an extra year of preparation to use English as the LOI in secondary school, Zanzibar introduced a new curriculum in 2006 that reintroduced English as the language of instruction from grade five in mathematics and science subjects (MEVT, 2006). There is a strange discrepancy between the terms of reference given to the researchers and the conclusions made in their consultancy report, since they were not asked to suggest a new language-in-education policy for Zanzibar. Rather, they were asked to evaluate the special orientation class designed to prepare pupils for English as LOI at secondary level, based on interviews with stakeholders. The consultants found low levels of English language proficiency among pupils and teachers, and noted that "primary English does not provide an adequate basis for the switch to English in the secondary phase" (MEVT/UoB, 2005: 4). One would expect such findings to lead to a discussion of the importance of using a language in which learners and teachers are proficient, e.g. Kiswahili, yet these consultants recommended the gradual introduction of English medium teaching, starting first with one subject at standard (grade) 4, increasing to core subjects, i.e. math, science or social sciences, by the end of standard 7 (ibid.: 5). The Ministry thus decided to reintroduce English as the LOI from grade five in mathematics and science subjects in all government primary schools (MEVT, 2006).

On 24 November 2009 I had a meeting with the Deputy Principal Secretary of the Ministry of Education and Vocational Training, who holds a Ph.D. in development studies from a well-known UK university. He told me that both he and the lead international consultant knew that children learn best in a language that is familiar to them. However, his job as a politician was to listen to what his constituency wanted, and he believed that parents want their children to be taught through the medium of English.

CHANGING A BELIEF SYSTEM WHICH HAS BECOME COMMON KNOWLEDGE

Having English as the language of instruction does not promote understanding of what is learnt in the majority schools in the so-called Anglophone African countries. As observed by Ayo Bamgbose, a long-term researcher and advocate for the use of African languages in education:

> Outside Africa, no one questions why the languages of countries with smaller populations in Europe should be used as a medium, even up to and including the university level. What seems to be lacking in many African countries is the political will to break away from the colonial policy and practice of limiting mother tongue education to lower primary classes. Where such a will exists, much can be done in a short period of time. (Bamgbose, 2005: 255)

Foucault (1988) claims that belief systems gain momentum (and hence power) as more people come to accept the particular views associated with that belief system as common knowledge. Some ideas, considered undeniable "truths," come to define a particular way of seeing the world. Unfortunately, at the moment, those who stand to lose the most from having a foreign language of instruction consider it as an undeniable "truth" that using English as LOI is the best way to learn English. This is a false belief, as years of research have shown. It is, however, a belief that some international donors, all of the former colonial powers, the publishing industry, and the African elite have an interest in promoting. These power groups are, as Sharp (1980) points out, dependent for their positions and political powers on the obedience, submission, and cooperation of their "subjects." Thus they have an interest in promoting and maintaining the misconception that using a language in which teachers and students can barely communicate will benefit education. In reality, such policies cause most African learners to miss out on important academic content, particularly in mathematics and science, and they exacerbate social and economic differences between people.

Misconceptions are possible to alter. When normal African people understand how this misconception holds them down and works to the advantage of the powerful, the allegedly powerless may unite to do away with the misconceptions. My work and that of others cited here helps to reveal the misconceptions and offer educational alternatives worth fighting for.

In an article on the 'values' dimension in evaluation, Avenstrup (2009) finds that much development aid in education engages in the rhetoric of improving access and quality, measuring these in terms of indicators such as enrolment, progression and completion rates, teacher/learner ratios, textbook/learner ratios and teacher formal qualifications.

This sort of instrumentalism completely ignores the debate about the reproduction of cultural capital and power structures in educational systems. It assumes that literacy and numeracy are relevant in themselves, and ignores the discussion about what content and values are conveyed in the official and hidden curriculum, or contested in curriculum appropriation (Avenstrup, 2009: 257). The curriculum which is hidden by having children study in a language in which they are not proficient is to make them look down on their own culture and to tell them that they are stupid when they do not understand what the teacher is trying to convey. African academics like Bamgbose (2005), Bgoya (1992), Desai (2006), Mazrui (1997), Makelela (2005), Mwinsheikhe (2007), Nomlomo (2007), Prah (2005), Qorro (2009), Rubagumya (2003) and Vuzo (2007) describe how the formal school sector is a re-colonization of education in Africa through the curriculum promoted and the language of instruction used. These academics and their arguments have sometimes been marginalized in language policy debates in their own countries, but the hope for African education lies in such people gathering sufficient momentum, and hence power, which will lead to political will, to have their views accepted as common knowledge.

At one point in time it was considered common knowledge that men and white people in general were more intelligent than women and black people. This is not common knowledge anymore. It was common knowledge that neither women[iv] nor black people[v] could learn mathematics. Now the common knowledge is that women and black people have the same ability to learn mathematics as anyone else.

In the future, it will become common knowledge in so-called Anglophone African countries that children learn better when they understand what the teacher is saying.

NOTES

[i] Editors' note: It must be acknowledged that these languages exist in "high" and "low" varieties, and that this diglossic situation may make it difficult for learners who enter school speaking local varieties of Tamil or Sinhala – but presumably not as difficult as learning in English, a foreign language.

[ii] LOITASA (Languages of Instruction in Tanzania and South Africa), a project sponsored by NUFU (Norwegian Universities Committee for Development, Research and Education), ran from 2001 to 2012. The researchers, from the University of Dar es Salaam, Tanzania, University of Western Cape, South Africa and the University of Oslo, have published nine books, with three more forthcoming in 2013. Eight students have completed PhDs, three are working on their doctorates, and twenty have completed MAs under the project (http://www.loitasa.org).

[iii] The LOISA (Language of Instruction in South Africa) project, funded by HSRC (Human Science Research Council) in South Africa and NRC (Norwegian Research Council) in Norway, ran from 2001 to 2006) and was closely connected to the LOITASA project.

[iv] When I attended elementary school in Norway, girls had fewer weekly lessons in mathematics than boys because of a belief that girls could not learn and would not need mathematics; instead we learned home economics. In our mathematics textbooks, some tasks marked with * after which it said, "Girls do not need to do this task," and the same was true for the final exam (Brock-Utne and Haukaa, 1980).

[v] My black South African students have told me that in the apartheid times of South Africa there was a belief that black people could not learn mathematics and they hardly had any teaching of this subject.

REFERENCES

AFP (2009). *Malaysia drops English for math, science classes.* Quoted from Agence France Press (AFP) 9/07/2009 on Mother tongue based learning in the Philippines: A blog for the MLE Consortium. (http://mothertongue-based.blogspot.com/)

Brock-Utne, Birgit (2005). Language-in-education policies and practices in Africa with a special focus on Tanzania and South Africa – Insights from research in progress. In Angel M. Y. Lin & Peter W. Martin (Eds.), *Decolonisation, globalisation. Language-in-education policy and practice* (pp. 173-194). Clevedon: Multilingual Matters.

Brock-Utne, Birgit (2007a). Learning through a familiar language versus learning through a foreign language – A look into some secondary school classrooms in Tanzania. *International Journal of Educational Development, 27*(5), 487– 498.

Brock-Utne, Birgit (2007b). Language of instruction and student performance: New insights from research in Tanzania and South Africa. *International Review of Education, 53*(5/6), 509-530.

Brock-Utne, Birgit, & Haukaa, Runa (1980). *Kunnskap uten makt. Kvinner som lærere og elever* [Knowledge without power. Women as teachers and pupils]. Oslo: Universitetsforlaget. (Reprinted 1981 and 1984. German edition in 1986, Wissen ohne Macht. Frauen als Lehrerinnen und Schülerinnen. Gießen: Focus Verlag.)

Brock-Utne, Birgit, & Skattum, Ingse (Eds.) (2009). *Languages and education in Africa: A comparative and transdisciplinary discussion.* Oxford: Symposium Books.

EFA GMR (2011). *Education for All global monitoring report. The hidden crisis: Armed conflict and education.* Paris: UNESCO Publishing.

Foucault, Michel (1988). Power, moral values, and the intellectual. An interview with Michel Foucault by Michael Bess. *History of the Present, 4*(Spring 1), 1-13.

Fredua-Kwarteng, Y., & Ahia, Francis (2005a). Ghana flunks at math and science: Analysis (1). Feature article. *Ghana News,* 8 January 2005.

Fredua-Kwarteng, Y., & Ahia, Francis (2005b). Ghana flunks at math and science: Analysis (2). Feature article. *Ghana News,* 23 February 2005.

Kimizi, Moshi. M. (2009). From a Eurocentric to an Afrocentric perspective on language of instruction in the African context – A view from within. In Kwesi Kwaa Prah & Birgit Brock-Utne (Eds.), *Multilingualism – An African advantage: A paradigm shift in African language of instruction polices* (pp. 195-219). CASAS. Cape Town.

Kosonen, Kimmo, & Young, Catherine (Eds.) (2009). *Mother tongue as bridge language of instruction: Policies and experiences in Southeast Asia.* Bangkok: Southeast Asian Ministers of Education Organization (SEAMEO).

Langenhoven, Keith Roy (2006). Teachers speak about the language of instruction in natural science classrooms in the Western Cape in South Africa. In Birgit Brock-Utne, Zubeida Desai, & Martha Qorro (Eds.), *Focus on fresh data on the language of instruction debate in Tanzania and South Africa* (pp. 251-265). Cape Town: African Minds.

Langenhoven, Keith Roy (2010). Teachers speak about the language of instruction in natural science classrooms in the Western Cape in South Africa. In Birgit Brock-Utne, Zubeida Desai, & Martha Qorro, & Allan Pitman (Eds.), *Language of instruction in Tanzania and South Africa – Highlights from a project* (pp. 133-144). Boston/Rotterdam/Taipei: Sense Publishers.

Lewis, M. Paul (Ed.) (2009). *Ethnologue: Languages of the world,* Sixteenth edition. Dallas, Texas.: SIL International. (http://www.ethnologue.com/)

Mammino, Liliana (1995). Teaching/learning theoretical chemistry at undergraduate level. *Southern Africa Journal of Mathematics and Science Education, 2* (1&2), 69–88.

Mammino, Liliana (2010). The mother tongue as a fundamental key to the mastering of chemistry language. In Charity Flener-Lovitt & Paul Kelter (Eds.), *Chemistry as a second language: Chemical education in a globalized society* (pp. 7-42). Washington DC: American Chemical Society Society Symposium Series.

Mehrotra, Santosh (1998). Education for All: Policy lessons from high-achieving countries. *International Review of Education, 68*(5/6), 461-484.

MEVT/UoB (2005). *Evaluation of the orientation secondary class Zanzibar.* An evaluation funded by SIDA and conducted by Pauline Rea-Dickins and John Clegg from the University of Bristol and Casmir Rubagumya, University of Dodoma. Ministry of Education and Vocational Training/ University of Bristol.

MEVT (2006). *Education policy.* Stone Town. Zanzibar: Ministry of Education and Vocational Training.

MoEC (1999). *Sera ya utamaduni* [Cultural policy]. Dar es Salaam: Ministry of Education and Culture.

Mwinsheikhe, Halima Mohammed (2002). *Science and the language barrier: Using Kiswahili as a medium of instruction in Tanzania secondary schools as a strategy of improving student participation and performance in science.* Education in Africa, Vol. 9. Oslo: University of Oslo, Institute for Educational Research.

Mwinsheikhe, Halima (2007). *Revisiting the language of instruction policy in Tanzanian secondary schools: A comparative study of biology classes taught in Kiswahili and English.* Ph.D. Dissertation. Oslo: Unit for Comparative and International Education.

Nomlomo, Vuyokazi, S. (2007). *Science teaching and learning through the medium of English and isiXhosa: A comparative study at two primary schools in the Western Cape.* Unpublished Doctoral Thesis. Bellville: University of the Western Cape.

Nomlomo, Vuyokazi (2008). IsiXhosa as a medium of instruction in science teaching in primary education in South Africa: Challenges and prospects In Martha, Qorro, Zubeida Desai, & Birgit Brock-Utne (Eds.), *LOITASA reflecting on Phase I and entering Phase II* (pp. 81-102). Dar es Salaam: E & D Vision Publishing Ltd.

NYT (2009). Malaysia drops English for 2 subjects. *New York Times, Asia Pacific.* The Associated Press, July 8, 2009. (A version of this article appeared in print on July 9, 2009, on page A5 of the New York edition.) (http://www.nytimes.com/2009/07/09/world/asia/09malaysia.html?_r=2)

Ouane, Adama (2009). My journey to and through a multilingual landscape. In Kwesi Kwaa Prah & and Birgit Brock-Utne (Eds.), *Multilingualism – An African advantage. A paradigm shift in African language of instruction polices* (pp. 52-62). Cape Town: CASAS.

Prah, Kwesi Kwaa, & Brock-Utne, Birgit (2009). Introduction. Multilingualism – An African advantage. In Kwesi Kwaa Prah & Birgit Brock-Utne (Eds.), *Multilingualism – An African advantage. A paradigm shift in African languages of instruction policies* (pp. 1-17). Cape Town: CASAS.

Prophet, Bob, & Dow, Peter (1994). Mother tongue language and concept development in science. A Botswana case study. *Language, Culture and Curriculum, 7*(3), 205-217.

Ranaweera, A. Mahinda (1976). Sri Lanka: Science teaching in the national languages. *Prospects, 6*(3), 416-423.

Rugemalira, Josephat, Rubagumya, Casmir, Kapinga, Maternus, Lwaitama, Azaveli, & Tetlow, Julian (1990). Reflections on recent developments in language policy in Tanzania. In Casmir M. Rubagumya (Ed.), Language in education in Africa: A Tanzanian perspective (pp. 25-36). Clevedon, PA: Multilingual Matters.

UNESCO (2011). *Education for All global monitoring report. The hidden crisis: Armed conflict and education.* Paris: UNESCO.

URT (1993). *The Tanzania education system for the 21st century: Report of the Task Force, 1993.* Dar es Salaam: United Republic of Tanzania (URT), Ministry of Education and Culture and Ministry of Science, Technology, and Higher Education.

Vuzo, Mwajuma (2007). *Revisiting the language of instruction policy in Tanzanian secondary schools: A comparative study of geography classes taught in Kiswahili and English.* Ph.D. Dissertation. Oslo: Unit for Comparative and International Education

Watson, Keith (2011). Education and language policies in South-East Asian countries. In Colin Brock & Lorraine P. Symaco (Eds.), *Education in South-East Asia* (pp. 283-304). Oxford: Symposium Books.

Wedikkarage, Lakshman (2006). *English as medium of instruction for collegiate level science classes in Sri Lanka: Theory, policy and practice*. Ph.D. Dissertation. Oslo: Unipub AS

Wedikkarage, Lakshman (2009). Science education and English medium: The Sri Lankan experience. In Birgit Brock-Utne & Gunnar Garbo (Eds.), *Language is power: The implicatons of language for peace and development* (pp. 260-267). Dar es Salaam: Mkuki na Nyota.

Birgit Brock-Utne
Department of Educational Research
University of Oslo, Norway

PART II:

COMMUNITY AND PARENT VOICES

LAURA MENCHACA BISHOP & PREMA KELLEY

5. INDIGENOUS MEXICAN LANGUAGES AND THE POLITICS OF LANGUAGE SHIFT IN THE UNITED STATES

ABSTRACT

Inin amatl kinititia in tlen onikitak kwak onikchih in tekitl ipan 2010. Nikan nikita kenin sekin masewalmeh, akinkeh otlakatkeh Mexico wan axan chantih EEUU, tlahtoah itech iminchantsitsin, tlen ika tlahtol in yehwan monotsah wan motlapwiah. Tikitaskeh tleka tetahwan kinnotsah in piltontsitsin ikan nin noso oksekin tlahtolmeh, katlie tlahtolmeh kinititiah iminpilwan. Namechititilis kenin in tetahwan kinitah in gobierno, in oksekin tlakameh, in tomin, in tlen opanohkeh, okchiwilihkeh ik tlahtoah se masewaltlahtol wan yenonik in yehwan amo noso kema kinekih kinititiskeh iminpilwan. Ipan nin tekitl, sekin tenantsitsin onechnankilihkeh in yehwan amo kinekih kinititiskeh iminmasewaltlahtolwan iminpilwan pampa ompa Mexico wan nikan EEUU in tlakameh amo kwalli kitah in masewaltlahtolmeh. In tenantsitsin san kinekih iminpilwan amo kimachiliah nochin in malda in yehwan okmachilihkeh. (*Translated to Central Nahuatl[nhn], a language of Mexico, by Lucero Flores Nájera from Tlaxcala and Irwin Sanchez from La Resurrección, Puebla.*)[1]

This chapter presents the findings of ethnographic research undertaken in 2010, which explores the language policies that Indigenous Mexican migrants in the US implement in their homes and with their families. The research examines how political, social, and economic stratification related to identity, as well as perceived experiences of discrimination, can influence how parents negotiate their children's linguistic repertoires. The findings suggest that because the Indigenous Mexican mothers interviewed believe there is a generally negative attitude toward Indigeneity in Mexico and the US, they have chosen not to pass their Indigenous language(s) onto their children to spare them from the discriminatory experiences they themselves have encountered.

INTRODUCTION

Many Indigenous Mexicans migrate to the United States seeking greater opportunities for their families. Language plays a vital role in achieving the socio-economic mobility they seek. Because Spanish and English wield significant socio-economic and political power in Mexico and the US respectively, Indigenous

C. Benson and K. Kosonen (eds.), Language Issues in Comparative Education, 97–113.

Mexican migrant parents often find themselves in a difficult position, having to make critical decisions regarding their children's linguistic future. This chapter presents the findings of ethnographic research undertaken in 2010, which explores the language policies that Indigenous Mexican migrants in the US implement in their homes and with their families. The findings indicate that Indigenous parents sacrifice their Indigenous language(s) in an effort to ensure the economic advancement of their families. Because the parents in the study see language as a marker of identity, and because they are acutely aware of the political, social, and economic stratification related to identity, they use language as a tool to "reinvent" their children's identities, hoping to elevate the social status of their families for future generations. Ultimately, this rationalization has led parents not to use their Indigenous language(s) with their children, and to encourage the acquisition of English and Spanish only. This chapter explores the factors that contribute to this decision.

To contextualize the language policies of the participants in our study, we use the first section of this chapter to consider how "one language, one nation, one state" ideologies influence power and identity. We then provide some historical perspective on Indigenous Mexican migration to the New York Metropolitan area before discussing and analyzing our findings.

LANGUAGE, POWER, IDENTITY AND THE PRESSURE TO "SHIFT"

In both the US and Mexico there is intense debate, often with racist undertones, over the use of language, suggesting that impassioned "one language, one nation, one state" ideologies are not merely an issue of linguistic preference, but also of the struggle over control, power, and identity (May, 2001: 91). For many years, liberal pluralists have argued that monolingual state policies are the most effective manner by which to distribute and equalize power in a society, and that in heterogeneous societies, institutionalized bilingualism causes fragmentation and threatens the "dream of one people" (Porter, 1965; Schlesinger, 1992: 109; Wong, 2008). Critics of these post-multiculturalist ideologies such as Anderson (1983) argue that this "dream" is no more than a psychological construct comprised of "affinities such as language" (as cited in Garcia, 2009: 25). As Young (1993) explains, these affinities are negotiated entirely by the dominant group; if some groups "have greater economic, political or social power, their group-related experiences, points of view, or cultural assumptions will tend to become the norm, biasing the standards or procedures of achievement and inclusion that govern social, political and economic institutions" (Young, 1993: 133). May (2001) stresses that as a result, the nation state "creates sociological minorities by establishing a civic language and culture that is largely limited to, and representative of, the dominant ethnie [ethnolinguistic group]" (p. 92). Subsequently, minorities are often prohibited from exercising their right to use their "existing" languages or practice their cultural traditions, since language policies of the dominant group are inextricably tied to the preservation of power for the dominant class (May, 2001).

This struggle for power demonstrates that matters of exclusion are as deeply rooted in issues of race and the preservation of power as they are in concerns over language use (May, 2001). Controlling language is thus one way that dominant groups have tried to limit the preservation of "undesirable" (non-dominant) cultures and identities. According to Skutnabb-Kangas (2000) this is accomplished by the "consciousness industry": formal education systems and mass media (p. x). She argues that educational systems in particular maintain and reproduce unequal power relations by using "deficiency-based models that ... invalidate the linguistic and cultural capital of minority children and their parents and communities ... [and] make the resources of dominated groups seem handicaps or deficiencies, instead of valued and validated non-material resources" (Skutnabb-Kangas, 2000: xi). For instance, a monolingual Spanish-speaking student entering a US public school is typically characterized as an "English Language Learner" or as being "Limited English Proficient." This labeling elevates the value of the English language while rendering the student's home language invisible, positioning the latter as an impediment to academic and intellectual proficiency. A deficiency-based orientation views the home language as an obstacle rather than as a resource for academic enrichment –the connotation is that students perform poorly because they do not speak English. Kaplan and Baldauf refer to this kind of rhetoric as "correction procedures" designed to "promote language spread and to prevent the development of a linguistic underclass" (1997: 36). Skutnabb-Kangas (2000) adds that this type of rhetoric seeks to veil the dominant group's efforts to subjugate minority groups by framing these efforts as "helping" them.

The media also promotes assimilation by routinely bombarding the public with images that seek to define desirability or normalcy. Dominant group notions of beauty, quality, and value are increasingly communicated via cable and satellite. If it is true, as Skutnabb-Kangas (2000) suggests, that there is a gross devaluation of minoritized[ii] peoples embedded in the signals received at school and through the media, then it is not far-fetched to assume that they might be internalizing these beliefs, prompting minoritized individuals, families, and communities to become proponents of language shift.

But can a shift in one's language directly cause a shift in one's culture and identity? Many scholars argue that because language is so integral to identity, losing a language can seriously jeopardize a person's sense of self and group membership (Crystal 2000; Garcia, 2008; May, 2001; Wright, 2004). Crystal (2000) notes that the "disappearance of the language of a group has immense repercussions for healthy self-regard," since language and identity are so tightly interwoven (Crystal, 2000: 225). Moreover, Norton and Toohey argue that "the language choices available to children and their parents, as well as the discursive practices that are encouraged and supported in school, have an important impact on children's identity and their possibilities of developing agency or resisting" (2001: 310). Thus, individuals who experience language shift are not only struggling with their sense of self and group membership, they are less empowered to advocate for their interests and rights.

It can thus be presumed that cultural shift can accompany language shift, by shifting political and cultural allegiances and engendering the "right" kind of "sameness." Because identity, culture, and language are so closely related, targeting one's sense of self-respect and belonging is clearly a means by which to subjugate. As Margalit and Raz suggest, "people's sense of their own identity is bound up with their sense of belonging to encompassing groups and their self-respect is affected by the esteem in which these groups are held" (1995: 86). When one's culture and language are devalued by a dominant culture, language shift becomes all the more desirable.

In the study reported here, the Indigenous Mexican migrant mothers we interviewed had, to varying extents, internalized negative societal understandings of their Indigeneity, and as a result, actively moved toward perpetuating their own family's language shift. The next section provides some cultural and social background to the study.

HISTORICAL AND CULTURAL CONTEXT OF THE STUDY

South of the Border

Mexico is a very diverse and multi-ethnic country. As the product of contact between many different groups, including Spanish and other European, African, and Indigenous people, it has a varied history informed by many cultures, religions, and languages. It is estimated that more than one in ten Mexicans come from a family in which an Indigenous language is spoken, challenging the stereotype that Mexicans speak only Spanish (Serrano Carreto et al., 2003; Machado-Casas, 2009).

Indigenous groups in Mexico are gravely stigmatized and, like many other Indigenous groups throughout the world, are often regarded as being "tradition bound" and thus irrelevant for the "post-industrial society" (John Porter, 1975: 303). Given the predominance of Spanish as a language of power in Mexico, many see linguistic homogenization as the only way to establish a national identity, and see the preservation of minoritized languages and cultures as an impediment to social cohesion, modernization, and progress.

In Mexico, this debate is particularly problematic, since in the last century, the country has sought to recover its Indigenous ancestral roots and exudes significant pride at this legacy. Regardless, Indigenous peoples continue to experience oppression and disproportionately comprise the lowest levels of the social stratum.

It is out of this socio-cultural, political, and historical context that many Indigenous Mexicans immigrate to the US. In addition to the regular ebb and flow of migration that has taken place over several centuries of fluctuating borders, the last 20 years have seen a relatively large-scale migration of Mexicans to the US. In addition to the well documented migration of Mestizos,[iii] there has also been an increase in migration among Indigenous Mexicans.

Over the last two decades, Mexicans immigrating to the US have primarily originated from central and eastern Mexico, areas heavily populated by Indigenous communities (D'Aubeterre Buznego, & Rivermar Pérez, 2007; Fox, 2006). According to Machado-Casas, the "Mixtecs, Nahuas, Purepechs, Triques, and Otomí are among the largest Indigenous groups currently migrating to the U.S." (2009: 85). The majority of Mexicans living in New York have migrated from Puebla and Guerrero, originating predominantly from rural areas. Financial concerns due to a poor economy along with unfavorable farming conditions due to climatic and political factors have forced many young men and women to seek employment north of the border (D'Aubeterre Buznego & Rivermar Pérez, 2007).

North of the Border

According to Durand and Massey (2003), approximately 20 percent of immigrants coming into the US establish residence in either New York or Los Angeles. Once migrants settle, they typically find jobs working as day laborers in agriculture, manufacturing, and construction industries; as domestic service workers, babysitters and nannies; as health workers caring for the sick and elderly; in restaurants; and as gardeners (D'Aubeterre Buznego, & Rivermar Pérez, 2007). Because their opportunities for formal schooling are often limited or constrained, Indigenous Mexican migrants tend to occupy jobs that require little training, offer low wages, involve long working days, and – often – incur high risk (D'Aubeterre Buznego, & Rivermar Pérez, 2007; Fox & Rivera-Salgado, 2004). Because many Indigenous Mexicans in New York began their migratory expeditions after the Immigration Reform and Control Act of 1986, they have not been able to take advantage of the status adjustments made to temporary and non-resident individuals and, consequently, have tended to remain "undocumented,"[iv] further exacerbating their economic and social marginalization in the US (D'Aubeterre Buznego, & Rivermar Pérez, 2007).

Moreover, when Indigenous Mexican migrants lack proficiency in English or Spanish, they are more vulnerable to exploitation by their employers, especially if they are undocumented. In her research of Nahuatl speakers in Xoyatla, a small town in Puebla that sends a large percentage of its population to the US, ethnographer Pérez has found that while many Indigenous Mexicans describe themselves as bilingual in an Indigenous language and Spanish, their ability to communicate in Spanish is often "limited" (2003: 208).

Another difficulty that Indigenous Mexican migrants face is racial categorization. In her ethnography, Machado-Casas (2009) argues, that "the use of pan-ethnic terms such as 'Latino'" reinforce the idea of mestizaje (p. 83) erasing Indigeneity and furthering the marginalization of Indigenous communities (Saldivar, 2010). She goes on to point out that "discriminatory and oppressive practices" experienced by many Indigenous Mexicans in Mexio, follow them into the US, where they experience similar discrimination at the hands of their "non-Indigenous 'Latino' peers" (Machado-Casas, 2009: 83).

These "discriminatory and oppressive" practices are often rooted in prejudices regarding language use. Because the use of an Indigenous Mexican language is such a strong marker of Indigeneity, and because many US Latinos and Mestizo Mexicans harbor prejudice against Indigenous Mexican peoples, Machado-Casas argues that many Indigenous immigrants feel the need to conceal their identities from "both White U.S. Americans and U.S. Latinos – or Latino immigrants – and teach their children to protect themselves from the same xenophobic practices they experienced in their country of origin" (2009: 84). Thus, Indigenous Mexican families in the US negotiate several identities that each carry their own societal prejudices and stereotypes that can affect which languages they cultivate.

METHODOLOGY

In the Spring of 2010, our research team of two graduate students undertook an ethnographic study to explore the language policies that Indigenous Mexican migrants in New York City implement in their homes and with their families. We wondered whether or not they were passing their Indigenous languages on to their children and what factors influenced their decisions. The research included data from interviews and classroom observations involving parents, their children, and bilingual educators, but this chapter focuses on the experiences of Indigenous Mexican mothers as they pertain to the transmission of their Indigenous languages to their children. The analysis draws occasionally from research interactions with the children and the children's bilingual teachers to offer insight into the mothers' described experiences.

The research team included Menchaca Bishop, a second generation Mexican-American Mestiza, bilingual in Spanish and English, and Kelley, an Anglo-American who also speaks Spanish and English. Both Menchaca Bishop and Kelley conceptualized the research design and collected the data; Menchaca Bishop interpreted and analyzed the data and wrote up the findings.

The research was conducted over a six-month period, with the aim of exploring: a) how, where, and when the participants use the various languages they speak; b) how they perceive the use of their linguistic repertoires; c) how their language use and perceptions are connected to their identities and cultures; and d) whether or not they are attempting to pass on their Indigenous languages to their children. Information was gathered through semi-structured interviews that lasted between 60 and 90 minutes. We utilized open-ended questions to encourage participants to offer their insights and ideas as freely as possible. At the beginning of each interview, we asked the participants to draw a language map that demonstrated which and how languages had been used throughout their recent family history in an effort to reveal where languages had been lost or acquired and ignite a conversation regarding why.

In addition to interview questions, we used a sentence completion tool to gather data regarding how speakers of English, Spanish, Mixteco and Nahuatl were perceived by our participants. Sentences beginning "People who speak Mixteco are …" and "People who speak Spanish are …" were used to capture snapshots of perception.

We recruited participants at a Spanish-English dual language school in New York City that serves a small population of Indigenous Mexican families. While our goal was to recruit more, we were only able to recruit three mothers, Marisol, Francisca, and Elena,[v] and their children. All three mothers are in their twenties and thirties, have been living in Manhattan for several years, and come from the same region of Guerrero. In addition to speaking Spanish and some English, Marisol and Elena both speak Mixteco and Francisca speaks Nahuatl. Marisol and Francisca both described having arrived in the western US before settling in New York City (NYC). Since Elena's husband had lived and worked in NYC prior to her arrival, she reported having migrated directly to NYC from Mexico. All three participants had prior contacts in the city, which they said helped to link them to the Indigenous communities in the area. As newcomers, these links offered them access to information regarding jobs, schools, and resources, making the adjustment to life in the US easier.

We understand that being limited to three participants means that we only have access to three points of view, and even these interpretations are limited since neither of us speak our participants' Indigenous languages, which forced them to express themselves in Spanish. We are also aware that this is a reinforcement of the dominant language issues at play in our participants' lives, and that had they used their Indigenous languages, they might have framed their answers in other ways. However, we are satisfied that we were able to gain significant insight into the perspectives of these three participants regarding their languages.

"WE KNOW WHAT THEY CALL US:" FINDINGS AND ANALYSIS

As mentioned previously, Indigenous Mexicans are often framed in their country of origin as unintelligent and traditional. Because this sentiment is so pervasive, it appears that some Indigenous people internalize negative ideas associated with their identities and consequently participate in their own assimilation to the dominant language and culture, a process which is supported and exacerbated by "Northern" frameworks. This section outlines our three most significant research findings in this regard.

Language Use in Public Spaces

The first finding was that all three participants had had negative experiences with people who did not speak an Indigenous language. Once they were identified as speakers of Indigenous languages, they were belittled by others in both Mexican and US contexts. In all three cases, their experiences were in public venues and directly impacted the women's decisions regarding language preservation. For example, Francisca said that when she is in public and receives a call from her brother on the phone, she speaks to him in Spanish since she feels that people stare at her when she speaks Nahuatl. When she is at home with her brother they only speak Nahuatl, since that is their shared language. As she explained:

Mostly, we protect ourselves from our own people. Even if they are Mexicans, so that they don't hear us because if they do, then they tell us we are *indios*, that we don't speak Spanish perfectly. This is because we are from Guerrero and they are from, well, they learn [Spanish – and we don't]. So, we don't speak it [Spanish] perfectly – we are lacking, there are some [Indigenous Mexicans] that don't speak it perfectly because we use Nahuatl more. Americans mostly are ok. We just protect ourselves from the people that are from over there. *We know what they call us.* (Francisca, April 22, 2010, my translation and emphasis)

For Francisca, being called *indio* indicated that she was perceived as inferior to others, presumably Mestizo Mexicans, and that it was her use of Nahuatl that signified her inferiority, since it connected her to an Indigenous identity. Though some Indigenous peoples have attempted to re-appropriate the term *indio* and redefine it in a more positive way, it is clear from Francisca's reaction that she is not one of these reformers, since she describes feeling *avergonzada*, "embarrassed" or "ashamed," that the term *indio* is used to describe her (Francisca, April 22, 2010; Gelles, 2010).

Experiences such as these, which Francisca describes as being rather frequent, have prompted her to eliminate Nahuatl from her children's linguistic repertoire; she hopes that by eliminating the marker of their Indigeneity, she will be able to protect them from similar discrimination. As Francisca's reflection illustrates, Spanish is used as a measure of belonging in which the stakes are high; if one is perceived as not speaking Spanish "well," it is understood that that person is not an authentic member of the group in power, in this case, Mestizo Mexicans. However, the notion of speaking Spanish "well" is relative, and often subjective. Although Francisca perceives that she does not speak Spanish well, we perceived her Spanish to be fluent. Francisca's feelings about how "well" she does or does not speak Spanish is likely influenced by the vigorous debate among Spanish and Latin American linguists regarding the standardization of the Spanish language and how it is "properly" spoken (Paffey, 2007). As Paffey (2007) observes,

Speaking a standard language is an index of power, prestige and membership ... standardisation can be and is used as a strategy of control, and not just in terms of language use. As official discourse excludes non-standard language varieties as 'sub-standard,' and even 'divisive,' so dominant languages (and their associated cultures) spread, and dominated languages and identities are subordinated. (p. 315)

Ultimately, preferences for standardization are made by the dominant, typically "educated" group, who favor their own language variety and usage (Lippi-Green, 1997). While Francisca may be able to effectively communicate in the Spanish language, her register, vocabulary, accent, as well as other linguistic characteristics of how she uses Spanish may influence how "well" she perceives herself to speak it and how "well" others perceive her speaking as measured against standardized norms of language use. This in turn affects the way in which her inclusion in or value to the dominant group is perceived, evaluated, and acted upon. Francisca feels that she is identified as Indigenous both because she speaks an Indigenous language and because she perceives that she does not speak "standard" Spanish "well," relative to "they," presumably Mestizo Mexicans, who "learn" Spanish in school, unlike Indigenous Mexicans who are "lacking."

Marisol, a Mixteco speaker, also described language discrimination experiences in public places:

> Sometimes, when I ride the subway with my country-people, we speak Mixteco and the people in the train stare at us as if saying, "... What could it be that they are speaking?" But no, they give us dirty looks, but I don't care. Yes, they look at us as if they are saying, "*indios!*" (Marisol, April 19, 2010)

When asked how the other passengers might have known that she was speaking Mixteco, she replied that:

> Maybe they don't know that it's Mixteco specifically, but they know that it is an indigenous language. (Marisol, April 19, 2010)

According to Marisol, simply knowing she is speaking an Indigenous language is enough for her fellow passengers to arrive at negative conclusions about her worth and her societal position. Marisol said she has experienced this sort of treatment not only from Mexicans and Mexican Americans, but also from White Americans and Dominican Americans, the latter comprising the second largest Latino population in New York City and experiencing significant discrimination themselves (Nyberg Sorensen, 2005).

Interestingly, Marisol reports that she "doesn't care" how people react to her use of Mixteco in public. Of the three mothers interviewed for our study, Marisol has the closest relationship to her children's bilingual teacher, Cassandra, a Mestiza born in Oaxaca, Mexico, a Mexican state with a large Indigenous population. This particular teacher is especially active in encouraging Indigenous Mexican mothers to use their languages with their children. She invites the mothers to Indigenous-focused events happening around the city, and has acquired children's books in Mixteco for Marisol specifically.

While this encouragement may have positively influenced the way that Marisol is able to brush off discrimination in public spaces, Marisol remains hesitant about using the language with her children as one of her family's primary home languages. Although Marisol reports "enseñando" ("teaching") her children Mixteco vocabulary in isolation, for instance, the Mixteco words for tortilla or "chair," she has made the conscious decision not to "hablar" ("speak") Mixteco when interacting with her children (Marisol, April 19, 2010). While Marisol takes a defiant attitude to public reactions to her use of Mixteco, at the same time, she expresses feeling uncomfortable with the discriminatory nature of people's reactions.

Elena had a similar reaction, stating that when she is on the street and speaks Mixteco, "People stare at you, shocked" (Elena, November 23, 2010). Elena referred directly to her experiences of discrimination and marginalization as the reason why she chooses to speak to her children in Spanish even though she and her husband continue to communicate with each other in Mixteco.

Later, when asked to elaborate on what she did not like about living in New York, Marisol referred back to her experiences in the subway and explained that she missed her community in Mexico. She explained that in the US:

> There are many racist people. They belittle you. When they look at me, like that … sometimes people look me over from head to toe. And in one's town, they aren't like that, because over there [in my town], we consider everybody to be equal. (Marisol, April 19, 2010)

In reflecting on the town she comes from, with which she clearly feels an affinity, she dichotomizes her experiences: in her hometown, people would never participate in such discrimination, whereas in the US, people do so regularly. Her comments signal that she feels safest and most valued in her own community, which is comprised largely of other Indigenous Mexicans. For Marisol, these types of experiences have likewise led her to refrain from speaking to her children in Mixteco.

Pride in Language Use and the Benefits of Multilingualism

The second finding from this study is that although all three participants made conscious decisions not to pass their Indigenous languages on to their children, they reported feeling proud about their ability to speak these languages. For instance, when asked how she feels when she speaks Nahuatl, Francisca's demeanor changed noticeably. Her face lit up, she smiled and her body became very relaxed, and she simply said "Oh, well, I feel great!" (laughing) (Francisca, April 22, 2010). She went on to describe how her home community, comprised mainly of Indigenous Mexicans, is afraid of Spanish speakers. To illustrate this point, she offered the example that if one of the researchers, a Mexican-American Mestiza, were to walk into her town, the people would shut themselves inside and hide; but if she – Francisca – showed up speaking Nahuatl, they would invite her in and offer her food. In other words, her ability to speak Nahuatl connected her very closely to her community and gave her a certain inclusivity that would not be afforded to everyone. This seemed to provide her with great comfort.

When asked about the benefits of speaking more than one language, all three participants in this study said there were multiple benefits. Francisca reported that when one speaks multiple languages, one is able to go places without feeling frightened, and that if a person speaks the language of the place she is in, she can "defenderse" ("defend herself") when she needs to. The manner in which Francisca used this term connotes an element of resistance; Francisca believed that speaking both English and Spanish "well" would maximize her ability to protect herself from discrimination, since she would be able to articulate a response to a negative comment. Interestingly, the notion of "defending oneself" was not identified as a motivating factor for speaking an Indigenous language "well," since discrimination was not seen as originating within one's own language community.

The participants also noted that the ability to speak many languages gives the speaker more freedom, confidence, and independence. According to both Marisol and Elena, speaking multiple languages is important, since it allows one to communicate with many other people. They found that multilingualism is also useful for its role in helping others; if one knows a non-dominant language, one can help others who speak that language, but who may not be well versed in the dominant language. Francisca illustrated this by relating the story of when she took her child to a hospital and encountered an Indigenous Mexican patient who did not speak Spanish or English. There was a Mexican American nurse trying, unsuccessfully, to communicate with the patient in Spanish, but the patient seemed very distressed. Francisca stepped in and translated for the woman, for which both the nurse and the patient were grateful. Francisca felt good being able to assist in this way (Francisca, April 22, 2010). Regardless, Francisca's negative experiences seem to outnumber her positive experiences of using Nahuatl in public, since she continues to perceive her Nahuatl as a primarily negative identifying marker that she prefers to withhold from her children's lives.

Regarding the benefits of speaking English, all three participants associated learning English with having more opportunities, and all three expressed a desire to improve their English:

If you speak English, the doors are open to you. (Marisol, April 19, 2010)

Marisol also mentioned her desire to learn Italian and expressed her hope that her daughter would learn more languages as she grew older.

Additionally, all three mothers were very aware of the value of multilingualism, since they had all chosen to enroll their students in a Spanish-English bilingual school. Elena reported having visited two different bilingual schools before settling on the one her children now attend. All three mothers said that one or more of their children were eager to learn their home language and often asked how to say things in Mixteco or Nahuatl. Marisol and Francisca, however, have chosen to speak only Spanish to their children, despite their clear support of multilingualism and despite their children's willingness and desire to learn their mother's Indigenous language. Elena noted that while she did try to teach her children Mixteco, she reported that they "didn't like it," so she decided to speak to them solely in Spanish at home (Elena, November 23, 2010). When Francisca, who speaks Nahuatl, was asked why she had made the choice to use only Spanish in the home, she explained:

Francisca: My husband, he speaks Mixteco, but we decided that we wouldn't speak in my language or his; only Spanish and English.

Interviewer: And why don't you want, or why haven't your children learned … to speak Nahuatl?

Francisca: It's because I don't speak to them … If I had accustomed them [to it] from when they were little, then they would know, yes, but no, I didn't teach them.

Interviewer: Was this a decision that you made as parents, or was it something that just happened?

Francisca: My husband told me that we would speak to them [in Mixteco and in Nahuatl] … [but] if he speaks to them in his language, Mixteco, and in my language, Nahuatl, I don't know, it's as if they'll get confused. They're already going to speak Spanish and English. And I tell my children, "You know what? At home, we speak only Spanish." And at school, since it's bilingual, they give them Spanish and English. So, she [my daughter] only speaks Spanish and English. And if she goes, if they teach her another language, then it'll be at the school, but they don't really teach more [languages]. Because, you know, if she speaks Nahuatl, or if she speaks English, it's like, sometimes, kids, they don't speak Spanish perfectly … they get confused. So I tell you, so that she will speak perfect Spanish, she only learns Spanish and English. (Francisca, April 22, 2010)

For Francisca, being able to speak Spanish "perfectly" is a major motivating factor for choosing Spanish as the child's home language. Given the fact that Francisca herself feels she does not speak Spanish "perfectly," she is also very concerned about her daughter's ability to speak it well. Francisca hopes her family will return to Mexico once her children complete their education, and thus she is concerned about her daughter's economic opportunities in Mexico, which are often dependent on fluency in Spanish. Francisca's expectation is that her children, by virtue of learning standard Spanish in school, will learn to speak it "well" despite her own perceived "imperfect" Spanish in the home. Because Francisca sees Spanish and English as languages of power in Mexico and the US, and thus as key languages to master to achieve upward economic and social mobility, she is most concerned with her daughter's fluency in these two languages. Because Francisca does not see Nahuatl or Mixteco as languages of power, and because she is concerned about the capacity for her children to learn more than two languages at a time, she does not prioritize passing on these languages.

Marisol offers yet another reason for not using her home language with her children:

My daughter, the oldest one, she likes to speak Mixteco. But I don't teach her because I can't speak Mixteco well either. That's why I say, if I teach her Mixteco, I'll teach it to her broken, but she likes it, she asks me, "Mommy, how do you say 'shut the door'? How do you say 'tortilla'? How do you say 'banana'?" She asks me and I tell her and she is proud that she knows those words. (Marisol, April 19, 2010)

Although Marisol perceives that she does not speak Mixteco well, she often uses Mixteco to communicate with others in her community, both in the US and in Mexico, but not with her children. She claims that she does not speak it well and is afraid that she will teach her children incorrectly, yet she also expresses fears about not speaking Spanish well, but does choose to use this language with her children. This contradiction may stem not so much from her language ability, but from the mixed feelings she has around themes of identity, home, economic aspirations, and what is best for her children's future. Unlike Francisca or Elena, Marisol has a strong desire to pass Mixteco on to her children. Throughout her interview, Marisol shared many fond memories of her home community in Mexico. She describes longing for home, often waking up in the middle of the night with the vivid sensation that she is walking through her town with her family. She dreams of going back with her children, of showing them all the beautiful things that her town and community have to offer. While she seems to strongly and positively identify with her Indigeneity in the context of particular themes, especially those of "home," "family," and "community," in the context of other themes, like "economic advancement," "upward social mobility," and "her children's futures," she sees Indigeneity as being problematic. She perceives her Indigenous community as inclusive and welcoming, but sees spaces outside of her community as exclusive, hostile, and difficult to navigate. All three women saw honing their own and their children's fluency in English and Spanish and downplaying their Indigeneity as the best strategy for easing this difficult navigation.

In summary, all three women considered several factors when they made decisions regarding their children's linguistic landscape. First, while they affirmed that multilingualism was valuable, they had real concerns about the number of languages one could learn "well." This concern may have been rooted in their feelings about speaking English, Spanish, and an Indigenous language, but not perceiving themselves as speaking any one language "well." Second, in choosing which languages their children would use, they were concerned about how many languages a child could learn at one time, ultimately deciding the ideal number was two. Regarding which two, they selected the ones they identified as being most economically and socially beneficial to their children: English and Spanish. Finally, all three women took into account their experiences of discrimination and acknowledged the importance of being able to "defend oneself" against discriminatory comments and attitudes, seeing the ability to speak English and Spanish fluently as a necessary component of survival and self-protection. Overall, their experiences and understandings of language and power appear to have directly impacted what languages their children acquire.

Indigenous Language as a Signifier and the "Reinvention" of Identity

The third finding of this study, related to the first two, is that all three participants believe there is a strong connection between language and identity, and this connection determines participation in or exclusion from a community as well as the opportunities that that community wields. Marisol, Francisca, and Elena all identified English and Spanish as important languages for upward social and economic mobility, English because it is the dominant language in the US, and Spanish due to the large communities of Spanish speakers living in the US. Because none of the mothers saw their Indigenous languages as marketable for their children's professional prospects in the US or in Mexico, they chose not to pass them on. Though they identified the importance of their Indigenous languages for their own social circles, they felt these languages ultimately stigmatized them in the wider society.

We believe that because all three women considered their identity to be signified first and foremost by their language, they were attempting to reinvent their children's identity through language. Spurred by the discrimination they experienced, they chose to spare their children the same fate by doing what they believed would help their children speak "perfect" Spanish and English. By refraining from speaking their Indigenous languages with their children, the women seemed to feel that their children would have more life opportunities and would experience less discrimination. None of the three women seemed concerned that their children would be breaking ties with their heritage or communities; rather, they seemed to see shedding their Indigenous language as a step forward in creating more opportunities for their children. Their reasoning seemed to be that the further removed one is from Indigeneity, the more economic and professional opportunities one has.

CONCLUSION

Essentially, all of our findings are connected to power, highlighting the idea that the value of a language is largely informed by those who speak it and the kind of power that the speakers possess. In Mexico, Spanish is the dominant language and wields the most power. In the United States, it is English. In neither country did these women experience that their home languages were valued. In fact, in both the Mexico and the US, they perceived that the devaluation of their languages signified the devaluation of their cultures and ultimately themselves as people. The means by which they saw that they could increase their "value" was to adopt the most "valuable" cultures and languages, which in this case, were perceived to be English and Spanish. In their interviews, all three women said that they had moved to the United States to improve the lives of their families. Paradoxically, all three spoke of facing discrimination, of longing for home, of working long hours in physically strenuous jobs, of regret, and of missing the acceptance, love, support and cultural reinforcement of their communities. The two most significant gains that they felt had "improved" their quality of life were the fact that their children were receiving a "more advanced" education and that they had a relatively stable income with which to provide for their families. One has to wonder, however, at what price these "gains" have been accomplished, both for these families, as well as for their communities.

Ultimately, the findings indicate that Indigenous Mexicans encounter grave challenges on both sides of the border when it comes to language maintenance. Though this research helps shed some light on the language practices of this relatively new population in New York, we were only able to present the practices of three families based on the women's interviews, and there is much left to be done to understand people's language practices and motivations. Clearly, further research with more participants is recommended to gain greater insight into the way that Indigenous Mexicans in New York perceive and use language. Though they were not included here, our research interviews with these women's children and their children's teacher indicated that the children were particularly eager to learn their parents' home languages. Further research could be done to explore whether their children's experiences in a bilingual school have influenced their desire to learn these languages.

NOTES

[i] Special thanks to Dr. John Sullivan from The Zacatecas Institute for Teaching and Research in Ethnology, Zacatecas, México for his support with the Nahuatl translation of the abstract.
[ii] The term "minoritized" refers to all non-dominant groups that are socially, economically, or politically marginalized by the dominant group in power regardless of their numerical representation.
[iii] The term "mestizo" refers to an individual of Mexican descent with mixed Spanish and Indigenous (and possibly other) heritages
[iv] The term "undocumented" refers to an individual living in a country without legal permission evidenced by official state-issued documents.
[v] Pseudonyms have been used to protect the identity of the participants.

REFERENCES

Anderson, Benedict (1983). *Imagined communities: Reflections on the origin and spread of nationalism.* London: Verso.

Baldauf, Richard, & Kaplan, Robert (Eds.) (2007). *Language planning and policy in Latin America: Ecuador, Mexico, and Paraguay.* Clevedon, UK: Multilingual Matters.

Crystal, David (2000). *Language death.* Cambridge: Cambridge University Press.

D'Aubeterre Buznego, Eugenia, & Rivermar Pérez, Leticia (2007). *Tres circuitos migratorios Puebla-Estados Unidos: Una lectura comparativa* [Three migratory circuits Puebla-USA: A comparative reading]. (http://nuevomundo.revues.org/10413)

Durand, Jorge, & Massey, Douglas (2003). *Clandestinos: Migración México-Estados Unidos en los albores del siglo XXI [The Clandestine: Mexico-US migration at the dawn of the twenty first century].* México: Universidad Autónoma de Zacatecas.

Fox, Jonathan, & Rivera-Salgado, Gasper (Eds.) (2004). *Indigenous Mexican migrants in the United States.* La Jolla, CA: The Center for U.S.-Mexican Studies, UCSD and the Center for Comparative Immigration Studies, UCSD.

Fox, Jonathan (2006). Reframing Mexican migration as a multi-ethnic process. *Latino Studies, 4,* 39-61.

Garcia, Ofelia (2008). *Bilingual education in the 21st century: A global perspective.* Oxford, UK: Wiley-Blackwell.

Gelles, Paul H. (2010). Cultural identity and Indigenous water rights in the Andean Highlands. In Rutgerd Boelens, David H. Getches, & Jorge Armando Guevara Gil (Eds.), *Out of the mainstream: Water rights, politics and identity* (pp. 119-137). Washington, DC: Earthscan.

Hidalgo, Margarita (Ed.) (2006*). Mexican Indigenous languages at the dawn of the twenty-first Century,* Chapters 5, 6, 12 [electronic resource]. Berlin/New York: Mouton de Gruyter.

Instituto Nacional de Estadística y Geografía (1995-2000). [National Institute of Statistics and Geography.] Ciudad de México. (http://www.inegi.org.mx/inegi/default.aspx)

Kaplan, Robert, & Baldauf Jr., Richard (1997). *Language practice: From practice to theory.* Bristol, PA: Multilingual Matters.

Lippi-Green, R. (1997). *English with an accent: Language, ideology, and discrimination in the United States.* London: Routledge.

Machado-Casas, Margarita (2009). The politics of organic phylogeny: The art of parenting and surviving as transnational multilingual latino Indigenous immigrants in the U.S. *High School Journal, 92*(4), 89-99.

Margalit, Avishai, & Raz, Joseph (1995). National self-determination. In Will Kymlicka (Ed.), *Rights of minority cultures* (pp. 79-92). Oxford: Oxford University Press.

May, Stephen (2001). *Language and minority rights: Ethnicity, nationalism and the politics of language.* Harlow, UK: Pearson Education Limited.

Norton, Bonny, & Toohey, Kelleen (2001). Changing perspectives on good language learners. *TESOL Quarterly, 35*(2), 307-322.

Nyberg Sorensen, Ninna (2005). There are no Indians in the Dominican Republic: The cultural construction of Dominican identities. In K. Fog Olwig & Kirsten Hastrup (Eds.), *Siting culture: The shifting anthropological object* (pp. 295-314). London: Routledge.

Paffey, Darren (2007). Policing the Spanish language debate: Verbal hygiene and the Spanish language academy (Real Academia Española). *Language Policy, 6*(3-4), 313-332.

Porter, John (1965). *The vertical mosaic.* Toronto, Canada: Toronto University Press.

Porter, John (1975). Ethnic pluralism in Canadian perspective. In Nathan Glazer & Daniel Patrick Moynihan (Eds.), *Ethnicity: Theory and experience* (pp. 267-304). Cambridge, MA: Harvard University Press.

Rivermar Pérez, Leticia (2003). Santa María de la Encarnación Xoyatla: A Nahua community of peasants and migrants. In Regina Cortina & Monica Gendreau (Eds.), *Immigrants and schooling: Mexicans in New York* (pp. 205-229). New York: Center for Migration Studies.

Rivermar Pérez, Leticia (2005). *Uno va agarrando otras culturas sin soltar la nuestra: Migración internacional e identidad étnica y cultural en una comunidad nahua del estado de Puebla* [One adopts other cultures without losing one's own: International migration and ethnic and cultural identity in a Nahua community in the state of Puebla]. Tesis de Doctorado en Antropología, Facultad de Filosofía y Letras, UNAM.

Saldivar, Martha V. (2010). From Mexico to Palestine: An occupation of knowledge, a Mestizaje of methods. *American Quarterly, 62*(4), 821-833.

Schlesinger, Arthur (1992). *The disuniting of America: Reflections on a multicultural society.* New York, NY: W.W. Norton and Co.

Serrano Carreto, Enrique, Embriz Osorio, Arnulfo, & Fernández Ham, Patricia (Eds.) (2003). *Indicadores socioeconomicos de los pueblos indigenas, 2002* [Socioeconomic indicators of indigenous peoples, 2002]. Mexico City, Mexico: Instituto Nacional Indigenista/Programa de las Naciones Undias para el Desarrollo.

Skutnabb-Kangas, Tove (2000). *Linguistic genocide in education – Or worldwide diversity and human rights?* Mahwah, NJ: Lawrence Erlbaum Associates.

Smith, Robert (2005). *Mexican New York: Transnational lives of new immigrants.* Berkeley/Los Angeles, CA: University of California Press.

Wong, Lloyd (2008). Multiculturalism and ethnic pluralism in Sociology: An analysis of the fragmantation position discourse. *Canadian Ethnic Studies, 40*(1), 11-32.

Wright, Sue (2004). *Language policy and language planning: From nationalism to globalisation.* New York, NY: Palgrave McMillan.

Young, Iris Marion (1993). Together in difference: Transforming the logic of group political conflict. In Judith Squires (Ed.), *Principled positions: Postmodernism and the rediscovery of value* (pp. 121-150). London: Lawrence and Wishart.

Laura Menchaca Bishop
Cornell University, USA

Prema Kelley
Columbia University, USA

KARLA GIULIANO SARR

6. "WE LOST OUR CULTURE WITH CIVILIZATION"

Community Perceptions of Indigenous Knowledge and Education in Senegal

ABSTRACT

Ci birr jëmuy Njàngale mu soxal ñépp akit ci njàngale mi ci daara yu ndaw yi di gën di nara soxal ñépp, xam ni nit ñi gise xam-xam yeek njàngle mi lu war la. Xamle mi mën naa jaadu akit dimbali ci tinki mi su fekkee akit doŋŋ su fekke te ni tëralin yooyu dëppoo na ñu. Pàcc bii mu ngi ame benn gëstu bu ndaw bu ñu amale ci gox bu feete ci Bundu ci Senegaal, doon sosu menn powum jàngale akit seetlum po moomu ak firnde yu jóge ci waxtaan yi. Gëstu boobu dafay seet nan la xale yi, jàngalekat yeek ñi dëkke ci goxi kow gi gise xeeti xam-xam ak jàngalem gox beek bu tubaab (waa xeetu tugal). Gëstu boobu wone na woroo ci diggante xeeti xam-xamu gox beek jàngale mu tubaab. Woroo boobu mu ngi wone boppam ci benn wàll cig tële akit ci gisin wu néewal caaday gox bi ci tëkkaloom ak xam-xamu tubaab. Ba tey it, jëfandikóom làkku farañse ngir jàngale mi dafay firndeel ni njàngale moomoo rekk a am solo, boole ci di jafeel bokksig xam-xami gox bi ci biir àlluway njàng mi. Seetlu gu wéru ci maanaa mi nekk ci dugal xale lekool, ak woroog doole yi, dañu wone ni ba tey nit ñi gem na ñu ni dese nañu mën-mënu jël dogali ëllëg. (*Translated to Wolof [wol], a language of Senegal, by Maam Daour Wade and Gary Engelberg.*)

In the context of Education for All goals and the push for universal primary education, it is critical to understand how people conceptualize Indigenous and non-Indigenous knowledges and education. Only when these conceptions align will schooling be genuinely relevant and promote liberation. This chapter is based on a small-scale research study in southeastern Senegal that involved the development and observation of a classroom game, supplemented with interview data. The study explores how children, teachers, and community members in a rural area conceive of Indigenous and Western (or Northern) forms of knowledge and education. Results show that there is a perceived tension between Indigenous and Western systems of education. This tension manifests in a sense of inadequacy and a negative view of local cultures in relation to Western knowledge. Similarly, the usage of French as the language of instruction (LOI) promotes the idea that only Western knowledge counts, and complicates the integration of Indigenous knowledge within the curriculum. An awareness of the importance of schooling

C. Benson and K. Kosonen (eds.), Language Issues in Comparative Education, 115–131.
© *2013 Sense Publishers. All rights reserved.*

and existing power differentials demonstrate that people nonetheless feel they have agency in making choices for the future.

INTRODUCTION

In the context of Education for All goals and the push for universal primary education, it is critical to understand how people conceptualize Indigenous and non-Indigenous knowledges and education. This analysis takes the position that schooling will only promote liberation when it is relevant to learners, i.e. when learners' conceptions of knowledge are aligned with education. This chapter is based on a small-scale research study in southeastern Senegal that involved the development and observation of a classroom game within the context of an NGO educational development project, supplemented with interview data. The game was chosen as a creative vehicle for the incorporation of local knowledge into the classroom. The study explores how children, teachers, and community members in a rural area conceive of Indigenous and Western (or Northern) knowledges and education.

Many comments and attitudes revealed by this study reflect the internalization of the development discourse by research participants. As the predominant paradigm in contemporary geo-political relations between North and South, the development discourse identifies factors and systems of relationships that contribute to development, as well as the experts that establish the rules of play (Escobar, 1997). According to Escobar, the development discourse identifies problems by creating pathologies of abnormalities in contrast to Western ideals. For example, the discourse refers to "illiterate," "underdeveloped," "malnourished," "small farmers," "landless peasants," to which it offers solutions of development (Escobar, 1997: 88). The most damaging effect of the development discourse is what Nandy (1997) refers to as the "colonization of the mind," and the conceptualization of Indigenous cultures and practices as inferior or underdeveloped, to which the response is to alter cultural priorities (see also Dei & Doyle-Wood, 2006). Similarly, Benson (2008) explores the internalization of oppression in relation to linguistic preferences, and how people self-limit their true choices with regard to languages of instruction (LOI). Oppressed people tend to demand Western-style education in a former colonial language, which in turn promotes culturally alien values like individualism and neo-liberal capitalism. They are not necessarily aware of other options that would support their own languages and cultural values, nor are they always responsive when these are proposed.

As this study shows, internalization takes a problematic form when people use notions from the development discourse to justify their own marginalization and the inferiority of their Indigenous knowledges in contrast to preferred aspects of Western "civilization." My findings demonstrate how community members in rural Senegal perceive school-based knowledge as being associated with high-status hierarchies of knowledge from the West. These findings stimulate reflection on the negative impacts of current formal schooling models on perceptions of culture. They also underline the need for purposeful methods that validate Indigenous knowledges, including the use of local languages as LOI and through culturally relevant learning content and approaches.

INDIGENOUS KNOWLEDGES IN AFRICAN CONTEXTS

Conceptualizing Indigenous Knowledges

The term Indigenous knowledges offers an alternative to the pejorative, patronizing and time-bound concept of "traditional knowledge" (Warren, 1996). I employ the plural form, "knowledges," in relation to both Indigenous and Western forms to highlight the heterogeneity of knowledge systems (Dei, Hall, & Goldin Rosenberg, 2000; Botha, 2010). There are many definitions for Indigenous knowledges, and some scholars argue that current debates about the definition provide greater precision as to what Indigenous knowledge is not rather than what it is (Fernando, 2003). Table 1 highlights the qualities of Indigenous knowledges present in the literature relevant to African contexts. While not explicitly addressed in the table, language is both a vehicle and component of Indigenous knowledges. Dei discusses its importance within Indigenous knowledge systems and as a form of resistance in the neo-colonial context, arguing that the continued development and use of local languages is one way Indigenous peoples can "own their past, culture, and tradition" (2002: 10).

The Mismatch of Francophone Schooling with Community Needs

The current school system in Senegal continues to display the influences of French education policies from the colonial era. These policies impact the form and content of schooling as well as people's perceptions of Indigenous knowledges. The French administration created an official educational system in Senegal in 1903 to indoctrinate youth into the language and culture of the French administration and diminish resistance to colonial rule (Robinson, 2000; Quist, 2001). The education system of Senegal was the most developed of all the colonies in French West Africa as the seat of the French colonial government (Blakemore, 1970).

French is the country's official language and remains the language of instruction (LOI) and the language of initial literacy instruction. Less than 1% of Senegalese speak French as a first language; the majority of Senegalese are speakers of approximately 37 Indigenous languages, of which the largest are Wolof (with an estimated 3.9 million speakers) and Pulaar (with an estimated 2.7 million speakers) (Lewis, 2009), both of which have the status of national languages. A pilot program using six languages as LOI began in 1981 (Obanya, 1995) but remains experimental. Implementation has lacked the appropriate materials, training for teachers, and advocacy at the community level necessary to support a successful program (Lexander, 2011). Within the country as a whole, Wolof functions as the lingua franca. In the geographical zone of this study, Pulaar is the home language for a majority of the population.

Table 1. Characteristics of Indigenous knowledges (IKs)

Characteristic	Description	Additional References
Time and place	IKs have developed over long periods of time in particular locations. Place references the "local," a fixed geographic area, a "fixed territorial space" (Fernando, 2003) or an "integral indigenous territory [sic]" (Viergever, 1999).	Warren, 1996; Mwadime, 1999; Dei, Hall, Budd, & Rosenberg, 2000; Fernando, 2003; Botha, 2010
Specific group of people	IKs are of a communal or collective nature and belong to an identifiable group of people. Their collective values elicit and define individual values.	Warren, 1996; Reynar, 1999; Semali, 1999; Viergever, 1999; Dei et al. 2000; Botha, 2010
Daily nature	IKs inform daily interactions and activities. They represent a way of life and incorporate mental constructs necessary to make sense of the world and resolve problems.	Semali, 1999; Dei et al., 2000; George, 1999
Dynamic nature	IKs are constantly changing and adapting. They do not exist in a vacuum but are influenced by and contribute to other knowledge forms and available resources, including Western knowledges.	Warren, 1996; Mwadime, 1999; Quiroz, 1999; Semali, 1999; Dei et al., 2000
Holistic	Religion and morality are key components of the overarching IKs that frame a group's worldview. This includes a respect for the universe and an assumption of interconnectivity among people and their surroundings.	Mosha, 1999
Orality	In addition to the contents of African written scripts that existed well before contact with Arabs or Northern powers (Zulu, 2006), oral histories and passage of information remain key attributes of IKs. Some oral forms of knowledge include stories, proverbs and sayings.	George, 1999; Mosha, 1999; Quiroz, 1999; Dei et al., 2000
Intergenerational transmission	The passage of IKs is from elders to youth, with elders identified and respected as the keepers and teachers of knowledge.	George, 1999; Viergever, 1999; Dei et al., 2000
Diversity	Adherence to and perceptions of IKs differ between community members. IKs are specialized among certain sub-groups or classes, and take the form of technical knowledge for skilled workers.	George, 1999; Mwadime, 1999; Reynar, 1999; Semali, 1999; Dei et al. 2000
Importance of relationships	Relationships among humans and between humans and the environment are central attributes of IKs.	Viergever, 1999; Semali & Kincheloe, 1999

Needless to say, the pedagogical techniques and foundational assumptions of colonial schooling reflected Western knowledges and assumptions and ignored Indigenous knowledges and approaches to learning (Altbach, 1971; Ouane & Glanz, 2011). Individual work and success were rewarded, in direct opposition to African Indigenous approaches that stress collective problem-solving and solidarity (Kanu, 2006). The positioning of French educational content as "modern," "new," and "innovative" greatly discredited African knowledges (Devisse, 1985). Eurocentric knowledge has remained dominant since Senegal's Independence from France in 1960 (Baker, 1998; Alidou, 2009), reflecting the current state of geo-political relations in *La Francophonie*, the French term for former and present colonies which continue to consider French their official and/or national languages. Alidou notes that the "francophone" African educational system is "essentially a French education system ill-implemented by Africans and Westerners on African soil" (2009: 107).

The use of colonial languages as LOI and accompanying emphasis on European literature "undermine the promotion, development and sustenance of African culture and traditions" according to Quist (2001: 306), and prioritize academic-literary skills over technical or vocational education (Quist, 2001). Criticizing the failure of education systems to incorporate Indigenous knowledges and languages, Alidou (2009) declares that there is a serious "mismatch" between the school language and culture and home languages and cultures, resulting in a perceived sense of failure and devaluation among communities.

Currently in Senegal, a country of 12 million inhabitants, nearly three-quarters of school-aged children attend some level of primary school (UNESCO, 2009). Primary schooling begins at age seven and entails six grades; this study focuses on children who are in the last two of these grades known as *cours moyen,* CM1 and CM2 (corresponding to grades 5 and 6), along with their teachers, school directors, and community members. French remains the LOI.

CONTEXT OF THE STUDY

Methodology

This study was conducted as part of a community development program in southeastern Senegal led by the Grandmother Project (GMP), an American-registered NGO,[1] in cooperation with World Vision Senegal.[ii] The project is based in a small town and works with a number of surrounding villages to recognize and promote grandparents as resources and partners in development efforts. Within this geographical area the majority ethnic group is Pulaar, which is also the dominant language. Other ethnic groups and languages present include Wolof, Sarakhole, Bambara, Mandingue, Sereer and Diola. Where possible, GMP work takes place in local languages, with translation as necessary for non-speakers. A key component of the project is to integrate the holders and teachers of Indigenous knowledges into school curricula and activities.

As part of efforts to introduce more culturally relevant content in the schools, I worked with GMP as a volunteer to develop an instructional game that teachers in village primary schools could use to discuss intergenerational relationships and Indigenous cultural practices in the classroom. Observations of game-play and resulting classroom interaction served as the primary data, which I supplemented with interviews with adults who were involved with GMP. In doing so, I used the convenience sampling method (Leedy & Ormrod, 2005), which entailed speaking with those who were willing and available. As a result, the majority of teachers, all school directors, and all interviewees were male. I took detailed observation notes of game trials and recorded interviews, which I then transcribed. I worked closely with a research assistant, who was chosen by GMP. He was a member of one of the village communities, spoke French, and showed interest in the project. All quotes below are my own translations from either the French of the participants or the translations from L1 or L2 into French provided to me by the research assistant or school personnel.

Table 2. Data collection

Instrument (#)	Population	Languages used
Game trials (10)	GMP and World Vision project team	French, Pulaar, Wolof
	Village #1 and #2 primary school teachers	French, Pulaar, Wolof
	Semi-urban town primary school teachers	French, Pulaar, Wolof
	Village #1 primary school students: combined grades 5 and 6; grade 5; grade 6	French, Pulaar
	Village #2 primary school students: multigrade 5 and 6	
	Town primary school students: grade 6	French, Pulaar, Wolof
	Middle school students: select group of grades 7, 8 and 9	French, Pulaar
	Village #2 community members	French, Pulaar
Semi-structured interviews (3)	Village #1 primary school director Former teacher/Politician/Artist, Town Village #1 Former PTA President	French
Structured interviews (2)	Village #1 primary school director Village #2 primary school director	French

The game comprised a set of cards with discussion prompts. Prompts included multiple choice, true and false, and open-ended questions. This simplified formulation was appropriate to students' ages (11-16 years old) and consistent with the terminology that GMP employed in its community discussions. Examples of game prompts included:
− Identify your three favorite activities. Are they traditional or modern activities?
− Cite three things in your traditional culture that you like a lot; and

– Choose the correct sentence: 'Children know traditional culture best' OR 'Children know Western culture best.'

Interviews solicited more in-depth information based on the broader research question: How do people conceive of knowledges and education within their community? Document review of NGO project reports provided additional background knowledge. Field notes and informal conversations also helped to triangulate data.

The game was designed in French, the LOI. With classes as large as 60 students, teachers facilitated the game with a group of 12 to 16 students as others looked on. Players organized as four teams of three to four students at the front of the classroom while classmates observed and either rotated into game-play or responded to questions directed toward the entire class. As an additional trial, we also played the game with a group of village community members to test its use outside of the school setting. The community trial involved eight players. All participants were male, as it was more culturally appropriate for such discussions to take place within gendered groups. An attempt was made to organize a trial with a group of women but this was not possible due to events in the village.

At the time of the research, I had over ten years of experience with the Senegalese context, having studied in Senegal and later worked at an NGO in Dakar with frequent travel to rural areas. I am married to a Senegalese man, which provides informal entry into dialogue with people, facilitating my research. I speak French and Wolof but not Pulaar, the dominant language of the geographical area of this study, so I worked with a Pulaar research assistant. Although this was his first experience as a translator and as a member of the project, he was extremely helpful in interpreting Pulaar conversation and helping me negotiate local customs and relationships with teachers and elders.

Because this research project was imbedded within a GMP development project, findings should be interpreted with care, since the focus on grandparents and cultural preservation may have influenced participant responses. However, my findings reveal attitudes that I believe to be widespread in Senegal, and that are consistent with the literature regarding the internalization of Western development discourse.

The School Community as Research Site

Through schooling, children acquire more Western-centric values such as structured time, progress, and individualism. It became clear throughout the research process that the school also plays the role as an entry-point to community-development projects and the services and institutions of the nation-state. The school serves as a mediator between students and community members with institutions and services that are important within the development paradigm. It is interesting to note that not only does this occur through the provision of knowledge during class, but through auxiliary services that the school provides informally and formally to the community. While school children are the main beneficiaries of schooling practices, the school is also influential with the community-at-large. In one village community, for example, the PTA President helps village members to register new births with the Senegalese government. The school director also helped a group of women to apply for development funds from the American Embassy and to begin a local garden project. Within this context, teachers often perform translation of documents from L1 and L2 languages of Pulaar and Wolof to the dominant language and LOI, French. In many ways, the school acts as translator between languages as well as between the home cultures and the more Western-based classroom culture.

Language Issues in Implementation

Communication difficulties due to language issues arose during the game trials and greatly impacted use of the game to facilitate discussion about culture and education. These issues provide insight into the complexities of education in non-dominant languages as well as the implementation of culturally relevant curriculum. In developing the game, we knew that Pulaar would be needed in the game-playing trials involving community members, but the extent of usage of L1 Pulaar and L2 Wolof during the trials with students and teachers was more extensive than originally thought. The game required participatory methods, with which students and teachers had little or no experience, so the use of home languages was necessary for teachers to explain the game prompts and to urge self-expression.

During the game trials it became even more evident that the L1 would best facilitate discussion about Indigenous knowledge and education, even for adult players with a strong command of French. During teacher trials, players demonstrated a preference to discuss amongst themselves in their L1 or L2 when responding to the prompts. In the village school settings, Pulaar most often served as the L1. In the town school setting, Pulaar and Wolof were used interchangeably. Switching to non-dominant languages may indicate a preference and increased comfort to address issues related to Indigenous knowledge in that language. If schooling was more culturally relevant and able to integrate issues pertaining to African culture and heritage more regularly, this may not have been the case.

One key finding throughout game-play was that students had heightened energy and expression abilities when responding to game prompts. Teachers commented positively numerous times about how certain students participated actively during the game, as opposed to during normal class time. They associated this new confidence with the use of the home language, a realization which alone was an important outcome for the teachers involved in this study. A member of the project team had shared a related anecdote from his own learning experiences. He described with great enthusiasm a primary school lesson about birds. When the teacher asked for a list of bird names in French, the LOI, the students could only provide three names. The teacher then led students to brainstorm a list of birds in their non-dominant languages and they came up with a over a hundred names. The NGO worker explained how he had been so excited and stimulated by this exercise that he kept his notes from that lesson for many years.

The experience with the game demonstrates the difficulties of bringing Indigenous knowledge into dominant language classrooms, further underlining the mismatch between school language and culture and home language and culture. Inability to access and influence classroom activities invalidates the knowledge of community members who are not French speakers.

CONCEPTIONS OF INDIGENOUS EDUCATION IN SOUTHEASTERN SENEGAL

The game encouraged participants to identify the content of Indigenous knowledges, and this content was consistent with the topics identified in Table 1 above. For example, grandparents do indeed play an important role in the education of children. Griots, who are the oral historians in many West African cultures, are also people who possess a great deal of knowledge in Senegalese society. Many game participants talked about how discussion and teaching occur on a daily basis during chores. They also emphasized the role that rites of passage such as male circumcision play in one's education. The communal imperative for education was also evident, meaning that any older person has the right and duty to educate younger members of the community.

People used concepts of education to express relationships within the larger society; as one respondent mentioned, the role of education is to prepare someone for life within society, or for "community life." This notion supports Kanu's (2006) assertions about the role of traditional education in an African context. Educational content differs for males and females; for boys, endurance, self-restraint, wrestling (Senegal's most prominent traditional sport), and soccer were most frequently mentioned, while for girls, content included singing, dancing, cooking, taking care of family members, sweeping and fetching water. One commonly cited example of Indigenous knowledge was traditional medicine, particularly knowledge of plants.

The game also encouraged participants to identify how Indigenous practices are manifested in their experiences. Participants associated the following with traditional culture/knowledge: music in general, instruments such as drums and flutes, songs and dancing, riddles and tales, stories and community/village history, pastoral activities, agriculture, male circumcision rituals, fishing, and clothing.

The game as well as the interviews allowed me to identify individuals in this predominantly Pulaar society who possess knowledge and are able to transmit it to others. Most identified various elders or griots as the possessors of traditional knowledge. Elders are seen as particularly informative about history and genealogy, giving advice, determining what is bad or good, and sharing traditional knowledge. During game-play students often said that "it is good to approach the elders because you can learn a lot of things." While this aligns with research on traditional culture (Moumouni, 1968; Kanu, 2006), GMP's particular focus on grandparents may have influenced participants to refer to extended family members and elders as possessing knowledge. Players used the term "elders" for anyone who was even slightly older, citing grandparents, fathers, aunts, sisters, and brothers as repositories of tradition. Perhaps an oversight, mothers do not figure on this list. It is also noteworthy that during a wrap-up discussion at the end of one trial, when students identified the names of two experts on Indigenous knowledge within their milieu, teachers were in agreement that these individuals were experts, confirming their prominence within the community.

The transmission of Indigenous knowledge occurs in a number of ways. As one participant articulated, Indigenous education is a continuous process with clear moments of heightened learning. More organized forms of education include the playing of games (the counting game known commonly as mankala for example), drumming sessions, family meetings, and rites of passage. In the past, children would go with grandparents into the bush to look for roots or trees, and would learn to identify plants useful in daily life for cooking, healing, and protection. They also learned pastoral knowledge by going with grandfathers to look after herds and by helping with the milking chores each evening. Once chores were done, children would receive advice or learn stories from elders. Grandmothers would also often gather children in the evenings to tell tales and teach dances and songs. While some of these activities continue to the present, there is a sense that these traditions are being lost. This will be explored in greater detail below.

While participants emphasized daily acts of education, the male circumcision ritual stood out as a highly organized practice where Indigenous knowledge is passed between the generations. This learning takes place according to age group, a typical societal structure in many West African societies, and one that GMP identifies as key to its own work. One adult interviewee compared the rigorous approach of rites of passage with military training. While this study did not explore the current state of rites of passage in such communities, it is clear that they remain a critical learning experience and space for transmission of Indigenous knowledge. As with other practices, there is a sense that the practice does not continue as it once did. Note that female rites of passage were not explicitly mentioned. This may be due to GMP's work to identify alternatives to female circumcision, or to the fact that most adult respondents were men.

Tension between Indigenous and Exogenous Forms of Knowledge

The data from observations of game-play and participant interviews reveal a palpable tension between modern and traditional forms of knowledge, particularly with regard to schooling. This section addresses the power dynamics between these forms of knowledge as articulated by research participants. It appears that the modern often wins out, as individuals indicated a sense of cultural loss.

Participant responses illustrate the contradictory and complex relationship between the value of exogenous and Indigenous knowledge. Although many students indicated that learning takes place both at home and in school, others indicated that school education is "more rigorous." This is evident, for example, in the notion that children who do not attend school play all day. Adults often revealed romanticism for the child who does not go to school by saying that he or she is then closer to his or her cultural heritage. The fact that the adults interviewed had relationships with the school, either as former teachers, current school directors, or members of the PTA, may explain this general sentiment. As one male adult articulated: "The child who does not go to school, in reality, does not have anyone as a reference other than his [sic] relatives ... He [sic] has a greater chance to respect society's norms" (Former Teacher, Town).

Similarly, during the initial game trial with a group of development workers and educators, there was a consensus that the students who live in towns are more familiar with the modern culture than students who live in the surrounding villages. This supports both rural and semi-urban students' assertions in subsequent trials that "children today are not familiar with traditional culture." Such a statement calls for further exploration, as the majority of these students live in villages and self-reported participation in agricultural and pastoral activities, activities which would be connected more closely to Indigenous knowledges.

Many participants also articulated a clear friction between Indigenous and Western forms of education. For example, during the community game trial, an older man expressed the tension that exists between those who function as knowledge repositories: "Teachers want the students to respect them, which puts them in competition with the elders." An interviewee identified the tension between the two institutions in more general terms:

> There's traditional education and also modern education, schooling. Today, there is a competition between these two and we see that modern education, or modern activities, are overtaking traditional activities because children spend more time at school. Even if they are at home, they spend more time listening to the radio, or watching TV ... Even though sometimes, for girls, they are taught to cook, to sweep, to fetch water ... Really, there is a terrible competition between modern education and traditional education ... This tension is killing our culture. (School Director, Village 1)

Not only does this participant illustrate the ambivalent relationship between modern and traditional cultures, but he identifies the radio and TV as factors in cultural loss. Even though there are programs in local languages, it is worthwhile to note that during this interview, the TV in this participant's living room was tuned to a news channel report in French, while his children were on the patio watching the Africa Cup of Nations soccer tournament (also in French) on a second television set. Modern influences permeate peoples' lives despite their recognition that they contribute to cultural loss.

Participants expressed cultural loss in terms of obstacles to Indigenous knowledge transfer. They expressed the weakened state of male initiation practices – a key institution of Indigenous education, as mentioned above – due to pressures such as work schedules, community members coming from overseas to participate, and even growing adherence to organized religion:

> Even if it isn't everyone, there are those who say that it is against Christian principles. You are going to a sacred forest. The sacred can only be in church. And for Muslims, the sacred can only be found at the mosque ... (School Director, Village 1)

This same participant also identified pressures that could be directly traced to the influence of development standards, e.g. the lack of purified water and the extended stay in the bush, as reasons for reducing the duration of initiation practices.

Changes in common forms of intergenerational communication also threaten the daily transfer of Indigenous knowledge. Many commented that whereas previously grandparents and children gathered in the evenings to share stories and other forms of cultural knowledge, children no longer seek out elders. Children are often in a hurry to finish pastoral chores in order to watch television. There also is a sense that children do not value traditional knowledge:

> In our time, we were often with our grandmothers or grandfathers in the evenings when they would tell us tales ... Today, grandmothers cannot even try to reverse or to transmit their knowledge to the kids, because for them, for the children, all of this is nothing. (PTA President, Village 1)

There also were comments that elders no longer have time for young people. The reason for this sentiment requires further investigation. While GMP's emphasis on intergenerational communication may have intensified people's awareness of these changes, the sense of tension that is present in people's statements cannot be overlooked.

Internalization of the Development Discourse – Expressions of Inadequacy

Individuals expressed negative views towards the local culture on a number of occasions. A frequent complaint cited the lack of teachers in rural areas. Many teachers live outside the villages and commute to their schools, resulting in missed class time if transportation breaks down. This is certainly the case for teachers who do not share the language or culture with the community where they have been assigned to teach. For others, it may be because they have acquired modern sensibilities through Western-influenced education and are unwilling to live in places with limited hygiene, access to infrastructure, and so on. As one village participant explained, he could understand the teachers' perspective because "they are going to suffer out here in the bush." This comment illustrates his internalized view of the development discourse on the uninhabitable nature of rural settings.

Similarly, some participants were critical of traditional forms of medicine. Whereas one teacher hailed its virtues alongside modern medicine, another teacher criticized its usage from a Western perspective, telling students, "Traditional practitioners, it's a risk. There isn't a dosage. Modern medicine uses laboratories so the medicine is properly dosed ..." (Teacher, Middle School). Other examples provide evidence of the internalization of the values of "civilization" and "progress," two notions fundamental to the concept of modernity, as referred to in the title of this chapter. During a discussion about changes in relationships between children and grandparents, the participant said, "At a certain moment, with this modernization and civilization ... there was television ... we have lost much of our grandparents' culture with civilization" (PTA President, Village 1). By identifying television with civilization, he implies that prior to the arrival of modern imports, people were not civilized.

This PTA President shared how his quest for advancement of the village school led him to disrupt the traditional power hierarchy some years ago, when he confronted his own father who was the previous PTA president. Having just returned from studying in another city and wishing for a more progressive school environment, he wanted his father to "cultivate contacts" and "develop" the school. Others in the village heavily criticized his actions as impolite, going against the order of things. Nevertheless, he succeeded in replacing his father and has had many accomplishments, such as adding several more classrooms, gaining the respect of many in his village and surrounding communities. As a colleague explained, "He is someone who is not lazy and who wants development ...." This description also exhibits internalization of the development discourse, which often attributes laziness to the non-Western "Other" (see Said, 1994).

Examples of Limited Agency

Many participants indicated a clear awareness of the multiple influences on their lives and the tensions that exist between Indigenous and Western knowledges and cultures. Parents make great efforts for their children to attend school, even while knowing that schooling may take their children out of the community and far away from them. Because French is the LOI, comments that underline the importance of schooling likely also imply the importance of acquiring French skills. Parental efforts include investment in "school supplies, clothing, everything in order to do well at school" (School Director, Village 1). One participant clearly understood the terms of such engagement and the impact of globalization and modernization on people's desire for certain positions within society:

It's a problem of survival ... because with schooling...with knowledge, diplomas, you can have a job. ... because with globalization, the infiltration of Western values is so strong, people are obligated to go to school in order to hold certain positions. Even to be a blacksmith, but a modern blacksmith. A modern woodworker .... Now, woodworkers don't only make stools, but they make dressers. They use centimetre measurements .... (School Director, Village 1)

Participants also expressed the need for school in terms of desperation and survival, even at the cost of cultural change and loss. One participant explained that people consent to schooling "because [they] are in difficult situations and are obligated to bring their children to school, even if they know that schooling will change them" (School Director, Village 1). Similarly, another participant identified one of the costs of education as future absence from the village. He said that people prefer to send a child to school, knowing that in the future he will "earn a lot from what he sends [in remittances] ... Even if he becomes lonely, he'll find a way ..." (PTA President, Village 1).

Expressions of agency remain constrained within the development paradigm, supporting Nandy's (1997) assertion that resistance takes place only within the limited space that hegemony allows (see also Benson, 2008 regarding language-related choices). For example, one participant described how educators organized French classes to empower community members:

And we had to, in order to be really taken into consideration, we needed to understand that official language ... It's French ... It's the language used in offices, right? You have to go to school in order to understand this language and there was even a time when we would organize evening classes for adults, for the elders, so that they could understand this language .... We organized evening classes so that people would be included .... (School Director, Village 1)

This commentary illuminates not only agency but awareness of the factors at play and how in order to counter marginalization, people need to establish familiarity with structures inherent to the development paradigm. Gaining French skills is one important way to open up opportunities for people and to resist exclusion. In sum, while the activities presented here work within the current structure and do not challenge the development discourse through truly counter-hegemonic acts, there is evidence of awareness and agency among community members.

CONCLUSION

Through this small-scale study, I have shown how young Senegalese students and their educators conceptualize both Indigenous and Western forms of knowledge and its transmission. Their examples align with the central characteristics of Indigenous knowledges present within the literature, particularly that Indigenous education is a continuous process whereby induction in local forms of knowledge occurs daily as well as during highly calculated and coordinated events such as rites of passage. Examples of Indigenous educational content include participation in chores and preparation for adult roles. Griots, and elders in general, are the most common possessors and transmitters of Indigenous knowledge.

People and especially youth gain exposure to Western knowledge through the media, such as television and radio, as well as through school activities. Schools induct community members into the development discourse through auxiliary activities and actions of the PTA, school directors and teachers. Indigenous and Western knowledges co-exist within local realities but in a tenuous relationship within the Senegalese communities involved in this project. Participants discussed numerous ways in which modern and traditional forms of knowledge contradict one another and compete. Given the inequality of the two forms of knowledge, this competition often results in the obstruction of the transmission of Indigenous knowledge, risking a loss of cultural heritage and practices. As one participant exclaimed, "This tension is killing our culture!"

The internalization of the development discourse is encapsulated by one participant's comment that his community lost their culture with "civilization." The emphasis of development on modern values and prioritization of education and market entry over cultural preservation complicates the relationship between Indigenous and Western knowledges. Many of the examples presented above demonstrate implicitly negative attitudes towards Indigenous knowledge and practices. Conscious acquiescence to participating in structures of modernity, like the school, offers insight into personal agency as existing within the confines of the development paradigm.

Issues of language use framed the experience of the game as a research tool and provided insight into the complexities of language issues in education. It was clear that players of all ages were most at ease discussing topics related to Indigenous education and knowledge using their home languages. The fact that students participated vigorously in game-play within the classroom was attributed by teachers to the use of L1 and L2 instead of French, the LOI. Like content related to Indigenous knowledge, the use of non-dominant languages in school is imperative for the validation of student identities and culture.

This study illuminates Senegalese community members' understandings of the interplay between Indigenous and Western knowledges, and highlights the internalization of the development discourse. While use of culturally relevant curricula represents one possible way to counter these influences, the current use of French as LOI and the practice of assigning teachers to areas where they are not familiar with students' home languages complicate the integration of Indigenous knowledge into classroom spaces. Increased sensitivity to Indigenous knowledges within communities themselves is necessary to address the current mismatch of Western-based schooling approaches with local realities. Only when that mismatch is addressed can education be truly liberating.

NOTES

[i] The Grandmother Project was recognized as an international non-profit organization by Senegal in 2011. For more information, see www.grandmotherproject.org.

[ii] Special thanks to the team at the Grandmother Project and World Vision Senegal for their support while conducting this project. This includes a number of key individuals at the regional IDEN. While I am unable to include their names due to ethical concerns for confidentiality, I remain wholeheartedly appreciative for their good work and collaboration.

REFERENCES

Alidou, Hassana (2009). Promoting multilingual and multicultural education in Francophone Africa: Challenges and perspectives. In Birgit Brock-Utne & Inge Skattum (Eds.), *Languages and education in Africa: A comparative and transdisciplinary analysis* (pp. 105-132). Oxford: Symposium Books.

Altbach, Philip G. (1971). Education and neocolonialism. *Teachers College Record, 72*(4), 543-558.

Baker, Victoria J. (1998). Literacy in developing societies: Native language versus national language literacies. In Aydin Y. Durgunoğlu & Ludo Verhoeven (Eds.), *Literacy development in a multilingual context: Cross-cultural perspectives* (pp. 21-36). New Jersey: Lawrence Erlbaum Associates.

Benson, Carol (2008). *Language "choice" in education*. PRAESA Occasional Papers, No. 30. Cape Town, South Africa: Project for the Study of Alternative Education in South Africa.

Blakemore, Priscilla (1970). Assimilation and association in French educational policy and practice: Senegal, 1903-1939. In Vincent M. Battle & Charles H. Lyons (Eds.), *Essays in the history of African education* (pp. 85-103). New York: Teachers College Press.

Botha, Louis R. (2010). Indigenous knowledge as culturally centered education in South Africa. *Africa Education Review, 7*(1), 34-50.

Dei, George J. Sefa (2002). *Rethinking the role of Indigeneous knowledges in the academy.* NALL Working Papers #58. New Approaches for Lifelong Learning.

Dei, George J. Sefa, & Doyle-Wood, S. (2006). Is we who haffi ride di staam: Critical knowledge/multiple knowings – Possibilities, challenges, and resistance in curriculum/cultural contexts. In Yatta Kanu (Ed.), *Curriculum as a cultural practice: Postcolonial imaginations* (pp. 151-180). Toronto: University of Toronto Press.

Dei, George J. Sefa, Hall, Budd D., & Rosenberg, Dorothy G. (2000). Introduction. In George J. Sefa Dei, Budd L. Hall, & Dorothy G. Rosenberg, (Eds.), *Indigenous knowledges in global contexts: Multiple readings of our world* (pp. 3-17). Toronto: University of Toronto Press.

Devisse, Jean (1985). The development of education and training in Africa: An outline of history for 1930-1980. In UNESCO, *The educational process and historiography in Africa,* Final report and papers of the symposium organized by Unesco in Dakar (Senegal) from 25 to 29 January 1982 (pp. 11-19). Paris: UNESCO.

Escobar, Arturo (1997). The making and unmaking of the third world through development. In Majid Rahnema & Victoria Bawtree (Eds.), *The post-development reader* (pp. 85-101). London: Zed Books.

Fernando, Jude L. (2003). NGOs and production of indigenous knowledge under the condition of postmodernity. *The Annals of the American Academy of Political and Social Science, 590,* 54-72.

George, June M. (1999). Indigenous knowledge as a component of the school curriculum. In Ladislaus M. Semali & Joe L. Kincheloe (Eds.), *What is Indigenous knowledge? Voices from the academy* (pp. 79-94). New York: Falmer Press.

Kanu, Yatta (2006). Reappropriating traditions in curricular imagination. In Y. Kanu (Ed.), *Curriculum as a cultural practice: Postcolonial imaginations* (pp. 203-222). Toronto: University of Toronto Press.

Leedy, Paul D., & Ormrod, Jeanne Ellis (2005). *Practical research: Planning and design.* Upper Saddle River, NJ: Pearson/Merrill Prentice Hall.

Lewis, M. Paul (Ed.) (2009). *Ethnologue: Languages of the World* (16th Ed.). Dallas, TX: SIL International.

Lexander, Kristin Vold (2011). Texting and African language literacy. *New Media & Society, 13*(3), 427-443.

Mosha, R. Sambuli (1999). The inseparable link between intellectual and spiritual formation in indigenous knowledge and education: A case study in Tanzania. In Ladislaus M. Semali & Joe L. Kincheloe (Eds.), *What is Indigenous knowledge? Voices from the academy* (pp. 209-225). New York: Falmer Press.

Moumouni, Abdou (1968). *Education in Africa.* London: André Deutsch.

Mwadime, Robert K. N. (1999). Indigenous knowledge systems for an alternative culture in science: The role of nutritionists in Africa. In Ladislaus M. Semali & Joe L. Kincheloe (Eds.), *What is Indigenous knowledge? Voices from the academy* (pp. 243-267). New York: Falmer Press.

Nandy, Ashis (1997). Colonization of the mind. In Majid Rahnema & Victoria Bawtree (Eds.), *The post-development reader* (pp. 168-177). London: Zed Books.

Ouane, Adama, & Glanz, Christine (Eds.) (2011). *Optimising learning, education and publishing in Africa: The language factor. A review and analysis of theory and practice in mother-tongue and bilingual education in sub-Saharan Africa.* Hamburg, Germany: UNESCO Institute for Lifelong Learning (UIL), the Association for the Development of Education in Africa (ADEA)/ African Development Bank.

Obanya, Pai (1995). Case studies of curriculum innovation in Western Africa. *International Review of Education, 41*(5), 315-336.

Quiroz, Consuelo (1999). Local knowledge systems and vocational education in developing countries. In Ladislaus M. Semali & Joe L. Kincheloe (Eds.), *What is Indigenous knowledge? Voices from the academy* (pp. 305-316). New York: Falmer Press.

Quist, Hubert O. (2001). Cultural issues in secondary education development in West Africa: Away from colonial survivals towards neocolonial influences? *Comparative Education, 37*(3), 297-314.

Reynar, Rodney (1999). Indigenous people's knowledge and education: A tool for development? In Ladislaus M. Semali & Joe L. Kincheloe (Eds.), *What is Indigenous knowledge? Voices from the academy* (pp. 285-304). New York: Falmer Press.

Robinson, David (2000). *Paths of accommodation: Muslim societies and French colonial authorities in Senegal and Mauritania, 1880-1920.* Athens: Ohio University Press.

Said, Edward (1994). *Orientalism*. New York: Vintage Books.

Semali, Ladislaus M., & Kincheloe, Joe L. (1999). Introduction: What is Indigenous knowledge and why should we study it? In Ladislaus M. Semali & Joe L. Kincheloe (Eds.), *What is Indigenous knowledge? Voices from the academy* (pp. 3-57). New York: Falmer Press.

Semali, Ladislaus (1999). Community as classroom: Dilemmas of valuing African indigenous literacy in education. *International Review of Education, 45*(3/4), 305-319.

UNESCO (2009). *UIS statistics in brief: Senegal.* (http://stats.uis.unesco.org/unesco/TableViewer/document.aspx?ReportId=121&IF_Language=eng&BR_Country=6860)

Viergever, Marcel (1999). Indigenous knowledge: An interpretation of views from indigenous peoples. In Ladislaus M. Semali & Joe L. Kincheloe (Eds.), *What is Indigenous knowledge? Voices from the academy* (pp. 333-359). New York: Falmer Press.

Warren, D. Michael (1996). Comments on article by Arun Agrawal. *Indigenous Knowledge and Development Monitor, 4*, 12-19.

Zulu, Itibari M. (2006). Critical indigenous African education and knowledge. *The Journal of Pan African Studies, 1*(3), 32-49.

Karla Giuliano Sarr
Center for International Education
University of Massachusetts Amherst, USA

PART III:

CLASSROOM PRACTICES AND TEACHER VOICES

GOWRI VIJAYAKUMAR, ELIZABETH PEARCE, &
MEHERUN NAHAR[i]

7. FIRST LANGUAGE-BASED PRESCHOOLS IN ADIVASI COMMUNITIES IN THE CHITTAGONG HILL TRACTS OF BANGLADESH

ABSTRACT

Bangla hani Hapong Chadigang-o Kokwansa saya cherokrok iskulo yapai bokmanibai wansa hukumuni bisingo kwlwgoi thango. Shishur Khamatayan projek kok-kainwi akhai hukumu-kainwi bisingtwi sakang yaprini phurungmarokbai cherokni swrwngnai lamani o kebengno nornani kha chungo. Iñ daio imotoi jaiti swrwngnai-no tengwi phunukjakkha. Amani kokbai swrwngnai bai amani kokbai swrwngya jaiti sakang yapri iskulo swrwngnai cherokrokni pharimanino chung iñ daio tengoi naikha. Tengmani nungjakkha amani kokbai swrwngnai SKP-ni cherokrok Koksanai, Thikinai samung, Soisima bai sakni hukumurokno gam khaiwi sio, klas-o kwsrang khaiwi tongo, akhai jomajori swrwngnani hamjago, tama hinkhai suinai bai suithaih sininai daio bok kisa rwngsukya. Hodani borokrokbo amani kokbai swrwngnaino lagwi simani baksaya. In bakhak daio klas bisingo kok-kainwi akhai hukumu-kainwi bisingtwi swrwngnai lamarokno tisagwi romjakkha, obobai baksa imotwi swrwngnai lamani kebengroknobo phunukjakkha, o bisingobo sakang yaprini swrwngnai lamano laiwibo kokrok sajkakkha. (*Translated to Tripura-Kokborok [trp], a language of Bangladesh, by Mathura Tripura*)

In Bangladesh's Chittagong Hill Tracts (CHT), school often represents Adivasi (indigenous) children's first encounter with the dominant Bangla culture. The Shishur Khamatayan Project (SKP) aims to transform this encounter through a bilingual and bicultural preschool curriculum. This chapter evaluates the approach. We compare SKP's curricular model to alternative preschool models prevalent in the CHT. The comparison reveals that SKP children significantly outperform their counterparts in language development, quantitative reasoning, and environmental and cultural awareness; are more engaged; and have more participatory learning environments. However, SKP is not significantly associated with performance in writing and in letter recognition, and community members face complex conflicts about language in education. This chapter highlights the promise of bilingual and

C. Benson and K. Kosonen (eds.), Language Issues in Comparative Education, 135–152.

bicultural education to enable learning in the classroom, but also points to the practical challenges of such an approach, especially in moving beyond preschool.

INTRODUCTION

The many Adivasi[ii] communities of Bangladesh share a rich and diverse cultural and linguistic tradition. At the same time, they are geographically, politically, economically and culturally marginalized within a country that is already one of the world's poorest. This paper examines the potential of first language (L1)-based bilingual preschool education to counter this deep-rooted marginalization at one of its most potent early encounters: an Adivasi child's first day at school. We compare child development, school readiness, classroom environments, and community perspectives in L1-based preschools with national-language-based[iii] preschools in the Chittagong Hill Tracts (CHT) to evaluate the strengths and limitations of L1-based bilingual education in this setting.

Efforts to provide bilingual and multilingual education in low-income countries have shown impressive results for learning, attendance, and overall self-esteem at the primary level, as a range of NGO-led project evaluations suggest (Dutcher, 2004). Such results have also been reported in a large cross-national data set focusing on attendance (Smits, Huisman, & Kruijff, 2008). While much of the literature focuses on primary schooling, Ball (2010) reviews the literature on bilingual and multilingual education at the early childhood level to find emerging evidence on the potential of L1-based models in the early years.[iv] Yet, as Ball points out, the evidence at the early childhood level remains limited.

This chapter contributes to filling this gap. In our study, children in L1-based bilingual preschools outperformed their counterparts in national-language-based preschools in several areas: communication, language and literacy; problem-solving, reasoning, and numeracy; knowledge and understanding of the world; and concepts about print. However, they performed less well in letter recognition and writing skills. Classroom observations revealed that L1-based classrooms were more participatory and culturally relevant than their national-language-based counterparts. Finally, focus group discussions with community members highlighted the diversity of opinions about language issues, but suggested that L1-based preschools may allow for greater participation from parents in reinforcing learning outside the classroom. In this chapter, we outline the context of the CHT and then describe our methods and results. Key concerns that emerged from the study about the long-term success of students, and about modes of evaluation, will be discussed at the end of the chapter.

HISTORICAL CONTEXT: POLITICS, EDUCATION AND MARGINALIZATION IN THE CHITTAGONG HILL TRACTS

Bangladesh is often cited as evidence that a low-income country can achieve impressive social development gains (UNDP, 2010). However, the complex history of the CHT serves as a reminder of continued inequality. Violent conflict in the CHT between militant Adivasi groups and the government began before Bangladesh's independence, and continued until the CHT Peace Accord in 1997. Some violence still persists, but to a lesser extent, today (Barkat et al., 2009).

The CHT region – a hilly region surrounded on two sides with neighboring India and Myanmar – is geographically and demographically distinct. The three districts that make up the CHT region in southeastern Bangladesh – Bandarban, Khagrachari, and Rangamati – are home to 1.6 million people out of a total national population of 142.3 million (Bangladesh Bureau of Statistics, 2011). Around 48% of the CHT population is Adivasi (Barkat et al., 2009: 17), while, nationwide, Adivasi groups make up closer to 1.5% of the population (Minority Rights Group International, 2008). In addition to being linguistically, geographically and culturally distinct from the rest of the country, the area also has a very different religious profile, with Adivasis following Buddhism, Hinduism, or Christianity (Minority Rights Group International, 2008), while the rest of the population of Bangladesh is predominantly Muslim.

Within this context of marginalization, the CHT faces continued poverty, with direct implications for educational inequality. Poverty is high in the region among both Adivasi and Bangla settler groups, with 86% of households living below the poverty line (Barkat et al., 2009: vii) and an average household income well below the average for rural Bangladesh overall, especially among Adivasi (Barkat et al., 2009: v). The three districts of the CHT have among the lowest human development index rankings in Bangladesh (Rangamati, Bandarban, and Khagrachari ranked 54, 59, and 63 out of 64 districts in 2001) and some of the lowest adult literacy rates in the country (World Bank, 2005: 47, 54).

Political and social marginalization manifests itself clearly in the education system. In one survey, only 7.8% of respondents had completed primary education, and although 82% of children aged 5-16 were enrolled in primary or secondary schools, 65% of children were reported to have discontinued their education before completion of primary school (Barkat et al., 2009: ii, vii). Further, 25.3% of children in CHT have no primary school in their local community, 19.2% are "not welcome in school," and 2.6% do not understand the medium of instruction (Barkat et al., 2009: 118).

The CHT region is highly diverse, with fourteen Adivasi groups speaking distinct languages; the national language, Bangla, is also spoken, as well as a regional dialect, Chittagonian. Table 1 shows the key languages spoken in Bangladesh that are relevant to this study, along with the number of speakers of each nation-wide. The rest of the chapter focuses specifically on two Adivasi groups, Chakma and Tripura.

Table 1. Speakers of languages relevant to this study (Bangladesh-wide).
(Source: Lewis, 2009)

First language	Population (thousands)
Bangla	110,000
Chittagonian	13,000
Chakma	150
Tripura	85
Marma	150

AN L1-BASED EDUCATIONAL MODEL: THE SHISHUR KHAMATAYAN PROJECT

In this context of marginalization, school can represent an Adivasi child's first direct encounter with the dominant national language and ideology. In 2006, Save the Children and a local NGO, Zabarang Kalyan Samity, founded the Shishur Khamatayan or Children's Action through Education Project (SKP) to transform this potentially alienating experience. SKP aims to provide a child-friendly and culturally meaningful bilingual and bicultural preschool curriculum. It intends to affirm children's cultural experiences and linguistic skills and build linkages between communities and schools, while preparing children for the transition to national-language schooling. SKP currently provides 2026 Adivasi children in 100 preschools with activity-based learning in their L1, with preschools in Chakma, Tripura, and Marma[v] communities.

SKP's preschool curriculum is grounded in best practices for supporting children's holistic development and readiness for school, as well as the experiences of Save the Children and other international agencies with language learning. The SKP curriculum was developed collaboratively by project staff, community language committees, and teachers. Community members and language committees chose the scripts to be used for teaching (Chakma script in Chakma preschools, Marma script in Marma preschools, and Roman script in Tripura preschools). Through a series of workshops, members of the language committees, teachers, project staff, and illustrators developed 40 big books, 40 small books, 48 listening stories, and 288 picture cards based on local stories, rhymes, songs, and riddles collected by the community. These learning materials are combined with early childhood development (ECD) materials, following the model Save the Children uses throughout Bangladesh. Parents' meetings complement preschool activities by facilitating child development and educational support at home.

These activities are designed to support children's holistic development and school readiness. At the same time, special focus is given to supporting children's language development by using their L1 as the primary language of instruction and gradually introducing elements of Bangla, the national language. Preschools are divided into K1 centers for 4-year-olds and K2 centers for 5-year-olds about to enter primary school. This two-year pre-primary sequence begins completely in the

LI for all classroom activities, with the introduction of writing through primers and storybooks. In the final six months of the second year, children are introduced to oral Bangla through child-centered second-language teaching techniques, with the aim of preparing learners as much as possible to begin grade 1 in Bangla-medium primary schools.

THE STUDY

Between June and July 2010, the NGO Zabarang, Save the Children, and a research fellow (Gowri Vijayakumar, the first author of this chapter) conducted a school readiness analysis of SKP children in comparison with children from mainstream national language-based preschools in 3 *upazilas* (sub-districts) in Khagrachari district in the CHT. The comparative framework is one of the key contributions of the study. Comparison preschools have roughly similar curricula to SKP preschools;[vi] the main difference is in the use of language in the classroom. While teachers in the comparison preschools use the first languages of children to some extent, SKP preschools build their entire curriculum around Chakma and Tripura, including early literacy in L1 and local stories and culture. In comparison preschools, L1 is used mainly to clarify instructions or ask questions, but not in its written form and not in any of the teaching and learning materials. For simplicity, we refer to the preschools as "L1" or "comparison preschools"; the latter use mainly Bangla as the language of instruction.

RESEARCH METHODS

Design and Tools

The research design consisted of three main components: one-on-one assessment, classroom observation, and focus group discussions.

1. *The one-on-one assessment* of children consisted of 2 sub-components:
– A school readiness assessment containing 30 questions in 4 competency areas: communication, language, and literacy; problem solving, reasoning, and numeracy; writing/fine motor skills; and knowledge and understanding of the world. These competencies were developed drawing on Save the Children's existing school readiness assessment tools (MacKenzie & Young, 2009) and checked for consistency against the government's pre-primary education framework.
– A pre-literacy assessment including 10 questions on "concepts about print" (Dowd & Friedlander, 2009) and a letter recognition chart. Letter recognition charts in Tripura, Chakma, and Bangla, show all the letters in the alphabet in random order; the child is asked to identify them one by one.
2. Classroom observations sought to systematically assess the learning environment and teacher-student interaction. A data collector observed each classroom for one hour, recording "snapshots" of classroom activities every 10 minutes as well as ratings of various aspects of classroom learning environment.

3. Focus group discussions with parents aimed to understand and document their attitudes toward language, preschool, and primary education.

The six data collectors were familiar with the community and the SKP program, fluent in Chakma, Tripura, and Bangla, and experienced in working with children. The assessment tools were piloted in one preschool and revised in collaboration with data collectors. The language of instruction of the evaluation was an important feature of the assessment. The questions were designed to transcend language and focus on child development, so enumerators spoke to children in whichever language was most comfortable (usually L1). Where writing or numerals were involved, data collectors were instructed to use the written form of the language of instruction in the classroom, L1 in SKP classrooms and Bangla in comparison classrooms. This approach also ensured the assessment was child-friendly, allowing children to demonstrate their skills in a comfortable, encouraging environment rather than pushing them to take on unfamiliar material.

The study had several limitations. Random selection of the sample had to be conducted twice in the comparison preschools because of logistical difficulties. There were time limitations on data collector training, low attendance in preschool during the rainy season, and a required police presence when any foreign nationals were present that may have distracted data collectors and children. Because data collectors were associated with SKP, there is also some possibility of bias. Finally, to strengthen the analysis, we would have benefited from more detailed information on children's home background, and on how parents made decisions about where to enroll their children in preschool.

Ethical Considerations

The research protocol was given ethical exemption by the Committee for the Protection of Human Subjects at the University of California at Berkeley, and was subsequently approved by an independent expert ethical review in Dhaka.

SAMPLE

Out of 44 SKP K2 centers (for 5-year-olds), a sample of 10, 6 Chakma and 4 Tripura, was selected randomly using Stata statistical software and stratified to ensure geographic representation. For comparison, a similar stratified random sample of 10 pre-primary centers was selected from a list of 445 mainstream comparison centers. Additionally, 4 randomly selected comparison centers run by another NGO were included in the analysis out of a list of 25. The final sample included 75 children in comparison preschools and 92 children in L1-based SKP preschools, in 10 L1 and 14 comparison centers. Table 2 details the study participants by language of instruction and *upazila* (sub-district).

Table 2. Study participants (n=167) in L1 and comparison preschools in Khagrachari

	Dighinala	Panchari	Sadar	Total
Comparison	16	17	42	75
Tripura (L1)	0	0	33	33
Chakma (L1)	38	21	0	59
Total	54	38	75	167

The focus of the analysis was children preparing to enter primary school. SKP classrooms are age-specific, with 4-year-olds in K1 and 5-year-olds in K2; only K2 classes were included. Comparison preschools include children of multiple ages in a single classroom, so teachers were asked to identify eligible children aged 5-6.

Focus group participants were recruited by the organization responsible for the pre-primary center in the community. Parents and any interested community members were invited. Four focus group discussions were conducted with an average of 10 participants.

Sample Characteristics

The SKP children and comparison children all came from similar communities in Khagrachari district in the CHT. However, basic differences between the two groups could not be avoided. Most prominently, SKP preschools tend to be located in more remote areas, so socio-economic status (SES) in SKP preschools was significantly lower than in comparison preschools. In addition, SKP children were significantly younger than comparison children.[vii] There was no significant difference in gender composition between the two groups. SKP teachers had significantly fewer years of experience than comparison teachers and tended to have lower educational qualifications. Table 3 shows descriptive statistics on the study participants and teachers.[viii]

Children were asked three questions relating to their exposure to print material: whether they had books at home, whether they had newspapers at home, and whether they had had a story read to them in the last week (at home or at school). As would be expected given their lower SES, a significantly lower proportion of children in L1 preschools reported having books and newspapers at home than non-L1 children. However, there was no significant difference in having heard a story read in the last week, probably because data collectors included hearing a story at school as a "yes" answer.

Table 3. Percent boys and girls, mean age, mean SES^a and teacher experience in L1 and comparison preschools in Khagrachari (n=167)

	L1 (n=92)	Comparison (n=75)	Total (n=167)	Difference	T
Boys	52%	41%	47%		
Girls	48%	59%	53%	0.11	1.44
N	92	71	163		
Age	5.2	5.8	5.5	0.6	6.57*
Sd	0.4	0.7	0.6		
N	88	70	158		
Range	4.5-7	5-9	4.5-9		
SES**	4.2	6.4	5.2	2.1	5.18*
Sd	2.6	2.7	2.8		
N	92	72	164		
Range	0-12	0-11	0-12		
Teacher experience	2.9	5.5	3.8	2.7	6.41*
Sd	1.2	3.7	2.7		
N	92	53	145		
Range	0.2-4	1-14	0.2-14		

*p<0.001 ^{a}SES is on a scale of 0-12, based on a list of self-reported home assets.

FINDINGS

One-on-One Assessments

On average, L1 children performed significantly better on the school readiness assessment and on the concepts about print assessment but not on letter recognition (Table 4). Because the L1 and comparison groups varied significantly on several demographic indicators, we report raw as well as adjusted mean scores that control for age, gender, SES, teacher experience, and exposure to reading. While adjusting the means does not change the overall trends, it does result in an increased gap between L1 and comparison children in school readiness and concepts about print and a smaller gap in letter recognition. While comparison children achieved higher raw scores on letter recognition than their L1 counterparts, the difference was not statistically significant when controlling for background variables. Analysis of the school readiness assessment by competency area shows that SKP children had the strongest advantage in the area of communication, language and literacy.

Table 4. Raw and adjusted[a] mean assessment scores (%) in L1 and comparison classrooms (n=167)

	L1 (raw) (n=92)	Comparison (raw) (n=75)	L1 (adjusted)[a] (n=92)	Comparison (adjusted)[a] (n=75)
School readiness	.89 (26.7/30)	.79 (23.7/30)	.91 (27.2/30)	.77 (23.0/30)
Writing/fine motor skills	.84 (2.5/3)	.87 (2.6/3)	.85 (2.6/3)	.85 (2.6/3)
Problem solving, reasoning and numeracy	.89 (14.2/16)	.85 (13.6/16)	.91 (14.5/16)	.83 (13.2/16)
Communication, language and literacy	.96 (5.8/6)	.70 (4.2/6)	.97 (5.8/6)	.69 (4.1/6)
Knowledge and understanding of the world	.84 (4.2/5)	.65 (3.3/5)	.87 (4.4/5)	.62 (3.1/5)
Concepts about print	.85 (8.5/10)	.80 (8.0/10)	.87 (8.7/10)	.77 (7.7/10)
Letter recognition[b]	0.66	0.77	0.68	0.74

[a]Controlling for gender, age, SES, teacher experience, and exposure to reading. [b]Letter recognition scores indicate percent of letters recognized. [c]Percentage scores are followed by (points scored/total points possible).

The only area in which SKP children did not significantly outperform their peers was letter recognition. However, disaggregating results by language of instruction shows that children in Chakma-medium preschools performed lowest on letter recognition (recognizing, on average, 57% of letters, or 60% when adjusted for background variables) while children in Tripura-medium preschools performed the best (recognizing, on average, 83% of letters, or 88% when adjusting for background variables. Comparison children recognized 77%, or 73% adjusting for background variables). This might be explained by the fact that Chakma uses a script that is largely absent from children's print environment and unfamiliar to most community members, while Tripura uses Roman script, which is more visible in children's day-to-day surroundings.

Analyzing Chakma- and Tripura-medium preschools separately yields important insights about children's overall performance. Both Chakma- and Tripura-medium preschools performed significantly better than comparison preschools on the school readiness assessment, but Tripura-medium preschools performed the best. Children attending Tripura-medium preschools tended, on average, to score 6.2 points higher (p<0.001) on the school readiness assessment (out of 30 points) than

143

children in comparison preschools, controlling for all other variables, while attending a Chakma-medium preschool was associated with scoring 3.6 points higher (p<0.001).[ix] Attending a Tripura-medium preschool was also significantly associated with higher scores on concepts about print (out of 10 points) (ß=2.8, p<0.001). In letter recognition, Tripura-medium preschool children on average scored 20 percentage points higher than their counterparts (ß=0.20, p<0.05) controlling for all other variables. Attending a Chakma-medium preschool was not significantly associated with performance on letter recognition or concepts about print.

Attending an L1 preschool was the strongest predictor of performance on all 3 assessment components. Other variables were also significantly associated with performance. On average, older children tended to perform significantly better in all areas (school readiness: ß =1.4, p<0.01, concepts about print: ß=0.5, p<0.05, letter recognition: ß=0.1, p<0.05). Being a girl was associated with a significantly higher score on school readiness (ß=1.7, p<0.01), though not on the other two components. Having heard a story in the last week was significantly associated with concepts about print (ß=0.9, p<0.01) and letter recognition (ß=0.1, p<0.05), though having books or newspapers at home was not. SES and teacher experience were not significantly associated with scores in any of the three assessment areas.[x]

After each one-on-one assessment, data collectors recorded subjective observations about the child's performance during the assessment. Data collectors noticed that children in L1 preschools were more confident attempting questions even when they did not know the answers, while comparison children tended to remain silent.

Classroom Observations

Two data collectors, both familiar with the community and the SKP program, were assigned to observe classrooms for a period of one hour; each data collector observed 10 classrooms, 5 L1 and 5 comparison classrooms, recording "snapshot" observations and rating the classroom on several indicators. Because of inconsistency between data collectors, here we report "snapshot" results from only one data collector and the rating scale for both.

Snapshot Observations. The snapshot tool provides a list of activities (teacher's activities and children's activities), languages used (teacher's language and children's language), and levels of visible child engagement.[xi] Data collectors checked off applicable activities, languages and visible child engagement levels 5 times, at 10-minute intervals for 50 minutes. Across 10 classrooms, this process resulted in 50 data points documenting teacher's activities, children's activities, languages used, and children's engagement.

The snapshot results confirm that L1 classrooms use the first language more than comparison classrooms despite the fact that many comparison preschool teachers describe themselves as providing instruction in children's first language.

Because the materials used in comparison classrooms are in Bangla, teachers are obliged to speak in Bangla when working with those materials, even if they use the first language at other times. In comparison classrooms, teachers were observed to be speaking Bangla about 71% of the time, as opposed to 28% of the time in L1 classrooms.

Despite the difference in languages used, the types of activities conducted in both L1 and comparison classrooms are roughly similar. However, children in L1 classrooms spent more time singing, saying rhymes, or dancing than their counterparts. Children in L1 classrooms spent a smaller proportion of their time doing silent exercises and, unlike their counterparts, no time silently listening to the teacher. Data collectors noted that children in L1 classrooms were more vocal and participatory than children in comparison classrooms. Data collectors also noted children's visible engagement levels, based on body language, participation (for example, joining the class in singing a song), or eye contact, as part of the snapshot observation. In both L1 and comparison classrooms, engagement levels seem to dip in the middle of class, and are highest at the beginning and end of the class period. However, at all points during the class period, children were more visibly engaged in L1 classrooms than in comparison classrooms (Table 5).

Table 5. Visible levels of engagement in 5 L1 and 5 comparison classrooms at 5 points in time (% of classrooms)

	Time 1	Time 2	Time 3	Time 4	Time 5
L1					
All children visibly engaged	.60 (3/5)	.40 (2/5)	.60 (3/5)	.80 (4/5)	.80 (4/5)
Most children visibly engaged	.40 (2/5)	.40 (2/5)	.40 (2/5)	.20 (1/5)	.20 (1/5)
Half of children visibly engaged	0	.20 (1/5)	0	0	0
Most children visibly not engaged	0	0	0	0	0
Comparison					
All children visibly engaged	.40 (2/5)	.25 (1/4)	0	.40 (2/5)	0
Most children visibly engaged	.60 (3/5)	.25 (1/4)	.40 (2/5)	.40 (2/5)	.75 (3/4)
Half of children visibly engaged	0	.50 (2/4)	.40 (2/5)	.20 (1/5)	.25 (1/4)
Most children visibly not engaged	0	0	.20 (1/5)	0	0

Rating Scale. Data collectors also rated classrooms on materials displayed in the classroom, learning environment, and teaching tools used on a scale of 1 to 4. As Table 6 shows, L1 classrooms had more participatory learning environments, involved more representation of culture in the classroom, displayed more child-made materials, and employed a greater variety of teaching tools.

Table 6. Rating scales of L1 and comparison classroom environments
(% of classrooms) (n=20)

	L1	Comparison
Materials made by children		
No materials	.10	.30
Some materials, but most not made by children	.30	.70
Children work makes up half the work displayed	.50	0
Children's work makes up most of the work displayed	.10	0
Language of materials		
Most of the materials displayed are in Bangla	.10	1
Half of the materials are in local language and half in Bangla	.60	0
Most materials are in local language	.30	0
Culture in the classroom		
Some materials are displayed but nothing to represent the children's culture	.10	.70
Some materials and decorations represent the children's culture	.20	.20
There are a variety of materials and activities that represent the children's culture	.70	0
Learning atmosphere		
Teacher creates a learning atmosphere where children are bored and uninterested in learning	0	.40
Teacher creates a learning atmosphere where most of children are enthusiastically involved in learning	.80	.50
Teacher creates a learning atmosphere that is interesting, friendly, and cheerful and all learners are enthusiastically involved	.20	.10
Teaching tools		
Teacher uses only the textbook, students' chalkboard, and the blackboard	.20	.70
Teacher uses one additional material apart from the textbook, slate, and blackboard	.20	.20
Teacher uses some materials that support learning and are relevant to learners	.40	.10
Teacher uses a variety of materials (including locally made items) that support learning	.20	0

Focus Group Discussions

Focus group discussions were held with four communities – two communities in which Save the Children and Zabarang run SKP Chakma- or Tripura-medium preschools, one community with a government-run comparison preschool, and one community with an NGO-run comparison preschool. An average of ten parents and community members participated in each discussion, which was facilitated by two Zabarang staff members in Chakma or Tripura. Discussions ranged from specific feedback about the preschool in the community, including its physical structure, to opinions about Adivasi language and culture.

When the discussion moved to language learning and culture, all four groups spoke of the importance of speaking Bangla well in order to function confidently and effectively outside of the village and get jobs, as well as their value for their first language and, in some cases, their concern that it was being lost. At the same time, in all groups, opinions varied widely as to the tradeoffs between learning in first language and learning in Bangla, with some participants declaring that Bangla was the national language and first language need not be studied at all, and others maintaining that the first language should be taught up to the college and university level.

Despite these similarities, some differences did emerge between the two groups. Most relevant to the research questions of this study, parents in comparison communities tended to feel less able to support their children's learning in preschool than parents in communities with L1-based preschools. In communities with comparison preschools, parents tended to speak of their children's success *despite* the lack of support from parents. If they did support their children, it was by asking older siblings to help, hiring tutors, or giving children story cards issued by the preschool teacher. In communities with L1-based preschools, by contrast, parents tended to say that they were able to support their children's learning by speaking to them, telling them stories, and asking them questions, even if they did not know how to read themselves. This difference reflects evidence from around the world that suggests parents are better able to support children's learning and development when it occurs in the first language (Ball 2010). SKP's parenting sessions and emphasis on locally generated learning materials may also contribute to parents' ability to participate in children's learning. Differences among curricular models other than language also emerged in the discussions. SKP parents tended to speak of the preschool more in terms of play and social interaction ("our children used to play alone, and now they play together"), while parents in comparison preschool communities focused more on study and learning ("our children used to play all the time, and now they study").

When asked about language in the classroom, participants in both groups felt that it would be good to learn their first language in school, though not at the expense of learning Bangla. However, while participants in comparison preschool communities spoke more of the functional utility of learning languages – Bangla to get jobs, first language to preserve culture – participants in SKP communities spoke more of the way the use of first language allowed for greater understanding in the classroom.

Several community members pointed to the transition to primary school as a key challenge in their communities. Participants in comparison preschool communities spoke more of their confidence that children would enter primary school already familiar with the Bangla skills that were expected of them in the government school system. This confidence was less evident in the L1-based preschool communities, who seemed to perceive a contrast between preschool and primary school. One parent in an L1-based preschool community told us that his son had entered primary school but was so scared of the teacher there that he had dropped out and now wanted to attend the L1-based preschool again. An important question emerges from this child's experience: if SKP provides children with a more play-oriented, culturally relevant, L1-based curriculum than other preschools, does it simply delay an eventual difficult encounter with the rote-based environment of Bangla-medium primary schools?

CONCLUSIONS

This study adds to the growing evidence that L1-based preschools offer children a significant advantage at the early childhood level. Children learning in an L1 setting had better quantitative, communicative, and environmental skills than their peers. They outperformed their peers on both school readiness and concepts about print, and – within the school readiness assessment – on every competency area except writing. The largest difference between L1 and comparison children was in the competency area of communication, language and literacy. These advantages emerge despite the fact that children in the L1-based preschools tended to have significantly fewer economic assets, less access to reading materials at home, and teachers with significantly fewer years of experience.

In addition to the better skills that children in L1-based preschools developed, they developed these skills in environments that involved more child engagement and participation and more integration of local culture. Classroom observation data show that, while activities appeared to be roughly similar in both L1 and comparison classrooms, teachers in L1 classrooms used more of the children's first language in the classroom. Related to this difference, we suggest, was the higher level of visible child engagement in L1 classrooms and a more friendly and participatory learning environment. L1 classrooms also incorporated children's cultural backgrounds into the classroom more often.

One key question emerging from this chapter is the following: how should an L1-based bilingual preschool program be measured? This pilot evaluation process offers important lessons. Quantitative measures of performance are increasingly popular in a range of low-income educational settings, and this study shows children in a rights-based educational program performing very well on such measures. Yet many of the positive results of such programs are not captured in quantitative indicators. We used a mixture of qualitative and quantitative measures to obtain a more fine-grained analysis of the preschools under study, paying attention both to the educational process and to learning outcomes. The classroom observation tool, in particular, attempts to quantify features of the classroom environment usually measured qualitatively, but also includes room for enumerators to complement quantitative data with structured and unstructured qualitative observations. This approach was not only useful from an evaluation perspective, but also made the process more meaningful for data collectors and program staff.

The evaluation also required careful attention to issues specific to providing education in an Adivasi context. Using mainstream measures – such as the Bangladesh government's school readiness competency that children must be able to sing the national anthem in Bangla by primary school – is an effective way to establish the effectiveness of an alternative model within the existing curricular framework. However, alternative measures must also be used to attempt to capture the value of the curriculum outside of this dominant framework. For example, our school readiness assessment also asked children to sing a song in their first language – a competency most of the children in both L1 and comparison pre-schools were able to demonstrate. We also evaluated measures such as the presence of local culture in the classroom. These measures helped the evaluation to affirm the skills and knowledge Adivasi children bring with them to the classroom – skills that national-language classrooms may simply ignore.

The areas in which L1 children did not uniformly outperform their peers were letter recognition and writing and fine motor skills, where scores were essentially indistinguishable. While Tripura children performed the best on letter recognition tasks, Chakma children showed the lowest performance. Tripura uses Roman script, which is available in the print environment and familiar to some parents and community members, while Chakma uses a unique script. Indeed, not only is Chakma script not visible in the print environment, but many of the children's parents themselves are not familiar with it. This difference suggests that, while the benefits of oral L1 instruction at home are evident, introducing written L1 scripts at the preschool level without support outside of the classroom may disadvantage children. There may also be other historical or socio-economic differences between the preschools in these two communities that our study could not capture.

The areas in which SKP children showed the lowest performance show some cause for concern for L1-based preschool education. At the time of research, primary schools in the CHT continue to follow a rote-based Bangla-medium curriculum. This system does not reward students with richer communicative or imaginative skills or a deeper understanding of quantitative reasoning. In fact, letter recognition and copying are likely to be emphasized at the primary level. Because our evaluation chose to focus on child development and used the language of the child's choice for evaluation, we still know little about SKP children's proficiency with Bangla. As primary schools in the area are conducted fully in Bangla, this gap must be addressed, or L1-based programs risk further disadvantaging Adivasi children when they enter primary school.

This challenge facing early childhood L1-based bilingual programming leads to a second key question: to what extent does an L1-based preschool model improve a child's long-term prospects if the primary school system is rigidly based in the national language? Existing research indicates that a structured bilingual model of several years is required for children to reap the full benefits of L1-based learning (Ball, 2010). In this context, SKP's two-year preschool model based in L1, with six months of introduction to the national language before primary school, seems inadequate to produce longer term advantages in learning outcomes within the currently existing primary school curriculum.

The importance of attention to primary school for Adivasi children in the CHT is clear in some survey data. These data indicate that preschool coverage in the area is relatively high compared to the rest of Bangladesh (38.5% of children in the study district of Khagrachari attend preschool, compared to the national average of 22.9%), while net primary school attendance is below average (79.4% in Khagrachari compared to the national average of 81.3%) (UNICEF, 2010: 87). Aside from being taught in the national language, Bangla, the government primary curriculum is grounded in the national culture and religion – for example, children receive Muslim holidays, not Hindu or Buddhist holidays they celebrate, off from school. Addressing these challenges requires more than NGO-provided preschools with bilingual curricula. Effectively addressing language issues in the CHT demands an approach that looks beyond the preschool classroom, and pays attention to the primary school environment children will enter once they leave preschool.

In the CHT, paying attention to the primary school environment also demands recognizing the fundamental link between rigid national language curricula and the deep-rooted political and social marginalization of Adivasi people in many spheres of life. In the CHT, the 1997 peace treaty that ended decades of violence between the government and Adivasi militant groups included a provision for primary education in the first language, and Bangladesh's 2010 National Education Policy also makes mention of the need to "facilitate" L1 instruction in primary school (Ministry of Education, 2010: 5). These commitments must now be translated into practice. Efforts to improve education access and quality for Adivasi children must address political and social conditions while simultaneously developing the most effective school- and classroom-based teaching and learning strategies.

These questions, of course, do not diminish the finding that children emerging from an L1-based learning environment, in this study, are in a better developmental position to succeed in school – as active, enthusiastic participants with a love of learning – than children who transition from a non-L1 preschool environment. The question is how the advantages of an L1-based curriculum can be translated into long-term academic success that can lead to broader social and political inclusion.

NOTES

[i] Many people made this study possible. The authors would especially like to thank Habibur Rahman, Margarita Clark, Mathura Tripura, Shubha Ranjan Tripura, Dayananda Tripura, Pongkaj Tripura, Gitika Tripura, Karandra Tripura, Sabina Tripura, Sunil Kanti Tripura, Ripon Tripura, Pramod Bikash Tripura, Jagadish Tripura and Amy Jo Dowd.

[ii] In this chapter, the term "Adivasi" will be used to refer to the Chakma and Tripura communities with whom this study was completed. Adivasi (literally meaning "first inhabitant") is used throughout South Asia to refer to a diverse set of groups variously referred to as "scheduled tribes," "indigenous groups," or "ethnolinguistic minorities" (Minority Rights Group International, 2008). We adopt the term "Adivasi" because communities themselves identify this way (Durnnian, 2007).

[iii] In this chapter, we use the term "national language" rather than "L2" to describe the preschools in this study, because Bangla, the national language, may or may not be a child's second language. For example, Tripura children may learn Chakma, a widely spoken language of wider communication in the CHT, or Chittagonian, a regional dialect of Bangla, before they learn the official version of Bangla used in school.

[iv] Ball (2010: 11) defines the "early years" as "up to about age 7"; here, because of the nature of the program under study, we focus on children aged 4-5.

[v] Marma preschools were not included in this study because of SKP's low number of Marma preschools at the time.

[vi] A more detailed comparative analysis of the curricula is planned that will extend this analysis.

[vii] Age was difficult to verify, especially in the multi-grade classrooms studied. Data collectors asked children their ages and cross-checked them with teachers, but some level of error is to be expected.

[viii] Missing data were generally minimal. Missing data were replaced with mean values within each organization – SKP, mainstream comparison preschools, and the other NGO.

[ix] These results are based on OLS regression results that are not shown here in full. Background variables, in addition to age, gender, SES, exposure to reading, and teacher experience, also included a dummy variable for the organization running the comparison preschool (there were two types of comparison preschool) and dummy variables for two of the data collectors whose results varied from the others. R^2 values were 0.37 for the regression with school readiness as the outcome variable, 0.26 for concepts about print, and 0.31 for letter recognition. Contact the first author for full data.

[x] Additional variables included in the regression are not reported in the text. Attending a preschool run by the smaller NGO was associated with significantly higher scores on letter recognition (ß=0.2, p<0.05). Two data collectors returned lower scores than their counterparts and we thus included dummy variables for them in our final regression. Data collector E was significantly associated with lower scores on school readiness (ß=-2.5, p<0.001) and letter recognition (ß=-0.1, p<0.05) and data collector F was significantly associated with lower scores on the same two areas (school readiness: ß=-2.5, p<0.05, letter recognition: ß=-0.2, p<0.01).

[xi] Data collectors were instructed to count the number of children *visibly* engaged in classroom activity. Visible engagement was defined quite broadly: during a group song and dance, a child not singing and sitting on the floor would be considered not engaged, for example. The measure was intended to give a very basic sense of how involved children were in classroom activities.

REFERENCES

Ball, Jessica (2010). *Enhancing learning of children from diverse language backgrounds: Mother-tongue-based bilingual or multilingual education in the early years.* Paris: UNESCO.

Bangladesh Bureau of Statistics (2011). *Population and Housing Census 2011: Preliminary results.*

Barkat, Abul, Halim, Sadeka, Poddar, Avijit, Badiuzzaman, Md., Osman, Asmar, Khan, Shahnewaz Md., Rahman, Matiur, et al. (2009). *Socio-economic baseline survey of Chittagong Hill Tracts.* Dhaka, Bangladesh: Chittagong Hill Tracts Development Facility.

Dowd, Amy Jo, & Friedlander, Elliott (2009). *Bangladesh Program: Emergent and early grades reading assessment validation study results.* Draft version. Save the Children USA.

Durnnian, Terry (2007). *Mother language first.* Dhaka: Save the Children.

Lewis, Paul (Ed.) (2009). *Ethnologue: Languages of the world* (16th ed.). Dallas, TX: SIL International.

MacKenzie, Pamela, & Young, Catherine (2009). *Multilingual education curriculum, pre-primary 1, basic education - Chittagong Hill Tracts.* Dhaka: Save the Children.

Ministry of Education (2010). *National Education Policy 2010.* Dhaka: Government of the People's Republic of Bangladesh.

Minority Rights Group International (2008). *World directory of minorities and Indigenous peoples – Bangladesh: Adivasis*. (http://www.unhcr.org/refworld/docid/49749d5841.html)

UNDP (2010). *The real wealth of nations: Pathways to human development*. New York, NY: UNDP.

UNICEF (2010). *Multiple Indicator Cluster Survey 2009, Progotir Pathey, Volume I: Technical report*. Dhaka: Bangladesh Bureau of Statistics and UNICEF.

World Bank (2005). *Targeting resources for the poor in Bangladesh*. Bangladesh Development Series. Dhaka: World Bank Office, South Asia Human Development Unit.

Gowri Vijayakumar
University of California, Berkeley, USA

Elizabeth Pearce
Save the Children, Bangladesh

Meherun Nahar
Save the Children, Bangladesh

JANELLE M. JOHNSON

8. TEACHERS AS AGENTS OF CHANGE WITHIN INDIGENOUS EDUCATION PROGRAMS IN GUATEMALA AND MEXICO

Examining Some Outcomes of Cross-Border Professional Development

ABSTRACT

Ja'i a'tel ini ja' ya yak ta na'el jun ilaw ta Guatemala sok ta Mexico. Ban la yich ilel te me beenem te bin chajpambil yu'un tej chapetik sakil winik antsetik yu'un Estados unidos te yakalik ta sp'ijubtesel jp'ijubteswanejetike. Sjok'oyel ¿bin ut'il a te jnopojeletik te ayik ta k'ubel nojptesel yu'un spamal balumilal yaxa tuunuk yu'uniok k'alal ya sujtik ta slumalik? Te bin ut'il la yich'ilel te a'tele la yich'tuuntesel jamal sjok'oyel, jukaw ta k'op, lok'ombail, stsajtayel sok tsibabil junetik, son nish sk'eluyel te a'tel. Ya stuuntes lekil sp'ijilal lumetik te tsibablilikixe. Yas skoltay ta sle'el bin ut'il yas slok'es ta mosoinel te lumetik sok nix yak'el ta na'el spijsil ta chajp chapetik te yak jelbellik te snael lekilale. Laj pas osh gojk' te jp'ijubteswanejetik j-a'tel-lekubtesguanejetik: yu'un máyuk tak'in, yuun p'ijutesteswanej ta cha'chajp k'op ta bayal ta chajp sp'ijilal lumetik sok nish euk te bin snael yuunik te bin ut'il ya xbeen te kuxlejalil. (*Translated to Tzeltal de Ocosingo [tzb], a language of Mexico, by Tomas Gómez Rodríguez.*)

This study is part of a qualitative research dissertation undertaken in Guatemala and Mexico. It examines the experiences and attitudes of teachers who participated in a US-based organization's efforts to provide transnational professional development for teachers. The study asks: How do participants in cross-border professional development make sense of their experiences when they return to their classrooms and communities? The research methods include open-ended questionnaires, interviews, document analysis, and participant observation within a critical sociocultural framework. The goals of the study are to contribute to the decolonization of society and academia, as well as to inform various types of organizations that carry out transnational educational exchanges. Here teachers are grouped into three categories of agents of change: in economic marginalization, in bilingual intercultural pedagogy, and in combating their own prejudices and stereotypes.

C. Benson and K. Kosonen (eds.), Language Issues in Comparative Education, 153–170.

INTRODUCTION

This chapter examines the experiences and attitudes of teachers in Mexico and Guatemala after participating in a USA-based capacity building program designed primarily for teachers in Indigenous communities. I analyze teachers as agents of change within the process I call *cross-border professional development.* "Cross-border" is a term employed by UNESCO (2005) and OECD (2007) to describe international cooperative educational projects and is seen by Knight (2007) as synonymous with "transnational," "borderless," and "offshore" education. The teachers described in this chapter participated in a year-long scholarship program called CASS (Cooperative Association of States for Scholarships) conducted by Georgetown University and USAID (United States Agency for International Development) and are henceforth referred to as "*exbecarios*," or former scholarship recipients who have returned to their communities.

One principal focus of the research is to understand how these exbecarios negotiate their roles as agents of change when they return to their classrooms and communities after participating in cross-border capacity-building. Though the exbecarios may work in community contexts where "practice is still enacted within idiosyncratic bases and local rules, impermeable by the official ideology of education modernization" (Mena, Muñoz & Ruiz, 2000: 51), my findings reveal that many exbecarios are able to carve out spaces for innovation, sometimes based on what they have learned and sometimes grounded in the empowerment gained through participation in the cross-border process (Cummins, 2000). Following the scholarly work of authors such as Luykx (1999a) and Valdiviezo (2009) on Indigenous education in Bolivia and Peru respectively, I examine how teachers' beliefs and practices "not only reproduce, but also challenge and transform government policy" (Valdiviezo, 2009: 62). Such teachers work to decolonize their classrooms, their communities, and even their own ways of thinking through a process of meaning-making (Johnson, 2011). I describe the exbecarios in three overlapping categories of teachers as agents of change: in recognizing and combating economic marginalization; in implementing authentic bilingual pedagogies; and in reflecting upon their own identities. Each of these activities addresses an important facet of the complex contexts in which Indigenous education takes place, helping us to rethink and reframe the meaning of innovation.

In this chapter I focus on both Indigenous and non-Indigenous exbecarios who act to support and/or revitalize Indigenous language and culture in their classrooms. Considering the histories and contexts where these teachers work, i.e. conventional educational systems that subjugate Indigenous identities, this in itself is a transformative act of resistance from within. I begin with an overview of the language-in-education contexts in Guatemala and Mexico, including relevant national language policies as well as shifts in the contemporary models of schooling. Then I situate the study in the breadth of definitions of teachers acting as agents of change offered by the literature. Next I describe the research settings and the methods utilized. Finally, I present my own definition of teachers acting as agents of change, supported with specific examples of *exbecario* practices that support Indigenous languages in schools.

LANGUAGE-IN-EDUCATION CONTEXTS IN GUATEMALA AND MEXICO

Mexico and Guatemala provide many examples of the ways Indigenous identity has been defined and redefined. In Guatemala, where close to half of the population of approximately 13 million identifies as Indigenous, Indigeneity is attributed by a combination of self-identification, language, dress and customs. Even though language shift to Spanish has already occurred in some urban communities, residents continue to identify strongly as Indigenous through maintenance of other cultural traits (Beckett & Pebley, 2003; Field, 2002). In Mexico, where only 6.7% of Mexico's 112 million people are identified as speaking an Indigenous language (INEGI, 2010), "the most important variable in identifying ethnicity and ethnic group is language" (Hidalgo, 2006: 97). In both countries, as in other parts of the world, identification as Indigenous is socially stigmatized (Field, 2002; Rockwell, 2002) and closely associated with poverty (Hidalgo, 2006). Anti-Indigenous attitudes have clear implications for ongoing language shift as assimilative and economic pressures cause families to focus on languages of wider communication (Brown, 1998; Montejo, 2005) and/or to migrate out of Indigenous communities (Garzon, 1998).

Whether or not language is an identifier, it is still an important characteristic of many Indigenous peoples in both countries, and the right to education in their own languages has been a contentious issue. Beginning in the 1980s, the most widely utilized model of schooling for Indigenous students in Latin America – *if* they have access to programs in their own languages – is called *bilingual intercultural education*.

Bilingual Intercultural Education

Advocates for bilingual intercultural education (*educación intercultural bilingüe*, EIB) describe the ways it can potentially draw on learners' own cultures and simultaneously "strengthen identity by drawing on ideas from other cultures" (Gow, 2008: 143; also see Aikman, 1997), which would call for an approach generated by Indigenous communities themselves. Unfortunately, because of the ways EIB programs have been implemented, they have been rightly criticized as top-down impositions by governments supported by large international development organizations (Benson, 2004; Gasché, 2010; González, 2009) – impositions that fail to disrupt existing linguistic hierarchies favoring dominant languages (Freeland, 2003; Luykx, 1999b). Though EIB has been promoted rather widely in recent years, in practice most models can be categorized as subtractive and transitional, replacing the students' L1 with the dominant language after the first three grades (Baker, 2001; Barnach-Calbó, 1997; López, 2008). Some approaches are even less empowering for Indigenous languages; for example, one teacher in Oaxaca, Mexico told me that at his "bilingual intercultural" school they are "lucky" because students are now allowed to speak their own language during recess, but that their language is never used for academic instruction (interview September 10, 2010). There are notable cases in which bilingual intercultural schools can be spaces of Indigenous linguistic and cultural vitality, as documented in Bolivia, Peru, Mexico, and Ecuador (see Aikman, 1997; Delany-Barmann, 2009; Gasché, 2010; King, 1997). Despite differences in the models and practices of EIB across Latin America, there is general agreement in the literature that due to ongoing economic, social, and political marginalization of the Indigenous communities EIB serves, it is an important site of political struggle (Howard, 2009; Lopez, 2008). This is true in Guatemala, for example, where Mayan organizations like Kaqchikel Moloj (an organization of Kaqchikel Indigenous people) support the implementation of EIB in their communities (2008; also see González, 2009; López, 2009).

The year 2003 saw crucial language legislation passed in both Guatemala and Mexico. Guatemala passed the Ley de Idiomas Nacionales [Law of National Languages] which, while naming Spanish as the country's official language, also recognized Guatemala's Indigenous languages for the first time. Similarly, Mexico passed the Ley General de Derechos Lingüísticos de los Pueblos Indígenas [General Law on Linguistic Rights of the Indigenous Peoples] (Hidalgo, 2006). Both contexts complicate understandings of *lengua materna*, which can be literally translated as "mother tongue" but is not necessarily equivalent to the L1 concept commonly utilized in North American sociolinguistics. As I found in my study (Johnson, 2011), some children raised by mothers speaking Indigenous languages may not speak or claim to speak an Indigenous language due to culturally-based racism and/or rapid language shift. One teacher told me that her students cannot speak well "*porque no tienen una lengua materna* [because they have no mother tongue]" meaning that while they came from Indigenous families, their parents attempted to raise them speaking only Spanish (interview, August 19, 2010).

Although schools supposedly use a model of EIB, the teachers in my study said that they and their colleagues are professionally underprepared to implement the model, and in addition are generally undersupplied with materials and may face serious opposition by community members. Further, teachers' oral skills in their Indigenous languages are typically far beyond their literacy skills, due to a combination of oral tradition and lack of formal schooling in Indigenous languages until very recently. This gap is problematic in both countries, where teaching EIB requires oral and written proficiency in Spanish, the regional Indigenous language, *and* English. The following sections review the evolution of language-in-education policies of Guatemala and Mexico up to present.

Guatemala

Small-scale local efforts at bilingual education for Indigenous students occurred throughout Guatemala during the 20th century, but leading directly up to current policy was a relatively large scale pilot project begun with USAID support in 1980. Materials and curriculum for the four most widely spoken Mayan languages –

Mam, Kaqchikel, K'iche', and Q'eqchi, representing more than 80% of Guatemala's Mayan language speakers – were produced and implemented in ten schools. USAID evaluators viewed the programs as successful in terms of lowering drop-out rates and improving results on Spanish language reading assessments (Richards & Richards, 1997). Civil war violence increased during the early 1980s, however, and the murder or disappearance of some of the program's senior Mayan technicians, teachers and bilingual promoters complicated its implementation (ibid). The Constitution ratified in 1985 marked the first time in the country's history that the pluralistic nature of the society was legally recognized, though no specific peoples were named (Barnach-Calbó, 1997; Richards & Richards 1997). Bilingual education for rural Spanish-Mayan language education was established and administered by PRONEBI (Programa Nacional de Educación Bilingüe/ National Bilingual Education Program). PRONEBI continued to expand throughout the 1990s, offering EIB at schools in larger geographic areas and developing additional Mayan languages. The final Peace Accords signed in 1996 officially ended the 36-year civil war during which more than 200,000 people – mostly Maya – were killed and/or disappeared. Several of the Peace Accords specifically addressed ethnicity, language, and identity, and peoples' right to education, such as the Acuerdo de Identidad y Derechos de los Pueblos Indígenas/ Accord on Identity and Rights of Indigenous Peoples signed in 1995. This accord recognized Guatemala's Indigenous peoples and called for increased access to bilingual education (Bastos, 2010).

Mexico

In 1984 Mexico's National Bilingual Education manual described bilingual schooling as a means of "*increasing the cultural level* of the Indigenous community" (SEP: 4, emphasis added) through the "promotion of community involvement in civic and sociocultural activities" (ibid.: 17). This illustrates the State's deficit view of Indigenous peoples as "traditional" and lacking in culture, limiting their official economic and civic participation. The Presidency of Salinas de Gortari from 1988-1994 emphasized modernization, dismantling the welfare state and centralizing norms and assessment for Indigenous education (Mena, Muñoz, & Ruiz, 2000; Street, 2001). Accommodating growing national and international pressures in the 1990s to address the needs of Indigenous peoples, Mexico adopted a neo-Indigenous discourse (González, 2009). Constitutional reforms passed in 1992 in response to ongoing cultural and political struggles defined Mexico as pluricultural (SEP, 2004); these reforms simultaneously initiated the process of decentralization by creating an Institute of Education in each Mexican state (Martin, 2009; Street, 2001). Within this decentralized system known as DGEI (Dirección General de Educación Indígena/General Direction of Indigenous Education) Educación Indígena/Indigenous Education or "EI" departments were created (Hernandez & Layton, 2006). The Larrainzar Accords of 1996 marked the first official recognition of pluriethnic Indigenous regions through negotiations with the EZLN (Zapatista National Liberation Army) (Barnach-Calbó,

1997). A total of 68 Indigenous languages are now officially recognized in contemporary Mexico, and the Instituto Nacional de Lenguas Indígenas/National Institute of Indigenous Languages recommends that linguistic varieties – referred to as *variantes* – be treated as distinct languages for provision of educational and other social services (INALI, 2010). While this should promote appropriate teacher placement, the hiring of teachers whose *variante* corresponds with that of the community is complicated by teachers' unions and teachers' rights to be placed in so-called preferred schools close to urban centers (Santibáñez, 2008). Another challenge is that DGEI concentrates on areas of extreme poverty, "focusing on schools located in the towns with a low index of human development and high social marginalization" (DGEI, 2008). Such difficult socioeconomic conditions add further complexities to the linguistic and cultural challenges in the provision of relevant education for Indigenous students. Transformation of such contexts requires agents of change, a concept reviewed in the next section.

AGENTS OF CHANGE IN THE LITERATURE

In contexts like the socially and economically marginalized regions of Guatemala and Mexico, teachers have played a key role as agents of change, but not always on behalf of Indigenous people. Largely due to processes of teacher education and assimilationist attitudes, teachers have often served a colonizing role (Fitzsimons & Smith, 2000; Luykx, 1999a). Another critique targets the "civilizing" role of education and educators; for example, Rosaldo (1989: 70) refers to agents of change in developing contexts as the bringers of a "civilizing process [that] destabilizes forms of life" when the values imposed in schools are distant from those of the community. The Western/Northern nature of schooling as a tool of colonization and development is similarly described by Leach (1994); she describes European teachers acting as agents of change during colonization through "the subject matter being taught (the formal or overt curriculum) and through the norms and values contained within that subject matter (the hidden curriculum)" (ibid: 218). These analyses demonstrate how teachers have served a colonizing function as agents of change, where "change" implies rejection of Indigenous language and culture and assimilation to the dominant one.

However, teachers may also become agents of change for social justice (Cummins, 2000; Zeichner & Flessner, 2009). In Guatemala, those who act politically to counter the hegemony of the elite oligarchy are referred to as agents of change by Sánchez (2008: 137). In Mexico, Hidalgo (2006: 364) describes the need for agents of change as those "committed to reversing language shift," which would specifically involve teachers participating in EIB. Specifically in the context of transnational educational efforts, McBurnie and Ziguras (2007) describe those who work to support local school reform efforts as agents of change, and García (2005: 32) highlights "the possibilities offered by transnational memberships that have reconfigured the foundations of the ideas of political and cultural belonging" present in transnational exchanges for bilingual teachers like the exbecarios in this study.

My own analysis, based on a larger study on the process of cross-border professional development for teachers, explores some ways in which transformative spaces can be carved out even within hegemonic processes where international development and formal education intersect. In this chapter, I describe how teachers act as agents of change when they work at the community level to reverse language shift (Fishman, 1991) and recover traditional knowledge (Kincheloe & Steinberg, 2008). This analysis is based on descriptions by CASS exbecarios from Guatemala and Mexico of the various ways they are striving to overcome social and linguistic discrimination in the communities where they work.

RESEARCH SETTINGS AND METHODS

In the research tradition of bilingual education scholars like Garcia (2005), the aim of this study was a "critical but engaged study of the local effects of development policies" (ibid: 14). In my dissertation research the development efforts occurred through capacity-building for teachers, and my analysis of the local effects focused on the teachers' experiences and voices. As a means of further centering teacher voices (following the precedent of Lykes, 1997; also see Hornberger & Swinehart, 2012) agency for self-naming is in the hands of the participants themselves; that is, all participants were given the option to have their actual names used in the research, and nearly all of them did.[i] My focus was on the teachers' experiences following their year-long scholarship in the USA to learn what strategies they were or were not able to put into practice. I did not propose to do an evaluation but rather a critical description of the process. My central research questions were:
- What institutions shape cross-border professional development in these cases?
- How are language policies enacted through CBPD?
- How do teachers make meaning of their CBPD experiences when they return to their classrooms and communities?
- What do these case studies tell us about cross-border professional development as a process?

CASS directors provided me with contact information of all program participants on record – a total of 73 teachers in Guatemala and 95 in Mexico had email addresses (see Table 1). I initiated contact with all exbecarios in both countries by email, an invitation to join a social networking site I created, and an open-ended questionnaire; I did not distinguish between which of the multiple sites of the CASS program the exbecarios had attended, but rather focused more generally on the cross-border process itself. In-person interviews were initiated based on location – I contacted exbecarios who lived near the routes on which I traveled.

Table 1 shows the number of participants and types of data collected. All fieldwork was conducted in Spanish, the language of wider communication in both Guatemala and Mexico and the primary language within the educational systems in which the exbecarios work. I carried out seven months of fieldwork in 2009 in the western highlands of Guatemala, largely in Kaqchikel-speaking regions, conducting a total of 10 interviews. In 2010 I undertook six months of fieldwork in

159

Mexico, interviewing a total of 10 participants in Zapoteco and Mixteco regions of Oaxaca and Tseltal and Tsotsil regions of Chiapas. The number of interviewees was based only on the distances I was able to travel during my fieldwork. Data was also collected remotely from exbecarios from other states in both countries via e-mail, use of a website where exbecarios could respond to discussion questions as well as dialogue with each other, and administration of open-ended questionnaires.

Table 1. CASS participants in the dissertation

	Guatemala (73)	Mexico (95)
Website members	18	16
Questionnaires	15	11
Visits/interviews	10	10

Teachers were asked for descriptions of community contexts, local views of bilingual education, and what strategies they were or were not able to put into practice after the scholarship. The data included in this chapter was contextualized in histories of institutionalized Indigenous education and national language-in-education policies.

TEACHERS AS AGENTS OF CHANGE IN GUATEMALA AND MEXICO

While national contexts in Guatemala and Mexico are distinct, in both countries the devaluing of Indigenous language and culture is so common that its perpetrators are not only in urban, elite, or dominant Spanish-speaking Ladino/Mestizo spaces but often among Indigenous communities themselves (Field, 2002). According to the teachers I interviewed, Indigenous teachers have at times been as guilty as the teachers in earlier eras who cultivated shame and fear among Indigenous students. "For many years, we teachers of [I]ndigenous education have been instruments of education policies that have tended toward the disappearance of original peoples by enabling their incorporation, assimilation, or integration into the dominant mestizo culture" (Soberanes, 2010: 105). Countering such histories requires teachers to take on leadership roles in ways that support, rather than marginalize, the communities where they work, as expressed by one teacher interviewed:

> El verdadero líder siempre está dispuesto a enfrentar obstáculos, retos y buscar soluciones al problema y ser un agente de cambio
> [A true leader is always ready to face obstacles, challenges, and look for solutions to problems to be an agent of change.] – Raúl T., Kaqchikel, Sololá, Guatemala (interview, November 25, 2009)

Both Indigenous and non-Indigenous Mexican and Guatemalan teachers who work against nationalist assimilationist forces in the schools are therefore working as agents of change. Teacher agency is described here in three overlapping categories that emerged during my analysis – combating economic marginalization, the challenges of implementing bilingual intercultural education, and internalized prejudices and stereotypes (Johnson, 2011). I will use teachers' own voices to illustrate each category.

Combating Economic Marginalization

The first category is teachers who work as agents of change to address the economically marginalized contexts where they work. This was one of the strongest themes of many respondents in both countries. Exbecarios described the parents of their students as strongly supporting their children's education but having very limited options for providing economically for their families while remaining in the community. "Poverty does not consist only of a lack of monetary income. It is about a subhuman state of existence: vulnerability, uncertainty, malnutrition, exploitation, lack of education, physical insecurity, absence of shelter, and actions and expectations constrained to the short term" (Gómez, 2001: 80). Planning limited to the short-term is a problem faced by many marginalized communities and one that has a direct effect on the structure and quality of schooling provided. Many rural schools are *escuelas unitarias*, with one teacher for grades K-6. Such remote schools are rarely served by a local teacher, but rather by an outsider who commutes on either a daily or weekly basis. As described by one exbecario,

En el caso de Chiapas, muchas personas prefieren vivir en San Cristóbal y no en sus comunidades. No sé porque.
[In the case of Chiapas, many people prefer to live in San Cristobal and not in their own communities. I don't know why.] – Ernesto T., Tsotsil, San Cristobal de las Casas, Mexico (interview, June 21, 2011)

The exbecarios and education officials I interviewed consistently described work in poor, non-dominant communities as undesirable, and therefore typically undertaken by new teachers, who remain only until they have a chance to locate to other schools closer to their homes or in urban centers (as in other countries; see Benson, 2004). Many teachers said that positive educational change supporting Indigenous language maintenance cannot occur if the economic marginalization faced by the communities in which they work is not addressed. The exbecarios I interviewed described community spaces as lacking in basic infrastructure such as running water, electricity, and roads. One teacher said he feels responsible to help deal with these issues:

Como exbecarios debemos hacer la diferencia, pero con hechos, actuando con humildad y buscar siempre los espacios para contribuir en mejorar las condiciones de vida de los comunitarios.
[As exbecarios we should make a concrete difference, acting with humility and continually looking for the spaces where we can contribute to improving conditions for community members.] – Moisés J., Kaqchikel, Santa Lucia, Sololá, Guatemala (interview, August 18, 2009)

Another teacher connected Indigenous identity with improved economic autonomy for his community:

> Aprecio aun más mi cultura, ya que es una gran riqueza de los seres humanos y no es ningún obstáculo para el desarrollo individual y social. Formo parte del comité de fundación del turismo que genera de manera práctico la producción cultural (escritos y artesanías).
> [I appreciate my culture even more; it is part of the richness of human beings and does not serve as an obstacle to individual or social development. I serve on the tourism committee that generates practical means of cultural production (writings and crafts).] – Joaquín G., Tseltal, Santa Cruz Oxchuc, Chiapas, Mexico (questionnaire, September 16, 2010)

This idea is supported by another teacher, who described how she

> ... adquirí otras experiencias en el ramo educativo, también me motiva a seguir buscando como poder conseguir apoyo social, política y económica, para ayudar a la niñez y a la juventud.
> [... acquired other experiences in the educational field that also motivated me to continue searching for the means to find social, political and economic support, to be able to help children and young people.] – Lucía S., Tz'utujil, Panul, Sololá, Guatemala (questionnaire, November 25, 2009)

The cross-border experience was transformative for the teachers in ways that helped to re-center their own identities as they worked to improve communities' sustainability; they work to "reduce economic impoverishment in their communities at the same time that they challenge the norms of wealth and poverty that are dominant in nonaboriginal society" (Blackburn, 2009: 75). The exbecarios' meaning-making processes in these cases facilitated their roles as agents of change to combat economic marginalization.

Challenges of Implementing Bilingual Intercultural Education

The second category of teachers working as change agents is using improved bilingual teaching methods as a means of supporting Indigenous language development. Bilingual education in and of itself is no assurance of Indigenous language maintenance and can actually facilitate transition to the dominant language (Luykx, 1999b). A more critical stance, as described by the exbecarios below, can help to counter such tendencies.

> La debilidad de los maestros es falta de concientización. Claro que es importante hablar la lengua materna, pero lo detalle es que la escribe. Entonces la mayor parte dan en español. Falta mucho para poner en práctica educación bilingüe.
> [The weakness of the teachers is their lack of awareness. Of course it's important to speak the students' first language but the key is to be able to write it. So most of the time teachers give classes in Spanish. There is a long

ways to go to put bilingual education into practice.] – Mariano R., Tsotsil, San Cristóbal de las Casas, Chiapas, Mexico (interview, June 21, 2011).

This teacher is acknowledging the difficulties of the contexts where Indigenous bilingual education is taking place. Another teacher provides similar insights:

Cuando usa mucho la lengua indígena es puras instrucciones, como "abrir tu libro en tal pagina," pero para construir su conocimiento es en español aunque el niño aprenda basado en sus proprio contexto y su propio cosmovisión.
[When they use the Indigenous language most is just to give instructions, like "open your book to this page," and although they are constructing knowledge in Spanish the child learns based on his/her own context and cosmovision.[i]] – Miguel Á., Tsotsil, San Cristóbal de las Casas, Chiapas, México (interview June 6, 2011)

For some of the research participants, stepping away from familiar contexts by having a cross-border experience in the USA provided this more critical perspective on bilingual pedagogies as practiced in their own contexts. For example, one teacher reflected that his experience:

… me ha dado los elementos pertinentes para reconocer, fortalecer y enriquecer la lengua indígena.
[… has given me the necessary elements to recognize, strengthen, and enrich the Indigenous language.] – Martin G., Tsotsil, Barrio San Sebastian, Chiapas, Mexico (questionnaire, May 22, 2010)

The theoretical and pedagogical tools this exbecario acquired during his cross-border experience improved his ability to be an agent of change in his own classroom (Hornberger & Swinehart, 2012). Other teachers reflected on the importance of inviting parent participation in transforming bilingual education, reflecting one of the typical focus areas of the CASS program. One teacher described the action plan she initiated, a requirement of the CASS scholarship, in the community where she works:

Ahora estoy trabajando con los padres de familia, organizándolos e involucrándolos en el aprendizaje de sus hijos. Es una colaboración entre la escuela, el estudiante y los padres. Ha tenido buen impacto … He notado muchos cambios en los niños. Es lo que estamos trabando mucho ahora, más que nada en el idioma – no soy hablante, pero estamos trabajando directamente con los padres a apoyar lectura y escritura en su lengua materna. Trabajamos con los padres en el abecedario, para que puedan escribir en su idioma indígena. También hacemos talleres en donde redactamos, y luego invitamos los padres a visitar cuando estamos trabajando con temas generados en la comunidad, o sobre la cultura para que puedan trabajar en conjunto con los estudiantes. Los padres ayudan con la pronunciación de las palabras, y ayudan en su idioma.

[Now I'm working with the parents, organizing them and involving them in the learning of their children. It's a collaboration with us, between the school, the student and the parents. It's had a good impact .... I've noticed lots of changes in the children. We're working really hard on that now, more than anything on the language – I'm not a speaker, but we're working directly with the parents to support reading and writing in their L1. We meet with the parents to work with the alphabet, so they can write the indigenous language. Also we do workshops where we write, and then we invite the parents to visit when we work on themes generated in the community or about the culture so they can work in conjunction with the students. The parents help with pronunciation of the words, and they help in their language.] – Adelaida Cruz Alavez, Spanish, Oaxaca, Oaxaca, Mexico (interview, September 25, 2010)

This example demonstrates the potential for teachers who may not write the Indigenous language they speak, who may not speak the same Indigenous language or variety as the community, or who may not speak an Indigenous language at all to act as agents of change by creating spaces in schools for community knowledge. This is a transformative act in communities whose experiences with schooling in previous generations have been either non-existent or culturally and linguistically subtractive. The quotes above also illustrate some of the contradictions around identity and language in both EIB hiring – where teacher placement is based on the individual's ranking within the educational hierarchy based on a combination of professional development, years of service, and union participation (Martin, 2009; Street, 2001) – and scholarship selection – where participants for programs such as CASS are selected because they are representatives of "underdeveloped" communities. Despite these contradictions, the cross-border experience offers transformative potential for both Indigenous and non-Indigenous teachers.

Internalized Prejudices and Stereotypes

Indigenous identity, knowledge, and language have historically been ignored, subjugated, and de-centered in public education. The third category of teachers as agents of change highlights the potential of the cross-border experience for helping participants to dismantle hegemonic structures and re-center Indigenous identity through language and culture.

Nuestra mentalidad cambia porque hemos entendido de que el maestro es un guia, ¿verdad? Es un orientador, y en donde tanto se aprende del alumno como el alumno aprende de maestro, ¿verdad? Ya no es un perfil asi [vertical], si no que ya es un espacio donde todos participan, todos colaboran. Entonces, pues básicamente la mitad de la educación en Guatemala, todavía se siguen patrones tradicionales y que muchos de los compañeros siguen ese línea.

[Our viewpoint changes because we've come to understand that the teacher is a guide, right? The teacher orients the students in a way that he/she learns as much from the students as the students learn from the teacher, you know? So it's not a vertical relationship anymore but rather a space where everybody participates and everyone collaborates. And well, basically half of the education in Guatemala continues in the same conventional patterns and a lot of the other teachers follow that pattern.] – Moisés J., Kaqchikel, Santa Lucia, Sololá, Guatemala (interview, August 18, 2009)

While this teacher learned to break away from common and longstanding ways of positioning oneself as a teacher, others had transformational experiences based on inter-Indigenous exchanges that occurred in some CASS sites. One teacher said that her ability to work as an agent of change was expanded through learning about various North American Indigenous communities through

... visitas a diferentes tribus Indígenas para que conozcamos el trabajo social y cultural que realizan.
[... visits to different Indigenous tribes to get to know the social and cultural work they are carrying out.] – Gloria R., Achí, Canton San Juan, Baja Verapaz, Guatemala (questionnaire, April 1, 2010)

Others talked about increased awareness of their community needs during a process of increased self-reflection. One teacher described a positive outcome of this process as working with rather than against the community:

Trabajar con el pueblo y para el pueblo con ideas y practicas, trabajar con proyectos comunitarios de beneficios a largo plazo.
[Working with the People and for the People with ideas and practices, and working with community projects that have long-term benefits.] – Joaquín S., Tseltal, Santa Cruz Oxchuc, Chiapas, Mexico (questionnaire, September 16, 2010)

Another adds:

He tenido mucha conciencia en lo colaboración con mi gente en el desarrollo de la misma y he trabajado mucho y me siento muy satisfecho por el programa que me cambio mi forma de ser.
[I have been very conscious regarding collaboration with my people in facilitating development and I have worked a lot and feel very satisfied with how the program has changed me.] – Adrián T., K'iche,' Aldea Nimasac, Totonicapán, Guatemala (questionnaire, April 8, 2010)

This same teacher also reflected specifically on language status and its connection with identity:

En momentos determinados antes de irme a EEUU no valoraba mi idioma porque pensé que solo es en mi país y que no tenga valor en otro lugar. Pero me di cuenta que si tiene mucha validez y por lo mismo se me dió la oportunidad de viajar y me cambió mi forma de pensar.

[At certain points before I went to the USA I didn't appreciate my language because I thought it was only spoken in my country and wouldn't be valued anyplace else. But I realized that it is very important because it gave me the opportunity to travel and it changed my way of thinking.] (Ibid.)

Such reflections speak to an interactional space known as a cultural interface (Delens, 1999; Nakata, 2007), which occurs as Guatemalan and Mexican Indigenous teachers are provided the opportunity to explore educational and social paradigms different than the systems in which they were educated and are now employed. They can potentially develop more critical lenses that facilitate the revaluing of community-based knowledge and cultural practices. For the teachers described here, transformation has occurred at personal and ontological levels, with clear implications for their classroom and community practices. They have gained tools for reflecting on their own identities and the ways in which racism and discrimination become normalized in the settings where they work. The cross-border experience has opened up new spaces for the exbecarios to act as agents of change, supporting Indigenous languages and cultures in Mexican and Guatemalan schools.

CONCLUSION

Schooling for Indigenous students in the Americas has historically used subtractive curricula and instruction to facilitate cultural and linguistic assimilation, which was considered "instrumental in embracing modernity, exploiting the past, and shifting the terms of identity" (Gow, 2008: 134). Contemporary national educational policy contexts in Mexico and Guatemala are described as bilingual and intercultural, yet many schools continue their subtractive legacy in practice. Teachers who work to counteract such processes and to support Indigenous linguistic and cultural vitality are therefore acting as agents of change. The voices of the exbecarios described here demonstrate the potential to carve out spaces for innovation within national systems of Indigenous education. While the experiences of these exbecarios do not represent those of a so-called typical teacher, they offer hope for the ongoing project of educational decolonization that involves "embracing the past, questioning the present, and imagining a different future" (ibid.: 134). As teachers work for change in challenging economic, pedagogical and epistemological contexts, their voices allow all of us to consider new ways of thinking about their roles as agents of change in Indigenous education not only in Mexico and Guatemala, but also in other contexts where education is being better adapted to the needs and wishes of non-dominant linguistic and cultural communities.

NOTES

[i] I adapted the methodology for purposes of this chapter, providing participants' last initials only.
[ii] Cosmovision is a spiritual worldview that is holistically integrated with Indigenous epistemologies.

REFERENCES

Aikman, Sheila (1997). Interculturality and intercultural education: A challenge for democracy. *International Review of Education, 43* (5/6), 463-479.

Baker, Colin (2001). *Foundations of bilingual education and bilingualism* (3rd ed.). Clevedon: Multilingual Matters.

Barnach-Calbó Martínez, Ernesto (1997). La nueva educación indígena en Iberoamérica. [New [I]ndigenous education in Latin America]. *Revista Iberoamericana de Educación, 13*, 13-33.

Bastos, Santiago (2010). *Indigenous rights and the peace process: Beyond cosmetic multiculturalism.* ReVista. (http://www.drclas.harvard.edu/publications/revistaonline/fall-2010-winter-2011/indigenous-rights-and-peace-process)

Beckett, Megan, & Pebley, Anne R. (2003). Ethnicity, language, and economic well-being in rural Guatemala. *Rural Sociology, 68*(3), 434-458.

Benson, Carol (2004). Do we expect too much of bilingual teachers? Bilingual teaching in developing countries. *Bilingual Education and Bilingualism, 7*(2/3), 204-218.

Blackburn, Carole (2009). Differentiating [I]ndigenous citizenship: Seeking multiplicity in rights, identity, and sovereignty in Canada. *American Ethnologist, 36*(1), 66-78.

Brown, R. McKenna (1998). A brief cultural history of the Guatemalan highlands. In Susan Garzon, R. McKenna Brown, Julia Becker Richards, & Wuqu' Ajpub' (Eds.), *The life of our language: Kaqchikel Maya maintenance, shift, and revitalization* (pp. 44-61). Austin, TX: University of Texas Press.

Cummins, James (2000). *Language, power and pedagogy: Bilingual children in the crossfire.* Clevedon: Multilingual Matters.

Delany-Barmann, Gloria (2009). Bilingual intercultural teacher education: Nuevos maestros para Bolivia. *Bilingual Research Journal, 32*(3), 280-297.

Delens, Michael (1999). Whose rules apply? Educational project management in less developed countries: Cultural considerations. In Fiona E. Leach &, Angela W. Little (Eds.), *Education, cultures and economics* (pp. 347-369). New York: Routledge Falmer.

DGEI (Dirección General de Educación Indígena) (2008). Mensaje de la Directora [Director's Message]. (http://basica.sep.gob.mx/dgei/pdf/inicio/mensajedir/MensajeDirectora.pdf)

Field, Les (2002). Blood and traits: Preliminary observations on the analysis of mestizo and [I]ndigenous identities in Latin America vs. the U.S. *Journal of Latin American Anthropology, 7* (1), 2-33.

Fishman, Joshua (1991). *Reversing language shift: Theoretical and empirical foundations of assistance to threatened languages.* Clevedon: Multilingual Matters.

Fitzsimons, Patrick, & Smith, Graham (2000). Philosophy and Indigenous cultural transformation. *Educational Philosophy and Theory, 32* (1), 25-41.

Freeland, Jane (2003). Intercultural-bilingual education for an interethnic-plurilingual society? The case of Nicaragua's Caribbean coast. *Comparative Education, 39*(2), 239-260.

García, Maria Elena (2005). *Making [I]ndigenous citizens: Identity, development, and multicultural activism in Peru.* Stanford: Stanford University Press.

Garzon, Susan (1998). Conclusions. In Susan Garzon, R. McKenna Brown, Julia Becker Richards, & Wuqu' Ajpub' (Eds.), *The life of our language: Kaqchikel Maya maintenance, shift, and revitalization* (pp. 188-200). Austin : University of Texas Press.

Gasché, Jorge (2010). De hablar de la educación intercultural a hacerla. [From talking about intercultural education to practicing it.] *Mundo Amazónico, 1*, 111-134.

Gómez Serrano, Pedro José (2001). La critica a la concepción economicista del desarrollo como base para una adecuada educación para el desarrollo. [Critique of the economic conception of development as the basis for adequate educational development.] In Antonio Monclús Estella (Ed.), *Educación para el desarrollo y cooperación internacional* [Education for development and international cooperation] (pp. 69-104). Madrid: Editorial Complutense.

González Apodaca, Erika (2009). The ethnic and the intercultural in conceptual and pedagogical discourses within higher education in Oaxaca, Mexico. *Intercultural Education, 20*(1), 19-25.

Gow, David (2008). *Countering development: Indigenous modernity and the moral imagination.* Durham: Duke University Press.

Hernandez, Martha B., & Layton, Heather M. (2006). *Determinants of [I]ndigenous schooling achievement.* World Bank.

Hidalgo, Margarita (2006). *Mexican [I]ndigenous languages at the dawn of the twenty-first century.* New York: Mouton de Gruyter.

Hornberger, Nancy H., & Swinehart, Karl, F. (2012). Not just situaciones de la vida: Professionalization and Indigenous language revitalization in the Andes. *International Multilingual Research Journal, 6*(1), 35-49.

Howard, Rosaleen (2009). Education reform, [I]ndigenous politics, and decolonisation in the Bolivia of Evo Morales. *International Journal of Educational Development, 29*, 583-593.

INALI (Instituto Nacional de Lenguas Indígenas) (2010). *Síntesis del Catalogo de las lenguas indígenas nacionales: Variantes lingüísticas de México con sus autodenominaciones y referencias geoestadisticas* [Synthesis of the catalog of national Indigenous languages: Linguistic varieties of Mexico with autodenominations and geostatistical references]. (http://www.inali.gob.mx/clin-inali/)

INEGI (Instituto Nacional de Estadística y Geografía) (2010). (http://www.inegi.org.mx/est/contenidos/espanol/metodologias/censos/sm_conteo2005.pdf)

Johnson, Janelle (2011). *Mapping a new field: Cross-border professional development for teachers.* Doctoral Dissertation. Teaching, Learning, & Sociocultural Studies, College of Education, The University of Arizona.

Kaqchikel Moloj/Fundación Kaqchikel (2008). *Rutzijol Samaj/Boletín Informativo* [Informational Bulletin]. Guatemala: Pestalozzi Children's Foundation/Ibis.

Kincheloe, Joe L., & Steinberg, Shirley R. (2008). Indigenous knowledges in education: Complexities, dangers, and profound benefits. In Norman K. Denzin, Yvonna S. Lincoln, & Linda Tuhiwai Smith (Eds.), *Handbook of critical and Indigenous methodologies* (pp. 135-156). Los Angeles: Sage Publications.

King, Kendall (1997). Indigenous politics and native language literacies: Recent shifts in bilingual education policy and practice in Ecuador. In Nancy Hornberger (Ed.), *Indigenous literacies in the Americas: Language planning from the bottom up* (pp. 267-284). Berlin: Mouton de Gruyter.

Knight, Jane (2007). Cross-border tertiary education: An introduction. In Stephan Vincent-Lancrin (Ed.), *Cross-border tertiary education: A way towards capacity development* (pp. 21-46). Paris: OECD and the International Bank for Reconstruction and Development/The World Bank.

Leach, Fiona (1994). Expatriates as agents of cross-cultural transmission. *Compare: A Journal of Comparative Education, 24*(3), 217-232.

López, Luis Enrique (2008). Top-down and bottom-up: Counterpoised visions of bilingual intercultural education in Latin America. In Nancy H. Hornberger (Ed.), *Can schools save [I]ndigenous languages? Policy and practice on four continents* (pp. 42-65). New York: Palgrave Macmillan.

López, Luis Enrique (2009). Plurinacionalidad y ciudadanía en Bolivia: Revisión de un largo recorrido y situación actual [Multinationalism and citizenship in Bolivia: Review of a long process and current situation]. *Revista Interamericana de Educación para la Democracia/Interamerican Journal of Education for Democracy, 2*(2), 145-178.

Luykx, Aurolyn (1999a). *The citizen factory.* Albany, NY: State University of New York Press.

Luykx, Aurolyn (1999b). *The historical contradictions of language maintenance: Bilingual education and the decline of Indigenous languages.* Paper presented at the Annual Meeting of the American Anthropological Association, Chicago, November 17-21, 1999.

Lykes, M. Brinton (1997). Activist participatory research among the Maya of Guatemala: Constructing meanings from situated knowledge. *Journal of Social Issues, 53*(4), 725-746.

Martin, Christopher (2009). Popular educational innovations in the hierarchical world of Mexican policy. *International Journal of Educational Development, 29,* 125-132.

McBurnie, Grant, & Ziguras, Christopher (2007). The cultural politics of transnational education. In *transnational education: Issues and trends in offshore higher education* (pp. 60-72). New York: Routledge.

Mena, Patricia, Muñoz, Héctor, & Ruiz, Arturo (2000). *Identidad, lenguaje y enseñanza en escuelas bilingües indígenas de Oaxaca* [Identity, language, and teaching in bilingual schools of Oaxaca]. Coedición de Sistema de Investigación Regional Benito Juárez, Universidad Pedagógica Nacional y Universidad Autónoma Benito Juárez de Oaxaca.

Monclús Estella, Antonio (2001). *Educación para el desarrollo y cooperación internacional* [Education for development and international co-operation]. Madrid: Editorial Complutense.

Montejo, Victor (2005). *Maya intellectual renaissance: Identity representation and leadership.* Austin, TX: University of Texas Press.

Nakata, Martin (2007). *Disciplining the savages: Savaging the disciplines.* Canberra: Aboriginal Studies Press.

OECD (2007). Executive summary. In Stephan Vincent-Lancrin (Ed.), *Cross-border tertiary education: A way towards capacity development* (pp. 11-20). Paris: Organization for Economic Co-operation and Development and the International Bank for Reconstruction and Development/The World Bank.

Richards, Julia B., & Richards, Michael (1997). Mayan language literacy in Guatemala: A socio-historical overview. In Nancy Hornberger (Ed.), *Indigenous literacies in the Americas: Language planning from the bottom up* (pp. 189-212). Berlin: Mouton de Gruyter.

Rockwell, Elsie (2002). Constructing diversity and civility in the United States and Latin America: Implications for ethnographic educational research. In Bradley A.U. Levinson, Sandra L. Cade, Ana Padawer, & Ana Patricia Elvir (Eds.), *Ethnography and education policy across the Americas* (pp. 3-20). Westport: Praeger.

Rosaldo, Renato (1989). *Culture and truth: The remaking of social analysis.* Boston: Beacon Press.

Sánchez, Omar (2008). Guatemala's party universe: A case study in underinstitutionalization. *Latin American Politics and Society, 50*(1), 123-151.

Santibáñez, Lucrecia (2008). Reforma educativa: El papel del SNTE. [Educational reform: The role of the National Union of Education Workers]. *Revista Mexicana de Investigación Educativa, 13*(37), 449-443.

SEP (Secretaria de Educación Pública) (2004). *Políticas y fundamentos de la educación intercultural bilingüe en México* [Policies and foundations of bilingual intercultural education in Mexico]. SEP/Coordinación General de Educación Intercultural y Bilingüe/Comisión Nacional para el Desarrollo de los Pueblos Indígenas. México: Disigraf.

Soberanes Bojórquez, Fernando (2010). Noam Chomsky and [I]ndigenous education in Oaxaca, Mexico. In Lois Meyer & Benjamín Maldonado (Eds.), *Noam Chomsky and voices from North, South, and Central America* (pp. 101-114). San Francisco: City Lights.

Street, Susan (2001). When politics becomes pedagogy: Oppositional discourse as policy in Mexican teachers' struggles for union democracy. In Margaret Sutton & Bradley A. Levinson (Eds.), *Policy as practice: Toward a comparative sociocultural analysis of educational policy* (pp. 145-166). Westport: Greenwood Publishing.

UNESCO (2005). *Guidelines for quality provision in cross-border higher education.* Paris: UNESCO.

Valdiviezo, Laura (2009). Bilingual intercultural education in [I]ndigenous schools: An ethnography of teacher interpretations of government policy. *International Journal of Bilingual Education and Bilingualism, 12*(1), 61-79.

Zeichner, Ken, & Flessner, Ryan (2009). Educating teachers for critical education. In Michael W. Apple, Wayne Au, & Luis Armando Gandin (Eds.), *The Routledge international handbook of critical education* (pp. 296-311). New York: Routledge.

Janelle M. Johnson
Department of Teaching, Learning, and Sociocultural Studies
The University of Arizona, USA

REBECCA STONE

9. EFFECTIVE ACTIVITIES TO SUPPORT TEACHERS' TRANSITION INTO THE MTBMLE[i] CLASSROOM IN THE PHILIPPINES

ABSTRACT

Su nia a sulat na ipebpagilay sia su napasadan nu kinapaganad'u 'bpamamandu pantag kanu MTBMLE. Su nalimud a ibpangingidsa na ebpun kanu nakatelu ulan a MTBMLE a kabpangagi kaped'u 'bpamamandu kanu ikaisa a 'bpangkatan taman kanu manga mapulu nilan lu kanu manga iskwilan a pedtabangan nu Save the Children sa Mindanao, Pilipinas. Su kinapangingidsa kanu lima kataw kanu 'bpamamandu sa ikaisa a 'bpangkatan na unan enggu ulian nu kinapaganad. Na sia kanu nauli den a kinangingidsa na inipatadem kanu namedtalabuk su embalang-balang a napaganadan nilan asal'a katawan u aden kambagu nilan sabap sa entu. Su ibpangingidsa na mailay sia i kapia na ginawa nu 'bpamamandu enggu pakapagkabagel sa ginawa nilan i kausal sa basa kanu kabpamandu nilan amaika (1) napangagian nilan den muna su basa nilan, (2) nakaumbal silan sa manga libelu enggu sulat a mausal'ilan sa kambpamandu sa basa nilan i inusal enggu (3) napagitung'ilan su danden a naukitan nilan sa kinapangagi. Pedsinantalen sia u ngin i makua kanu kinapangingidsa asal'a maliwanag i kasabut sa panun i kapaganad enggu katabang sa 'bpamamandu a 'bpeludsu pagusal sa basa nilan sia kanu kabpamandu nilan. (*Translated to Maguindanaon [mdh], a language of the Philippines, by Lito Jose Endong and Xinia Skoropinski.*)

This paper examines the effect of specific training activities on teachers' attitudes towards MTBMLE. The research data was derived from a three-month MTBMLE training with a group of indigenous first grade teachers and their school principals in Save the Children's outreach areas in rural Mindanao in the Philippines. The researcher conducted pre- and post interviews with a subset of five teachers. At the final interview participants were asked to recall various training activities and what effect if any these activities had on their attitude change. The data showed that teachers were more positive and confident using the mother tongue as the language of instruction and teaching mother tongue literacy when they had the opportunity to: 1) spend time learning about their own language, 2) create L1 teaching and learning materials, and 3) reflect on their early learning experiences. The research findings and discussion provide a clearer picture of how to train and support teachers who are transitioning into mother tongue-based multilingual education.

C. Benson and K. Kosonen (eds.), Language Issues in Comparative Education, 171–187.

INTRODUCTION

Throughout Asia and the Pacific, like many other regions of the world, there is a mismatch between the language of instruction in primary schools and the home language of learners. This sets up a challenging situation for young children: they enter primary school having to learn about schooling norms and content, often in a language with which they have little familiarity. The World Bank estimates that half the world's out-of-school children do not have access to the language of school in their homes (Bender et al., 2005: 1).

Evidence from empirical research around the world indicates that teaching children in their home language is an effective strategy and policy. A recent World Bank Education Note (ibid.) labels the use of colonial languages as media of instruction as one of the "non-productive practices that lead to low levels of learning and high levels of dropout and repetition" and deems this "the biggest challenge to Education For All" (p. 1). According to the same Note, L1 instruction results in (i) increased access and equity, (ii) improved learning outcomes, (iii) reduced repetition and dropout rates, (iv) sociocultural benefits, and (v) lower overall costs (ibid.).

Mother tongue-based multilingual education (MTBMLE) provides schooling through a language in which children are familiar, and starts with what they already know before moving to the unknown, including the second language (UNESCO, 2007). Research from around the world shows that the longer the students learn in a familiar language, the better they will perform on both content and second language proficiency tests (Ouane & Glanz, 2011; Hovens, 2002; Thomas & Collier, 2002). However, there are many challenges inherent to implementing a first language-based educational system. Research shows that one of those challenges is teachers' attitudes and beliefs about instruction in learners' home languages, which are usually non-dominant languages.

Because of my interest in this challenge, I took a consultancy in the Philippines with Save the Children, an international non-governmental organization (INGO), to help design and implement a professional development program that would prepare teachers to teach multilingually in their home languages of Ilonggo, Tboli and Maguindanaon. Schools selected to participate in the program serve the Tboli, Ilonggo and Maguindanaon communities, which were chosen due to their remote location and high levels of poverty, marginalization and lack of access to Filipino and English, the official languages of schooling.

In this chapter, I use data from my experiences with these teachers to investigate the effectiveness of four specific professional development activities designed to support and encourage teachers during their transition into teaching in an L1-based multilingual education program. The research question that guided this study was:

How are teachers' knowledge, attitudes, and skills affected when they participate in professional development that seeks to build their capacity to:
– Critically reflect on their previous language, learning, and literacy experiences and beliefs in light of their own teaching practice;

- Teach English and Filipino as foreign languages;
- Shift roles from authoritative figure to facilitator of learning;
- Design and use locally relevant mother tongue teaching and learning materials, including graded storybooks.

This question emerged from my previous research, including a review of the literature around MTBMLE at the primary level in West Africa (Paulson Stone, 2010a) and interviews with experts in the field of MTBMLE (Paulson Stone, 2010b). Based on recommendations from the literature and from the experts, I developed a professional development program, in consultation with Save the Children staff, for first grade teachers and their school principals consisting of three separate training modules of two and a half days each for a total of 69 contact hours. This chapter will focus on four training activities found to be particularly effective at building teachers' capacity to carry out the above four strategies.

The Linguistic Situation in the Philippines

The Republic of the Philippines is an archipelago consisting of 7,107 islands in the southwest Pacific Ocean, about 800 kilometers from mainland Southeast Asia (Quijano and Eustaquio, 2009: 84). The population and their languages are spread throughout these islands: estimates show that between 120 and 180 separate languages are spoken in the Philippines. Lewis (2009), for example, reports that there are 181 languages spoken in the Philippines, of which 171 are autochtonous, making the Philippines the 25th most linguistically diverse country in the world. Of the countries in Southeast Asia, the Philippines is second only to Indonesia in terms of number of languages.

Table 1. Languages spoken in the Philippines by over one million people (year 2000)
(Source: adapted from Nolasco, 2008: 1-2)

Language	Population of L1 speakers
Tagalog	21.5 million
Cebuano	18.5 million
Ilocano/Ilokano	7.7 million
Hiligaynon/Ilonggo	6.9 million
Bicol/Bikol	4.5 million
Waray	3.1 million
Kapampangan	2.3 million
Pangasinan	1.5 million
Kinaray-a	1.3 million
Tausug	1 million
Meranao	1 million
Maguindanaon	1 million

Table 1 highlights this linguistic diversity by listing all groups with over one million speakers according to the 2000 census. Note that the first eight of these are considered major regional languages in different parts of the country, and represent 66 million people (86% of the population of 76.5 million). There are still about 159 languages with under a million speakers. Interestingly, because of missionary work and organizations like SIL International which focus on language development, orthographies exist in most of these languages, and there are written materials in more than 100 of them (Kosonen, 2009).

Language-in-Education Policy in the Philippines

The Bilingual Education Policy of 1987, which was in effect at the time of this research, decrees that English and Filipino be used as the media of instruction (MOI).[ii] The goal of the Bilingual Education Policy is the "achievement of competence in both Filipino and English" (Quijano & Eustaquio, 2009: 87). The policy specifies that the regional languages should be used in grades one and two. In fact, the government, in collaboration with SIL, even produced a "bridging" plan showing which languages should be used as media of instruction in the classroom, and at what point second and third languages should be taught (DepEd order 74). The plan shows that teachers should use one of the regional languages as MOI through grade three, while progressively teaching oral and written English and Filipino. Up to the time of this research, however, there had been no wide-scale training of teachers in how to manage these three languages in the classroom, and so in most places, English and Filipino were the only languages being used, particularly since textbooks were only printed in English and Filipino. In order to help the government meet the need of training so many teachers, Save the Children and local Department of Education staff began the above-mentioned pilot project to train first grade teachers and their school principals in ten project areas.

METHODOLOGY OF THIS STUDY

The professional development program (a set of three 23-hour training modules conducted in two and a half day increments for 15 primary schools teachers and their principals) was designed based on the evidence gathered from the literature on high-quality professional development, teacher attitude change, and recommendations for MTBMLE teacher training. The three training modules were intended to equip teachers with the knowledge, attitudes and skills needed for the MTBMLE classroom. I chose a small sample of the participating teachers and conducted in-depth interviews before and after the program to gauge the effectiveness of the modules in bringing about attitude change.

Sampling

Approximately 15 first grade teachers and 15 school principals from 10 schools in the Save the Children project area of the Southern Philippines participated in the program. Of these, a sample of five teachers participated in the pre- and post-interviews. The sample was selected for representativeness based on a range of characteristics including: gender, age, first language, classroom language (majority language of their students), years teaching, and educational qualifications. Teachers agreed to share their real names for the study.

Sources of Data

This chapter makes use of data from three sources: 1) My personal observations of participants during the training, 2) Recordings of participants' explanations of their reflective drawing during training one, and 3) Final interviews with five teachers, including an "early school experience" reflection drawing and explanation, and teachers' reflections on the impact of training activities. To obtain data on the effectiveness of training activities I gave a brief description of each activity, after which I asked the following three questions:
– What do you remember about this activity and why?
– What do you think was the purpose of this activity?
– What does it mean for how you teach in your classroom?

With these questions as my framework, I attempted to gain a better understanding of how and if these teachers' attitudes and beliefs about language and education had changed during the course of their professional development, and if so, what activities or other elements were responsible for that change.

EXAMINATION OF THE PROFESSIONAL DEVELOPMENT PROGRAM

As a professional development consultant, my main task was to help develop and implement a training that would prepare grade one teachers and school principals in the ten target schools to implement multilingual education based on learners' L1s. As mentioned above, in my earlier work (Paulson Stone, 2010a, 2010b) I identified four specific strategies for training MTBMLE teachers. Figure 1 outlines these four strategies along with specific activities and objectives that were conducted during the professional development program to address each one.

Strategy 1: Activity and Results

For strategy 1, the activity was designed to reveal early experiences that may have been influential in forming these teachers' attitudes and beliefs about language, literacy and learning. By critically reflecting on them, the participants could become aware of unconscious ways of thinking that affect the way they teach in the classroom. For this activity, I asked participants to close their eyes and reflect on their own early language and school experiences guiding them with prompts such as:
– Think about what it was like for you to learn English and Filipino.
– How did you feel when you learned math in English?
– Remember what it was like to learn to read in Filipino and English.

– How did you feel? What did it make you think about yourself? About your home language?

Strategy 1: Build teachers' capacity to examine their early learning and literacy experiences
Activity: Reflection activity and drawing of teachers' early learning experiences.
Objectives: By the end of the activity participants will be able to: 1) express their memories of their own first grade experience; 2) recognize the difficulties they may have had in learning to read and how that related to the language of instruction in their classroom; 3) relate their own early learning experiences to those of the students they now teach in their classroom.
Strategy 2: Build teachers' capacity to teach English and Filipino as foreign languages
Activity: The meaning of language – Hausa story-telling
Objectives: By the end of the activity participants will be able to: 1) express what it feels like to try to learn in a language in which they are unfamiliar; 2) recognize that teaching English by immersing their students in the language is not the best way to help them learn, since they cannot make meaning in a language they do not understand.
Strategy 3: Build teachers' capacity to adopt a facilitative approach to teaching and learning
Activity: Modeling through professional development training
Objectives: By the end of the training participants will be able to: 1) identify several activities they could use in their classroom to facilitate learning; 2) confidently teach a lesson to their peers using different teaching approaches and strategies learned in the training.
Strategy 4: Build teachers' capacity to design and use local language materials and graded stories in the classroom
Activity: Creation of local language primers & practice teaching them
Objectives: By the end of the activity participants will be able to: 1) differentiate the sounds and symbols of their language; 2) understand the frequency of different symbols in their language and how the frequency affects the order in which the symbols are taught; 3) explain the purpose of a primer and the essential elements which make it up; 4) demonstrate how to teach a lesson using the primer.

Figure 1. Professional development strategies and related activities

Participants were then given time to share with a partner their memories of early language learning experiences, individually represent their experience on paper, and share those experiences and drawings with the large group. Drawings were put up on the walls for all to see. At the end of the professional development program, a sample of teachers was interviewed and asked to complete a new drawing of what their early experience would have looked like if it took place in an MTBMLE classroom.

Activity Data. During the Guided Reflection Activity everyone participated so animatedly that I had to ask them several times when they would be ready to stop sharing. They seemed to appreciate the opportunity to represent their experiences in a visual way, not just using words. The majority of the teachers volunteered to share their drawings in front of the large group, and participants listened intently to the experiences of others. They were proud to put their drawings up on the wall, and during lunch hour I found many participants browsing through the drawings.

One teacher, Maria-Lyne, touched on many ideas and experiences that were shared by the other teachers in the sample. Figures 2 and 3 below display Maria-Lyne's drawings from the first training and her final interview, respectively.

Figure 2. Maria-Lyne's initial drawing   *Figure 3. Maria-Lyne's final drawing*

When she stood to describe her initial drawing representing her experiences in grade one, Maria-Lyne said:

> I am in school, entering grade one. Here is my teacher [...] an Ilonggo. And in our classroom I think one percent of the total population is Tboli like me. So here are my classmates, they are busy playing, they are busy interacting with each other, and here is me. Because I don't understand what my teacher is telling us, what my teacher's spoken language is .... I finished grade one without any ... I don't know how to read, since the instructions of my teacher is hard for me to understand it. (Reflection Activity, Training 1)

Maria had strong memories of how she wanted to be able to communicate with her classmates and teacher and wanted desperately to be able to express herself. Even the desire to establish friendships was blocked since she could not speak the language. Maria: "I wish to mingle with my classmates, with my teacher, but the problem is I couldn't express myself, I couldn't express myself ... that's why I placed myself here (points to girl in corner in the drawing)" (Interview 2).

Maria-Lyne's second drawing showed how her first grade classroom might look if MTBMLE were implemented (Figure 3). She explained that the instructions

177

would be in a language she understood and she would be able to express herself and participate along with her classmates. "Here is our teacher and my classmates, and it's me, not at the corner anymore, because I can express myself and I can mingle with them. Maybe instructions for me is now easy to understand [...] maybe I felt that I was not alone anymore, I felt the spirit of belongingness"[iii] (Interview 2).

When I asked how her learning was affected in the two different classrooms, Maria responded that in the MTBMLE classroom she could learn more easily because even if she did not understand the lesson, at least she could ask for help, whereas in the traditional classroom, "questions are still in my mind without bringing it out because I couldn't express myself, I couldn't express myself with this classroom because foreign dialects are being used" (Interview 2).

Conclusion. Maria-Lyne's drawings and explanations showed how difficult it was for her going to school in a language she did not speak or fully understand. She described her isolation and inability to participate or interact because she could not speak the language. Maria's understanding of MTBMLE, however, showed that she viewed it as inclusive and participatory, and as bringing a sense of belonging to children by increasing their self-confidence, making them feel happier and allowing them to understand and thus express themselves and participate in the lessons.

Strategy 2: Activity and Results

For strategy 2, the activity was designed to help participants see the link between language and learning. For this activity, I read aloud a short story in the Hausa language.[iv] I then asked participants to explain what the story was about. Most looked at me quizzically and a few tried to guess based on the few words they had understood. We then discussed as a group why they believed they did not understand. Afterwards I told the same story in English (a language everyone in the room was familiar with), and we discussed the difference between their understanding of the first and second stories. We then reviewed Figure 4 below showing the relationship between thinking, language, and learning.

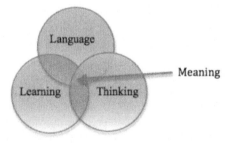

Figure 4. The meaning of language. (Source: adapted from AusAID, 2005: 40)

Activity Data. During their final interviews, when asked what they remembered about this activity, every one of the teachers remembered it. Three of the teachers specifically remembered that when I read the story in Hausa they did not understand. Rosalie: "We do not understand, we laugh, we frown, because we cannot understand." Dinah: "The first language you used, I can't understand what you're saying," and Maria-Lyne: "We keep on staring, we keep on listening, but I couldn't understand actually when you used that different language." They remembered not understanding, and according to their descriptions, just staring, laughing, frowning, and trying to listen because they could not understand the language being spoken. Each of the five teachers made the connection between what they experienced during the activity and what their students experience in the classroom when the language spoken is not their mother tongue. Rosalie: "When you translate it in English, we understand it and … we say to ourself that … when you are teaching to pupils in a language that they do not know, same experience maybe, they are just frowning, they are just laughing maybe because they do not understand you" (Interview 2). She connected what she had just experienced with how her own students react when she speaks in a language they are not familiar with. Fely also made this connection: "I realized that in our pupils also, if we are always talking English, they don't understand also, like for us, we don't understand the words that you have said, the only thing we can remember is your name, Rebecca" (Interview 2). Out of the entire story I read to her, my name was the only thing that stuck with her because that was the only word she recognized.

The conclusions that each of these teachers came to as a result of this activity are as follows. Dinah felt that:

> Speaking in a foreign language, especially the first graders, is very difficult for them to understand. Even in […] grade six, if we'll just speak English all the time, they don't understand you. … you have to say it in their language so that they will understand fully what you are telling them. (Interview 2)

For Dinah, this activity helped her make the connection between language and understanding. As a result, she recognizes that she must use the students' language if she wants them to understand what she is saying.

Maria-Lyne felt that: "better learning and better instruction should start with what the learners know" (Interview 2). When I read the story in English, instead of Hausa, "I [Maria-Lyne] could relate with story, so maybe […] learning that starts with what the children doesn't know, make the children a stranger, but learning that starts with what the children already know, make them belong" (Interview 2). In our professional development activities, language was discussed as one of the many ways teachers could start with what the children know, others included bringing their culture into the classroom through relevant lesson material, use of the community, etc.

Conclusion. Perhaps for the first time, teachers were able to experience what it is like for their students when they speak to them only in Filipino or English. They experienced frustration and were not able to answer my questions or respond about the story I read to them. This seemed to really jar them, as each one of them remembered this activity almost a month later when I interviewed them to find out the effect training activities had on their attitudes, knowledge and skills.

Strategy 3: Activity and Results

In order to help participants adopt a facilitative approach to teaching, the most important thing we did during the professional development program was to model what good facilitation looks like. We asked participants to work individually, in pairs or in small groups, to move around the room for various activities, to engage in discussions with their peers, and even to lead portions of sessions. My colleagues and I, as facilitators, attempted at all times to model good facilitation so that teachers could have the experience firsthand of observing and participating in a group process that was being facilitated.

We tried to make this explicit so that participants could consciously reflect on the teaching style being used. For example, one activity we did early in the training was called *Definitions of MTBMLE.* During this activity, we placed five different definitions of MTBMLE around the room, and participants stood next to the one they most agreed with. We asked people from each group why they chose that particular definition and what was it about other definitions that made them not choose those. This created a dialogue among the participants that I only had to facilitate with a few leading questions here and there.

At the end of the activity, I asked them what they thought the purpose was. We discussed how what they learn in the training was not just the content from the different activities but the activities themselves could be learned from. We discussed how I as the "teacher" was not at the center of the activity, but that I had set it up to create dialogue and interaction and only needed to interject questions when necessary to keep ideas flowing. I then asked participants to pay close attention to how the other activities during the program were led, in order to learn both content and process.

Participants had many opportunities to facilitate portions of the training, and conducted microteaching exercises where they facilitated a lesson for their peers. It is hard to measure if they learned the skill of facilitation during the professional development program, as it is a skill that takes time, both through participating in facilitation to observe and learn how it is done, and from practicing the skill.

Strategy 4: Activity and Results

The purpose of this activity was to develop primers in Tboli, Ilonggo and Maguindanaon and understand their application in the classroom and their importance for developing early literacy. Creating the primers was an iterative process that continued during all of the training modules across the professional development program. We first showed participants a sample primer in a language they do not speak and then taught a sample lesson showing how they would eventually teach new letters, words, and sentences. Once teachers had the basic idea of how it would work, they got into groups by language (there were three language groups present: Tboli, Maguindanaon and Ilonggo), and went through the process of primer creation.

Each language group started by writing two stories, each one about 300 words long. They were told to write one story about something familiar in their community and to write the other story as a dialogue. Once participants had their two stories, they conducted a sound count. They were provided with charts (Malone, 2006) to record all of the sounds/symbols and to count how many times each symbol was found in the stories. They then ordered the symbols by frequency so that they had a list of which symbols were used most frequently down to those that were used least frequently.

At this point participants created their key words. The idea was to start by teaching the letters most frequently used and add one letter at a time to form new words with the other letters students have already learned. To do this, teachers wrote each symbol from their language on a note card, and used these to try and form different key words. Participants then developed other primer activities for each lesson, including word making and breaking (syllables), a big box (separate symbols for building new words), sentence making and breaking, and other short sentences or paragraphs for extra reading using only learned symbols. Figure 5 shows a sample of a page from the Tboli primer teachers developed.

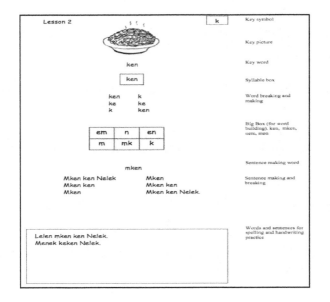

Figure 5. Tboli Primer Page

Activity Data. A written evaluation of training module one revealed that the majority of teachers listed the Symbol Count as one of their most enjoyable activities. This was fascinating to me, as it was tedious reviewing every word and counting the symbols throughout two 300-word stories. Three out of five teachers I interviewed for my sample listed the Creation of the Primer as the activity that they most enjoyed or was most memorable. Dinah: "My favorite parts is especially making the primer, and creating some words that would rhyme, and sometimes it is very enjoying" (Interview 2). Imelda: "The most memorable and the most interesting part of that seminar is ... how to create primer and how to introduce that to the pupils" (Interview 2).

These teachers reported that although enjoyable, the process was not easy. Rosalie: "it was difficult" and Fely: "At first we experienced it's hard, it's hard for us" (Interview 2). When prompted to discuss what exactly was hard she replied that it was "the making of symbols ... because we wrote some words that did not go with the key words, key letters" (Interview 2). Here she is referring to the process of developing key words that had to be very exact and could only use one new letter plus the letters previously taught. The word had to be picturable which meant that many words that were created had to be thrown out, as they did not fit one of the two criteria. It was a complicated process that required many iterations, but it seems that rather than being frustrated by this process, the teachers really enjoyed the challenge. According to Maria-Lyne it was: "very exciting" to work within those given limitations and this sense of challenge seemed to motivate the teachers and make this activity fun (Interview 2). Aside from being memorable and enjoyable, the interviews with my sample showed that teachers learned from this activity. Rosalie gained experience and confidence in writing stories and using her mother tongue. In her final interview, Rosalie reported: "What I was learned in making the book ... I can say to myself that I **can** [her emphasis in bold] make it ... before I did not try to make stories, but when you can make one, two, you are eager to make more." Rosalie seems to be saying that the mere experience of writing stories and creating the primer gave her the confidence to do more, and that it is now something she enjoys doing.

After the *Primer Activity*, Fely had a better understanding of the importance of pictures and visual aids in helping her students learn. Fely: "the pictures that we will use ... easy for them to understand, and to recognize the letters through the pictures," referring to the importance of having a key word and recognizable picture to represent each new letter (Interview 2). Maria-Lyne learned that "you should not teach symbols, or you should not insert symbols when it has not been taught already" (Interview 2). She went on to say that in her classroom, even though they have not yet implemented mother tongue, "for now, thanks to the idea, I never show a symbol that has not been gone through with my previous lessons" (Interview 2). So she took the idea of teaching only one new symbol at a time and applied it to her current teaching of Filipino and English.

Conclusion. Since such a large proportion of the professional development program was spent working on the primers, perhaps it is logical that this would be the most memorable activity, although it does not explain why participants would enjoy the activity so much. Participants really seemed to enjoy the process of developing stories, seeing their language in print, and solving the puzzle of finding key words that fit with the right letters. I think this activity was so successful because it valued and allowed teachers to contribute to the development of their language. It made the teachers the creators of what they would be teaching, they were able to work together with their peers, and it was seen as a motivational challenge.

ANALYSIS

These four professional development activities were demonstrated to be effective at building teachers' capacity according to the four target areas. However, there is evidence that changes could be made to improve their effectiveness for future trainers and program designers. This section analyzes the strengths and weaknesses of the activities and discusses how each could be improved.

Reflection and Drawing Activity

The first activity, the *Reflection and Drawing Activity* of teachers' early learning experiences, was effective because it allowed participants to critically reflect on how their own early learning experiences and attitudes affected their current teaching and to consider how they might need to change. Most of these teachers went through an education system that was heavily focused on memorizing facts and learning language through submersion,[v] and we know that teachers reproduce the way they were taught. As Richards et al. explain, "The most resilient or 'core' teachers' beliefs are formed on the basis of teachers' own schooling as young students while observing teachers who taught them. Subsequent teacher education appears not to disturb these early beliefs, not least, perhaps, because it rarely addresses them" (2001: 2).

If teachers' beliefs about teaching are formed based on their own schooling experiences, then it stands to reason that in order to change these beliefs, teachers must consciously recognize what they are. According to the same authors, effective professional development "gives participants the opportunity to reflect on their beliefs and make those beliefs explicit" (Richards et al., 2001: 12). By giving teachers the opportunity to reflect on their attitudes and beliefs about teaching, which are often below the surface, this activity opened the doors to potential changes in practice and acceptance of new innovations.

I would not change much about this activity. In fact I would suggest adding another similar activity to help teachers reflect on how they were actually taught to read and write in English and Filipino. As already noted, most were never explicitly taught English or Filipino as a second or third language, so getting them to reflect on the process they went through would be beneficial in helping them understand what research tells us about language teaching and learning and how they might need to adapt their teaching practices in the classroom.

The Meaning of Language – Hausa Story-Telling

The Meaning of Language activity was meant to address the strategy of building teachers' capacity to teach English and Filipino as foreign languages. The reason this activity was so memorable to each of the five teachers, is that it put them in the position of the learner and gave them the chance, although brief, to experience what their pupils go through every day when the language of instruction is unfamiliar. This activity was a quick and easy way to drive home the point that language and understanding are directly related to making meaning. The teachers were able to experience it first hand and it helped them to identify with what their students were experiencing on a daily basis.

This activity was only one brief opportunity for the teachers to become the students, and I think it could have gone much further. To be truly effective, this activity should have been the first in a series of language modeling exercises to help teachers experience and learn about how to teach a foreign language. This activity only gave them the experience of what it was like to learn in an immersion classroom. The next step, then, should have been to model good practices for teaching a foreign language. One strategy for doing this would be using the TPR (Total Physical Response) method developed by James Asher (1969). The TPR technique encourages students to learn the new language through hearing, seeing, and doing. They hear meaningful language (directions), they see others responding to what was said and then they respond to the directions through physical action. This technique can easily be modeled for the teachers in a language that is unfamiliar to them, so that they actually participate as learners.

Modeling through Professional Development Training

The practice of *Modeling* good teaching practices was incorporated to build teachers' capacity to adopt a facilitative approach to teaching and learning. Modeling is an evidence-based strategy for changing practice. Because attitudes and beliefs about teaching and learning are deeply ingrained and often unconsciously held, changing these beliefs and therefore ways of teaching, can be very difficult. According to Hunzicker (2004: 45), "Changing a teacher's beliefs requires that new information be presented repeatedly over time, to the point that the person begins to feel disequilibrium between current beliefs and new information." Through professional development programs, we have the opportunity to present information about an innovation, model it in action, and give teachers the opportunity to practice using it, hopefully resulting in changed attitudes and beliefs about that innovation.

Given that most teachers were themselves taught by teachers using rote memorization and an authoritative style, they adopt these same familiar methods.

Helping teachers reflect on the kind of teaching that they experienced along with modeling what good child-centered, active teaching and learning looks like, can help them to change their beliefs and adopt a more facilitative approach to teaching. The key is that they have to understand how they were taught, experience being taught in a different way, and be given the opportunity to practice teaching using this new method. Microteaching is one important way that teachers can practice using the new strategies they are learning and to receive constructive feedback in a safe environment before taking them into the classroom.

Creation of Local Language Primers and Practice Teaching Them

This activity was designed to address the goal of building teachers' capacity to design and use local language materials and graded stories in the classroom. The process of creating, illustrating, and learning to use and teach the primers was extremely time consuming, but the feedback from teachers and my own personal observations tell me that the benefits gained from this activity were worth the time. Although it was time-consuming, I found that the process of creating stories, counting symbols and developing a list of symbol frequencies was one of the most enjoyable (for the teachers) and effective activities that we did during the entire program. Teachers became intimately familiar with their own writing systems, became more confident in teaching literacy in their mother tongue, and gained a deeper understanding of the process for teaching reading skills to young children. They also developed a deep knowledge of how their language works, their grammatical and orthographic structures, how to build from letters, to sounds, to words to sentences, and how to help their students master reading and writing in their own language. Most of these teachers had never explicitly taught reading in their classrooms, so going through the process of primer creation helped them understand how to explicitly guide students through the process of learning to read.

I would strongly recommend that program designers incorporate this process of allowing teachers to participate in the primer production process. Even if there is a primer already in existence, it is worthwhile to go through the steps so that teachers gain a deeper understanding of the language they will be teaching as well as increase their confidence in how to teach students to read in that language.

CONCLUSION

Research shows that in order to help teachers effectively adapt to teaching in the MTBMLE classroom, we need to give them the chance to reflect on their ingrained attitudes and beliefs about teaching and learning, develop their knowledge, attitudes and skills through modeling good practice, and practice those new skills in a collaborative learning environment where they can receive constructive feedback. The four activities discussed in this chapter aim to do just that. Although some will require further reinforcement, all are beneficial to teachers, and the recommendations I suggest would make them even more effective. We know that MTBMLE, when done well, is the most effective way to help ethnolinguistic minority children learn. We also know that teachers are the vehicle through which MTBMLE is implemented. This chapter is an attempt to further our knowledge of how best to prepare teachers for the challenges of adapting to an MTBMLE classroom.

NOTES

[i] The term MTBMLE is contested in many circles as children may have multiple mother tongues. However, this was the term I used during my professional development program with teachers, and so for this research I will continue to use the term with the understanding that it refers to a home language of the learners.

[ii] The recent DepEd Order No. 16 of February 17, 2012 titled "Guidelines on the Implementation of the Mother Tongue-Based Multilingual Education (MTB-MLE) lays out a new policy for the 2012-2013 school year. It states that MTB-MLE should be implemented in all public schools, and specifies that the L1 should be used as the MOI in all subject areas in grades K-3 except for the subjects of English and Filipino.

[iii] This non-standard use of English is common among the teachers due to their lack of exposure to the language, and the fact that their own teachers had limited English skills. You will notice this in the teachers' quotes throughout the document.

[iv] I chose to speak Hausa, a West African language spoken primarily in Niger, Nigeria and Mali because I knew that none of the participants would understand, and I could simulate the situation for learners when a foreign medium of instruction is used.

[v] When the L2 or L3 is used as the primary language of instruction for children who do not have access to those languages at home, or other supports to keep them "afloat", this is considered submersion. Children either sink or float, and unfortunately in these circumstances, most sink.

REFERENCES

Asher, James J. (1969). The total physical response approach to second language learning. *The Modern Language Journal, 53*(1), 3-17.

AusAID (2005). *Vernacular literacy trainers' manual.* Department of Education, Papua New Guinea. (http://sites.google.com/site/mlephilippines/Home/mle-resources)

Bender, Penelope, Dutcher, Nadine, Klaus, David, Shore, Jane, & Tesar, Charlie (2005, June). *In their own language, Education for All.* Education Notes. Washington, DC: The World Bank..

Desimone, Laura (2009). How can we best measure teacher's professional development and its effects on teachers and students? *Educational Researcher, 38*(3), 181-199.

Guskey, Thomas R. (2002). Professional development and teacher change. *Teachers and Teaching: theory and practice, 8*(3/4), 381-391.

Hovens, Mart (2002). Bilingual education in West Africa: Does it work? *International Journal of Bilingual Education and Bilingualism, 5*(5), 249-266.

Hunzicker, Jana (2004). *The beliefs-behavior connection: Leading teachers toward change.* (www.naesp.org)

Karavas-Doukas, Evdokia (1996). Using attitude scales to investigate teachers' attitudes to the communicative approach. *ELT Journal, 50*(3), 187-198.

Kosonen, Kimmo (2009). Language-in-education policies in Southeast Asia: An overview. In Kimmo Kosonen & Catherine Young (Eds.), *Mother tongue as bridge language of instruction: Policies and experiences in Southeast Asia* (pp. 22-41). Bangkok: SEAMEO.

Lewis, M. Paul (Ed.) (2009). *Ethnologue: Languages of the world* (16th ed.) Dallas, TX: SIL International.

Malone, Susan (2006). *Teaching the sounds of your language – Guide to developing an alphabet-teaching book*. Adapted from "The Sounds of Your Language", published 1991, by the Department of Education, Papua New Guinea, Written by R. Litteral and S. Malone: ISBN 9980-58-659-1

Nolasco, Ricardo (2008). *The prospects of multilingual education and literacy in the Philippines*. A paper presented at the 2nd International Conference on Language Development, Language Revitalization, and Multilingual Education in Minority Communities in Asia. 1-3 July 2008, Bangkok, Thailand. (http://www.seameo.org/_ld2008/doucments/Presentation_document/ NolascoTHE_PROSPECTS_OF_MULTILINGUAL_EDUCATION.pdf)

Ouane, Adama, & Glanz, Christine (Eds.) (2011). *Optimising learning, education and publishing in Africa: The language factor. A review and analysis of theory and practice in mother-tongue and bilingual education in sub-Saharan Africa*. Hamburg, Germany: UNESCO Institute for Lifelong Learning (UIL), the Association for the Development of Education in Africa (ADEA)/African Development Bank.

Paulson Stone, Rebecca (2010a). *Medium of instruction or medium of obstruction? A Review of the literature on language of instruction at the primary level in West Africa*. Unpublished. Comprehensive Exams, University of Massachusetts Amherst.

Paulson Stone, Rebecca (2010b). *Enhancing learning through the use of mother tongue language: Analysis of the forces for and against mother tongue education*. Unpublished. Comprehensive Exams, University of Massachusetts Amherst.

Quijano, Yolanda, & Eustaquio, Ofelia (2009). Language-in-education policies and their implementation in Philippine public schools. In Kimmo Kosonen & Catherine Young (Eds.), *Mother tongue as bridge language of instruction: Policies and experiences in Southeast Asia* (pp. 84-92). Bangkok: SEAMEO.

Richards, Jack C., Gallo, Patrick B., & Renandya, Willy A. (2001). Exploring teachers' beliefs and the processes of change. *The Pan Asia Consoritum (PAC) Journal, 1*(1), 41-62.

Stern, Carolyn, & Keislar, Evan R. (1975). *Teacher attitudes and attitude change*, Volume 1, A *handbook for educational practitioners*. Los Angeles, CA: National Institute of Education.

Thomas, Wayne, & Collier, Virginia (2002). *A national study of school effectiveness for language minority students' long-term academic achievement*. Santa Cruz, CA and Washington, DC: Center for Research on Education, Diversity & Excellence.

UNESCO (2007). *Advocacy kit for promoting multilingual education: Including the excluded*. Bangkok: UNESCO Asia and Pacific Regional Bureau for Education.

Rebecca Stone
University of Massachusetts Amherst, USA

PAULINE REA-DICKINS & GUOXING YU

10. ENGLISH MEDIUM INSTRUCTION AND EXAMINING IN ZANZIBAR

Ambitions, Pipe Dreams and Realities

ABSTRACT

Sura hii inaanza kwa kuuchunguza kwa kina mchango wa 'lugha' katika ufundishaji, ujifunzaji na upimaji nchini Zanzibar, mahali ambako Kiswahili ni lugha-mama na vilevile ni lugha ya kufundishia katika shule za msingi, wakati ambapo Kiingereza ni lugha ya kufundishia katika shule za sekondari. Aidha, sura hii inatumia matokeo ya tafiti zilizochunguza michango ya lugha kwenye matokeo ya wanafunzi katika mitihani yao ya mwisho wa masomo ya msingi. Makundi matano ya taarifa kutoka kwenye eneo moja la utafiti yamewasilishwa, ikiwa ni pamoja na utafiti uliochunguza uwezo wa wanafunzi kuyaelewa maswali katika lugha ya kingereza (ambayo ni lugha ya pili au ya kigeni), na mahitimisho yatokayo kwenye matokeo ya mitihani ya Hisabati, Bailojia, na Kemia iliyotungwa ama kwa Kingereza tupu, ama kwa kiswahili tupu, au kwa lugha mchanganyiko, yaani kwa Kiswahili na Kingereza pamoja. Majadiliano yanaangazia maswala ya sera za kitaifa na ya matarajio binafsi katika utumiaji wa lugha isiyofahamika vyema katika maswala ya elimu ukilinganisha na jinsi matarajio ya wanafunzi yanavyooanishwa na ukweli halisi wa mambo. (*Translated to Kiswahili [swh], the lingua franca of Tanzania, by Simon Karuku and Peter Kajoro.*)

This chapter begins by exploring the 'language' factor in teaching, learning and assessment in Zanzibar, where Kiswahili is the first language (L1) and medium at primary school, with English the medium in secondary schools. It then draws on empirical studies investigating the dynamics of language in student performance as assessed at the end of basic education. Five different data sets from the same research context are presented, including an exploratory study investigating students' abilities to access examination questions through English, a second or foreign language, and findings from three different language versions (English only, Kiswahili only, bilingual English-Kiswahili) of the same school subject examinations for math, biology and chemistry. The discussion addresses issues of national policy and of individual aspiration for the use of an unfamiliar language in

C. Benson and K. Kosonen (eds.), Language Issues in Comparative Education, 189–207.

education, referenced to how learner ambitions align with the realities on the ground.

INTRODUCTION

A widely held assumption is that English – as a language of wider communication – is *the* gateway to higher education or to skills and knowledge that access workplace opportunities as the basis for participating socially and economically in society. Aspirations for English have been the driving force behind language policies mandating the use of an international language as medium of instruction in schools. Parents as well as students voice their support for schooling to be through the medium of an international language with a pervasive view of 'the earlier the better' (Rea-Dickins, Clegg, & Rubagumya, 2005; Rea-Dickins, Yu, & Afitska, 2009). However, research demonstrates that students are considerably challenged in trying to develop simultaneously their linguistic skills and school subject knowledge (e.g., Abedi, Courtney, Leon, Kao, & Azzam, 2006; Abedi & Gándara, 2006) and that examinations, which have become high-stakes worldwide, have particularly negative consequences for many low-income countries where large numbers exit basic education[1] as unsuccessful learners.

This chapter explores the dynamics between two languages – English and Kiswahili – in the formal examining of Form II Secondary school students in Zanzibar (in which Kiswahili is the L1 for over 98% of the population) in three core curriculum areas: math, biology and chemistry. It draws on empirical studies investigating the dynamics of language in student performance as assessed at the end of basic education (Student Performance in National Examinations: the dynamics of language/SPINE).[ii] Five different data sets from the same research context are presented, including: 1) an exploratory study investigating students' abilities to access examination questions through English, a second or foreign language; 2) results of an English vocabulary test; 3) findings from three different language versions of the same examination (English only, Kiswahili only, bilingual English-Kiswahili) for math, biology and chemistry; 4) an analysis of national data captured at the end of basic education examinations; and 5) survey responses on students' exposure to English both inside and outside of school. The central aim of this research was to investigate the impact of both the language of instruction and the language of examinations on the exam performance (achievement, underachievement) of students acquiring subject knowledge and understanding through a language that is not their first language. The research sought to provide insights into factors that impact on students' demonstration of subject knowledge and understanding, at a macro-level by analyzing longitudinal national exam and the micro-level of the classroom in the three subject areas.

THE LANGUAGE FACTOR IN TEACHING, LEARNING AND ASSESSMENT

Children in many African classrooms face considerable cognitive and linguistic challenges in acquiring conceptual understanding across the curriculum when they are taught through a language that is not their first language. Classroom observation studies in African contexts (e.g. Benin, Burkina Faso, Guinea-Bissau, Mali, Mozambique, Niger, South Africa, Togo, Tanzania, Ethiopia, Ghana, and Botswana) show that teaching processes are often not conducive to fostering conceptual, linguistic or literacy development and that a key factor is the use of a language of instruction (LOI) which is unfamiliar to the children and in which teachers themselves may not be proficient. This can lead to teacher-centered interaction in which the children are predominantly silent, any participation tending to take the form of choral repetition and recall (Alidou, 1997, 2003; Brock-Utne, 2005; Brock-Utne & Holmarsdottir, 2004; Hovens, 2002; Rubagumya, 2003). In addition, research shows the prevalence of code-switching (despite the fact that this may be prohibited by official policy) and 'safe talk' where interaction lacks meaning (Brock-Utne, 2005; Heller & Martin-Jones, 2001; Rubagumya, 2003).

Research in Africa has also shown that the use of an unfamiliar language can inhibit children from speaking in class, particularly if they fear punishment for not using the official LOI. Girls may be particularly at risk, fearing ridicule (see Ouane & Glanz, 2011), as this "may [incorrectly] be interpreted as evidence of limited academic ability, rather than lack of exposure to the language of instruction" (Benson, 2005: 3). On the other hand, learning in a familiar language can have considerable benefits for girls, leading to their staying in school longer, being perceived as 'good students,' performing better on achievement tests, and repeating grades less often (Hovens, 2002; Benson, 2005). An increasing body of research shows that the use of familiar languages in African classrooms, particularly through late-exit or additive bilingual instruction, leads to greater interaction and communication, facilitating teaching and learning (Heugh & Skutnabb-Kangas, 2012 in Ethiopia; Walter & Davis, 2005 in Eritrea; see also Walter, Chapter 14 this volume). Use of learners' home languages in school has particular benefits for the development of conceptual understanding in core curriculum subjects such as science and math (Kaphesi, 2003; Mwinsheikhe, 2002, 2003; Wilmot, 2003). Further, Levine (2011) argues against code switching – which operates under a deficit model – and for a multilingual community of practice in classrooms where several languages are represented. All of the above work identifies the use of an unfamiliar language as a factor in school ineffectiveness and low academic achievement (Brock-Utne, 2005, and Chapter 4 in this volume), contributing to school dropout.

Furthermore, research shows that the use of unfamiliar languages in instruction can lead to incorrect assessment of children's understanding, with very early evidence of this as far back as 1978 in Tanzania (Mlama & Matteru, 1978; see also Luckett, 1994 in South Africa and Wilmot, 2003 in Ghana). The tests used in many African countries are often both linguistically and culturally inappropriate (e.g. Fredua-Kwarteng & Ahia, 2005a; 2005b) and lack validity and reliability (Ouane & Glanz, 2011). A further issue is that teachers are not given adequate training in monitoring and assessing learning, particularly for formative purposes (Ouane & Glanz, 2011). Long ago, writing from the Tanzanian experience, Nyerere (1968) highlighted the role of testing and assessment in driving the curriculum in African contexts, reflecting recognition of the importance of testing and assessment worldwide (e.g., Kellaghan & Greaney, 2004; Shohamy, 2006). Despite this, the topic of assessment has been under-represented in discussions of educational reform and language policy in Africa. We find this somewhat surprising, since effective assessment practices will be crucial in ensuring that any policy has a positive impact on teaching and learning practices for all children, who have a right to benefit from full participation and not to suffer discrimination as a consequence of the language of examinations (see e.g. Skutnabb-Kangas & Heugh, 2012 regarding the detrimental effects of English examinations in Ethiopia).

In Tanzania, Kalole (2004) found that the majority of markers of test papers along with test designers recognized language incompetence in English as the main factor contributing to low performance and favored a switch to Kiswahili. However, this may not benefit all children if, as Luckett (1994) found in South Africa, pupils are unable to explain in English what they know in their first language, or are similarly unable to transfer to their first language what they have learnt in English. Contributors to Ouane and Glanz (2011) advocate language choice in testing: pupils can respond in the language in which they can best express themselves. The findings from the SPINE project resonate with these last two points. Although research in the USA on language-related accommodations (e.g. translating the instructions) has found little evidence that they significantly improve students' performance (e.g., Castellon-Wellington, 2000), these have tended to relate to test procedure, such as providing extra time or reading test items aloud, rather than test modifications (Butler & Stevens, 2001). Allowing children to select the language of response may avoid the predicament that "when the language of instruction is English, translating test items and tasks into students' native languages may not actually serve as an accommodation, but rather may confuse students who have begun to associate certain content material and concepts with English" (ibid: 8) and they may not yet have the requisite level of formal academic proficiency in Kiswhili, their first language.

The details of the research and some findings are presented next.

THE STUDIES

The aim of the SPINE research studies,[iii] therefore, was to investigate the dynamics of two languages – English and Kiswahili – in the formal examining of subject content in the achievement of learners at the end of basic education. The key research questions around which the progressively focused research studies in SPINE were shaped were related to the wide question: Why do so many children underachieve? Specifically, the study was designed to explore:

– To what extent can underachievement be attributed to language factors?
– What are the dynamics of English, an unfamiliar L2, and Kiswahili, the L1 in this research context, in the achievement of learners at the end of basic education?

This research comprised a series of progressively focused studies.[iv] Here we present findings from five of these: the initial exploratory study (Data Set 1), the study investigating students' levels of English language proficiency through a specific purposes vocabulary test (Data Set 2), sample findings from the larger roll-out of school subject examinations in three language versions (Data Set 3), an analysis of national examination data sets (Data Set 4) and finally, findings from a survey questionnaire, part of which aimed to capture the extent to which students who took the three different language versions of the tests were exposed to English both inside and outside of school (Data Set 5). Our findings are reported by data set in the following sections.

Initial Exploratory Study: Data Set 1

Exploratory in design, this study aimed to investigate whether achievement in formal Form II examinations may be inhibited through language factors.

Procedure for Phase 1:
- 6 target students in 8 schools were asked to respond to a set of *original* examination items (in English) from past papers (N=48) in English, math, biology and chemistry.
- Interviews were conducted with each target student using both English and Kiswahili.

Procedure for Phase 2:
- Original items from Phase 1 that were particularly problematic were modified.
- Learner workshops took place 6 to 9 months later.
- The same students were asked to respond to the modified items, followed by structured activities designed to identify more specifically some of the challenges that students faced in writing their exams.

Insights from the exploratory study:
From the learner interviews in Phase 1, we gained insights into the kinds of problems students experienced in responding to examination items. These included the following – not necessarily mutually exclusive – problems such as not understanding the task, difficulty understanding specific words and phrases or the meanings or functions of tables and diagrams, as well as non-linguistic reasons having to do with subject content, such as partial or no knowledge of the topic. Typical student responses are exemplified below.

Extract 1 (MT-Q1; B3:153-154)
I: What was the problem with this examination question?
B3:   Silifahamu [I don't understand it]

One of the strategies used by the interviewers, Kiswahili and English speakers, was to encourage student to respond in the language of their choice, i.e. in either the L1 or the L2, or both, so as to better discover the nature of the students' difficulties. For example, students were asked to translate questions orally from

English into Kiswahili. One of the word problems on the math examination was as follows:

> Question 6: The combined ages of Juma and Asha are 10 years. The difference of Asha's age from twice Juma's age is 8 years. Find the ages of each one.

Extract 2 below provides one of a number of examples where students were unable to understand very basic English vocabulary in the instructions of the exam.

Extract 2 (MT-Q6; C1)
I: Do you understand this instruction?
C1:   Some of instructions
I: … 'Combine' and what? … Can you translate it …? So what do you think that means 'the combined ages of Juma and Asha are ten'?
…
C1:   Mayai ya Juma na Asha [Juma and Asha's eggs]
I: Eeh [okay]
C1:   Mayai ya Juma na Asha yalikuwa ni kumi miaka kwa miaka [Juma and Asha's eggs were ten years]

In this case, the student had confused the word 'ages' with 'eggs,' translating 'ages' into Kiswahili as 'mayai' (meaning eggs). A further example comes from the Reading Comprehension section of the English examination, where the instruction for one of the questions on mammals was:

> Give out short, clear and meaningful answers:
> Q3. What are the four things that man could resemble whales?

The student in the extract below had been identified to us as an able student but one who had left this particular question blank in his answer paper. His interview was entirely in English, unlike the majority of students who relied on Kiswahili to respond. When asked why he had not answered the question, he explained:

Extract 3 (Eng; D1:122-133)
D1:   Because I did not understand this question … I do not understand by this this one … resemble" [student pointed to the word *resemble* on the examination paper]
I: If I tell you that resemble means 'to look like' … can you do the question now?
D1:   Yes
I: OK so what's the answer?
D1:   Man … Is warm-blooded … and whales also … Whales have lungs and man also have lungs …

In the second phase of the exploratory study, we modified some of the original examination questions, in particular those that appeared to cause students most problems. The modifications included greater contextualization of the questions, simplification of instructions and rephrasing of items, for example by removing low-frequency lexical items such as "suffocate" and "immersed." As appropriate, we also provided visual clues to support retrieval of knowledge and altered the layout and format of the questions.

The main conclusions drawn from both phases of the exploratory study were as follows:

- Students *do* experience language problems in processing examination questions and producing responses in English
- Restructuring and modifying the original items generally impacted positively on student performance in respect of overall response rates and the number of correct or partially correct responses
- Insights were gained into some of the learning that *had* taken place that was not evident using the original exam items
- There is evidence to suggest there are threats to test reliability and validity on account of language introducing construct irrelevant variance.

Whilst not a central focus of this research, several other factors emerged as inhibitors to student learning, for example non-linguistic factors such as examining topics that had not been taught, a lack of qualified teachers, teacher absenteeism, and lack of subject knowledge. These non-linguistic factors appear to compound the challenges for learners who are already challenged by having to use English as a language of learning and assessment.

This first exploratory study paved the way for further studies, for which the findings from the specifically constructed English vocabulary levels test are presented next.

English Language Proficiency – Vocabulary Levels: Data Set 2

The second study was designed to probe student vocabulary levels more systematically since, as seen above, vocabulary emerged in the exploratory studies as a significant problem for students in their processing of examination instructions and questions. The earlier data revealed frequent student comments about 'not understanding the words,' and in some cases students reported and demonstrated that they did not know the majority of the content words of the English Reading Comprehension passages. Across all the school subjects, students reported difficulty in understanding words or phrases in the instruction rubrics for the examination items as well as within the test items themselves. When students were asked to provide synonyms or to provide Kiswahili equivalents, they were often not able to do so. In addition, it became clear that even words students reported 'knowing' were often incorrectly interpreted.

For the second study, given the lack of suitable English vocabulary tests for use in this particular educational context, it was decided to develop, pilot and use a specifically designed vocabulary measure. Our aim was to determine the extent to which vocabulary was a major inhibitor to school achievement as measured through the national exams at the end of basic education. In addition, we wanted to establish a benchmark in terms of students' English vocabulary knowledge based on their actual exposure to English through teaching, learning and assessment processes, as opposed to some general measure developed and validated on students with different educational experiences and levels of exposure to English.

Both language and subject specialists on the SPINE research team worked on the selection of words for this English vocabulary test based on a corpus developed throughout the project based on school textbooks and past examination papers. All lexical items in the corpus were classified in terms of process, objects/parts, properties, and function, as shown in Table 1, with examples for each category.

Table 1. Vocabulary selection criteria

Process	Objects/Parts	Properties	Function
expand, multiply, use, recall, rearrange, draw	unit, square, brackets, rectangle, esophagus, locust, mammal	same, solution, inside, distance, accurate	by, and, with, also, to

The aim was to capture a range of vocabulary knowledge including everyday words, everyday words with specific meaning in subject specialist contexts (e.g. under, square), and specialist word knowledge (e.g. canines) within a framework that captured subject specialist language use, exemplified by process, objects and their parts, properties, and grammatical function words. A 90-item vocabulary test was constructed from this vocabulary list based on the textbooks in use in schools and past examination papers, and was piloted, analysed and revised prior to administration. An exemplar item, with the correct answers, is presented next. Students were asked to choose the most appropriate word from the list of six words on the left to match the definitions on the right.

```
1 FOLLOWING
2 BOTH
3 VARIOUS      _5_ a lot
4 FIRST        _1_ next
5 MANY         _6_ like another
6 SAME
```

The vocabulary test with 90 items of this type was completed in 8 schools (selected to capture the diversity in schools in the research context) by 837 Form II students who were in their last year of basic education.

Our findings revealed:

– Exceedingly low levels of English vocabulary amongst some of the students, with raw scores ranging from 3-97 (scores were converted to percentage), with a mean of 33 and standard deviation of 22.41.

– Statistically significant differences in students' English vocabulary knowledge between the eight research schools ($F=300$, $p.<0.001$).

– Two schools with significantly higher English language proficiency than the other six schools, possibly because of greater exposure to English in or out of class.

These findings raise several questions: How can the significant differences between schools be explained? Given the very low attainment on this vocabulary measure, how can these students engage productively in English-medium instruction? If students were given the opportunity to respond in Kiswahili, their L1, in examinations, what would be the effects on their performance? These questions led to the third and fourth studies, presented next.

Investigating the Effects of Language on Student Achievement: Data Set 3

The research team, including language testers and science and math specialists, constructed a new examination for three school subjects: math, chemistry and biology. These examinations were then produced in three language versions, with significant iterative engagement with the English and Kiswahili language specialists and verification of meanings and subject content through back translation.

The three language versions – Kiswahili only, English only, and bilingual Kiswahili-English – were randomly allocated in each class of our 8 targeted schools, around 1/3 in Kiswahili (n=182), 1/3 English (n=169), 1/3 bilingual (n=179) in the three subjects: biology, chemistry and math. A total sample of 530 students' performance provides the basis for the analyses below. Given the findings from the vocabulary test that two schools outperformed the other six, the results from these two schools (G and H) are excluded from the first round of analysis of the results for biology, which are presented in Table 2 below.

Table 2. Biology mean scores for schools with limited exposure to English (Schools A-F)

Language version	N	Subset for alpha=0.05	
		1	2
English	130	10.17	
Bilingual (English-Kiswahili)	135	12.19	
Kiswahili	134		17.71
significance		0.052	1.00

Means for groups in homogeneous subsets are displayed

These results show that the students in these six schools that had limited exposure to English outside the school performed best on the Kiswahili version of the biology examination and lowest on the English version. Table 3 provides the results from Schools G-H, where students appeared to have greater exposure to English.

Table 3. Biology mean scores for schools G-H with likelihood of greater exposure to English

Language version	N	Subset for alpha=0.05	
		1	2
English	39	25.77	
Bilingual (English-Kiswahili)	44	27.73	
Kiswahili	48		12.60
significance		0.320	1.00

Means for groups in homogeneous subsets are displayed

From the above we see a different performance pattern, with School G-H students achieving the highest scores on the bilingual version, followed by English, and lowest on the Kiswahili version. Why the scores for Kiswahili are so low would need further investigation, but might be explained by students having relatively less classroom exposure to Kiswahili than English.

From the illustrative findings and analysis of the results on the chemistry and math exams (not presented here), we come to the following conclusions. First, it is clear that some students in some schools do better on the English versions of the three subject tests (math, chemistry and biology), that others perform better on the Kiswahili versions but that, overall, more students do better on the bilingual version of the tests (English and Kiswahili). We also found variation in student performance within subject areas (from analyses not presented here), and established that both Kiswahili and English may have introduced construct-irrelevant variance into the formal examinations of student achievement in their various school subjects. In other words, the measurement of student achievement may have been muddied by the use of either language which is, in traditional measurement terms, not necessarily part of the construct of what was actually being measured here (i.e. students' achievement in their school subjects). Thus for educational decision-makers these findings demonstrate that a switch in the language of exams will not resolve the inequalities in this high-stakes examining context. The analyses of the national data sets described next provide additional insights into the language-related effects on student performance.

Language in National Examination Performance: Data Set 4

Data from the 2007 and 2008 national Form II examination results were initially subjected to analysis at three levels (district, school and pupil) using MLwiN (Yu & Thomas, 2008), comprising a total of 44,455 students from 10 districts and 161 schools (14,603 students in 2007 and 29, 852 in 2008). All results were standardized for analysis to facilitate comparison of the findings across the school subjects. Because the initial round of analysis showed that district-level variances for biology, chemistry, math, and English were not statistically significant, we dropped district and conducted the following 2-level (school and pupil) analyses: first, we used a cons model to identify the variances between schools and pupils

(Model 1); next, students' English language proficiency (i.e. Form II English examination results) was added as the single explanatory variable (Model 2); and finally, the school average English exam results was added as an indicator of the school's overall English achievement as a school-level contextual variable (Model 3). The key purpose of these analyses was to determine the effects of English language proficiency on students' examination performance in biology, chemistry and math, as shown in Table 4.

Table 4. Effects of English language proficiency on biology, chemistry and math performance on Form II exams (2007 and 2008 data)

Fixed part	Biology			Chemistry			Math		
	Model 1	Model 2	Model 3	Model 1	Model 2	Model 3	Model 1	Model 2	Model 3
Cons	0.052	0.053	0.053	0.084	0.086	0.086	0.106	0.107	0.107
	(0.036)	(0.026)	(0.026)	(0.039)	(0.030)	(0.030)	(0.046)	(0.038)	(0.037)
English		0.644	0.644		0.647	0.647		0.484	0.484
		(0.004)	(0.004)		(0.004)	(0.004)		(0.004)	(0.003)
English school mean			0.008			0.033			0.282
			(0.057)			(0.065)			(0.079)
Random part (variances)									
Between school	0.197	0.109	0.109	0.238	0.143	0.142	0.337	0.229	0.212
	(0.023)	(0.012)	(0.012)	(0.027)	(0.016)	(0.016)	(0.038)	(0.026)	(0.024)
Between pupils	0.851	0.489	0.489	0.841	0.476	0.476	0.759	0.556	0.556
	(0.006)	(0.003)	(0.003)	(0.006)	(0.003)	(0.003)	(0.005)	(0.004)	(0.004)
Total	1.048	0.598	0.598	1.079	0.619	0.618	1.096	0.785	0.768
A	18.8	18.2	18.2	22.1	23.1	23.0	30.7	29.2	27.6
B	81.2	81.3	81.3	77.9	76.9	77.0	69.3	70.8	72.4
C	---	42.9	42.9	---	42.6	42.7	---	28.4	29.9
D	---	44.7	44.7	---	39.9	40.3	---	32.1	37.1
E	---	42.5	42.5	---	43.4	43.4	---	26.8	26.8
−2*log (likelihood)	119570	94990	94990	119084	93796	93796	114608	100738	100726

Notes: (1) N=44, 455 students in all models, (2) ( ) stands for standard errors.
A=intra school correlation (%), B=intra pupil correlation (%), C=% of total variance explained, D=% of school-level variance explained, E=% of pupil-level variance explained

As shown for Model 1, the school level differences in the mean exam scores in the three subjects vary, with biology having the smallest difference and math having the largest difference between schools. In other words, the difference in math examination results between schools was the biggest among the three subjects. English language proficiency as the single explanatory variable was found to explain 28.4% of the total variance in math, 42.6% of the total variance in chemistry, and 42.9% of the total variance in biology. A similar amount of school and pupil level variances can be explained by this single explanatory variable: 32.1% of the school level variance in math, 39.9% in chemistry and 44.7% in biology; 26.8% of the pupil level variance in math, 42.5% in biology and 43.4% in chemistry. In other words, English language was found to be a significant predictor of students' performance in biology, chemistry and math. Adding school mean scores in English as another explanatory variable (i.e. Model 3) did not seem to improve the model fit for biology and chemistry examination results. However, it was significant as a school-level factor for modeling math examination results. A further 5% of the school-level variance (from 32.1% to 37.1%) was explained by school mean scores in English, which explained a further 1.5% of the total variance (from 28.4% to 29.9%). As shown in these models, students' English language proficiency is clearly a significant and substantial predictor of their performance in all three subjects, particularly biology and chemistry. Furthermore, although the total school-level variance is largest in math, English language proficiency, both as a pupil and a school level variable, is less capable of predicting math performance than biology and chemistry. This could be because student exam performance in math is less affected by language proficiency, but previous research has shown that word problems cause significant difficulty for English L2 speakers (e.g. Barwell, 2002). Other factors like teacher qualifications may play a more significant role in math, as anecdotal evidence indicated that there is a shortage of qualified math teachers in schools. However, it should be noted that nearly one-third of the total variance in math can be explained by the English language proficiency variable, which provides sufficient evidence that English language proficiency plays a significant and substantial role in student exam performance overall.

Students' Opportunities to Learn English at School and at Home: Data Set 5

In order to increase the explanatory power of our findings, we administered a student questionnaire at the time we administered the different language versions of the exams. The purpose was to investigate factors other than language and their effects on student achievement. These included question items indicating socio-economic status such as possessions in the home and parent/guardian education levels and work. To explore student opportunities for English exposure at home, we asked for example whether students spoke English outside of school, if they watched TV or videos in English and/or Kiswahili, and if they read English and/or Kiswahili magazines and books. Table 5 provides descriptive statistics on students' self-reported frequency of exposure to English in and outside of school, with 1 representing "never," 2 "rarely," 3 "sometimes," 4 "often" and 5 "all of the time." Please note that while the means are highest for "using English in school," a rating of 3 indicates only "*sometimes*" speaking English, suggesting that actual opportunities for using the language outside of school are insufficient to develop the requisite language skills for successfully engaging in learning through the medium of English.

We used these data of student exposure to English as independent variables to model the relationship between student opportunities to use English and their performance in the three different versions of the subject examinations, but none of them significantly predicted exam performance. At face value, this result may seem to contradict our finding, as demonstrated in Data Set 4 above, concerning the significant and substantial predictive power of English proficiency on exam performance.

Table 5. Descriptive statistics of students' self-reported exposure to the English language

Variable	N	Minimum	Maximum	Mean	Std. Deviation
Speaking English outside of school	453	1	5	2.46	1.005
Speaking English at home	456	1	5	2.30	0.993
Reading English at home	447	1	5	2.54	1.103
Watching TV/videos in English	453	1	5	2.18	1.145
Speaking English in English lessons	455	1	5	3.29	1.341
Speaking English in other school subjects	462	1	5	3.16	1.288
Read English books from school library	463	1	5	2.69	1.221

However, we would argue that this consolidates and strengthens our key findings on the importance of student English proficiency in determining their performance on content exams that are administered in English. Indeed, we have observed that students with greater exposure to English, i.e. Schools G and H, have higher English vocabulary test scores and are thus more likely to achieve high scores in the Form II exams administered in English. This seems to represent a vicious circle: little exposure to English in and outside of school leads to lower English proficiency which, in turn, leads to poorer exam results. In the context of this research, there was little sustained exposure to English in school observed, in spite of the prevailing national language policy promoting English as the sole medium of instruction. The reality is that most learners use Kiswahili in and outside of school. The lack of opportunities to use English has an impact going far beyond educational policy implementation issues; it dramatically affects the quality of teaching and learning processes in the classroom and the extent to which school-aged children will be able to perform well in national exams if they are administered only in English.

DISCUSSION

From the findings of the SPINE research project, we have gained considerable insight into the specific challenges that school children face when working through an unfamiliar language to try and demonstrate their school achievement in national exams. In this section we focus on two issues: first, the political and individual aspirations for English use; and second, the mismatch between these aspirations and the realities on the ground.

Aspirations for English versus On-the-Ground Realities

For governmental and educational policymakers, an international language, in this case English, embodies a country's aspiration for economic development and globalization as well as individual upward mobility. Widening access to education is seen as crucial to the achievement of scientific and technological innovation and increasing industrialization. It is also seen as important to the creation of new knowledge to manage some very real societal challenges arising from, for example, increasing rural-urban migration and high proportions of national populations living below the poverty line, in order to secure socio-economic advancement. These decision-makers frequently represent the elite, who have been successful at English and in school. By and large, their children will receive privileged educations and be surrounded by literate and numerate environments at home. Many of these leaders have been influential within their countries' universities prior to entering the policy arena, and their higher education modeled on Northern Anglo-Saxon values has determined their entry into the emergent middle and upper classes. It is unsurprising therefore to encounter amongst a country's educational leaders a strong entrenched belief that English-medium education is the means to economic development, societal well-being and bringing a population out of poverty.

It is now a widely held view amongst development professionals that whilst significant advancements have been made in terms of widening educational access, this has not been matched by quality or equity for all learners. Free access to education has led to inadequate numbers of trained teachers, teaching and learning resources, and suitable buildings with even the most basic of facilities. Compounding these factors is that teachers' own low proficiency in the language of instruction, English in this case, further hampers their ability to use English effectively to teach. Children in such classes may attend school for several years yet learn very little, as evidenced by the data reported here, (see also Rea-Dickins, Khamis, & Olivero, 2013; see also Walter, Chapter 14 in this volume).

Returning to the decision-makers, if they were to be convinced by data such as ours and those included in this volume and were to implement bilingual assessment for all students, their concerns would immediately turn to resourcing such a strategy. But which carries the highest resource demand: implementing bilingual assessment or developing a teaching force fully competent in both subject knowledge and with a high-level of English proficiency? A system of bi- or multilingual assessment would also be considerably fairer and more inclusive for all students.

Meanwhile, there are challenges from stakeholders themselves. An ADEA report (2004) quotes a village parent who describes the aspiration for English:

> It's not skill in his mother-tongue which makes a child succeed in life, but how much English he knows. Is it going to be one type of school for the rich and another for the poor? At the end of the day we are expected to pass examinations in English! (ADEA, 2004: 38)

Put another way, any employment opportunities based on English language proficiency will be determined by the quality of an individual's exam performance through and in English. Yet, in our view, the majority of school children simply cannot cope with being taught and tested in a foreign language. Huge numbers fail their school examinations, drop out of school and fail to complete their primary basic or upper secondary educations successfully.

In terms of individual aspirations, parents and students too are emphatic in their thirst for English and its use in schools. An earlier study in the same research context using questionnaire and interview data (Rea-Dickins et al., 2005) demonstrated that parents overwhelmingly supported the introduction of English-medium instruction before the transition to secondary school and for English to be used as sole medium of instruction when the switch has been made. However, if we recall the results on the English vocabulary results (Tables 2 and 3 above), the reality is that students are not ready for English-medium instruction and examining. In other words, the realities are holding back the achievement of their tenaciously held aspirations for English.

The following are some further questions that remain to be addressed:

Firstly, does or could one language-in-education policy, regardless of the use of the first language or the aspired international language, fit all? What are the implications and the potential impact for rural or marginalized contexts vs. the growing middle classes whose children have more opportunities and resources to use the international language in and out of school? What impact does a monolingual language policy in a bi- or multilingual setting have on student achievement in different subjects, given, for example, the differential effects of different languages evidenced in our data sets? Does a monolingual policy discriminate against and disadvantage certain groups of learners because of their different language proficiency levels in different languages?

Secondly, to what extent would the implementation of any change in language-in-education be gradual or otherwise? Change in students' and teachers' language proficiency and other skills takes time, yet policy-makers often look for quick and 'simple' solutions. If English is to remain an important international language, then it becomes imperative for countries with a strong legacy of English as the language of instruction to have a robust strategy in place for the gradual development of a variety of systems to support students' learning of English in preparation for its use as the language of instruction. Crucial to any action plan would be the strengthening of human resources and infrastructures for teacher professional development *and* quality language development opportunities for all teachers, i.e. not only English teachers. But how realistic is it to achieve these goals?

Thirdly, irrespective of what government or policy-makers determine regarding the language of instruction, in the interest of justice for all children and the empowering of parents to become knowledgeable decision-makers, other actions are called for. This goes beyond support for teacher professional development. For example, awareness campaigns should be mounted for improving understanding of the issues by the general public and parents on the advantages and disadvantages of language of instruction choices (English, Kiswahili or non-dominant languages). This would need to educate parents sensitively, within the social and political backdrop of a country, so that they can understand that English is not the only useful language for their children's academic development, as well as their social integration and contributions within the localized globalised contexts. How achievable and effective would this campaign be?

In the light of the findings and this discussion, we return to the title of our chapter in our concluding section.

CONCLUSION: AMBITIONS & PIPE DREAMS

It is a basic human right to aspire to a better life, to richer opportunities for the next generation and to exodus from poverty. There is, thus, a strong 'economic' factor underlying the use of English as a medium of instruction. The reasoning of policy-makers, and of parents, is related to the view that an international language is essential to a country's social, economic and industrial development. Because international languages such as English are seen as the panacea for stemming the inter-generational transfer of poverty, large numbers of children in Sub-Saharan Africa are not taught or examined in their first or home languages when they go to school. The reality on the ground frequently runs counter to this ambition for international language proficiency, as the majority of children cannot cope with being taught and tested in a foreign language. Huge numbers fail their national school tests and many do not get beyond primary, with fewer still completing basic secondary education. Examining through English is thus a 'high stakes' issue, impacting significantly on the consequential validity of the examinations in use (Messick, 1980).

The ambition for English is actually something of a 'pipe dream,' with respect to the overwhelming evidence from the SPINE research, some of which we have presented in this chapter. Our conclusion, therefore, is to reject a monolingual blanket policy in exams in favor of offering bi/multilingual testing choices. The consequences of continuing to test only in international languages that are foreign to students remain considerable for large numbers of students, the majority of whom will be kept on the periphery of society, unable to gain an education that will allow them to escape from poverty. Our conclusion is that language is a major gatekeeper for the majority: in spite of intense motivations and aspirations to 'do better' what remains are pipe dreams in face of what is possible given the realities on the ground.

NOTES

[i] Basic education includes primary and junior secondary education, i.e. grades 1 through 8.

[ii] ESRC/DfiD Major Research Grant, RES-167-25-0263S; see www.bristol.ac.uk/spine. Researchers include Mohamed Abeid, Dr Oksana Afitska, Professor Sibel Erduran, Professor Harvey Goldstein, Dr Neil Ingram, Zuleikha Khamis, Abdulla Hemed Mohammed, Dr Haji Mwavura, Dr Federica Olivero, Professor Pauline Rea-Dickins, Shambana Said, Professor Rosamund Sutherland and Dr Guoxing Yu.

[iii] For details on our respective roles and on study design, see www.bristol.ac.uk/spine

[iv] See also http://www.bristol.ac.uk/spine/publication%20and%20reports/study5.1report.

REFERENCES

Abedi, Jamal, Courtney, Mary, Leon, Seth., Kao, Jenny, & Azzam, Tarek (2006). *English language learners and math achievement: A study of opportunity to learn and language accommodation.* CRESST Technical Report 702. Los Angeles: University of California, Los Angeles.

Abedi, Jamal, & Gándara, Patricia (2006). Performance of English language learners as a subgroup in large-scale assessment: Interaction of research and policy. *Educational Measurement: Issues and Practice, 25*(4), 36-46.

Alidou, Hassana (1997). *Education language policy and the bilingual education: The impact of French language policy in primary education in Niger.* Unpublished PhD, University of Illinois Urbana-Champaign, Urbana-Champaign.

Alidou, Hassana (2003). Language policies and language education in Francophone Africa: A critique and a call to action. In S. Makoni, G. Smitherman, A. F. Ball, & A. K. Spears (Eds.), *Black linguistics: Language, society, and politics in Africa and the Americas* (pp. 103-116). London: Routledge.

Barwell, Richard (2002). *The development of a discursive psychology approach to investigation of participation of students with English as an additional language (EAL) in writing and solving arithmetic problems with peers.* Unpublished PhD Dissertation. Bristol, England: University of Bristol.

Benson, Carol (2005). Girls, educational equity and mother tongue-based teaching. Policy document. Bangkok: UNESCO Bangkok.

Brock-Utne, Birgit (2005). Language-in-education policies and practices in Africa with a special focus on Tanzania and South Africa – Insights from research in progress. In A. M. Y. Lin & P. W. Martin (Eds.), *Decolonisation, globalisation: Language-in-education policy and practice* (pp. 173-193). Clevedon, England: Multilingual Matters.

Brock-Utne, Birgit, & Holmarsdottir, Halla B. (2004). Language policies and practices in Tanzania and South Africa: problems and challenges. *International Journal of Educational Development, 24*(1), 67-83.

Butler, Frances A., & Stevens, Robin (2001). Standardized assessment of the content knowledge of English language learners K-12: Current trends and old dilemmas. *Language Testing, 18*(4), 409-427.

Castellon-Wellington, Martha (2000). *The impact of preference for accommodations: The performance of English language learners on large-scale academic achievement tests.* CSE Technical Report 524. Los Angeles: University of California, Center for the Study of Evaluation/National Center for Research on Evaluation, Standards and Student Testing.

Fredua-Kwarteng, Eric Y., & Ahia, Francis (2005a). Ghana flunks at math and science: Analysis (1). Feature article. *Ghana News* (8 January 2005).

Fredua-Kwarteng, Eric Y., & Ahia, Francis (2005b). Ghana flunks at math and science: Analysis (2). Feature article. *Ghana News* (23 February 2005).

Heller, Monica, & Martin-Jones, Marilyn (Eds.) (2001). *Voices of authority: Education and linguistic difference.* Westport, CT: Ablex Publishing.

Hovens, Mart (2002). Bilingual education in West Africa: Does it work? *International Journal of Bilingual Education and Bilingualism, 5*(5), 249-266.

Kalole, Safarani Alli Mndeme (2004). *Answering essay and summary type questions in English and Kiswahili: Problems in the certification of secondary education examination in Tanzania.* Unpublished Master, University of Oslo, Oslo.

Kaphesi, Elias (2003). The influence of language policy in education on mathematics classroom discourse in Malawi: The teachers' perspective. *Teacher Development, 7*(2), 265-285.

Kellaghan, Thomas & Greaney, Vincent (2004). Assessing student learning in Africa. Washington, D. C.: World Bank.

Levine, Glenn. S. (2011). *Code choice in the language classroom.* Bristol: Channel View Books.

Luckett, Kathy (1994). National additive bilingualism: Towards a language plan for South African education. *Southern African Journal of Applied Language Studies, 2*(1), 38-60.

Messick, Samuel (1980). Test validity and the ethics of assessment. *American Psychologist, 35*(11), 1012-1027.

Mlama, Penina, & Matteru, Martha (1978). *Haja ya Kutumia Kiswahili Kufundishia Katika Elimu ya Juu* [The need to use Kiswahili as a medium of instruction in higher education]. Dar es Salaam: Bakita.

Mwinsheikhe, Halima M. (2002). *Overcoming the language barrier: An in-depth study of the Tanzanian secondary school science teachers' initiatives in coping with the English-Kiswahili dilemma in the teaching-learning process.* Paper presented at the NETREED Conference.

Mwinsheikhe, Halima M. (2003). Using Kiswahili as a medium of instruction in Tanzanian secondary schools. In B. Brock-Utne, Z. Desai, & M. Qorro (Eds.), *Language of instruction in Tanzania and South Africa (LOITASA).* Dar es Salaam E&D.

Nyerere, Julius (1968). *Education for self-reliance, in Ujamaa, Essays on Socialism.* Dar es Salaam: Oxford University Press.

Ouane, Adama, & Glanz, Christine (Eds.) (2011). *Optimising learning, education and publishing in Africa: The language factor. A review and analysis of theory and practice in mother-tongue and bilingual education in sub-Saharan Africa.* Hamburg, Germany: UNESCO Institute for Lifelong Learning (UIL), the Association for the Development of Education in Africa (ADEA), African Development Bank.

Rea-Dickins, Pauline, Clegg, John, & Rubagumya, Casmir M. (2005). *Evaluation of the orientation secondary class in Zanzibar.* A consultancy report. Bristol: University of Bristol Graduate School of Education.

Rea-Dickins, Pauline, Yu, Guoxing, & Afitska, Oksana. (2009). The consequences of examining through an unfamiliar language of instruction and its impact for school-age learners in sub-Saharan African school systems. In L. Taylor & C. Weir (Eds.), *Language testing matters* (pp. 190-214). Cambridge: Cambridge University Press.

Rea-Dickins, Pauline, Khamis, Zuleikha, & Olivero, Federica (2013). Does English-medium instruction and examining lead to social and economic advantage? Promises and threats: A Sub-Saharan case study. In E. J. Erling & P. Seargeant (Eds.), *English and international development.* Bristol: Multilingual Matters.

Rubagumya, Casmir M. (2003). English medium primary schools in Tanzania: a new 'linguistic market' in education? In B. Brock-Utne, Z. Desai, & M. Qorro (Eds.), *Language of instruction in Tanzania and South Africa* (pp. 149-169). Dar es Salaam: E & D.

Shohamy, Elana (2006). *Language policy: Hidden agendas and new approaches.* Abingdon, Oxon: Routledge.

Skutnabb-Kangas, Tove, & Heugh, Kathleen (Eds.) (2012). *Multilingual education and sustainable diversity work. From periphery to centre.* New York: Routledge.

Walter, Stephen, & Davis, Patricia (2005). *Eritrea national reading survey: September 2002.* Ministry of Education, Asmara, Eritrea. Dallas, TX: SIL International.

Wilmot, Eric (2003). *Stepping outside the ordinary expectations of schooling: Effect of school language on the assessment of educational achievement in Ghana.* Paper presented at the 47th Annual Meeting of CIES.

Yu, Guoxing, & Thomas, Sally. (2008). Exploring school effects across southern and eastern African school systems and in Tanzania. *Assessment in Education, 15*(3), 279-301.

Pauline Rea-Dickins
Aga Khan University, East Africa
Institute for Educational Development

Guoxing Yu
University of Bristol, UK

NUZZLY RUIZ DE FORSBERG & ALICIA BORGES MÅNSSON

11. IMPLEMENTATION OF LOCAL CURRICULUM IN MOZAMBICAN PRIMARY SCHOOLS

Realities and Challenges

ABSTRACT

Kubulikira caka ca piiri na pi chanu pisaoneka muno Mocambique m´bazawaza pa m'pimo wa kuonevera curriculo m'ma funzisiro pa mabhuku onesesa macitiro adacitwa m'pimo pa mabhuku a mfendo ia kutoma. M'funziro uyu usafuna onesesa macitiro adalongwa, pondho na kupisandiks tewera pioniwe mwa uthambaruki pabozi na mapika, peno m'pingizo udacitika pa ku mwadzwa kwa m'sobo unou wa ku funzisa. Na pinango pia ku funa kuona utambaruki na undhabwalabwa si wacitika pakati pa ufundjisi m'mum m'zinda wa kuNyungwe. Mufunziro awa adacitwa m'ghiriza pa uthubo pabozi na ufunzi wa m'tundo peno wa cisa pondho na mivunzo kuna ape asogoleri a m'mafunziro tewera kunyerezevana kupi penula kuti tany piri kufamba pindhu pida citwa pondho na macindiro apyo mwa andhu. Pondho pasa dikhirwa na khulipirwa kuti panaoneka uthambaruki m'ma funziro a ku pasana ku suzuka mwa uundhu. (*Translation to Sena [seh], a language of Mozambique, by Amalia Dickie.*)

Since 2005, Mozambique has attempted to devolve some control over the national curriculum to the local level within the overall context of education decentralization. The aim of this paper is to examine the implementation of the country's *local curriculum* component for primary schools. The progress and challenges posed by implementation are assessed along with the manner in which the policy has been interpreted by school directors in three districts of the Province of Tete, situated in central western Mozambique. This study is based on a review of official documents and reports. A qualitative approach is taken to examine the extent to which the local curriculum component has been implemented, and the underlying attitudes as revealed by observations and interviews with primary school directors. The findings take into consideration those elements of school background and contextual factors that facilitate or restrict attainment of the aims of the reform policy. Our interpretations are based on a combination of constructivist and liberation pedagogy frameworks. From these perspectives, knowledge is socially constructed and learners draw meaning out of a multiplicity of stimuli.

C. Benson and K. Kosonen (eds.), Language Issues in Comparative Education, 207–223.

INTRODUCTION

At first glance, Mozambique appears to be a prosperous country, with abundant natural resources (water, land, hydroelectric energy, forestry, coal deposits, minerals, etc.). In light of recent economic and social analyses, however, it is clear that the country is still confronted by major challenges. First, more than half of the population lives below the poverty line, particularly those in the central region of the country (Ministry of Planning and Development, 2010). Almost half of all children are malnourished; one out of every two children under 5 years of age cannot achieve physical, mental or cognitive growth potential (Government of Mozambique, 2010). The HIV-AIDS epidemic continues to threaten development by robbing families of wage earners and reducing available human resources. According to the results of a recent national survey, the prevalence of HIV infection among adults (15-49) is 11.5%, with a greater number of women than men infected (INSIDA, 2009). Rural infrastructures need rehabilitation (Government of Mozambique 2010), and ensuring an inclusive system of education is among the most important needs. Much of schooling is still provided in Portuguese, a language that few children understand outside the capital city.

The explanation for this paradox rests, in part, in the history of Mozambique. In 2010 the country celebrated 35 years of independence from Portuguese colonial domination, which was characterized by little colonial investment in the training of local staff or in the construction of basic rural infrastructure in the country. Disparities developed between districts and provinces; some were chosen for investment and others not. Mozambique experienced successive waves of destruction as a consequence of long periods of war before and after independence: first, the war for independence from 1964 to 1974, and then a civil war from 1977 to 1992 (Brito et al., 2010). The agricultural sector was one of those sectors most disrupted by the civil war, as well as by the various droughts affecting local food supply.

Another aspect of Mozambican development is its transition from a centrally planned economy with close links to Eastern Europe and the Soviet Union to a market-oriented economy with close links to the high-income countries of the North and West as well as with international financial institutions. The dialectic of 1980s Marxism was replaced by capitalist discourse in the 1990s. A combination of internal and external factors has affected the implementation of structural changes in the education system, which is subject to donor aid and influence.

The entire curriculum was reviewed following political changes in the country, and since 2004 a major *Reforma Curricular* or Curriculum Reform has been taking place. Two of the innovations introduced into basic education is the component known as *currículo local* or local curriculum (LC) within the primary curriculum and the integration of local languages into initial literacy and for teaching and learning. The aim is to bring the community closer to the school and allow children to find meaning in what they learn with respect to their home and community lives. Prior to this Reform, school instruction and materials were entirely in Portuguese, a language foreign to most learners, reflecting the culture and aspirations of the dominant elite.

The aim of this study is to provide deeper insight into the evolution of LC implementation by investigating individual schools in three districts of Tete province in Mozambique. The study is organized around the following questions:
- How is local curriculum understood and implemented?
- How does the centrally defined national curriculum relate to the local curriculum?
- What kinds of difficulties have school directors encountered during the course of implementation?
- What still needs to be done to consolidate implementation of this aspect of the Reform?

BACKGROUND OF THE STUDY

This study was undertaken by the authors during a one-month period in 2010 as a result of our previous work experience in Mozambique and our interest in following up on developments related to the curriculum reform. Based on our experiences, we decided to conduct a small study on how the local curriculum component was being implemented in eight public schools of three districts of Tete province. It was possible to collect the desired data during this short period of time due to the support of the school authorities, to whom we extend our deepest thanks.

Conceptual Framework

The conceptual framework underlying the present analysis is organized on two levels:
- The national level and its interconnections, taking a combination of World Systems and Neo-Marxist perspectives; and
- The school level along with Reform implementation, taking a combination of constructivist and liberation approaches.

The first analysis offers a solid explanation of significant connections between structural forces at the global level and contemporary reforms and changes in national education systems around the word. As is the case in many African countries, Mozambique embarked on decentralization reforms that are driven by neoliberal thinking regarding the use of financial, material and human resources. Values with an emphasis on competition, quality, deregulation and efficiency have influenced public policies (Farrell, 1999). In his analysis of the 1999-2003 Strategic Plan for Education, Cossa points to two underlying rationales, both of which are linked to economic aspects, namely "to respond to the exigencies of the Mozambique economy" and "to respond to the pressures and opportunities from a more integrative and competitive global economy" (Cossa, 2011: 9). Education is clearly seen as a means to respond effectively to economic needs. As stated by the government, students need to be prepared for the new working world, and Mozambique must be ready to participate in the new global economy (Guro &

Weber, 2010). In this context, changes in education are felt to be necessary to respond to challenges beyond the local and the national.

Regarding the overall Reform, the proposed integration of subjects in the classroom is consistent with constructivism. Bottom-up analysis is important to highlight the relationship between policy and practice, providing the meaning of the local, or the situation at the grassroots level. The constructivist approach views learning as an active process in which learners construct their own understandings and knowledge of the world through action and reflection. In this framework, education must engage with the languages and experiences of learners, as stated by Freire (1970), which means that teachers must understand the experiences and world views of their students and build on these to further the learning process. Students themselves need to be engaged in meaningful and relevant activities that allow them to actively seek after knowledge – providing a multiplicity of stimuli though practices such as collaborative learning – and apply this knowledge to future problems. Critical reflection demands opportunities for students to reflect on their experiences and express their thoughts. Education is thus conceptualized by Freire as a vehicle for human emancipation and transformation.

In the case of the curriculum reform in Mozambique, Guro and Weber (2010) find that a great deal of emphasis is put on problem solving and the development of cross-disciplinary higher-order thinking skills. New meanings and understandings are seen as being socially constructed, unlike traditional approaches using more technical and mechanistic methods. Teachers are considered critical for successful implementation of curriculum reform, and they should be prepared to implement methodologies that help students move to new levels of understanding and development.

It is interesting to examine the school level, where educators implement their understandings of the proposed changes in specific institutional settings, and where the meaning or significance of these changes in people's lives is emphasized. We assume that these interpretations are subjective, and that the social and cultural settings of each school and community influence the implementation of any particular reform policy. In order to promote a deeper understanding of the curriculum reform process, we aim to reveal how changes are perceived by school directors in the context of their work.

Methodology Used

This study is based on qualitative research methods and analysis, which allow for in-depth descriptions and interpretation of the processes involved in implementation of the local curriculum component of the educational Reform. In addition to the review of policy documents, studies and reports, we solicited the insights of eight school directors, one in each of eight public schools (both urban and rural) in three districts of Tete province where the LC component is being implemented. We conducted the investigation in February 2010, a month after the beginning of the school year, eliciting data of two types:

– Questionnaire for school directors: Each school director completed a written questionnaire in Portuguese containing 12 open-ended questions designed to solicit her/his perceptions of what the local curriculum component entails, how it is being implemented and how it can meet the local learning needs of students.
– Focus group interviews with school directors: After reviewing the questionnaires, we carried out two focus group sessions with the same eight school directors, allowing them to comment on and confirm their responses and to add relevant information concerning the different stages of reform implementation.

Unfortunately, due to limited time and resources, we were not able to assess the contributions of LC in terms of learners' educational attainment, which would have required more in-depth observations and assessment. We are thus limited to describing implementation of the local curriculum component as perceived by these school directors, and analyzing their responses in terms of the available literature.

CURRICULUM REFORM IN MOZAMBIQUE

Education in Mozambique

In general, two main periods of economic and social development can be distinguished in Mozambique since the country gained independence from Portugal in 1975 under the leadership of the Front for the Liberation of Mozambique (FRELIMO) party. The first period lasted from 1975 to the 1990s, during which time the country's political, economic and social structures were transformed in the transition to a socialist regime. The second period began with the signing of the peace accord in 1992, which set the country on a new course of development, establishing contacts with the major international financial institutions, implementing structural reforms (beginning in 1987 with the Economic Rehabilitation Program), developing a multiparty system, and transitioning gradually from a planned economy to a liberal market-oriented one. Since then, economic growth has been considerably more positive. The external context, including the breakdown of both the Socialist block and the Apartheid system in South Africa, also played a role in the political and economic transformations of Mozambique, and foreign assistance has fueled growth and financed social development. These political and economic changes, both internal and external, have influenced the vision and nature of the education system in Mozambique. The system established during the Portuguese colonial administration was replaced in 1983 by the New National Education System, which made possible the adoption of a new curriculum structure, with new programs and teaching materials, and a new model for pre-service teacher training (Dhorsan & Moreno, 2008). The new curriculum that has introduced the local curriculum component has also introduced English, music, moral and civics education, and the use of Mozambican languages as languages of instruction.

Public primary education today is free and is divided into two compulsory levels: 1st level primary education (EP1, 1st to 5th grades) and 2nd level primary education (EP2, 6th and 7th grades). Many primary schools have two five-hour shifts, one in the morning and another in the afternoon. In order to accommodate the expansion of the system, some urban primary schools even have three 3.5-hour shifts, and/or offer EP2 at night. Less than 2% of all primary students attend private schools. Upon completion of primary education, students may continue their studies at the general secondary level or at the basic level of technical-professional education. Secondary education is not free; school fees are charged. Later, higher education is offered at both private and public universities.

The present five-year Strategic Plan for Education and Culture (*Plano Estratégico para Educação e Cultura* or PEEC) 2006-2011 was the first plan that is truly comprehensive, covering all levels of the system from early childhood education through to higher education, and the first to incorporate culture, following the merger of the Ministries of Culture and Higher Education into the Ministry of Education in 2006. The PEEC underlines government efforts to cope with existing challenges in the education sector, focusing on extending access to all school-aged children, out-of-school youth and adults and improving quality and relevance to ensure that increasing numbers of learners (particularly girls) have access to post-primary education.

There has been significant progress with respect to the following indicators: the number of students in primary and secondary education increased from 3.6 million in 2003 to 6.3 million in 2010; gender as well as geographic and economic disparities are decreasing, particularly in primary education; an increased number of teachers and improvements in the provision of educational materials (including teaching materials), contributed to a significant increase in the primary education completion rate from 34.1% in 2004 to 47.9% in 2009 (MoE, 2010). Through the national Education for All (EFA) Movement, civil society organizations participate in the annual review and planning meetings, as well as in Ministry working groups.

Despite these efforts, significant challenges remain in strengthening the sustainability of the expanded system, improving the quality of education and learning as well as ensuring an inclusive system, particularly for the most vulnerable populations, i.e. girls and students in rural areas. The results of an evaluation of the PEEC 2006-2011 (CesoCi, 2010) point to insufficient and deficient infrastructure, lack of appropriate training of staff (teachers and school managers), and inadequate or non-existent teaching materials as key factors affecting implementation of the Reform.

Decentralization

Responsibility for the administration of education services and the management of human, material and financial resources is increasingly being decentralized, and schools are receiving growing financial authority and decision-making power. The central government stipulates the main education objectives, strategic plans, regulations, standards and control over the system, while the provincial and district levels are given a wider scope for decision-making with respect to planning, financing and management of resources. However, there are obstacles to sustainability linked to weak capacity at the provincial and district levels to plan, manage and monitor implementation of decentralized programmes such as accelerated classroom construction for primary education (MoE, 2010).

At the school level, decentralization has been strengthened through the creation of local school councils (*Conselho de Escola*), which consist of the principal and elected members including representatives of the parents, teachers and students, where any member of the council other than the principal is eligible to be president. The areas of decision-making of the council include planning, administration of resources, curriculum development and school infrastructure among others (MEC, 2005).

Also at the local level, the Zones of Pedagogical Influence (ZIPs) have been progressively reintroduced to support in-service teacher development at the school level, which is one of the cornerstones of decentralization efforts. The ZIPs are defined as centers where local schools have the opportunity to organize in-service teacher training, adapt teaching programs to the local reality, assure the integration of local curriculum content into the national one, produce didactic materials and establish and develop cooperation between schools and ZIPs (MEC, 2008)

The Local Curriculum Component

In the context of the primary education Reform initiated in 2004 (Guro & Weber, 2010) several innovations have been introduced in addition to the local curriculum (LC) component that is the focus of this study, which overlaps considerably with the introduction of bilingual education (MEC, 2008).The aim of the LC is to introduce content that is relevant at the local level to meet local learning needs and develop life skills, attitudes and values. In the process, it aims to promote greater local participation in education, bringing the economic, social and cultural life of the students and their communities into the schools. In Tete province, districts like Angonia which hosted the earlier bilingual experiment (Benson, 2000) have even introduced local languages as part of the LC.

To facilitate implementation of the LC component, manuals and guidelines have been developed with support from international organizations such as UNDP and UNESCO. The LC is organized to delve into topics defined in the central curriculum or to include new topics that will develop experiential knowledge, attitudes and practices of students that are relevant to the local community situated. These topics are related to local culture, history, geography, agricultural practices, health and nutrition, and life skills (INDE, 2006). According to curriculum developers, the LC "enables the development of the necessary competences to solve basic problems concerning health, food, habitat, technology transfer for the production of plants and animals, among many other topics that have been identified by the communities as relevant" (Dhorsan & Moreno, 2009: 203).

The LC is supposed to be integrated into the primary curriculum, and is allocated 20% of the total time given to teaching each subject, to deal in an integrated manner with relevant topics (INDE, 2006). These topics, which are meant to be identified by the local communities, should be relevant to the children's lives, families and communities. The notion of "local" is not limited to the immediate geographical area where the school is situated, but can be extended to the ZIPs at the district and provincial levels. The process of developing the LC is carried out at the school level, where a committee of teachers is set up and given responsibilities for data collection in the community. Parents and other members of the community should participate in the provision of content related to health education, traditional practices, nutrition, gastronomy, geography, history and so on. Once the data is collected, the teachers are to systematize this information by inserting it into the various disciplines, taking into account:

- the objectives identified in the basic education curriculum plan as defined at the central level;
- the skills that should be developed;
- the need for further study to add detail to topics defined at the central level, taking into account their relevance to the community;
- the need for extending knowledge, adding new content to topics defined at the central level.

Once this is done, the school council is to select and approve those topics that are considered to be most relevant to the students. The topics and teaching plan are organized in a school booklet known as a *brochura*, which should be assessed and approved by the education authorities at the district level. An example of how the relevant information and/or topics for the LC can be structured is given in Table 1.

Table 1. Example of LC grid proposed by the ZIP2* in Tete City

LC Topic	Subject	Thematic Units	Teaching Themes	Content	Class	Participants in the teaching process
Ceramics	Natural Science	Environment	Fighting erosion	Fighting erosion in the region	3rd, 6th & 7th	Participation of teachers, students and community

*ZIP2 includes three primary schools in Tete City

It should be noticed that the example in Table 1 is not fully elaborated according to the LC approach established in the policy (INDE, 2006). However, the brochure of ZIP 2 does include topics related to the particular characteristics of the area where the schools are located, including:

- Health: Diseases that occur most frequently in the community; means for prevention and care
- Culture: Traditional songs and musical instruments; tales, myths, traditional practices for requesting rain; the making of ceramics
- Agriculture and fishing: Methods practiced in the community

- Gastronomy: Typical foods in the community (with terms in Nhongwe) such as *phunde* (leaves), *nkhongue* (goat intestines), *mulenguera* (tree leaves), *ntanga* (pumkin leaves), *quiabo* (okra) and *chiombo* (curry of pumpkin and watermelon seeds)
- Geography: Main rivers of the province such as the *Zambeze, Róvubwe, Luia* and *Capoche*

The LC booklet lists all the topics of local interest to be taught in the school. When planning the lesson, teachers must consult not just the centrally defined content but also the LC booklet. Concerning the management of the 20% time allocated to the LC, the local topics can be handled in the following ways:

- The LC topics are integrated into the teaching-learning process in the classroom during the time allocated to the lesson;
- The teacher can plan some classroom activities, such as asking a parent to come in and explain how a local dish is made;
- The teacher can organize activities outside the school, such as visits to local factories or places of historical interest, among others.

The LC is a flexible curriculum which can be developed systematically in accordance with the specific needs of a given community. As the findings of this study will show, a few schools have proceeded with policy implementation, while others are far behind.

LOCAL CURRICULUM IMPLEMENTATION IN TETE

This section reports on our investigation of the manner in which local curriculum implementation has been organized in eight schools of three districts in Tete province to pursue the objectives stated in the Reform policy. The LC reform was initiated in 2006 after an intensive in-service training meant to orientate school directors and ZIP coordinators with regard to conceptual aspects and the steps necessary to implement the LC.

In this section we begin with a brief description of the conditions for implementation in Tete province. We then examine the perceptions and meanings attached to Curriculum Reform implementation by school directors in the three districts. For the purpose of this analysis we have organized the findings and discussion under the following headings: meanings of the Reform, potential impact of the Reform (advantages), constraints on the implementation of the Reform (disadvantages) and perceptions of the actual changes resulting from the reform. In the realm of meanings and perceptions, we demonstrate that it is possible to trace how current practices diverge from the original intentions.

Background on Tete Province

The province of Tete is the third largest in Mozambique after Niassa and Zambezi, covering an area of 100,724 square kilometers in the west-central region bordering Malawi, Zambia and Zimbabwe. According to the 2007 population census (INE, 2007) Tete has almost two million inhabitants but one of the lowest population densities in the country. Administratively, the province comprises 13 districts, including the district around its capital, Tete City; as noted above, we worked in three districts with both rural and urban schools represented.

Tete has large coal deposits and substantial hydroelectric power generation potential in the Zambezi River, including the Cahora Bassa Dam, which is the main source of electrical energy in Mozambique and supplier to other neighboring countries. As a result there has been an influx of private companies (both local and foreign) in search of business opportunities such as the Brazilian VALE Company and the Australian Riversdale, along with Portuguese and Chinese investors. As a result, as shown by data from the last population census (INE, 2007), the population of Tete has rapidly expanded over the last ten years, making it the second fastest growing province after Maputo province. This would indicate a positive development outlook, at least from an economic perspective, but one limited mainly to the provincial capital, causing large intra-province inequalities. There is thus a high incidence of poverty comparable to other parts of the country, as illustrated by some comparative indicators presented in Table 2.

Table 2. Selected Millennium Development Goals: Tete vs. National Indicators. (Source: Cumbi & Warren-Rodríguez, 2007)

Indicators	1997	2003
Percentage living below the poverty line		
Tete	82.3	59.8
Central region	73.8	45.5
National	69.4	54.1
Infant mortality rate (per 1,000 live births)		
Tete	160	125
National	147	124
Nampula (worst off province)	216	164
Maputo City (best off area)	49	51
Illiteracy rate		
Tete	66.8	59.2
National	60.5	53.6
Cabo Delgado (worst off province)	75.0	68.4
Maputo City (best off area)	15.0	15.1

Considering the conditions present in Tete province, we felt that collecting data in three of its school districts would give us a reasonably good idea of how implementation of the Reform might be going in other parts of the country. In comparative terms, as shown in Table 2, Tete reports about the same level of development as the rest of the country, with the exception of Maputo, the capital city.

Perceptions of the Local Curriculum

The local curriculum component, as discussed partially above, aims to provide an education that meets the real needs of learners with respect to acquiring those life skills, attitudes and values that will enable their full participation in the political, economic, social and cultural life of their communities and country, ultimately helping to alleviate extreme poverty and vulnerability (as stated in a manual for teachers; see INDE, 2006). The LC should guarantee that learners gain basic health knowledge and should promote values and attitudes for better integration of students in their communities – yet in many places Portuguese, a foreign language, remains the medium of instruction, alienating students from their communities. In fact, so far, none of the schools we investigated is implementing mother tongue-based bilingual education as offered by the Reform. However, through the participation of community members and use of local themes, learners' home languages are beginning to enter classrooms where previously only Portuguese was used.

Findings from the questionnaire show that seven of the eight school directors seem to be informed and aware of the LC objectives and benefits. The following comments from the focus group discussions illustrate these views (our translations from Portuguese):

The LC is relevant to local learning needs because it helps students to be creative problem-solvers, with the life skills that will support them in the future. (School Director, district of Moatize)

The LC creates opportunities to appreciate local culture, to support students to develop creativity and capacity to use local means ... to keep children in school ... and to improve the linkages between the school and the parents. (School Director, district of Changara)

Among the main contributions of the LC that can be recounted are those that are related to the development of entrepreneurship and life skills knowledge. (School Director, city of Tete)

As noted above, there was an intensive in-service training held in 2006. However, according to the school directors, very little follow-up has been done to supervise or advise policy implementation. According to our respondents there was insufficient orientation with respect to methodological and pedagogical aspects, and very few practical exercises. There was a limited amount of informative material offered that would have supported effective orientation and dissemination of Reform objectives in their schools. Consequently it could have been foreseen that LC implementation would make no further headway and would be limited to superficial results. Respondents were asked to describe two aspects of Reform initiation: (i) How was the process of identifying LC subjects carried out? and (ii) What support was given by parents and community members with regard to the approach to LC topics?

217

Responses given to the first question indicate that the schools have indeed been primarily responsible for collecting local topics from the communities. Firstly, the schools have organized brigades (*brigadas*) or committees (*comissões*) of teachers who are authorized to carry out the task of informing parents, religious leaders and other influential people in the community about the objectives of the LC; they should also gain these people's support to provide topics of local interest to be taught. According to all eight school directors, early in the process a large proportion of parents were willing to collaborate by providing information relevant to students' learning needs. Below are some comments related to this issue:

> The response of the parents was positive ... they were willing to share their knowledge on the elaboration of handicraft items. (School Director, city of Tete)

> The support of parents was very positive ... they provided ideas, experiences and lessons ... they came to school to show how to make handicraft items, cook, dance traditional dances like Njolo, play games and so on. (School Director, district of Moatize)

Judging by their responses, the school directors responded to implementing the LC in their own ways, using available resources. According to them, their efforts have not been properly supported by systematic monitoring on the part of the Provincial Directorate, but they are doing what they can. This might explain why the example in Table 1 was not elaborated in the detail called for by the LC policy.

Integration and Contributions of the LC within the National Curriculum

The school directors were requested to indicate how the integration of the LC was being carried out at the time of the study. Their responses reveal that the LC has been integrated within the centrally defined curriculum during weekly lesson planning, which means that teachers must consult not only the centrally defined program but also the LC booklet. Only one director stated that he had encountered difficulties in integrating these topics into the teachers' lesson plans. One indication of weakness concerning the management of the LC is the fact that with the exception of one city school, the schools under investigation have not properly elaborated LC booklets covering all of the topics needed. In many instances, the booklets do not have the content that supports the teaching of topics of local interest. It seems that school directors were not aware of these inconsistencies at the time of data collection. This situation indicates a lack of proper supervision and technical orientation on the part of provincial education authorities, who have been charged with these tasks but who for various reasons (like technical staff mobility or limited resources) have not been able to carry them out.

Despite the challenges, the study participants still have a sense that the LC is making positive contributions regarding the development of student competencies, as shown in the following comments:

The LC has contributed to the improvement of the life skills of the students that will guarantee their self-sufficiency in the future ... The LC has also contributed to the retention of the child in the school and to improving the interaction between the school and the parents. (School Director, district of Changara)

The students have made progress and show they have knowledge and skills of the local topics. (School Director, district of Moatize)

We are using different local items as resources in the teaching of mathematics. (School Director, city of Tete)

Constraints on LC Reform Implementation

Our findings show that there is inconsistency in the way schools elaborate their study plans in relation to what is expected by curriculum developers. In addition, the majority of the schools that we investigated lack the necessary content of LC that would support lessons as requested by the policy, because they conducted only limited data collection and did not analyze or even organize the information collected. Our findings point to the need to strengthen technical support to policy implementation.

In the interviews, the school directors indicated that they have encountered some major difficulties during the LC implementation. Among these are the following:
– Insufficient manuals and other informative teaching materials to support LC implementation;
– Weak participation on the part of parents and/or community members in delivering instruction at the times allocated to LC because of lack of time and willingness. According to the respondents, parents would be more willing to participate if they were offered financial incentives;
– Shortcomings with regard to classroom conditions for the delivery of some LC instruction – for instance, lack of sufficient time to teach cooking skills;
– Shortage of training for those involved in the LC; and
– Insufficiency of financial and material resources for the elaboration of local themes.

The last difficulty is concerned with the need to provide more orientation and/or training to key actors such as parents who will deliver instruction. Interestingly, none of the respondents referred to the performance of teachers with respect to teaching the LC. This has in part to do with the general assumption among school directors that teaching the LC is being carried out in accordance with the procedure that has been established for its implementation. However, as mentioned above, the majority of the schools did not have an appropriate booklet for supporting teaching plans, which in turn has led to superficial teaching of the LC in many cases. A further issue pointed in the focus group discussions is the lack of systematic supervision, along with communication blockages between schools and districts offices.

Based on the school directors' comments, proposals to overcome the difficulties above can be summarized as follows:
- Training community leaders in the elaboration of LC;
- Sensitizing parents and school communities regarding the LC and gaining their participation;
- Seeking collaboration, experiences and financial support from non-governmental organizations to further develop the LC;
- Providing orientation for teachers in the teaching of the LC; and
- Updating the LC.

One school director also suggested the continuous training of teachers for management of the LC. It is clear from these responses that the difficulties will have to be tackled in a holistic manner if the curriculum reform is to have a meaningful future.

DISCUSSION AND CONCLUSIONS

It is well known that implementing educational reform and assessing outcomes in general is a complex matter. One aspect of this complexity is the simultaneous changes that involve different parts of the system; another is the roles played by different groups from the central level to the grassroots level, particularly when decentralization is at the forefront of the Reform. A descriptive and qualitative approach has been adopted for this study in order to examine the implementation of the local curriculum component of the Reform at the school level, using a sample of eight primary schools in three districts of Tete province.

Mozambique has embarked upon the transformation of its education system in response to the transition of the country to a market-oriented and competitive economy in a democratic system. There has been a shift with respect to the organization of the national education system, where decentralization and community participation policies have been dominant. The scope of curriculum reform includes the introduction of new disciplines and even a new bilingual approach, in addition to a local curriculum component. Education authorities are concerned not only with the knowledge and skills to be transmitted to the younger generation in order to facilitate their entrance into the labor market, family life and exercising their rights as citizens, but also with the reinforcement of Mozambican identity and recognition of cultural heritage. In this context, bilingual education and the local curriculum component are innovations that have been introduced into basic education since 2005 in response to challenges posed by the transition to a more authentic national orientation in a multilingual, multicultural country such as Mozambique. This transformation is related to Liberation and Constructivist theories in terms of developing individuals who are capable of constructing their own knowledge and understandings of the world through action and reflection while also taking into account their local environments. This is reflected in the school directors' expressions, such as, "The pupil becomes independent and creative"; "They gain the ability to solve their own life problems"; "The pupil becomes a man [sic] of the future"; "They gain practical skills for life." In all of these expressions, education is conceptualized as a vehicle for liberation and transformation.

The initiation of the LC reform in the schools under investigation was clearly fraught with difficulties with regard to the provision of technical support and informative materials as part of the process of change. The majority of schools have not yet elaborated their booklets in accordance with the established model (see Table 1). At this point in Reform implementation, parents are reluctant to collaborate with schools' efforts. They now seek financial incentives in return for their participation, which indicates that something is amiss with regard to implementation. One possible explanation is that the parents have not been well informed or have not fully understood the purpose of their involvement, and therefore do not feel motivated to participate without compensation. They might feel that the time required for their participation was too long and took them away from their daily work. Further, in contexts such as the district of Moatize (where coal exploitation is planned) and the city of Tete (the center of economic power in the province), people have become more centered on their own individual needs rather than on common social issues. It would appear that the language of economics, together with globalization and structural reforms, has entered into the domain of family contributions to education.

With regard to school directors' perceptions of the LC, they see the potential contributions and benefits of the LC despite the constraints they have identified in its implementation. The emergence of a primary education system with centrally and locally defined curricula requires a lot of effort to implement. Some recommendations made by the school directors during the course of the study, for example that more supervision be given to policy implementation, may serve as points of departure for making the LC a reality in their schools. In addition, the perceived positive contributions of the LC, such as the production of knowledge relevant to children's lives and cultural identities, should serve as reference points for policymakers, not only in education but also in other public sectors. We believe that the LC component may contribute to a more inclusive education system by increasing community participation, guaranteeing the rights of the learners and laying down the basis for better school performance, provided that implementation mechanisms like quality supervision, continuous teacher training and improved communication between schools, parents and communities are in place—and more importance is given to the use of local languages as mediums of instruction.

Implications for Further Research

This study has given voice to the school directors in part of one province of Mozambique. Today, in the context of a new Strategic Plan for Education 2012-2015, it is essential that more in-depth studies on the LC be carried out, along with studies on the processes of its implementation, in order to consolidate the existing models and progress made in the province of Tete and beyond.

REFERENCES

Adams, Martin (2008). *Evaluation of development cooperation between Mozambique and Denmark, 1992-2006*. Working Paper 01. The Political and Social Context. Rotterdam. ECORYS.

Benson, Carol (2000). The primary bilingual education experiment in Mozambique, 1993 to 1997. *International Journal of Bilingual Education and Bilingualism, 3*(3), 149-166.

CesoCi & Cambridge Education (2010). *Reforma do currículo do ensino primário: Avaliacão do plano estratégico para a educacão e cultura 2006-2010/11* [Primary education curriculum reform: Evaluation of strategic plan for education and culture 2006-2010/2011]. Mozambique.

Cossa, José (2011). System transfer, education, and development in Mozambique. *International Journal of Education Policy and Leadership, 6*(2). (http://journals.sfu.ca/ijepl/index.php/ijepl/article/view/93/107)

Cumbi, Amélia, & Warren-Rodríguez, Alex (2007). *Evaluation of development cooperation between Mozambique and Denmark, 1992-2006*. Working Paper 10: Geographical Patterns of Danish Assistance and Danish AID to the Province of Tete. Draft. Rotterdam. ECORYS

De Brito, Luis, Castel-Branco, Carlos, Chichava, Sérgio, & Francisco, António (2010). *Desafios para Moçambique* [Challenges for Mozambique]. Maputo: Instituto de Estudos Sociais e Económicos.

Dhorsan, Adelaide, & Moreno, Albertina (2008). The local curriculum in Mozambique: The Santa Rita Community School in Xinavane. *Prospects, 38*, 199-213.

Farrell, Joe (1999). Changing conceptions of equality of education: Forty years of comparative evidence. In Robert Arnove & Carlos Torres (Eds.), *Comparative education. The dialectic of the global and the local* (pp. 149-177). Oxford: Roman & Littlefield.

Freire, Paolo (1970). *Pedagogy of the oppressed*. New York & London: Continuum.

Government of Mozambique (2010). *Report on the millennium development goals*. Maputo: GOM.

Guro, Manuel, & Weber, Keith Everard (2010). From policy to practice: Education reform in Mozambique and Marrere Teachers' Training College. *SA Journal of Education, 30*(2), 245-259.

Klees, Stephen J. (2008). Reflections on theory, method, and practice in comparative and international education. *Comparative Education Review, 52*(3), 301-328

INDE (2006). *Sugestões para abordagem do currículo local. Uma alternativa para a redução da vulnerabilidade. Manual de apoio ao professor* [Suggestions for local curriculum approaches. An alternative to reduce vulnerability. Teacher support manual]. Maputo, Moçambique.

INE (2007). *Censo 2007* [Census of 2007]. Maputo: Instituto Nacional de Estatística.

INSIDA (2009). *Inquérito nacional de prevalência, riscos comportamentais e informação sobre o HIV e Sida em Moçambique* [National survey on HIV/Aids prevalence, behavioural risks and information in Mozambique]. Maputo: Ministério da Saúde.

Ministry of Education (2010). *Programme document for the funding request to the Catalytic Fund*. Maputo: Ministry of Education.

MEC (2005). *Manual de Apoio ao Conselho de Escola* [Guide to support the School Council]. Maputo: Ministério da Educação e Cultura.

MEC (2008). *Regulamento da ZIP* [ZIP regulation]. Maputo: Ministério da Educação e Cultura.

Ministry of Planning & Development (2010). *Poverty and wellbeing in Mozambique: Third National Poverty Assessment*. Maputo: Ministry of Planning & Development.

Muzima, Joel (2006). *Lessons of the experiences with direct support to schools mechanism in Mozambique*. Working Document. Presented at ADEA 2006 Biennial Meeting, Libreville, Gabon, March 27-31, 2006.

Osei, George (2010). The implementation and impact of curriculum decentralization in Ghana's junior high chools. *Comparative Education Review, 54*(2), 271-293.

Ribeiro, Calisto (2007). Education decentralization in Mozambique: A case study in the region of Nampula. In Daun, Holger (Ed.), *School decentralization in the context of globalizing governance. International comparison of grassroots responses* (pp. 159-173). Dordrecht: Springer.

Nuzzly Ruiz de Forsberg
Stockholm University, Sweden

Alícia Borges Månsson
International Consultant in Education Development

KERRY WHITE

12. CULTURE AS A VEHICLE, NOT A BRIDGE

Community-Based Education in Autonomous Regions of Nicaragua and in the Navajo Nation, USA

ABSTRACT

Ameriki Indianka tasbaia kau tarka ba Navajo Nation. 1923 wina klaunka laka brisa. Nicaraguara 1987 Atlantik Kus klaunka laka yan, RAAN an RAAS baku. RAAS an RAAN tanira klaunka laka takisa tawan nani smalkanka mihta. Nicaragua lakara skul nani smalkisa, sakuna witin nani ai bila nani slp lan munisa.an ai smalkanka ulbisa. Nicaragua Kus an Navajo Nation walsut trabil kaikisa tawan smalkanka dauki taim. Atlantik Kus skulka tawan an tuktan ailal wal blistu wark takisa. Navajo uplika nani ai skulka yus munisa ai bila raya brikaia, bikas prua man sa talia sa. Navajo an Kus uplika nani sim apia sakuna pas taim an naha taim sturka nani wina pain pali smalkanka nani sim sat dukia nani takisa. Plis walsut ra pain pali smalkanka tawan sturka laki kaikisa, tawan laka kulkisa, an tawan uplika wina ilp an kupia kumi laka brisa. (*Translated to Mískito[miq], a language of Nicaragua, by Mark Jamieson.*)

America's largest Indian reservation, the Navajo Nation, has been recognized as autonomous since 1923. In Nicaragua, the Atlantic Coast was granted autonomy as Región Autónoma del Atlántico Norte (RAAN) and Sur (RAAS) in 1987. In both regions, this autonomy is being enacted through community-controlled education. While still accountable to national regulation, schools can educate in non-dominant languages and write their own culturally-relevant curriculum. The Nicaraguan coast and Navajo nation face unique challenges in community-based education: Atlantic Coast schools have to accommodate pluricultural communities and children, while the Navajo use schools to preserve their language on the brink of virtual extinction. Despite these differences, common characteristics of successful programs emerge from an analysis of history, current trends, and case studies. In both regions, successful programs take into account the social-historical context of each community, address cultural values beyond language, and garner investment and involvement from the community at large.

C. Benson and K. Kosonen (eds.), Language Issues in Comparative Education, 225–241.

INTRODUCTION

From the Basque region of Spain to Inner Mongolia in China to Iraqi Kurdistan, many modern nations have negotiated intranational cultural differences by offering autonomy or semi-autonomy to ethnolinguistic minorities, Indigenous people or other non-dominant groups. The USA has had autonomous American Indian reservations since the 19th century, the largest of which is the Navajo Nation, home to the Diné people. In Nicaragua, the department formerly known as "Zelaya" (and informally known as "the Coast") was granted autonomy and divided into two regions: Región Autónoma del Atlántico Norte (RAAN) and Región Autónoma del Atlántico Sur (RAAS) in 1987. While the majority of Nicaraguans declare themselves Spanish-speaking Hispanic Mestizos, the "Costeño" communities have a unique mix of Indigenous (Miskitu, Mayagna, Ulwa, and Rama); Afro-Caribbean (Creole and Garifuna); and British cultural influences.

Various degrees of educational autonomy are practiced in the Navajo Nation and in Nicaraguan RAAN and RAAS. While still accountable to national education standards and regulation in each country, these community-controlled education systems are in effect decentralized because they are surrounded by mainstream systems; further, their schools can educate in Indigenous/non-dominant languages and write their own culturally relevant curricula.

The success of these schools depends on more than a simple translation of national curriculum into learners' home languages. Each linguistic and cultural group faces its own set of unique challenges. Many Costeño children are not only bilingual, but plurilingual,[i] using multiple viable and vibrant languages depending on the context. Meanwhile, the Diné have a vested interest in protecting and maintaining their language through education, as it faces virtual extinction due to long-term domination by English. Both are facing the challenge of using the freedom afforded to autonomous schools to revitalize not only their languages but also local cultures to counteract assimilation to dominant culture, without losing sight of the overarching need to improve learner achievement.

In this chapter I examine recent literature and case studies from both contexts, explore current educational issues in each, and compare their situations to reveal common characteristics of successful educational programs, focusing on programs that utilize learners' home languages and cultures not only to revitalize culture but also to encourage achievement and completion. I examine how educational programs take into account the social-historical context of the languages that learners speak, how they address cultural values and practices that go far beyond language, and how they garner investment and involvement from the non-dominant ethnolinguistic and autonomous communities they serve, so that community-controlled education can be a vehicle for history and culture rather than only a bridge to the dominant culture.

HISTORICAL CONTEXT OF COSTEÑO EDUCATION

Language has been an educational issue on the Atlantic Coast since the arrival of Europeans. The English encountered the Miskitu, the largest Indigenous group, as early as the 17th century while protecting Jamaica from eastward Spanish expansion. The region was declared "The Kingdom of the Mosquitia" and Miskitu the lingua franca (Sollis, 1989). As British settlers attempted to communicate in Miskitu, the Miskitu began informally learning English, taking pride in their bilingualism because it made them more "European" (Holm, 1978: 39). When the Treaty of Versailles forced the English out in 1849, their government encouraged settlement in the independent, strategically located Atlantic Coast region by Saxon Moravian missionaries from Jamaica (Freeland, 1995).

The Miskitu continued to use rudimentary conversational English (Freeland, 1995), and English-medium Moravian day schools became the first instances of official education in the region. The Moravian missionaries became concerned about the lack of written English in Miskitu communities, which were abandoning English in an attempt to separate themselves from Afro-Caribbean immigrants (Sollis, 1989). The Moravians then turned to Miskitu, the lingua franca among the Miksitu, Mayangna,[ii] and Rama Indigenous populations, to continue their educational work. Between 1850 and 1900 the bulk of Moravian day schools were taught in Miskitu in the early grades with increasing exposure to English; the notion of sending children to Miskitu-medium schools in order to learn English thus took hold among all Indigenous groups, including speakers of Rama, Mayangna, and the closely related language of the Southern Mayangna, Ulwa (Freeland, 1995).

This early bilingual education program was not sustained, however, due apparently to cultural misunderstandings. Moravian missionaries were discouraged by children's constant requests for the retelling of lessons and failure to take written notes, mistaking elements of oral culture for laziness and declaring the Indigenous population incapable of learning (Freeland, 1995). These early lessons on the role of culture in the classroom illustrate issues with which Coastal programs continue to struggle today.

During the second half of the 19th century, growing American economic presence favored Afro-Caribbeans who spoke an English-based Creole[iii] and were more culturally assimilated prior to their emancipation from slavery. Whereas the Miskitu had previously demanded Miskitu-medium education to separate themselves from the Afro-Caribbeans, they reacted to loss of socioeconomic power by demanding English-medium education from the Moravians, who were the sole source of education in the independent Coastal region. The Moravians resumed their educational mission, insisting on teaching in Miskitu to develop a local, literate clergy, but agreeing to offer English as a second language (Freeland, 1995).

Miskitu-medium education with English taught as a second language became the dominant paradigm until 1893, when José Santos Zelaya united Nicaragua and imposed "universal national Hispanic culture" to foster unity (Freeland, 1995). Part of this unity campaign was to force the Indigenous and Afro-Caribbean populations to learn Spanish and become "civilized" (Kain, 2006: 4). Zelaya urged Nicaragua's Spanish-speaking Mestizo citizens to "hispanizar" or Hispanicize the region by migrating, obtaining civil servant positions and settling in the sparsely populated Coastal region (Sollis, 1989). The Nicaraguan government took over the responsibility for education, banning education by foreigners or religious sects as well as teaching in any language other than Spanish (Freeland, 1995). Suddenly Costeños were no longer considered "British"; they were a non-dominant group with few or no rights, and their demands for continued local, bilingual education were systematically ignored (Freeland, 1995).

After Zelaya was deposed in 1911, renewed freedom on the Coast led to resumed discussions on local education. The pendulum swung once again, and local Indigenous communities reacted to their release from Zelaya's cultural repression by demanding Miskitu-medium education in the now-government run schools. Bilingual education in Miskitu and Spanish was resumed to conform to local demands along with the requirement of Hispanic national identity. Still seeking jobs with American companies, many Miskitu communities nonetheless continued to ask for English-Miskitu bilingual education (Freeland, 1995).

Isolated from the landlocked Coastal communities, the national government struggled to provide education to the region during the mid-20th century. Hispanic teachers attempted to teach in Miskitu in the 1950s but were rejected by the communities. In response, the government returned to Spanish-language education (Freeland, 1995), but communities grew to resent and fear forced Hispanicization, and it became commonplace for Hispanic teachers to return to the west for school holidays and never return to the Coast (Freeland, 2003).

Despite increasing tension between Hispanic teachers and local communities, monolingual Spanish education continued on the Atlantic Coast until 1980 (Freeland, 2003). As Mestizos continued to move into the area, the Indigenous advancement organization ALPROMISU (Alianza por el Progreso de los Miskitus y Sumus) attempted to promote assimilation among the Indigenous as a way to parlay the increasing Hispanic presence into infrastructure improvements and economic investment from Managua. After the Sandinista revolution, however, the first generation of college graduates from the Coast rose to assert themselves.

The youthful intelligentsia formed a political organization known as MISURASATA, representing MIskitu, SUmu, RAma, and SAndinistas TAnaka [united]. MISURASATA became the principal mass organization on the Coast, simultaneously launching a public awareness campaign proclaiming language rights as a symbol of resistance to repression under the Sandinista regime. L1-based bilingual education was at the core of their demands. MISURASATA appealed to parents, claiming that a bilingual education would be less traumatic for children than a Hispanicization education (Baracco, 2011).

MISURASATA succeeded in cementing its non-dominant group base in favor of community-controlled education. In 1980 during the Spanish-language Sandinista Literacy Project, MISURASATA set up boycotts that eventually spurred the government to produce revised literacy materials in Miskitu, English, and Mayanga, the second largest Indigenous population. (Freeland, 1995)

Following shortly after was the legalization of bilingual primary education through 4th grade for the Atlantic Coast region, beginning with 215 Miskitu children in kindergarten and first grade in 1984, and in 1985 adding Creole and Mayagna classrooms (Ministerio de Educación, Cultura, y Deportes, 2002). When the government preoccupation with the civil war between the Coastal guerrillas and the Sandinista forces diverted attention from the language sovereignty acts, both federal implementation support and local development of bilingual-bicultural education stalled (Freeland, 1995).

Education was finally put officially and definitively in the hands of the Atlantic Coast community through the 1987 autonomy law. Local parents were of the generation that had been indoctrinated into valuing education as an entrance to the dominant culture, and no longer embroiled in civil war, parents began to express desire for dominant language skills to provide perceived socioeconomic opportunities for their children. The educational pendulum began to swing again towards rejection of programs that used non-dominant languages and cultures. Through the 80s and early 90s, local populations continued to construe education as a means of acquiring Spanish, the dominant national language, despite campaigns for local cultural empowerment (Freeland, 1995).

The national government responded with the dual approach of placing control of education into the communities themselves while providing a state-supported bilingual curriculum, the Bilingual Bicultural Education Program (PEBB), which evolved in the 1990s into the Bilingual Intercultural Education Program currently known as PEIB. The PEIB offers bilingual curriculum with a cultural education element tied to the language of instruction, e.g. Afro-Caribbean culture lessons taught in Creole schools, and Mayagna and Miskitu culture taught in their respective schools. The PEIB has expanded beyond initial offerings in Miskitu to develop and offer curriculum in the RAAN serving Mayagna children, in the RAAS for Creole (Ministerio de Educación, Cultura, y Deportes, 2002); Rama and Garifuna have been officially recognized as languages of instruction as well, though materials and teacher training to support these languages have not yet been fully developed (Koskinen, 2010).

The legal foundation for autonomous education was reaffirmed in the Law 162 on languages (Government of Nicaragua, 1993) which authorized Regional Autonomous Governments to place intercultural bilingual education under their direct administration, converting teacher training programs into decentralized bilingual institutions, and the General Law for Education of 2006, stating that "intercultural education in their mother tongue is a right of the indigenous peoples of the Atlantic Coast" (Government of Nicaragua, 2006). In 2007, the number of children enrolled in intercultural-bilingual programs was totaled at 30,218 at the primary level and an additional 10,600 in the pre-school level (Koskinen, 2010).

Higher education also followed the autonomy law. The national higher education council founded the Universidad de las Regiones Autónomas de la Costa Caribe Nicaragüense (URACCAN) and Bluefields Indian Caribbean University (BICU) to support political autonomy in the area of junior college education. Both schools run specific programs intended for non-dominant groups, training local civil servants and recruiting in remote rural areas (Brunnegger, 2007). URACCAN has taken an active role in teacher training, offering programs specifically designed to train teachers in PEIB and acting as implementing agent for educational development programs of UNDP and the Finnish Government to strengthen bilingual intercultural education (UNDP, 2005).

HISTORICAL CONTEXT OF NAVAJO EDUCATION

For Native Americans, as for Indigenous people of the Nicaraguan Coast, education has been paradoxically both a force to strip them of their culture and a way to reclaim and strengthen their culture. Similar to Nicaraguan education, local schools and seminaries that respected Indigenous language and lifeways were in existence until forced acculturation policies pushed these programs aside. As the federal government via the Bureau of Indian Affairs (BIA) began sending teachers to reservations, reports from the field showed an agreement that "a large number speak and write their own, and are able to hold correspondence [in local languages]" (United States Bureau of Indian Affairs, 1871: 189), with one teacher writing "we have found it far better to instruct them in their own language, and also to teach them English as fast as we can" (United States Bureau of Indian Affairs, 1871: 168).

Faced with forced acculturation and tribal suppression, the Diné specifically held education as a high priority in negotiating with the US government. In response for demands of public education, the Navajo Treaty of 1868 specifically stated that for every 30 Navajo children, the government would provide at least one classroom and one teacher. While the Navajo did try to use these provisions to develop education on the reservation, they were unsuccessful in the face of government manipulation of the treaty's stipulations. For example, in 1943 when a small day school was built in the Ramah Navajo community, the Bureau of Indian Affairs of the US government provided one teacher for grades 1 through 3 and capped enrollment at 30. After grade three, students were transferred to BIA boarding schools (Baum, this volume; Manuelito, 2005).

The federal boarding schools were the most common avenues of education for Navajo children for the hundred years following the 1868 treaty. The exceptions were children taken in by Mormon missionaries and sent to public schools while living with Mormon families. While some Navajo children had access to warm beds and regular meals, being spared from the poverty experienced on the reservation, boarding schools were overwhelmingly negative experiences for them. They were expected to keep buildings clean and complete their studies without personal attention. The boarding schools sought to eradicate Navajo language and customs and used physical forms of punishment to "civilize" the children. It is public record that many children died from malnourishment and abuse in federal boarding schools (Manuelito, 2005).

Organized resistance to the boarding school system arose in the 1960s when reports of psychological and physical abuse brought local education to the forefront of Navajo social justice campaigns. In 1965, the United States Office of Economic

Opportunity (OEO), the BIA, and a group of Navajo leaders incorporated under the name Demonstration in Navajo Education, or DINÉ, joined with a newly-appointed Diné School Board in the Rough Rock area, and with $600,000 in funding built the Rough Rock Demonstration School (Collier, 1988). The OEO included funding for community-controlled curriculum development using a bilingual, bicultural model (Manuelito, 2005) and created a contract between the tribal trustee board and the USA federal government (Lipka & McCarty, 1994).

Rough Rock formed the first all-Indian governing board and dedicated itself to teaching in and about Navajo language and culture using the so-called "both/and" approach—acknowledging and teaching both local and dominant languages and cultures. Through this approach students were exposed to important cultural values, both Navajo and dominant, and never asked to make a choice. Visitors to Rough Rock found a school "saturated in Navajo culture" where students spoke the Navajo language without shame (Collier, 1988: 163). Much like PEIB in Nicaragua, however, the school suffered from high teacher turnover and inadequate federal funding (Lipka & McCarty, 1994).

The solutions to these issues came both from within and outside the Navajo community. The Navajo Teacher Corps was formed during the 1970s to cultivate a corps of teachers from the community who had experience as students in the Navajo system, who were committed to working with local children, and who would be able to infuse the curriculum with Navajo values. Outside intervention in the form of teachers and researchers from the Hawaii-based Kamehameha Early Education Program (KEEP) visited Rough Rock in 1983. KEEP participants viewed teachers as agents of change in Indigenous communities, and encouraged them to take ownership over their roles in schools, their pedagogical philosophies, and their curriculum (Lipka & McCarty, 1994). KEEP had achieved this in Hawaii by implementing classroom models based on years of ethnographic research that reflected the adult-child relationships of Hawaiian homes. An approach known as "The Open Door" incorporated children into the organizing, cleaning up and operation of educational centers, similar to children's work at home. Each teacher took on a Hawaiian adult role as "modeler of skills, setter of tasks, and overall supervisor" (Tharp et al., 2007: 295).

KEEP did not apply the same principals to Rough Rock, but rather placed one anthropological researcher and one pedagogical specialist in Rough Rock to work with the community for one semester to develop a community-based curriculum. After training Diné teachers, KEEP staff were so invested in Rough Rock that they continued to visit regularly from 1984 to 1988, offering financial support for professional development and supporting administrators in encouraging local teacher-led improvements. With the encouragement of KEEP's pedagogical expert, teachers gained confidence to adapt the curriculum to the local context, and slowly Rough Rock staff wrote their own curriculum. In 1989, as KEEP's partnership with Rough Rock ended, a grant from Title VII allowed them to continue to develop their bilingual curriculum (McCarty, 2005).

Because Rough Rock "provided a model for contract schools that were locally controlled and ... became centers for the development and dissemination of Navajo language curriculum materials" (Lockard & DeGroat, 2010: 4), community-based schools appeared in other Navajo communities. Fort Defiance was one such community, initiating bilingual education in 1986. Its location outside the southeastern border of the Navajo Nation meant that the majority of Diné children entering school were English monolinguals – in other words, they had lost their heritage language. At the program's inception, less than 10% of children beginning kindergarten were "reasonably competent" in Navajo. Students in the Navajo immersion program learned to read and write Navajo first, then English. The lower grades taught only in Navajo, after which instruction transitioned to English; by grade 4, instruction was in English but an hour of day was spent teaching functional language skills in Navajo using a cooperative learning model developed at Rough Rock. To revitalize Navajo language in the community, the Fort Defiance program required "homework assignments" for all students to speak Navajo at home. Fort Defiance demonstrated that communities whose ties to Navajo language and culture had been weakened could strengthen their ties through bilingual, bicultural education programs (McCarty, 2003).

Navajo-controlled secondary and higher education programs also developed following the founding of Rough Rock. Ramah High School, the Navajo Nation's first community-controlled secondary school, was born when Navajo elders and boarding school graduates protested at the doorway of the BIA until funding for the school was approved. Much like the promised but not always fulfilled support for bilingual education from the Sandinista government in Nicaragua, the American government never provided Ramah High School with the attention it deserved. While President Nixon was declaring Ramah "an important new direction," those on the ground faced resistance from non-Indigenous community members and lack of support for curriculum and facilities (Manuelito, 2005).

While locally-controlled Navajo education came primarily from the ground up, it was bolstered by many legal cases. In 1971, for example, the Coalition of Indian-Controlled Schools was formed to create a clearinghouse for curricular and developmental information. This directly influenced the passing of 1975's Indian Self-Determination and Educational Assistant Act, which codified Native American rights to a culturally sensitive and appropriate education (Manuelito, 2005). This legislation encouraged proliferation of community-controlled schools and colleges, which thrive to this day under the Association of Navajo-Controlled Schools within the Department of Diné Education. With increased political agency, the Diné people can pursue new initiatives with vigor, including community-controlled charter or grant schools funded by the BIA, state-sponsored schools with local advisory boards, and completely autonomous cultural survival schools governed entirely by the community (Lipka & McCarty, 1994).

COMMUNITY CODE-SWITCHING AND PLURICULTURALISM: CURRENT ISSUES AMONG THE COSTEÑOS

Currently, Nicaraguan Costeños appear to understand of the role of language in identity and ethnic pride, and the pendulum seems somewhat fixed in the arena of education as a means of cultural preservation. PEIB has evolved into using community input to design and select local curricula. Some Miskitu communities have begun writing their own textbooks and producing literature in Miskitu that also represents values of the Indigenous culture. These must first be assessed by the Ministry of Education, however, and civics books are allowed no such liberty as they must be exact translations of the state-crafted Spanish versions. The Ministry of Education is more than 200 miles away in Managua, accessible only by plane, a physical divide that underscores the cultural one; however, local leaders are becoming more vocal with their representatives (Freeland, 1995).

Another development in Costeño education is the inclusion of languages in addition to Miskitu. The 1987 autonomy law granted economic, political, and cultural rights for all local communities on the Coast, but earlier efforts focused on Miskitu. Modern PEIB has bilingual programs pairing Spanish with English/Creole,[iv] Mayagna, and more recently Garifuna and Rama, (Koskinen, 2010). These modern programs follow the PEIB model of teaching in the community language during preschool and early primary, introducing Spanish orally from grade 2 and in writing from grade 3, and using both languages for teaching and learning until grade 6, when the curriculum is entirely in Spanish (Freeland, 2003).

According to Freeland (2003), however, this model of bilingual education does not fit the real needs of Coastal communities. The PEIB model in Nicaragua was based on models used in Peru, Guatemala, Bolivia, Ecuador, and Mexico, which in turn are based on North American/European traditions in which a discrete, homogenous, dominant linguistic/cultural group is assimilating non-dominant groups. This is not the case in Coastal Nicaragua, where Costeño interethnic practices are much more diverse. With the Moravian church still using Miskitu as their lingua franca, a growing Pentecostal church presence preaching in Creole, and intermarriage among non-dominant groups common (even encouraged as a means of social mobility), most Costeño children grow up in plurilingual settings (Freeland, 2003).

This is not to say that the languages have equal footing; many parents still speak English or Spanish to their children even if Creole or Miskitu is their first language, and if Spanish-speaking "gangs" police schoolyards to be sure no Hispanic student uses a non-dominant language. With four Indigenous minorities, two Afro-Caribbean minorities, and four languages commonly used with varying power implications, Costeño children's code-switching identities are not adequately accommodated by the oversimplified state model of bilingual education (Freeland, 2003). Thus the Coast has evolved into a "contact zone ... where disparate cultures meet, clash, and grapple with each other, often in highly asymmetrical relations of domination and subordination" (Pratt, 1992: 4).

Freeland did a comprehensive study of URACCAN university students and their cultural-linguistic experiences, documenting nuances that PEIB ignores. She found that not only were many children raised in one non-dominant language and educated in another, several developed "defensive" skills in a third language, such as a Mayagna child who used Miskitu to bond with other Indigenous students, and a Miskitu child who developed Creole to be able to tell when other students made fun of her. According to Freeland (2003), language is "not digital, but analogic" (248); in other words, children do not speak single non-dominant languages but rather different combinations of languages depending on context and need.

PEIB has had the most success in rural, mono-ethnic communities. In areas where multiple ethnic identities co-exist, the program's choice of a single non-dominant language mirrors dominant language programs by creating an in-group, thus distorting PEIB's inclusive intent. In Kakabilla, for example, the Pearl Lagoon Miskitu have reportedly requested an English PEIB program so that Miskitu children can attract English-speaking husbands and wives. This has led to a sharp decline in the maintenance of the Pearl Lagoon variety of Miskitu. On the opposite end of the autonomous region, the El Muelle Indigenous people speak Creole and English, but are only offered Spanish/Miskitu programs, as English-medium PEIB has not yet been implemented in the RAAN. Even when English PEIB is introduced, all cultural elements of the program will focus on the Afro-Caribbean culture, ignoring the area's Miskitu heritage (Freeland, 2003).

Complicating the situation even further are campaigns to revitalize the Ulwa, Rama, and Garifuna languages and cultures, even while many Ulwa learn Miskitu as their first language, and many Rama and Garifuna have spoken English for many generations. The government has responded by incorporating lessons in "heritage languages" in the primary school PEIB English texts. A 1993 law promised Ulwa/Rama/Garifuna programs but failed to provide funding until European NGOs intervened, including the Finnish government's work with URACCAN in developing new curricula for both schools and teacher training programs. As of 2008, PEIB has been revised to include Rama and Garifuna programming, but lacks orthographies to use Ulwa (Koskinen, 2010).

These issues all underscore a common problem with PEIB as identified by Freeland (2003): seeing language as synonymous with culture. The need to address cultural elements beyond language was recognized in initial demands for bilingual education, which included "knowledge of their own culture" alongside "wide knowledge of our country" (MISURASATA, 1980: 8), but incorporating culture into curricula has been hard. The PEIB model encourages teachers to teach in the "community culture" by using Indigenous and other non-dominant languages, but within each of the distinct non-dominant cultures are multiple sets of practices, beliefs, values and rituals. Until PEIB uses community input to individualize curricula, considering local cultures separately from community languages, these programs will continue to fall short of providing culturally relevant content and legitimizing education for all learners.

Despite these problems, there is definite improvement in Nicaraguan Coastal education from the blatant Hispanicization of the mid-twentieth century, to Sandinista Spanish/Miskitu programs, to current bilingual offerings. PEIB has successfully legitimated Coastal languages against a "wall of prejudice" (Freeland, 2003: 254), as Creole is now acknowledged as a language in itself, URACCAN is researching lexicons and orthographies of lesser-used non-dominant languages, and URACCAN is vocally encouraging multilingualism among all sectors of

Coastal society including Hispanics (Koskinen, 2010). Indeed, URACCAN provides all staff and students the opportunity to learn a Coastal language, and its teacher training courses stress interculturalism and take a locally-controlled approach to plurilingual education (Freeland, 2003). As education has embraced non-dominant languages, so too have other elements of community life, with election propaganda and local government documents being produced in non-dominant languages as well as Spanish (Freeland, 1995).

PEIB's most important effect is on student achievement. PEIB programs have lowered school anxiety, achieved higher passing and retention rates, increased pride in multilingualism, and used local cultural research to inform new teaching materials. Unfortunately, inadequate financial support, poor infrastructure and shortage of trained teachers inhibit this work (Freeland, 2003).

The Regional Autonomous Education System (SEAR) has set goals for 2015 that include 50% adult literacy, 80% of boys and girls in primary education, and training for all teachers in regional intercultural bilingual training centers (Arrien, 2006). SEAR aims to strengthen institutional management, build budget support and cultivate technical resources to address shortcomings through wider multicultural awareness and increased state support. According to Freeland, all this is needed for "PEIB to progress from being a symbol of autonomy to one of its best examples" (2003: 254).

ENCOURAGING ACHIEVEMENT, REVITALIZING CULTURE:
CURRENT ISSUES IN THE NAVAJO NATION

Issues in Navajo education mirror many of those in coastal Nicaragua. As of 1999, there were more than 114 tribally-controlled schools registered in the Navajo Nation (Manuelito, 2005). While free from following national curricula, these autonomous Navajo schools lack community input into local curriculum, which makes them only marginally different from state-run schools. Community control does not equal community involvement, and where teachers take a mainstream perspective, the results are often low expectations and a lack of investment from parents and communities, who lament the loss of previous generations' wisdom and feel ostracized from their children's education (Lipka & McCarty, 1994).

Conflicts between political and personal interests in language maintenance further complicate self-determination via education. While Nicaraguan education authorities struggle to develop policy to meet the diverse linguistic needs of local communities, the Navajo Nation is endeavoring to rescue its one Indigenous language from virtual extinction. Although Navajo is one of the most widespread Indigenous languages in North America, the percentage of incoming Kindergarteners who can speak Navajo has fallen over the last three decades from 95% to an estimated 30-50% (McCarty, 2003).

The loss of Navajo is tied to the educational history of the Diné, as the BIA boarding school era forced many to stop speaking Indigenous languages. These Diné parents may use English exclusively at home despite their lack of fluency, and thus their children have no Navajo skills while being categorized as "limited

English proficient" in the classroom (McCarty, 2003). Thus a community still recovering from generations of attempted linguistic and cultural annihilation must cope with the academic struggles of its children who have limited proficiency in both the community language and the dominant one.

This is the context of the current push for bilingual Navajo-English education. In communities like Fort Defiance this takes the form of Navajo immersion transitioning to English, while in communities like Rough Rock the emphasis is on bilingual education as a means of language maintenance. Results are positive for both models. In Rough Rock, RRENLAP (Navajo/English) students regularly outperform non-RRENLAP (English only) students, though both score below national norms on United States nation-wide standardized tests. Comparable data on the Fort Defiance program demonstrates that bilingual immersion programs are highly effective for monolingual students acquiring Navajo language skills. By upper elementary, bilingually taught students perform as well as or better than their peers in monolingual English programs, the former developing Navajo language proficiency and the latter progressively losing Navajo as they age (McCarty, 2003). Studies have demonstrated success not only in revitalizing the Navajo language but also in improving school achievement.

The Rough Rock Community School also continues to set precedents in bilingual education for language preservation. RRENLAP reading scores rose steadily as teachers flushed the curriculum of outdated materials, designed cooperative learning centers with culturally relative themes, and involved parents and elders in educational programming and curriculum design. RRENLAP aggressively pursued grants, and developed a teacher corps from the local community prepared to teach bilingual classes with culturally relevant themes (McCarty, 2003).

A further development that supported Rough Rock as it paved the way for other community schools was the organic creation of a teacher-study group. While meeting to create alternative assessment forms, teachers discovered the benefits of linking classroom observations with reading professional literature. The group met throughout the early 1990s to create checklists designed to evaluate students in Navajo and English writing skills. Meanwhile, they cultivated a body of research and literature to help educators understand Navajo learners and, most importantly, they developed confidence in their own ability to effect change and "reverse the type of schooling [they] went through" (Dick, 1998: 25). As one RRENLAP teacher said, "If we want to be powerful, we have to exercise our power" (as cited in Lipka & McCarty, 1994: 273). Another added, "[Our group] gave us ways of how to develop appropriate materials and assessment .... It gave us that confidence and empowerment" (McCarty, 2005: 58).

The Ramah High School, now known as the Pine Hill School, also develops curriculum on an ongoing basis for Kindergarten through post-secondary levels. Studies have thus far provided support for community-controlled Navajo language education, which has the highest rate of matriculation and graduation in the Navajo Nation (Lipka & McCarty, 1994).

COMMON CHARACTERISTICS AND LESSONS LEARNED

While both the Navajo Nation and the Atlantic Coast of Nicaragua are home to non-dominant populations, their historical attitudes to intercultural bilingual education have been markedly different. In between campaigns for bilingual education, the Costeños first embraced foreign education in English and later in Spanish. Their association of education with social mobility according to dominant cultures has plagued campaigns for intercultural bilingual education, underscoring the need for community-level awareness to secure support from non-dominant group members.

The Navajo, on the other hand, have a long history of resisting missionary and outsider education in favor of local education, and have had to fight outside forces to pursue implementation of relevant bilingual intercultural education. While Nicaraguan Coastal community-controlled schools must adapt to how learners embrace languages from outside their cultural backgrounds, Navajo community-controlled schools are tasked with saving their own single endangered language.

Just as the common challenges of inconsistent funding and vacillating government support hinder education in both regions, both cases have shown that local community involvement, integrated elements of culture beyond language, and an understanding of the socio-historical context of language and education are keys to implementing successful programs.

The primary element of success for both education systems is community involvement. Much of what Rough Rock and Fort Defiance have aimed to do for Navajo learners mirrors what URACCAN/PEIB is beginning to do now for Costeños, i.e. implementing a fully bottom-up education system and empowering community members. This has been a challenge in both areas for different reasons: in Nicaragua, parents still hold onto the vestiges of previous education paradigms and seek assimilationist education policies, while the trauma and cultural suppression of the BIA boarding schools stifles Navajo parents' desire for Navajo cultural elements in education.

A central element of community involvement is fostering a sense of pride in non-dominant cultures. In the Navajo Nation, this is promoted at schools like Fort Defiance by requiring Navajo language "homework." On the Nicaraguan Coast, activities like production of government documents and electoral propaganda in Miskitu and other local languages are a first step to legitimizing local culture and spreading the message that socioeconomic success and Indigenous cultures are not mutually exclusive. De-stigmatizing local languages may encourage parents from non-dominant communities to continue or revive the practice of speaking non-dominant languages at home, which will potentially counteract the difficulties plaguing students with limited proficiency in both dominant and local languages.

An additional element of community involvement is the cultivation of local teachers. In the Navajo Nation, teacher preparation programs outside the Navajo Teacher Corps routinely neglect Native epistemologies in favor of assimilationist models. A 2003 survey by the Native Educators Research Project found that only 26 percent of 238 Native American participants in 27 Native American teacher education programs felt prepared to teach their languages and cultural practices (Manuelito, 2005). If the demographic is expanded to include non-tribal teacher preparation programs, this number is proportionately even lower. Similar issues are seen in Nicaragua, where poor educational outcomes have previously limited the number of trained Coastal teachers, but where there is distrust for dominant Hispanic teachers, who exhibit high attrition rates. Like the Navajo Teacher Corps, URACCAN's teacher training program is attempting to produce a critical mass of teachers who are locally grounded and prepared to implement intercultural curricula.

The inclusion of local teachers also supports the next element of successful programs: integrating cultural elements beyond language into education. Teachers raised in local communities aid in the creation of curricula steeped in local knowledge that legitimizes the history and cultural traditions of students. This is integral to engaging students in an education where they feel validated. Coastal cases like that of the Muelle, who are of Indigenous background but speak Creole, illustrate the error of conflating language with culture.

Navajo community-controlled schools like Rough Rock and Ramah High School promote cultural education as well as language, and the Nicaraguan Coast is beginning to catch up with such ideas. The shifting focus from language to a wider definition of culture is seen in the evolving name of Nicaragua's Coastal education program: originally PEBB (bilingual bicultural education program), then broadening the cultural definition with PEBI (bilingual intercultural education program), and finally most recently adjusting the focus to culture rather than language with PEIB (intercultural bilingual education program). Critics note that these name changes also reflect debates in European education policy and might speak to dependence on imported models (Freeland, 2003), but nonetheless they reflect an awareness of the broadening scope of non-dominant/Indigenous education.

The local curricula developed for relevant community-controlled education can also be used for inclusion in national curricula to promote change beyond non-dominant communities. URACCAN already attempts to reach out to dominant students by offering non-dominant language classes and requiring them in many programs, including teacher training. One suggestion Freeland makes to effect even greater change is to incorporate non-dominant language awareness into the national curriculum, and to offer dominant Hispanic children across Nicaragua an opportunity to study a Coastal language (2003: 254). Navajo education proponents also urge educators and policy makers to look beyond local schools; for example, Manuelito suggests that Indigenous epistemologies be included in public school curricula for "Natives and non-Natives alike" (2005: 84).

Running through these themes is an acknowledgment and legitimization of social and historical context. Community campaigns should acknowledge the effects of traumatic assimilationist education, while underscoring the potential for achieving success through a culturally-rich and relevant education. The dynamics of language use and code-switching must also be recognized and legitimized as realities for both Costeño and Diné children. Non-dominant languages should be viewed not just as stepping stones to dominant languages but active parts of children's identities worthy of development and maintenance.

Moving away from subtractive models, where non-dominant languages are replaced by dominant ones, classrooms would benefit from dynamic programs where code-switching is incorporated into education through what Garcia calls "translanguaging" (Garcia, 2011: 389). Translanguaging incorporates the complex practices plurilingual speakers employ to make sense of their language identity, including but not limited to internal translation and code-switching. Classroom translanguaging, involving processes like reading texts in a dominant language and responding orally in a language of the student's choosing, removes the discrete time and place regulations often ascribed to languages in plurilingual classrooms (Garcia, 2011). Translanguaging could help education systems avoid the trap of simply adding languages to address all cultural groups without considering "when, how, and even whether" (Freeland, 2003: 254) to teach them, an issue in Nicaragua faced by non-dominant groups within non-dominant groups, who are beginning to assert their cultural sovereignty rights. Translanguaging also inevitably localizes education, as each multilingual community has its own unique set of connotations, mores, and guidelines that influence individuals' language choices.

Ironically, help from organizations and institutions outside the community often facilitates the integration of local culture into local curriculum. The Rough Rock School was founded with the help of DINÉ and reforms were set in motion by KEEP; both organizations offered strategic guidance for empowering local communities. Similarly, URACCAN and PEIB utilize USAID funding; the first of three intermediate results of the recently completed "Excelencia" project, which had a budget of 11.5 million dollars, includes "implementing the active learning model ... and, in the Atlantic Coast, incorporating bilingual education approaches" (American Institutes for Research, 2005: 3). In addition to strategic consultation and specialist perspectives, the benefits of collaboration with outside organizations are augmented by the funding they provide.

Pattanayak once said of globalization and homogenization, "[b]y luring people to opt for globalization without enabling them to communicate with the local and the proximate, globalization is an agent of cultural destruction" (2000: 46). As such, the reclamation of culture through local education has become an exercise in democracy, social justice, and self-determination. Both in Hispanicization campaigns in Nicaragua and American English-only education in the Navajo Nation, the loss of language and culture is caused by the exercise of power by the dominant over the non-dominant. Interestingly, just as it was the schools that led these campaigns to disenfranchise, it is now the schools that have the opportunity through autonomous education to revitalize Indigenous and other non-dominant cultures and languages (McCarty, 2003).

As the Costeños and the Diné continue their struggles, using their autonomy to craft school systems that revitalize culture and non-dominant language learning, pockets of success show what could come out of schools tied to communities, building pride and understanding in both non-dominant and dominant cultures (McCarty, 2003). As a college-educated Navajo professional and member of the first Ramah High School graduating class said when asked to define education: "And so those are the niléí jiniyááld ę́ ę́do hwiłhane' éédoo bee ha' átishii hak' I áadoolyaay ę́ ę́ bee nahidinaast' ą́ ą́ éi bee ájit' éełe. [And so those are, from birth to adulthood, the instructions you were given, ceremonies that were done for you as well as your teachings, that make you the person you are]" (as cited in Manuelito, 2005: 82). In this statement we see the potential for education to be a holistic entity that incorporates – not excludes – local cultures in an inclusive, appropriate education.

NOTES

i   Plurilingual is used intentionally because it implies knowledge of languages that make up a whole person, while multilingual implies two or more languages learned discretely and kept separate.

ii The Mayangna people are referred to in some literature and in early political groups as "Sumo" or "Sumu;" however, this term is derived from a derogatory Miskitu term for the group, and "Mayangna" is therefore the preferred term.

iii This English-based Creole is also known as "Miskitu Coast Creole" or "Nicaraguan English Creole." It is nearly identical to Belizean kriol and similar to most English-based Central American and Caribbean Creoles. Within this paper it will be referred to simply as "Creole" as that is the term used in relevant literature.

iv The Afro-Caribbean population was originally offered an English-medium curriculum, which was invariably taught through Creole, the dominant spoken language. The 2007 curriculum reform legitimized Creole as L1 and introduced English as L3 after L2 Spanish. In Coastal vernacular, "English" describes both standard English and Creole.

REFERENCES

American Institutes for Research (2005). *Excelencia quarterly report*. Washington, DC: American Institutes for Research. (pdf.usaid.gov/pdf_docs/PDACI565.pdf)

Arrien, Juan B. (2006). Background paper prepared for the Education for All Global Monitoring Report 2006 Literacy for Life: Literacy in Nicaragua. (http://unesdoc.unesco.org/images/0014/001459/145937e.pdf)

Baracco, Luciano (Ed.) (2011). *National integration and contested autonomy: The Caribbean Coast of Nicaragua*. New York: Algora Publishing.

Brunnegger, Sandra (2007). From conflict to autonomy in Nicaragua: Lessons learnt. *Minority Rights International*. (http://www.minorityrights.org/969/micro-studies/from-conflict-to-autonomy-in-nicaragua-lessons-learnt.html)

Collier, John Jr. (1988). Survival at Rough Rock: A historical overview of Rough Rock demonstration school. *Anthropology & Education Quarterly, 19*(3), 253-269.

Dick, Galena Sells (1998). I maintained a strong belief in my language and culture: A Navajo language autobiography. *International Journal of the Sociology of Language, 132*(1), 23-25.

Freeland, Jane (1995). "Why go to school to learn Miskitu?:" Changing constructs of bilingualism, education and literacy among the Miskitu of Nicaragua's Atlantic Coast. *International Journal of Educational Development, 15*(3), 245-261.

Freeland, Jane (2003). Intercultural-bilingual education for an interethnic-plurilingual society? The case of Nicaragua's Caribbean Coast. *Comparative Education, 39*(2), 239-260.

Garcia, Ofelia (2011). Pedagogies and practices in multilingual classrooms: Singularities in pluralities. *The Modern Language Journal, 95*(3), 385-400.

Government of Nicaragua (1993). *Ley No.162 o Ley de Uso Oficial de las Lenguas de las Comunidades de la Costa Atlántica de Nicaragua* [Law number 162 – Law on the Official Use of Languages of the Atlantic Coast of Nicaragua]. Managua: National Assembly.

Government of Nicaragua (2006). *Ley No.582 o Ley General de Educacion* [Law number 582 – General Law on Education]. Managua: National Assembly.

Holm, John (1978). *The Creole English of Nicaragua's Miskito Coast.* Unpublished PhD Dissertation. University College, London.

Kain, Myrna Cunningham (2006). *Racism and ethnic discrimination in Nicaragua.* Puerto Cabezas, Nicaragua: Center for Indigenous People's Autonomy and Development.

Koskinen, Arja (2010). Kriol in Caribbean Nicaraguan schools. In Bettina Migge, Issabelle Leglise, & Angela Bartens (Eds.), *Creoles in education: An Appraisal of current programs and projects* (pp. 133-166). Amsterdam, the Netherlands: John Benjamins.

Lipka, Jerry, & McCarty, Teresa L. (1994). Changing the culture of schooling: Navajo and Yup'ik cases. *Anthropology & Education Quarterly, 25*(3), 266-284.

Lockard, Louise, & DeGroat, Jennie (2010). "He said it all in Navajo!": Indigenous language immersion in early childhood classrooms. *International Journal of Multicultural Education, 12*(2).

Manuelito, Kathryn (2005). The role of education in American Indian self-determination: Lessons from the Ramah Navajo community school. *Anthropology & Education Quarterly, 36*(1), 73-87.

McCarty, Teresa L. (2005). The power within: Indigenous literacies and teacher empowerment. In Teresa L. McCarty (Ed.), *Language, literacy, and power in schooling.* Mahwah, NJ: Lawrence Erlbaum Associates.

McCarty, Teresa L. (2003). Revitalising Indigenous languages in homogenising times. *Comparative Education, 39*(2), 147-163.

Ministerio de Educación, Cultura, y Deportes (2002). *Seminario-taller sobre la calidad de la educación en contextos multiculurales: Programa de Educación Bilingüe Intercultural* [Seminar-workshop on the quality of education in multicultural contexts: Program of Intercultural Bilingual Education]. (http://www.oas.org/udse/seminario_mx/nicaragua.doc)

MISURASATA (1980). Lineamientos generales/General directions. Published in English in Klaudine Ohland & Robin Schneider (Eds.) (1983), *National revolution and indigenous identity: the conflict between Sandinists and Miskito Indians on Nicaragua's Atlantic Coast* (pp. 48-63). Copenhagen, Denmark: International Work Group for Indigenous Affairs.

Pattanayak, D. P. (2000). Linguistic pluralism: A point of departure. In Robert Phillipson (Ed.), *Rights to language: Equity, power, and education* (pp. 46-47). Mahwah, NJ: Lawrence Erlbaum Associates.

Sollis, Peter (1989). The Atlantic Coast of Nicaragua: Development and autonomy. *Latin American Studies (UK), 21*(3), 481-520.

Tharp, Roland G., Jordan, Cathie, Speidel, Gisela E., Au, Kathryn Hu-Pei, Klein, Thomas W., Calkins, Roderick P., Sloat, Kim C. M., & Gallimore, Ronald (2007). Education and native Hawaiian children: Revisiting KEEP. *Hūlili: Multidisciplinary Research on Hawaiian Well-Being, 4*(1), 269-319.

UNDP (2005). *Finlandia apoya grandioso programa de educación bilingüe en la Costa* [Finland supports large bilingual education program on coast]. (http://www.undp.org.ni/noticias/127)

United States Bureau of Indian Affairs (1871). *Annual report of the board of Indian commissioners.* Washington, DC: United States Government Printing Office.

Kerry White
Education Development Center
Washington DC, USA

PART IV:

RESEARCHER VOICES

LEILA SCHROEDER

13. TEACHING AND ASSESSING INDEPENDENT READING SKILLS IN MULTILINGUAL AFRICAN COUNTRIES: NOT AS SIMPLE AS ABC

ABSTRACT

Angu, okugenderesya obhuturo bhwa abhaana bha Echiafrika mu-kusoma bheyagaarire, eyiija okusakira abheyigisya okusooka bhuraaya na jifurumbendo jeebhwe okwikirisimbwa mu-bhyaro bha Abhaafrika na mu-nyaika jinyafu? Anu echirora ati, okusoma emisango jinu jikaamirwe era, okukora abheyigisya okwiigisya mu-kanariiye era, amatokeo ga obhuyenjeresi bhwone inguru ya abhayiki bha inyaika ya Echijungu aamwi na rikusyo/obhutinge bhwa obhukaami na jinyaika ja Abhaafrika mu-bhwiganirisya ara. Nawe anye nitakwikirisyanya na ati, jiri-wo njira ebhiri ja ebhikaame era (Coltheart na Baron 1978, 2005) ja okusoma inguru ya okwiigisya abhaana mu-mbaga nyafu nyafu ja okwandika Afrika. Mwanya mwafu, obhutinge bhwa injira ya omusamiati (emisango) eitumika muno Afriko nooro obhwererwa uri inguru ya okutegeresya obhuraka amwi obhuku bhwa jinyaika ejo. Amwi na okurema okubha-wo kwa ebhiimu bhyafu na echiwango chitooto cha emirimu ja risoma, jinjira joone joone jinu jitakwikirisyanya na abhaanu bhanu, ejitura okwimusya echitimaato mu-bhataaramu bha risoma na amagenderero. (*Translated to Jita [jit], a language of Tanzania, by Samson Zablon.*)

Developing independent reading skills for African children: will strategies familiar to Western educators be appropriate in multilingual African contexts? The purpose of this chapter is to identify effective pedagogical strategies for African readers. The chapter re-examines certain reading theories and resulting instructional practices – all products of research on monolingual English language speakers – with African linguistic and orthographic characteristics in mind. Specifically, I challenge the applicability of Dual-Route theories (Coltheart & Baron, 1978, 2005) to reading pedagogy in most African writing systems. Lexical route strategies are often used in Africa, almost to the exclusion of phonological route strategies. With limited resources and low levels of functional literacy across the continent, any mismatch of methodologies should raise concern for literacy and development professionals.

C. Benson and K. Kosonen (eds.), Language Issues in Comparative Education, 245–264.

INTRODUCTION

Developing independent reading skills for speakers of African languages: will Northern Anglophone educators' familiar strategies be effective in an African context? Experience shows that it's not as simple as ABC. The purpose of this chapter is to examine the context of indigenous African languages and writing systems in order to identify effective pedagogical strategies for future readers.

Research has made it clear that reading is a complex psycholinguistic process (Adams, 1994; Morris, 1992; Seymour, 2006). Since writing represents speech, linguistic skills and proficiency in the target language are integral to reading. In order to decode new words and develop fluency in blending sounds and syllables, the reader must be able to recognize the phonemes of the target language, and intuitively grasp its syllable structures and morphology. Reading is also a visual process. It requires visual discrimination skills of various sorts, from whole word recognition to analyzing words into their component parts and blending those components into fluid, comprehensible speech. Most importantly, since comprehension, or "accessing meaning," is actually the goal of reading, teachers in the North usually assume that learners are familiar with the vocabulary and syntax of the text they encounter in our schools (Snowling & Hulme, 2005: 101). Any authentic reading experience, teachers in the North assume, will involve a language the child is familiar with, both for decoding and comprehension.

In Africa and the rest of the South, it is very rare to find educators with that expectation (Klaas & Trudell, 2011: 6). Kenyan educators, for example, were asked about norms for reading comprehension as part of a follow-up to the Early Grade Reading Assessment (EGRA)[1] testing in Kenya. Their response was that they expect children to attend school for about 4 years before they understand what they "read" – in English, a language that is not their first. By a Northern definition of the reading process, people are not even reading if they do not understand a text, because they associate reading with more than breaking a visual code for speech. Northerners, accustomed to school-taught reading taking place via their mother tongue, assume that decoding letters and words gives the reader access to meaning. The obvious conclusion for children of the South is that their initial reading experiences, too, should be in a language they speak and understand. This chapter begins by examining the pedagogical implications of this conclusion for African learners.

LINGUISTIC FACTORS IN APPLYING ANGLOPHONE STRATEGIES TO AFRICAN LANGUAGES

To begin with, linguistic and cultural differences affect people's responses to pedagogy. Native English speakers, for example, often respond negatively to syllable drills such as "mu me mi ma mo." An explanation for this may be that English has thousands of monosyllabic words, so to mix a nonsense syllable in with actual words – bag, hag, sag, nag, *cag* – disturbs Anglophones. The same aversion has been expressed in Ndogo, a Sudanese language which has many monosyllabic words (Coombs, 2006). Speakers of such languages expect focused practice to be with meaningful units. Yet for speakers of many other African languages, notably those with long, polysyllabic words, practicing sets of syllables is a thoroughly enjoyable activity. In my experience, teachers, literacy learners and participants in various literacy workshops often express pleasure in participating in focused practice experiences, called "drills" elsewhere. Decoding skills in many African settings seem to be valued for immediate, practical reasons, and the means for developing those skills just may be part of the pleasure (Klaas & Trudell, 2011:15). Many basic literacy learners are part of strongly oral societies and they may especially enjoy the rhythm and repetition which come with the visual and auditory practice of syllable recognition.

Appropriate and effective methodologies, then, will reflect the contexts of their use. Methodologies that have been developed and tested on learners using languages such as English or French in Northern contexts may not be applicable in different social, economic, or linguistic situations. While social and economic factors certainly influence the success of a pedagogical approach, I will focus on three crucial linguistic factors for reading methodologies: depth of the orthography, phonological properties and morphological properties of the language in question. I will challenge the applicability of English-based research such as Coltheart and Baron's Dual Route models (1978, 2005) to reading pedagogies in African languages.

Depth of the Orthography

Most European and African languages have alphabetic writing systems, or *orthographies*, which represent the phonology of a language to some extent. Those with clear sound-symbol links are called *shallow*, while those which less obviously represent the sounds of the language are called *deep*. Cook and Bassetti (2005: 7) put the world's deep and shallow orthographies on a continuum; at the deep end are meaning-based writing systems such as Chinese which represent *morphemes* (the primary units of meaning) graphically, and at the shallow end are alphabetic systems like Spanish or Luganda that represent phonemes, the minimally contrastive sounds of a language. Deep orthographies thus represent the morphology more than the phonology of a language, while alphabetic systems aim to represent the sounds of speech by mapping them directly onto letters. However, as we have noted elsewhere, "even within alphabetic writing systems a variety of depth exists, between the more morpheme-preserving orthographies such as English and French, and the more phoneme-based orthographies of Swahili and Lugungu" (Trudell & Schroeder, 2007: 167).

Readers of very shallow orthographies are able to decode words using simple letter-phoneme conversion, while readers of phonologically deeper systems such as English or French must rely on strings longer than a letter; this amount of orthographic information readers must process in order to read is called the *grain size*, which varies depending on orthographic shallowness (Cook & Bassetti, 2005: 16). For languages like English, it has been natural to develop learning strategies which help the reader focus on larger sequences which are full of meaning like morphemes and whole words (Seymour, 2006: 457). Examples of English grain size are shown in Table 1.

Table 1. English grain size

man	main	mane	champagne
pan	pain	pane	campaign
ran	rain	lane	reign
plan	plain	plane	feign
can	cain	cane	Duquesne
List 1.1	List 1.2	List 1.3	List 1.4

The examples in the four lists illustrate the grain size a reader of English must visually distinguish in order to read. In list 1.1, readers must recognize a digraph, a vowel followed by a consonant, in order to recognize the short sound of the vowel a. In list 1.2, readers must look at a three-letter string. The same is true for list 1.3, just in order to recognize the phoneme /ɛ'/. In fact, readers must look far beyond the individual grapheme <a> to a four letter sequence in order to recognize the long sound of <ɛ'> before <n> in list 1.4.

More recently developed orthographies, like many writing systems developed for education in African languages, are on the shallow end of the orthographic depth continuum, partly because the languages they represent have not yet had time to change. Their simpler connections between graphemes and sounds allow readers to attend to a smaller grain size than that of English. Unlike the English orthography, one of the deepest in the world, many African orthographies stick fairly closely to one grapheme-one phoneme (one letter-one sound) mapping (Trudell & Schroeder, 2007).

The orthographic depth hypothesis proposed by Frost and Katz (Mattingly, 1992: 71) predicted that readers using a shallow orthography would depend on phonological encoding more than readers of a deep orthography. The results of ensuing research seem to bear this out. Readers of a deep orthography such as English (or even French or Portuguese, ironically the most common official languages in Sub-Saharan Africa)[ii] use whole word recognition strategies much more frequently than readers of German, Italian or Spanish, presumably because their deep orthographies do not consistently make clear connections between the graphemes and the phonology of the language (Scholfield & Chwo, 2005; Seymour, 2006; Cook & Bassetti, 2005). Figure 1 illustrates the connection between orthographic depth and time needed for mastery of reading skills.

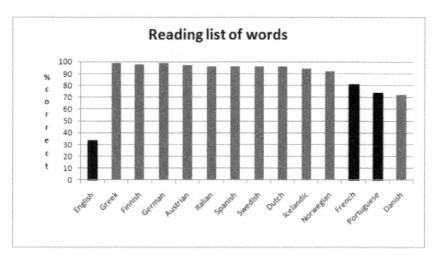

Figure 1. Reading levels compared. (Source: Seymour, 2006)

Although the developmental trajectory of children's phonological awareness is the same across different alphabetic systems, the rate of development/mastery varies, with English at one extreme. Children who are learning to read in a shallow orthography (e.g. Greek, Italian, or Finnish) develop phonological awareness, and as a consequence reading skill, faster than children who are learning in a deep orthography (e.g. English). Evidence for this comes from studies carried out with individual language groups as well as from cross-linguistic studies (Aro, 2004; Bishop & Snowling, 2004; Hutzler & Wimmer, 2004; Ziegler & Goswami, 2005).

Because of the depth of English orthography it takes mother tongue speakers of English far longer to learn to read – an estimated 2.5 years more (Aro, 2004: 541) – than speakers of all other European languages studied! Many compensatory strategies that supplement straightforward decoding for English have been developed, including use of context clues and sight word memorization. Pedagogical approaches include Whole Language, language experience approaches, and many other global strategies.

In studying the cognitive processes and strategies that L1 Anglophone readers use, Coltheart and Baron (1978, 2005) developed the Dual Route model of reading. According to the Dual Route model illustrated in Figure 2, readers use two routes, or strategies, when deciphering new words: a lexical one that links orthography and meaning, and a phonological one, relying on grapheme-phoneme conversion. The model was based on research conducted in the UK using English.

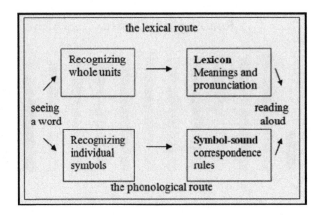

Figure 2. The Dual Route Model of Reading Aloud (Source: Cook and Bassetti, 2005)

Despite the fact that the English orthographic system is so much deeper than that of other languages, the results of Coltheart and Baron's research have been considered applicable and generalizable far beyond English-speaking contexts. Yet linguistic, orthographic and educational evidence seems to contradict the model's generalizability to shallow (or "transparent") orthographies (Nikolopoulos & Goulandris 2000; Patel, Snowling & de Jong 2004; Scholfield & Chwo, 2005; Seymour, 2006; Lau & Liow, 2005).

Specialist David Share refers to English as having an "outlier orthography," adding:

> Although no individual study has controlled for all relevant items and subject variables, the body of evidence, collectively, is unanimous in showing that, for the developing reader, English is truly exceptional. By the end of the 1st year of schooling, hyperlexic-style reading is the norm in transparent alphabetic orthographies; most children are capable of tackling almost any printed (monosyllabic) word. In English, though, such proficiency is delayed for several years. Moreover, this 'great divide' between early English and non-English reading appears to be more than quantitative and clearly extends to the nature of the reading strategies employed. (2008: 586)

An example of the compensatory strategies needed to teach children to read English is the Dolch word list.[iii] In his 1948 book, Problems in Reading, Dolch published a list of 220 frequently used 'service words' and a separate list of 95 common nouns. These lists are estimated to contain 50-75% of the words in children's books. Many of the 220 Dolch words cannot be 'sounded out' and must be learned by 'sight,' or memorized. The list includes pronouns, adjectives, adverbs, prepositions, conjunctions, and verbs. It excludes nouns, which make up a separate 95 word list. Because recognition of these frequently occurring words is considered essential to literacy (Perkins, 2010), a variety of techniques are used to teach them, including: use of context clues, reading books with repetition of these words, using flash cards, playing games, and writing activities. It should be noted that industrialized Anglophone countries have the means and the will to accomplish this daunting task.

Research indicates a series of stages in reading acquisition for mother tongue learners of English reading (Ellis et al., 2004). New readers move from recognizing whole words (logographic reading), through a stage where they begin to apply sound-symbol correspondences (alphabetic reading), to skilled reading that predominantly involves direct lexical access by way of the orthography, at least for high-frequency words (Seymour, 2006). In the last twenty years much has been said in the North about the importance of children being able to "access meaning" and adapting whole language strategies to make this possible, which means taking the lexical route. Global approaches will always be an integral part of reading instruction in any language, especially in the pre-reading phase, for accessing meaning. However, an emphasis on the lexical route for readers of shallow orthographies may lead to an avoidance of the very things that enable independent reading in these orthographies: immediate sound-symbol recognition, syllable recognition, ability to visually segment words, ability to blend sounds/syllables from left to right, recognition of morphemes within words and sentences, and practice of those skills with text.

From the Dual Route model and widespread research (Patel, Snowling, & de Jong, 2004[iv]; Seymour, Aro, & Erskine, 2003[v]) it can be inferred that shallow orthographies promote faster rates of decoding, so it seems illogical to promote lexical route strategies over phonological route strategies in the early years of reading, in a context where the orthographies are very shallow. Research suggests a strong link between reading methodologies and orthographic depth (Aro, 2004). A look at the *phonology*, or the sound systems, of African languages will further illustrate the need for relevant pedagogy, and for that matter, for reading assessments which also reflect the linguistic and orthographic characteristics of the languages used.

Studying the orthographic context before developing curricula also applies, of course, to assessing children's reading abilities in a given language. The effective use of educational assessments to improve learning is not just a good idea; it is essential. Early Grade Reading Assessments used to be given only in English, but gradually they are being applied to local languages. One challenge is that little consideration has been given to the linguistic and sociolinguistic contexts where EGRA is applied and pedagogies developed. Next I examine some of the features of African languages which set them apart from English and other Indo-European languages – in fact, from the rest of the world.

Nature of the Phonology

Some 30% of the world's languages are spoken in Africa (Lewis, 2009). While there is immense variety across its six linguistic regions, linguists have identified several very unique phonological features occurring only, or almost exclusively, in

African languages. Among the unique consonantal phenomena in Africa are *co-articulated labial-velar* stops (complex consonants whose constituents are pronounced simultaneously, resulting in syllables like <gba>), clicks, and *implosives* (consonant sounds which are made while the speaker inhales sharply). Word-initial prenasalized consonants (words preceded by an m or n, and in which the two consonants fuse into one sound) are quite common, and add to the visual complexity of syllable onsets. For example, Malila, spoken in southern Tanzania, uses complex syllable onsets such as <mbw->, <ndy->, <mpw->, and <nk->, for a total of 25 *prenasalized consonants* (Schroeder, 2010: 8-9).

African vowels are not to be outdone in their own complexity: some require tone-marking, or have oral-nasal contrasts in meaning, and vowel length distinctions as well[vi]. There are three types of vowel harmony systems which do not exist anywhere else in the known linguistic world (Heine and Nurse 2008: 49), meaning that sets of vowels in affixes and even roots of words change their sound, and hence their spelling, so word roots and affixes can change in appearance. The phenomenon of changing vowel sounds and letters adds to the challenges for readers trying to immediately recognize words and the morphemes that are within them. These readers will need to use the *phonological route* to reading, sounding out the words in order to access their meaning.

For Bantu languages, spoken by roughly 200,000,000 people in central, southern and eastern Africa, phonological rules cause nouns and verbs to mutate considerably with affixation, meaning that the word changes quite dramatically when prefixes or suffixes are added. As we (Trudell & Schroeder, 2007) have noted, these changes in pronunciation may make it difficult for readers to quickly identify morphemes due to their small size (often 1-3 letters) and changing visual images. I will refer to this phenomenon, with lots of morphemes packed into words, as *dense morphology.*

Verbs in Bantu languages, for example, are usually very long and packed with morphemes. In Swahili, widely spoken as a first or second language in Kenya, Tanzania and cross-border areas, the phrase 'she baked me a cake yesterday' is <alinipikia keki jana>. The polymorphemic verb <a-li-ni-pik-i-a> contains the following: 2nd pers.-sing.-past-1st person singular object-verb root-applicative-verb-final. Readers must quickly recognize syllables and morphemes in order to read fluently and with comprehension. Skills such as automatic syllable recognition take on much greater value for Bantu readers than whole word memorization or other global strategies. Considering the affixation issues, Bantu language speakers are not likely to benefit from memorization of a list of frequently occurring 'sight' words. Indeed, it would be highly challenging to make a sight word out of a verb which has a tiny root surrounded by an exponential number of constantly changing affixes.

From this sprinkling of examples, it is obvious that even with the shallow orthographies most common on the continent, readers of African languages face challenges which with mother tongue English readers – and assessors – are completely unfamiliar.

Nature of the Morphology

Awareness of the morphology of a language makes an important contribution to literacy acquisition in that language (Koda, 2005: 315). Unlike the relatively few grammatical words on the English Dolch word list, however, Bantu grammatical words are multitudinous in their variety because they vary depending on the class of noun they modify. For example, simply saying "of," or "belonging to," requires a familiarity with up to 23 noun classes and their prefixes. The associative marker takes these forms in the Ikoma language of Tanzania (Higgins, 2010: 25), as demonstrated in Table 2. It is clearly impractical for readers to memorize a long list

Table 2. Ikoma associatives. (Source: Higgins, 2010)

Noun class	Noun	Associative	Noun class	Noun	Associative
1	omutɛmi	o	10	changibɔ	che
2	abatɛmi	ba	11	orosiri	ro
3	omugaate	o	12	agakɔ	ka, ga
4	emigaate	ge	14	obutɔɔti	bo
5	erishɛrɛ	re	15	ogogoro	ko, go
6	amashɛrɛ	ga	16	ahagiro	ha
7	egetumbe	ke, ge	18	–	–
8	ebetumbe	be	19	ehikɔ	he
9	angibɔ	e	20	ogukɔ	go

of variants for associatives as well as for conjunctions, locatives and possessives. Instead, incipient readers of Ikoma, like readers of other shallow orthographies (e.g. Randall, 2005: 129), will quickly need to develop visual discrimination of a variety of open syllables.

These are common linguistic and orthographic features which merit attention for reading skill development in African languages. The following section examines some of the implications of these features for reading methodologies.

METHODOLOGICAL IMPLICATIONS

Implication 1: Attend to the Morphology

The dense morphology of Bantu words, especially verbs, has been mentioned above, with the example of Swahili. Since a word can contain several affixes, those affixes and their variant forms call for specific focus in teaching so that readers can gain fluency and immediate access to meaning (Klaas & Trudell, 2011: 11).

Most of these complex words are spoken as part of a noun phrase, where they are fairly predictable to the reader. Nevertheless, grammatical words and particles tend to be unstressed phonologically, meaning that there is no stress when they are spoken, and they carry little meaning in isolation. Their recognition as units of meaning helps readers to process words and phrases more rapidly and with comprehension. Recent research on Greek, Portuguese, English, Russian and other languages indicates that explicit instruction in morpheme recognition benefits reading and spelling (McCutchen, Logan, & Biangardi, 2009; Bryant, Deacon, & Nunes, 2006; Grigorenko, 2006). Two pedagogical strategies can help readers recognize morphemes whether they are affixes or words.

The first strategy is helping readers recognize the position of a morpheme in a word or phrase. The second is helping readers recognize the function of that morpheme. Both of these strategies should help support and maximize the predictability of morphemes for the reader, but the reader will always have to attend to the visual distinctions between such a multiplicity of variants as those shown in Table 2. To teach the position of a particular morpheme, one strategy is to show that morpheme repeatedly in a set of phrases or words.

Another strategy is to contrast it with related morphemes in the same position. Such a contrastive activity also helps learners recognize the functions of the morphemes and learn to expect to see them in particular locations. For a Bantu language such as Swahili, with its obligatory polymorphemic verbal phrases, readers benefit from awareness of the location of a particular morpheme, as in:

Wa-li-ni-pat-i-a (They got for me)
3rd person plural-past-1st person singular object-verb root-applicative-final

One way to help readers quickly identify a verb root is to substitute various verb roots while keeping the rest of the phrase the same:

Wa-li-ni-**pat**-i-a (They **got** for me)
Wa-li-ni-**pik**-i-a (They **cooked** for me)
Wa-li-ni-**imb**-i-a (They **sang** for me)

Finally, to develop comprehension and fluency a bit further, ensuring that the reader is engaging fully with the text, a cloze activity can be very helpful, forcing the reader to think about the text and choose the only morpheme which will actually be appropriate in the context:

Walini ___ ia viazi. pik imb (They ___ potatoes for me. cooked sang)
Walini ___ ia saa. pat pik (They ___ a watch for me. got cooked)

In sum, reading development for these languages should develop morphemic awareness, both for spelling skill and recognition of particular morpheme slots within words. It should provide practice in remembering long series of syllables, supporting decoding of long words. There is supportive evidence from Verhoeven, Baayen and Schreuder (2004) that it may be appropriate to include chunking of meaningful word particles bigger than the syllable because reading comprehension and fluency are facilitated by such exercises. Attention to immediate morpheme recognition may be even more important with shallow orthographies (Verhoeven and Perfetti 2003), since words for these languages are spelled as they sound, and changes in morpheme appearance or spelling are conditioned by their environment within a word. For example, in Kiswahili the person-marking morpheme /mu-/ in muntu *man* changes to <mw> before a vowel, so /mu-alimu/, *teacher,* is written <mwalimu>.

Implication 2: Attend to the Phonology

Early reading pedagogy for any alphabetic language should encourage auditory awareness of phonemes and teach sound-grapheme correspondences, for example <B> is for /b/ (Pearson & Hiebert, 2010). While English readers have to substitute grapheme-phoneme decoding strategies for larger grain-size strategies, readers of shallow orthographies appear to rely more on phoneme-grapheme correspondence rules as they acquire reading fluency (Cook & Bassetti, 2005: 16). Their decoding strategies include attention to syllables, analogical recognition of new syllables, (for example initial consonant substitution as shown in Figure 2), and the joining of syllables into words. As Adams (1994) observes, frequent exposure to series of letters which bond together phonologically can aid recognition of long letter series. Adams points out that with practice, the association between an ordered pair of letters becomes encoded in memory as a cohesive, ordered sequence. Complex syllables, then, represented by a series of letters such as <nywrra>, are not impossible to decode if readers are taught how to recognize them. Automaticity of complex syllable recognition is crucial for fluency in some languages.

New readers of many African languages need to develop visual discrimination of syllables, depending upon the nature of the syllable structures of the language involved, and help with visual contrast between open and closed syllables as needed. They should benefit from focused auditory-visual practice with syllables, especially since syllables are often easier than individual segments for incipient readers to recognize auditorily (Seymour, 2006: 460). Analogy strategies like that in Figure 3 for teaching <bw>, <hw>, then adding <fw> can be useful in teaching a variety of similar syllable structures in many African languages. As part of developing syllable and phoneme awareness and recognition, a focus on tone and vowel length may also be needed, in languages where these make a difference in meaning.

Another methodological point worth noting relates to the degree of complexity of syllable structures for a given language. Many African languages have unusually complex syllable structures, especially in their *onsets*, or beginnings. All of these need to be taught directly during the stage when learners are recognizing the forms of monosyllables (Seymour, 2006: 459). This means that even if learners are reading a shallow orthography, some special teaching strategies are needed. For example, readers of Irigwe, not a Bantu language but a Central Benue-Congo language of Nigeria (Lewis, 2009), must decipher such syllable onsets as <yhwrr>,

<nnyw>, <nywrr>, and <ngwrr>. Irigwe has an inventory of 188 consonant *graphemes* (including letters, letter combinations and other relevant symbols such as tone markings). Many are complex syllable onsets. These onsets should be taught as wholes in a setting which makes their constituents easy to recognize, as shown in Figure 4 (NBTT, 2011).

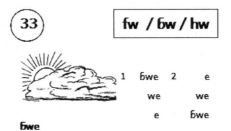

Figure 3. Complex syllable onsets

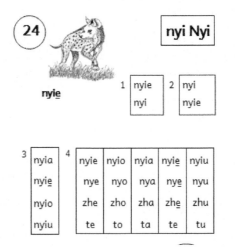

Figure 4. Irigwe Consonant Clusters from Draft Irigwe Primer 2011

One of the first steps in developing a reading pedagogy is identifying all of the graphemes of a particular language so they can be taught systematically. As implied by the title of this article, these are not just letters like A, B or C. The inventory of elements to be taught will reflect the number of vowel forms (including nasality and tone), consonants, clusters and syllable *codas* (syllable-final consonants) in a given language. If a letter can occur both syllable-initially and syllable-finally, for example, it will need to be taught in both positions.

Implication 3: Attend to the Nature of the Orthography

Orthographic depth and reading methodologies should be closely linked. In fact, there is little evidence that taking a lexical route to reading shallow orthographies will be effective. As Aro (2004: 30) states, "[w]hen the orthography allows for teaching of grapheme-phoneme correspondences, that is also the natural choice for a reading instruction method."

There is a paucity of research literature on the reading of African language orthographies, but Malaysian provides another example of the deep-shallow orthography contrast. As Randall concludes in comparing reading pedagogy in Malaysian and English, "A reader in BM [Bahasa Malaysia], with its highly consistent grapheme-phoneme relationships (an orthographically highly regular language), will have no need to use a whole-word route to gain lexical access; a phonological assembly route will always produce successful lexical access. However, use of the phonological route alone will not always produce successful word recognition in English" (Randall, in Cook & Bassetti 2005: 128). He concludes that for English the dual route model of lexical access is a necessity, unlike most other languages.

Shallow orthographies also lend themselves well to identifying and blending of word parts. Comparative data from Ellis (2004) indicate that among readers of shallow orthographies there is a much more linear relationship between successful word-naming time and word length, so the importance of instant recognition of syllables is magnified for readers of languages with long words. "This is the pattern that would result if pronunciation were assembled by means of left-to-right parsing of the graphemes that constitute each word, with concomitant decoding of the corresponding phonemes; the more graphemes to process, the longer is the assembly time" (ibid.: 39). In contrast, readers of English are not so affected by word length, often memorizing unique spellings of entire words such as <whole> and <hole>. The average English word length is 5.1, based on "normal written prose" (Solomon, 2011). This means that readers of English do not have to focus as much on instant recognition of syllables in words as do readers of hundreds of African languages.

Since readers of shallow orthographies tend to use a strictly phonological (letter-sound decoding) route to understanding, word length directly corresponds to word recognition time (Seymour, 2006). A very simple beginner text in Malila, a language of southern Tanzania, is displayed in Figure 5. The average word length for the text is seven letters, and if only nouns and verbs were counted, the average would be 8.2.

> Abhaana bhatatu bhabhalolile abhiibha uwusiku. We bhakumuloleela utaata nu Shaali. Abhiibha bhiibhile ukalulu, amakawiilu na matuuli.

Figure 5. Text in Malila primer book 1, lesson 8

An appropriate reading methodology for this orthography would develop readers' ability to quickly recognize sequences of both graphemes and syllables, because if new readers must decode letter by letter, they will forget the entire sequence by the time they reach the end (Koda and Zehler 2008: 30). Memorization of such long words loaded with exponential morphological variants, as shown in the section on morphology, will be impossible. The need for their automatic recognition takes on greater importance for long strings of syllables than it would for shorter strings as in English. In Figure 6, a page from the Malila primer (SIL 2005) shows some syllable analysis strategies which help pupils recognize syllables quickly.

Figure 6. Polysyllabic words

In the example above, beginning readers are shown the whole words at the bottom of the page, then the syllables, initially focusing on the digraph <bh>. They are then helped to recode the new syllables by analogy with other syllables they have studied before, recognizing the new digraph in combination with vowels they already know. Such practice through drills, in words, and on a controlled-vocabulary text promotes automaticity of recognition and fluency in decoding.

CONTEXTUALIZING READING INSTRUCTION AND ASSESSMENT

When broad generalizations from Northern English-based research are applied to pedagogy for non-Indo-European languages (such as the Bantu and Benue-Congo languages given as examples here) and to very new orthographies, it is often learners themselves who must compensate for inadequacies in the teaching approaches used. Ironically, it is these learners who are already marginalized and lacking the resources we assume to be needed who are forced to find their own ways to master the complex skill of reading. In other words, if teaching methodologies do not appropriately reflect the linguistic context, they put an unnecessary burden on learners who are already at a disadvantage. In fact, the lack of linguistically contextualized pedagogies may go a long way toward explaining poor educational achievement in Africa.

Studying the phonological, orthographic and morphological characteristics of the target language and applying this knowledge to pedagogy is not a simple matter – it is clearly not as easy as ABC. Designing methodologies, materials and evaluation strategies which focus on the details within the words on a page, while accessing and utilizing the reader's skills and perceptions, requires time and hard work, but the payoff is the ease with which learners master reading. Once appropriate pedagogies are developed, speakers of these languages find learning to read easy – and even enjoyable.

The linguistic context should also be studied before developing curricula and before developing tools to assess children's reading abilities. As mentioned above, the EGRA instruments are a case in point. As recently as 2009, EGRA instruments ignored the first language of the child (USAID, 2009). This changed a year later, when the EGRA was administered in four Kenyan languages: English, Gikuyu, Dholuo and Kiswahili (Piper, 2010). The 2010 assessment examined children's reading skills in their mother tongues, quantified use of these languages in classrooms, and in some cases evaluated syllable recognition rather than letter recognition, which was an improvement. However, actual adaptations based on the linguistic characteristics of individual languages are still quite limited, and it will be important to establish developmental benchmarks for assessments like the EGRA that reflect the orthographic and linguistic contexts where they are used.

Another aspect of developing appropriate assessments is determining ways to assess previously ignored skills such as bilingual oral language skills in L1 and L2. This might provide major clues as to the reasons for greater success of the EGRA Plus in Liberia (2009), where English is spoken more widely, than of the Kenyan intervention (Korda & Crouch, 2009). If reading fluency and comprehension are goals for instruction in a second language, reading (and writing) skills in the L1 combined with oral language skills in the L2 are prerequisites, and determining whether or not they are being developed will lead the way to improved reading methodologies and reading test scores as well.

The Eritrean National Reading Survey, carried out in 2002 for eight language groups, is an example of assessment which has directly impacted pedagogy. Because children were expected to switch at grade 6 from mother tongues to English medium, their English skills were assessed for word-object recognition, listening skills, understanding word meanings, understanding sentence meaning, reading and answering in English, and reading accuracy, fluency and comprehension (Walter, 2005: 64). The results of the survey then impacted development of these skills, especially in grade 5. It should be noted that this assessment utilized many more measures of understanding than the EGRA instruments do.

I propose, then, that there are best practices to promote reading fluency and comprehension in these languages, and that they involve using orthographic, phonological and morphological characteristics in reading methodologies. The significance of lexical route strategies for these languages is diminished in African language contexts. Phonological route strategies – which are much more important for shallow orthographies – need to be developed, and should reflect the unique properties of each language.

APPLICABILITY IN AFRICAN CLASSROOMS

Curriculum designers may be forgetting that learners are highly motivated not only by understanding what they read, but by an ability to access that meaning for themselves, rather than depending upon a teacher to tell them what is written on the page. What I am proposing here is giving new readers of African languages the confidence and skill to do just that, while also developing their comprehension skills and their enjoyment of the reading experience.

Independent reading skills are highly valued by adults who attend literacy classes, who tend to have utilitarian reasons for learning to read (Trudell & Klaas, 2010: 126-128). A bit of focused practice supports automaticity of syllable and morpheme recognition and self-confidence in one's ability to figure out a new word. When adults as well as children find they can do this, they are often highly motivated to keep on reading?

How can literacy be promoted by teachers, whose training is often highly limited (Goody, 2001: 181)? I suggest an approach which forces an interactive teaching style and leverages the relative transparency of a given orthography. Direct learner involvement, rather than passive memorization and repetition (Schroeder, 2004), would encourage learners to engage with text from the very beginning, and force them to recognize sound-grapheme connections, syllable patterns, and word parts. Step-by-step teachers' guides, paired with a strictly sequenced set of learning activities to promote automaticity in decoding (Abadzi, 2006), and interesting, authentic texts providing built-in access to meaning (Schroeder, 2007) would be effective in most African school settings. A reading curriculum should also include:

– a pre-reading skill set which is culturally and linguistically contextualized,
– an early reading skill set which includes analysis and synthesis of word parts and even phrases, and
– reading and writing fluency development for upper levels with graded texts.

The latter texts should be embedded in daily lessons through keywords and discussion, stories and other literature learners actually want to read, and a variety of comprehension questions, using the language and meta-linguistic skills that learners bring from home and develop in effective programs (Schroeder, 2001, 2007).

CONCLUSIONS

This chapter has challenged the generalizability of Coltheart and Baron's English reading research (1978, 2005) to reading in other linguistic and orthographic systems. Lexical route strategies have sometimes been used almost to the exclusion of phonological route strategies, the latter holding more promise for effective literacy education in African languages.

I am not the first to advise caution regarding reading strategies for shallower orthographies. Dual route theorists themselves had misgivings in extending the model to German, which has a highly regular orthography (Coltheart, Rastle, Perry, Langdon, & Ziegler, 2001). Ziegler and Goswami (2005: 15) find that the "dual route architecture (i.e., two separate routes in the skilled reading system) may in fact only develop for English." More recently, Share (2008: 588) observes that "[a] growing number of reading researchers have begun to question the generalizability of the Dual Route Model beyond English."

Viewed collectively, findings from both phonological and morphological awareness studies provide clear implications for pedagogy, curriculum and assessment to facilitate literacy learning. Northern, English-based research findings and models must be subjected to further scrutiny when applying them to teaching and assessing readers of African languages.

NOTES

[i] This EGRA was conducted by RTI in two provinces in Kenya. Reading skills of 2,000 children in 100 schools were assessed, using four languages.
[ii] Less than 10 million Africans combined, out of a population of one billion, speak any of these four former colonial languages to any degree. See e.g.
http://en.wikipedia.org/wiki/Languages_of_Africa#Official_languages
[iii] Edward William Dolch compiled these lists of words which occur very frequently in American English texts. Many of them are of course grammatical words, and beginning readers in schools are often encouraged to recognize them by sight.
[iv] This recent study comparing reading in English (deep orthography) and Dutch (relatively shallow orthography) found that phonemic awareness was a significant predictor of reading ability in both languages, whereas naming speed was not.
[v] Seymour, Aro, and Erskine (2003) of the EC COST Action A8 network conducted cross-linguistic studies of foundational levels of literacy in 12 European countries. Results revealed that English-speaking children in their first two years of schooling in the UK have the poorest outcomes

regarding familiar word identification and non-word reading when compared with children from other countries/languages tested.

[vi] Examples of some of these vowel contrasts can be found in the Bantu Orthography Manual, pages 25-47 (Schroeder, 2010).

REFERENCES

Abadzi, Helen (2006). *Efficient learning for the poor: Insights from the frontier of cognitive neuroscience*. Washington, DC: World Bank.

Adams, Marilyn (1994). *Beginning to read: Thinking and learning about print*. Cambridge, MA: MIT Press.

Aro, Mikko (2004). *Learning to read: the effect of orthography*. Jyväskylä Studies in Education, Psychology and Social Research 237. Jyväskylä: University of Jyväskylä.

Bishop, Dorothy, & Snowling, Johannes (2004). Developmental dyslexia and specific language impairment: Same or different? *Psychological Bulletin, 130*, 858-886.

Bryant, Peter; Deacon, Hélène, & Nunes, Terezinha (2006). Morphology and spelling: What have morphemes to do with spelling? In R. Malatesha Joshi & P. G. Aaron (Eds.), *Handbook of orthography and literacy* (pp. 601-616). Hillsdale, NJ: Lawrence Erlbaum.

Coltheart, Max (1978). Lexical access in simple reading tasks. In Geoffrey Underwood (Ed.), *Strategies of information processing* (pp. 151-216). London: Academic Press.

Coltheart, Max, Rastle, Kathy, Perry, Conrad, Langdon, Robyn, & Ziegler, Johannes (2001). DRC: A dual-route cascaded model of visual word recognition and reading aloud. *Psychological Review, 108*, 204-256.

Coltheart, Max (2005). Modeling reading: The dual route approach. In Margaret J. Snowling & Charles Hulme (Eds.), *The science of reading: A handbook* (pp. 6-23). Oxford: Blackwell.

Cook, Vivian, & Bassetti, Benedetta (Eds.) (2005). *Second language writing systems*. Clevedon, England: Multilingual Matters.

Coombs, Craig (2006). *A case study on teaching of tone in primers. Ndógó, Western Bahr al Ghazal, Sudan*. Unpublished report. SIL International.

Dolch, Edward (1948). *Problems in reading*. Champaign, IL: The Garrard Press.

Ellis, Nick, Natsume, Miwa, Stavropoulous, Katerina, Hoxhallari, Lorenc, van Daal, Victor, Polyzoe, Nicoletta, Tsipa, Louisahalis, & Petalas, Michalis (2004). The effects of orthographic depth on learning to read alphabetic, syllabic, and logographic scripts. *Reading Research Quarterly, 39*(4), 438-468.

Goody, Esther (2001). Literacy for Gonja and Birifor children in Northern Ghana. In David Olson & Nancy Torrance (Eds.), *The making of literate societies* (pp. 178-200). Oxford: Blackwell.

Grigorenko, Elena (2006). If John were Ivan. In R. Malatesha Joshi & P. G. Aaron (Eds.), *Handbook of orthography and literacy* (pp. 303-320). Hillsdale, NJ: Lawrence Erlbaum.

Heine, Bernd, & Nurse, Derek (2008). *A linguistic geography of Africa*. Cambridge: Cambridge University Press.

Higgins, Holly (2010). *Ikoma orthography sketch*. Unpublished report. SIL International.

Hutzler, Florian, & Wimmer, Heinz (2004). Eye movements of dyslexic children when reading in a regular orthography. *Brain and Language, 89*, 235-242.

Klaas, Anthony, & Trudell, Barbara (2011). Effective literacy programmes and independent reading in African contexts. *Language Matters, 42*(1), 22-38.

Koda, Keiko (2005). Learning to read across writing systems: Transfer, metalinguistic awareness, and second-language reading development. In Vivian Cook & Benedetta Bassetti (Eds.), *Second language writing systems* (pp. 311-334). Clevedon, England: Multilingual Matters.

Koda, Keiko, & Zehler, Annette (2008). *Learning to read across languages: Cross-linguistic relationships in first- and second-language literacy development*. Routledge: New York.

Korda, Medina, Crouch, Luis, & Mumo, David (2009). *Improvements in reading skills in Kenya: An experiment in the Malindi District*. Malindi, Kenya: RTI International and Aga Khan Foundation.

Lau, Lily, & Liow, Susan (2005). Phonological awareness and spelling skill development in bilingual biscriptal children. In Vivian Cook & Benedetta Bassetti (Eds.), *Handbook of orthography and literacy* (pp. 145-177). Hillsdale, NJ: Lawrence Erlbaum

Lewis, Paul (2009). *Ethnologue: Languages of the world* (16th ed.). Dallas, TX: SIL International.

Mattingly, Ignatius (1992). Linguistic awareness and orthographic form. In Ram Frost & Leonard Katz (Eds.), *Orthography, phonology, morphology and meaning* (pp. 109-110, 129-140). Haskins Laboratories Status Report on Speech Research. New Haven: Elsevier Science Publishers.

McCutchen, Deborah, Logan, Becky, & Biangardi, Ulrike (2009). Making meaning: Children's sensitivity to morphological information during word reading. *Reading Research Quarterly*, Oct/Nov/Dec, 1025-1040.

Morris, Darrell (1992). Concept of word: A pivotal understanding in the learning-to-read process. In Shane Templeton & Donald Bear (Eds.), *Development of orthographic knowledge and the foundations of literacy* (pp. 53-77). Hillsdale, NJ: Lawrence Erlbaum.

Nikolopoulos, Dimitris, & Goulandris, Nata (2000). The cognitive determinants of literacy skills in a regular orthography. In Michael Perkins & Sara Howard (Eds.), *New directions in language development and disorders* (pp. 261-270). New York: Plenum Publishers.

NBTT (2011). *Reading and writing in Rigwe*. Jos, Nigeria: NBTT. Unpublished.

Patel, Tanya, Snowling, Margaret, & de Jong, Peter (2004). A cross-linguistic comparison of children learning to read in English and Dutch. *Journal of Educational Psychology, 96*(4), 785-797.

Pearson, David, & Hiebert, Elfrieda (2010). National reports in literacy: Building a scientific base for practice and policy. *Educational Researcher, 39*, 286-294.

Perkins, Jill (2010). Mrs. Perkins' Dolch words: Helping your children read. (http://www.mrsperkins.com/what_are_dolch_words.html)

Piper, Benjamin (2010). *Kenya early grade reading assessment: Findings report*. RTI International.

Randall, Mick (2005). Orthographic knowledge and first language reading: Evidence from single word dictation from Chinese and Malaysian users of English as a foreign language. In Vivian Cook & Benedetta Bassetti (Eds.), *Second language writing systems* (pp. 122-146). Hillsdale, NJ: Lawrence Erlbaum.

Scholfield, Phil, & Chwo, Gloria (2005). Effect of teaching on reading processing. In Vivian Cook & Benedetta Bassetti (Eds.), *Second language writing systems* (pp. 213-137). Clevedon, England: Multilingual Matters.

Schroeder, Leila (2001). Mother-tongue education in schools in Tharaka language group of Kenya. *Notes on Literacy, 27*(3), 8-22.

Schroeder, Leila (2004). Mother tongue education in schools in Kenya: Some hidden beneficiaries. *Language Matters, 35*(2) 376-389.

Schroeder, Leila (2007). Promoting cognitive development in children from minority language groups. *International Journal of Learning, 14*(7), 7-14.

Schroeder, Leila (2010). *Bantu orthography manual*. Version 1.2. (http://www.sil.org/silepubs/abstract.asp?id=50630)

Seymour, Philip, Aro, Mikko, & Erskine, Jane (2003). Foundation literacy acquisition in European orthographies. *British Journal of Psychology, 94*(2), 143-174

Seymour, Philip (2006). A theoretical framework for beginning reading in different orthographies. In Malatesha Joshi &P. G. Aaron (Eds.), *Handbook of orthography and literacy* (pp. 441-462). Hillsdale, NJ: Lawrence Erlbaum.

Share, David (2008). On the anglocentricities of current reading research and practice: The perils of overreliance on an "outlier" orthography. *Psychological Bulletin, 134*(4), 584-615.

SIL International (2005). *Ishitabu isha kumanyila kubhaazya*. Mbeya, Tanzania: SIL International. Unpublished.

Snowling, Margaret, & Hulme, Charles (Eds.) (2005). *The science of reading: A handbook*. Oxford: Blackwell.

Solomon, N. Watson (2011). *Sentence and word length*. (http://ds.nahoo.net/Academic/Maths/Sentence.html)

Trudell, Barbara, & Klaas, Anthony (2010). Distinction, integration and identity: Motivations for local language literacy in Senegalese communities. *International Journal of Educational Development 30*, 121–129.

Trudell, Barbara, & Schroeder, Leila (2007). Reading methodologies for African languages: Avoiding linguistic and pedagogical imperialism. *Language, Culture and Curriculum, 20*(3), 165-180.

USAID (2009). *EGRA Plus: Liberia: Data analytic report*. (https://www.eddataglobal.org/documents/index.cfm/LI%20Manual%20Year%202_gph.pdf?fuseaction=throwpub&ID=201)

Verhoeven, Ludo, & Perfetti, Charles (2003). Introduction to this special issue: The role of morphology in learning to read. *Scientific Studies of Reading, 7*(3), 209-217.

Verhoeven, Ludo, Baayen, Harald, & Schreuder, Rob (2004). Orthographic constraints and frequency effects in complex word identification. *Written Language and Literacy, 7*(1), 49-59.

Walter, Kelly (2005). *The Eritrean English curriculum: Grades 2-6: Assessing academic readiness*. Unpublished MA Thesis. Arlington: University of Texas.

Ziegler, Johannes, & Goswami, Usha (2005). Reading acquisition, developmental dyslexia, and skilled reading across languages: A psycholinguistic grain size theory. *Psychological Bulletin, 131*, 3-29.

Leila Schroeder
SIL International, Kenya

STEPHEN L. WALTER

14. EXPLORING THE DEVELOPMENT OF READING IN MULTILINGUAL EDUCATION PROGRAMS

ABSTRACT

Gheli nkɨŋ ila' nɨ gheli ghɨ baŋnɨ keli meyn ɨfyê' sɨ ɨyaŋsɨ-ɨ kèsa izɨlì i jàŋ, ifaytɨ ijàŋ nɨ ɨjâŋ i atu a baynɨ-a sɨ chɨyntɨ sɨ dyèyn sɨ fì sɨ keli ilema kûm ɨye'i sɨ jàŋ sɨ dyèyn a nzɨtɨ ndô ŋwà'lɨ nɨ woynda i bol. Ɨfyê' nâ wèyn ta wu n- ghɨ nɨn nî na ghɨ na bɨfɨ sɨ kfeynsɨ aninɨ iye'i ta nkɨ̂ŋ lvɨ̂yn dyèyn meyn na ilema i ijàŋ a tɨ̂la' tɨ ànfɨf nɨn laynî keli ɨfyê' nâ wèyn. Ɗwà'lɨ yèyn nɨn bô'lɨ kɨ̂tɨ mɨwôlɨ nâ mèyn ta mɨ n-dyêyn ilema ijàŋ a tɨ̂la' tɨ ànfɨf fɨ̀ boŋ dyêyn na itaŋi zɨ a ghɨ chò' meyn lèm sɨ isa' kà' sɨ a mo' a yi na ghɨ sɨ dyèyn ikfɨnɨ nô sɨ a ŋaŋ ta ghɨ kɨŋ yèyn izɨlì sɨ lema ijàŋ a tɨ̂la' tɨ ànfɨf. (*Translated to Kom [bkm] a language of Cameroon, by Godfrey Kain Chuo*.)

Researchers in the West have developed detailed standards – reading rate, reading accuracy, and comprehension – to both characterize and track progress towards learning to read in early basic education. The existence of such standards raises the obvious question of whether or not they can be extended to broader educational practice, since recent research has established that the development of reading skills in lower-income countries tends to lag far behind these standards. This chapter investigates some of the data on reading development from low-income countries and provides evidence that educational policy on language of instruction may, in fact, be the most salient explanatory variable in explaining the widely observed deficit in reading skill development in such countries.

INTRODUCTION

Reading is foundational to basic education. After spending the first few years of school learning to read, children must be able to read to learn, i.e. to read academic content in textbooks and other materials, which helps them develop linguistically and cognitively. Because reading is essential to school learning, there is an abundance of research, publications, and attention given to remediation when children fail to achieve established *norms* for reading speed, reading accuracy, or reading comprehension When this happens, policy makers and researchers normally ask, "*Why* did children fail to achieve these norms" – and then, "*What* should we do to fix the failure"?

C. Benson and K. Kosonen (eds.), Language Issues in Comparative Education, 265–281.

In recent years, the Western construct of *reading norms* has been invoked with reference to reading development in low-income countries (Abadzi, 2010). What gives reading norms salience and credibility? How broad or universal is or should be their scope? What norms are appropriate (if any) for reading development in non-Western or low-income countries? What major variables – language and quality of instruction, availability of materials, amount of instruction time, etc. – affect reading development in such countries?

This paper undertakes an empirical investigation of recent research on reading development in low-income countries with a particular focus on one variable – language of instruction. The research findings are being reported primarily to shed light on the abundant dissimilarities between what we know about reading in developed countries of the North and West, particularly research on monolingual Anglophone learners, and what we are discovering about reading development in multilingual low-income countries. Implications include such issues as the universality (or not) of reading norms developed in the North, the impact of language of instruction on learning to read, and the consequences of transitioning to a second language both for reading and for instruction. While the findings reported reflect on the adequacy of reading instruction in low-income countries, they are not intended as a critical commentary on this subject.

THE ISSUE OF READING NORMS

Reading Norms as Proposed for the USA

Barr, Blachowicz, Katz, and Kaufman (2002) have published sets of reading norms – reading rate (based on words read correctly per minute), reading accuracy (number of words read correctly as a percentage of all words read), reading comprehension (percent of comprehension tasks answered correctly) – that both reflect and guide educational practice and expectations for English speakers in the USA. At the same time, the Early Grade Reading Assessment (EGRA)[i] research carried out by RTI,[ii] the World Bank, and USAID has starkly reminded us that reading norms such as those popularized by Barr et al. do not come even remotely close to describing reading achievement in most low-income countries. Not only do rates of reading speed and reading comprehension fall far below those established by Barr et al. in Tables 1, 2, and 3, but the achievement of even modest levels of proficiency happens years later than the norms suggested by Barr and her colleagues.

The contrasting realities raise a number of compelling questions. Are the reading standards prevailing in the North in general and for English speakers in the USA in particular applicable in low-income countries? Are they applicable to children who are not learning to read in a language they understand? Are they the product of an excessive Northern preoccupation with early reading achievement? Are the deficits documented by the EGRA work indicative of specific instructional problems in the South which can be easily remedied, or are they rather the product of structural issues in education which are not being addressed in any fundamental manner or which have no simple solution? What types of reading norms might be reasonable or appropriate for basic education in developing countries if/when the necessary research has been completed?

For ease of reference, the widely cited norms proposed by Barr et al. (2002) for primary education in the USA – as one exemplar of a high-income Northern country – are summarized in Table 1.

Table 1. Norms for levels of reading proficiency suggested by Barr et al. (2002)

Reading Level	Accuracy	Comprehension
Independent	98–100%	90–100%
Instructional	95–97%	75–89%
Borderline	90–94%	50–74%
Frustration	<90%	Below 50%

Barr et al. (2002) have also published norms for reading rates which are tied to school grades. These suggested norms appear in Table 2.

Table 2. Grade-level norms for reading rates proposed by Barr et al. (2002)

Grade Level	Oral Reading Rate (normally based on words read correctly per minute, wcpm)
First	30–70
Second	50–100
Third	70–120
Fourth	90–140
Fifth	100–150
Sixth	110–150

In Table 3, Hasbrouck and Tindal (1992) provide additional specificity based on performance by selected percentiles as well as gains made during the course of a school year based also on US educational practice.

The data from Hasbrouck and Tindal show clearly that reading skills, as measured by reading rate, vary quite dramatically within a grade and across the span of a school year, an observation to keep clearly in mind as we examine the data from a range of programs in low-income countries.

Investigating Reading Norms in Rural Cameroon

We now examine data similar to results achieved through EGRA instruments for general primary education in low-income African contexts. These data were collected in Cameroon in 2006 for a baseline study on reading performance in rural African schools. The data establish a second frame of reference for this study in the

267

Table 3. Reading rate norms (wcpm) for grades 2-5. (Source: Hasbrouck & Tindal, 1992)

Grade	Percentile	Beginning of year	Middle of year	End of year
	75	82	106	124
2	50	53	78	94
	25	23	46	65
	75	107	123	142
3	50	79	93	114
	25	65	70	87
	75	125	133	143
4	50	99	112	118
	25	72	89	92
	75	125	143	151
5	50	105	118	128
	25	77	93	100

Table 4. Data illustrating typical results in the development of reading proficiency in a low-income country. (Source: Walter, 2007)

	Decoders (percent)		Rate	Accuracy	Comprehension
	No	Yes			
Grade 1	98	2	.1	3.6	0
Grade 2	99	1	.1	2.0	.2
Grade 3	95	5	1.4	23.4	2.4
Grade 4	25	75	29.2	78.4	27.5
Grade 5	3	97	67.1	93.6	66.9
Grade 6	0	100	83.6	97.1	66.1

sense that they appear to typify the development of reading when children are taught and learn to read in a second language AND when the quality of instruction is rather low, e.g. where teachers have relatively low levels of knowledge and/or training.

In Table 4, the term *decoders* is used to identify children who have mastered enough of the English writing system to be able to orally articulate words encountered during the reading process. Decoding does not necessarily entail comprehension, as the data will show.

Table 4 indicates clearly that these children do not begin to decode until they reach grade 4. In addition, it is evident that reading comprehension lags even further behind, reaching a minimally acceptable level only at grade 5. However, as demonstrated later in this chapter, even the level of comprehension reflected in Table 4 is not as hopeful as it first appears.

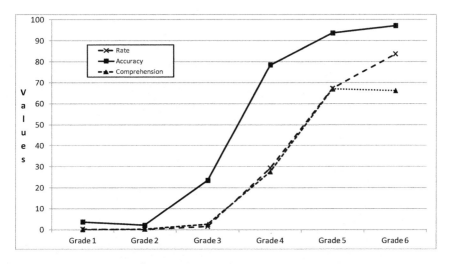

Figure 1. Development of reading metrics by grade level in standard schools in rural Cameroon. (Source: Data from Walter, 2007)

The data in Table 4 are graphically rendered in Figure 1 to give a visual model of the development of the relevant reading measures in this population.

The Y axis in Figure 1 is a percentage scale for the metrics of accuracy and comprehension but indicates the absolute number of words read correctly per minute (wcpm) in the case of reading rate. As the curves demonstrate, children are essentially non-readers through grade 3. By the end of grade 4, 75% have become decoders at a rudimentary level. Grade 5 students meet the borderline norms suggested by Barr et al. (2002) for accuracy and comprehension, but lag behind on reading rate. Grade 6 readers have risen to the instructional level in accuracy but lag in rate and comprehension with the latter still at the borderline level.

The results for grades 5 and 6 in Figure 1 are less positive when we note that these students were tested on a grade 1 text. When the same students were tested on a grade 6 text, the results were substantially lower, as Table 5 illustrates.

Table 5 is troubling in several regards. First, the reading skills of grade 5 students are still weak as highlighted by the significant drop in performance when asked to read a grade 6 text. Second, the performance of the fifth and sixth graders – regardless of level of difficulty – makes them approximately equivalent to Northern end-of-year grade 2 students (taught and tested in English, their home language or L1) according to the norms posited by Hasbrouck and Tindal (1992). Finally, when asked to read a grade level text, students in grades 5 and 6 suffer a dramatic drop in comprehension to a level identified by Barr et al. (2002) as being "frustration" level, i.e. non-readers. The fact that they appear to be able to decode highlights an unfortunate but widespread reality about reading development in low-income multilingual countries – skilled decoding may look like reading but too often it is not when there is limited comprehension.

Table 5. Comparison of grade 5 and 6 reading performance by level of text used for testing

	Performance on a grade 1 text		
	Rate	Accuracy	Comprehension
Grade 5	67.1	93.6	66.9
Grade 6	83.6	97.1	66.1
	Performance on a grade 6 text		
Grade 5	47.4	85.3	31.0
Grade 6	82.3	97.9	38.1

Reading Norms from MLE Programs in Low-Income Countries – A Brief Sample

Data like that reported in Table 4 give the reader the impression that reading instruction is extraordinarily difficult and unproductive in low-income multilingual countries. Fortunately, other data are not so grim. We turn now to an examination of data from several countries which have used the L1 as a language of instruction for reading, either as a matter of policy or as an experimental innovation. In doing so, the focus is not so much on making an argument for L1-based education, though its advantages will be apparent, but rather on probing the research data that exist to see what additional insights we might be able to gain about reading norms in low-income countries. We begin with data from Eritrea, which has used a mother tongue-based instructional model since independence in 1993. As the data in Table 6 illustrate, learners are reading at much higher rates in Eritrea than in Cameroon.

Table 6. Reading performance of Eritrean children instructed in their L1. (Source: Data from Walter & Davis, 2005)

	Decoders (Y or N)	Rate	Accuracy	Comprehension
Grade 1	Yes (49.5)	11.9	68.1	49.4
(No = 0 words read)	No (50.5)	0	.06	>1
Grade 3 (L1 text)	Yes (96.5)	47.9	87.2	87.7
(No = <5 words read)	No (3.5)	.7	3.0	14.8
Grade 3 (L3 text)	Yes (95.0)	39.4	85.0	62.1
(No = <5 words read)	No (5.0)	.1	2.7	5.8
Grade 5	Yes (98.5)	52.5	91.6	62.5[iii]
(No = <60 words read)	No (1.5)	3.9	12.9	36.0

The similarities and differences between Tables 6 and 4 offer some interesting insights. First, the percentage of learners who are non-decoders differs markedly. In the Cameroonian data (Table 4), more than 90% of children remain non-decoders through grade 3 whereas, in the Eritrean data, just over 50% are non-decoders at the end of grade 1, with the proportion of non-decoders dropping to just 5% by the end of grade 3. The contrast in reading comprehension is also dramatic when we compare performance at the end of grade 3 – a mean of less than 3% in the Cameroon data versus 75% in the Eritrean data. (This mean of 75% is a composite of performance on two separate reading tasks given to grade 3 children.)

At first glance, the grade 5 results for reading comprehension from both programs look quite similar at around 60%. However, this is misleading in that the grade 5 result from Cameroon was based on a grade 1 text, while the grade 5 result from Eritrea was based on a more challenging set of academic tasks including identification of antonyms and synonyms, interpretation of figures of speech, solving logic problems, and ability to identify the main point of a text.

Table 7. Measures of reading comprehension in an MLE program in Cameroon.
(Source: Walter & Trammell, 2010)

	Traditional Model		MLE Model	
	Decoders (percent)[iv]	Comprehension	Decoders (percent)	Comprehension
Grade 1	4.1	17.5	78.8	64.2
Grade 2	26.6	25.0	87.3	73.3
Grade 3	29.6	23.9	92.9	70.4

Next, Table 7 contains data from an experimental program of multilingual education (MLE) – the Kom project in Cameroon, the same linguistic area from which the baseline data in Table 4 were compiled. The experimental project consists of 12 experimental schools using Kom as a language of instruction to teach reading in Kom, matched with 12 control schools using English, a foreign/second language for learners, for all instruction, which is the standard model for the entire province.

The data in Table 7 were taken from a written assessment of reading proficiency, so only reading comprehension scores can be reported. All comprehension measures were based on grade-level texts. Of primary interest is the fact that comprehension scores are in the 60-70% range right from grade 1 for those in the MLE program. However, while representing a marked improvement over the performance of those in control schools, this level of comprehension is still in the "borderline" category as defined by Hasbrouck and Tindal, probably due to one or more of the following factors: (a) lack of reading practice, (b) lower quality of instruction, (c) inadequate instructional time in school, or (d) measurement error.

The final example comes from research done in the Philippines (Walter & Dekker, 2007). Students in an MLE project were given an assessment of reading skills in their L1. The results are reported in Table 8. In this case, data were collected only for grade 1.

Table 8. Reading performance of grade 1 children in Lubuagan District in the Philippines. (Source: Walter & Dekker, 2007)

	Decoders (percent)	Reading rate	Reading accuracy	Reading Comprehension
Grade 1	69.0	16 wcpm	92.5	81.4

The observation of greatest interest is the fact that both reading accuracy and reading comprehension are high despite the low reading rate of just 16 words read correctly per minute (wcpm), well below the 40-60 words per minute posited as necessary for basic comprehension (Abadzi, 2010). Based on direct classroom observation, I would suggest that the primary reason for this "low" rate relative to the Northern standard is the lack of regular reading practice.

Generalizing across MLE Programs

Even though we have data from three separate programs in three separate countries, the data are not yet extensive enough to draw definitive conclusions. However, we can extract some hints from the data as to a set of norms which are attainable *when instruction in low-income countries is provided in the learners' first language*, even if all other educational factors remain (essentially) the same.

– It is realistic to expect that 50-70% of grade 1 students can master basic reading by the end of grade 1.
– Reading rates of 10-20 words per minute (wcpm) appear to be normal for grade 1 students who do master basic reading by the end of grade 1.
– Rates of reading accuracy of 70-95% are reasonable for grade 1 students who do master basic reading by the end of grade 1.
– Reading comprehension percentages of 50-80% are reasonable for grade 1 students who master basic reading by the end of grade 1.
– Even through grades 5 and 6, all measures of reading proficiency tend to remain below the norms such as those of Barr et al. (2002) established for English speakers in the USA.

In contrast to the trends noted in MLE programs, the Cameroonian data reported in Table 4 (Walter, 2007) suggest that children in non-MLE programs (in which literacy and instruction are not in the L1) only begin to decode in grade 4, and only start becoming reasonably fluent readers in grade 5. Comprehension rates are in the range of 30-40% for grades 5 and 6 when reading grade level material, which means that children learning to read in a language that is not their L1 can read very basic material with limited comprehension, but cannot "read to learn" standard grade-level material.

READING RATE AND COMPREHENSION IN MLE AND NON-MLE PROGRAMS

Is there a reliable relationship between reading rate and reading comprehension? If so, what is a reasonable correlation between these two metrics for reading development in low-income countries? If the correlation is weak or non-existent, what does this tell us about reading instruction in such countries? Research done on English speakers nearly a century ago (Traxler, 1932) suggested positive correlations of 0.6 to 0.8 though some of the correlation may have been partially a product of methodological limitations. Abadzi (2010) has suggested that there are psycho-physiological reasons to support a claim that comprehension is difficult to impossible with a reading rate of less than 40 correct words per minute. Her evidence, however, is based primarily on cognitive and psycholinguistic research done on L1 speakers in the US and Europe. Whether the linguistic character of a language in terms of word length, agglutination, and tonality matters is largely undetermined. Valencia et al. (2010) suggest that the question itself may be suspect in that reading rate and comprehension may be mutually dependent measures, an observation made by Traxler (1932) as well. If Valencia's argument is sound, the relationship between these measures of reading may not be so direct as once supposed.

All the data from Southern countries reported here show relatively high comprehension with relatively low reading rates. What does this mean? Consider Figures 2 and 3.

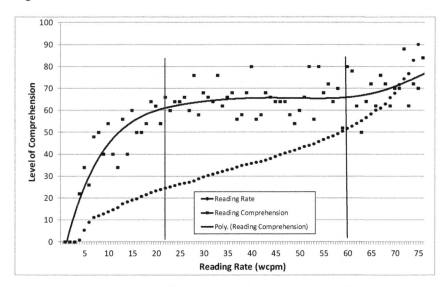

Figure 2. Relationship between reading rates and comprehension for grade 3
students in Eritrea when reading grade-level textual material (N = 763).
(Source: Walter & Davis, 2005)

As described earlier, virtually all children in Eritrea receive their primary education in their first language. To generate the Figure 2 data, 763 children attending grade 3 in five randomly selected schools in each of eight different linguistic communities were tested for progress in the development of reading skills. The dotted line plots reading rates (number of words correctly read per minute) from low to high. The scatter plot tracks corresponding scores in reading comprehension for each reading rate data point. The solid line is a trend line for the comprehension scatter plot (a fifth order polynomial). The vertical lines identify what appear to be transition zones between levels of comprehension. It can be seen that at rates below 22 words per minute (wcpm), reading comprehension drops quickly to zero. Between 22 and 60 wcpm, reading comprehension is nearly constant at 65%. Reading rates above 60 wpm appear to be associated with further increases in comprehension above 65%.

The data in Figure 2 appear to suggest several observations about the relationship between reading rate and reading comprehension in this type of educational setting. First, a causal relationship does appear to exist at the lower end of the performance curve, with comprehension dropping rapidly as reading rates decline. It seems likely that this portion of the figure reflects the process of "learning to read." Secondly, we note that an increase in the rate of reading fluency (or speed) between 22 and 60 wcpm appears to have little or no impact on comprehension, which remains fixed at 65% throughout the range. Finally, we note another upward tendency in comprehension levels as fluency exceeds 60 wcpm. The 22 wcpm threshold is well below the 40-60 wcpm boundary identified by researchers working with English speakers/readers as the necessary threshold for reading comprehension.

Additional perspectives on the relationship between fluency and comprehension are reflected by Figure 3, which uses baseline data gathered in rural Cameroon in 2006 on students in grades 5 and 6 learning to read in English rather than in their first languages. As reported above (Tables 4 and 6), reading achievement for these grades was first measured using a grade 1 text, and then using a grade 6 text. In the figure, the weaker lines indicate performance data on the three measures of speed, accuracy, and comprehension for these students when tested using the grade 1 text. The darker lines give corresponding performance data for the same students when tested using the grade 6 text.

Figure 3 provides at least four categories of information about reading performance: (a) level of performance on a given metric, (b) differential performance on grade 1 and grade 6 texts, (c) improvement between grades 5 and 6, and (d) an indication of the relationship between the three performance metrics.

On the measure of accuracy, grade 5 students are at the borderline level (applying the scheme of Barr et al., 2002) when reading a grade 1 text, but are effectively non-readers (below frustration level) when confronted with a grade 6 text. However, by the end of grade 6, students have achieved an instructional level of accuracy (approximately 97% accuracy) regardless of the level of difficulty of the text. These students have "mastered the code" and can do what has variously been described as word calling, rote reading, or mechanical reading.

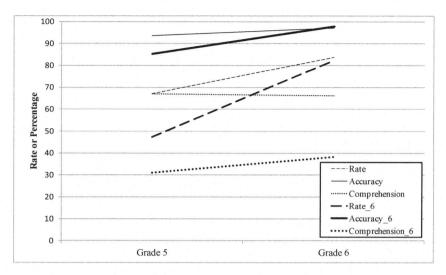

Figure 3. Impact on reading metrics of textual difficulty for children in grades 5 and 6. (Source: data from Walter, 2007)

On the measure of reading fluency (or rate), grade 5 students meet the norms established by Barr et al. for grade 2 students (in the US) whether tested with a grade 1 or grade 6 text. However, by the end of grade 6, students have made a substantial improvement in reading rate, with a mean rate of approximately 82 wcpm, placing them at a low grade 3 level according to the norms proposed by Barr et al. Interestingly, the reading rate at the end of grade 6 is the same regardless of the level of text difficulty. Again, this performance profile reflects a mastery of the code (which is largely, but not completely, independent of text difficulty or content).

Especially fascinating are the findings for reading comprehension. There is a very large difference in comprehension between grade 1 (68%) and grade 6 texts (35%). Furthermore, there is very little improvement between grade 5 and grade 6 (indicated by the fact the lines for comprehension are nearly flat between grades 5 and 6).

The analysis in Figure 3 suggests certain tendencies about learning to read through a second or foreign language in a low-income country. First, children can and do master decoding (reading accuracy), which is necessary but not sufficient for developing reading comprehension. Second, the development of reading fluency is significantly dependent on actual reading practice (indicated by low rates of reading despite high accuracy rates). Third, reading comprehension, especially of grade-level material, severely lags behind the other measures of reading, a finding consistent with the assertions of various researchers (Cummins, 1984; Hakuta et al., 2000) that children need five to seven years or more to learn a language well enough to be effectively educated in that language.

This lag in the development of skill in reading comprehension is further highlighted by the next set of data in Table 10, in which there is a three-way contrast between (a) Kom-speaking students in English-medium schools (abbreviated English) learning to read entirely in English and tested in English (23.2% comprehension), (b) Kom-speaking students in the bilingual Kom Experimental Project schools (abbreviated KEP) being taught in Kom but tested in English (39.6% comprehension) and (c) Kom-speaking students in bilingual schools (KEP) tested in Kom, the language of primary instruction (67.9% comprehension).

Table 10. Comparison of reading performance by program and language of instruction for grade 3 (N = 575). (Source: Walter & Chuo, 2011)

| | Tested in English | | Tested in Kom | |
	English	KEP	KEP Students	Gain (%)
Language Arts	24.2	41.1	66.4	174
Grammar	27.4	42.1	65.8	140
Word recognition	21.0	41.4	*	*
Reading comprehension	23.2	39.6	67.9	193

The level of reading comprehension for grade 3 students taught and tested in English is at the level of random guessing (which would be 25%) and is thus effectively zero. The KEP bilingual students, taught and tested in their L1, have learned to read with comprehension, as indicated by their performance on this measure (67.9% comprehension), but can apply this skill in only a limited way when reading in English (39.6% comprehension) almost certainly due to limited knowledge of this language.

In summary, the data presented in this section suggest the following tentative conclusions. First, the norm for accuracy appears to have broader scope than just reading performance in Northern contexts based on the evidence that children in both L1 and L2 educational programs can achieve high rates of accuracy regardless of their performance on the measures of reading rate and comprehension. Second, when children are taught to read entirely in a second/foreign language, English-based norms for reading rate and comprehension are, at least in part, a function of language proficiency, and thus are difficult to attain.

TRANSFERRING READING SKILLS TO A SECOND LANGUAGE – EVIDENCE
FROM EARLY-EXIT[v] MLE PROGRAMS

Thomas and Collier (1997) and others have argued – with substantial research support – that early-exit MLE programs are inherently weaker than late-exit MLE programs; therefore they are less desirable for use in multilingual educational contexts. Practically speaking, however, educational authorities are often reluctant to authorize late-exit models presumably because they see such models as being too costly, too difficult and politically unacceptable (Ouane & Glanz, 2011). In the case study which follows, data is presented from recent research (Walter & Chuo, 2011) on the Kom bilingual program, shedding light on the claims made about early- versus late-exit programs.

The Kom Experimental Project (KEP) in northwest Cameroon is conducting an extended investigation of the relative effectiveness of MLE in a rural region of a low-income country. During the 2010-2011 school year, the first cohort of children were sent along to English-medium instruction after having completed three years of instruction in and through Kom, their first language, having also been taught English as a subject. The results of the first three years of this project have been reported elsewhere (see Walter & Trammell, 2008, 2009, 2010). In April and May of 2011, standardized testing was done to evaluate educational progress in general, as well as to examine in more detail the levels of learner achievement in an early-exit MLE model.

Tests based on the learning standards specified in the national curriculum were administered to measure progress in reading and mathematics. The reading test was divided into two main parts: reading comprehension and language structure (punctuation and grammar). All assessment was done in English, testing reading comprehension and knowledge of English, since English becomes the language of instruction in grade 4. The comprehension testing was based on English texts drawn from the grade 4 reader. All test items were four-item multiple choice questions.

The section on reading comprehension can be further divided into four sections: (1) superficial comprehension (finding factual information directly stated in the text); (2) general comprehension (finding factual information directly implied or stated differently in the question than in the text); (3) global comprehension (ability to summarize or to identify and express the main idea of the text); and (4) knowledge of English vocabulary used in the texts. The test results are given in Table 11.

Table 11. Data on the impact of an early-exit MLE program on measures of reading among grade 4 Kom-speaking learners in Cameroon. (Source: Data from Walter & Chuo, 2011)

	English	KEP (MT)	P value
Structure	29.2	45.0	0.000
Punctuation	22.9	45.7	0.000
Grammar	34.2	44.5	0.000
Comprehension	28.7	40.5	0.000
Superficial	32.3	46.8	0.000
General	30.0	43.3	0.000
Global	19.4	23.3	0.082
Lexical knowledge	24.9	24.9	0.986
Overall English	28.1	38.9	0.000

The first two columns of numerical values are mean scores based on percentage of correct responses. The P value is a measure of statistical significance (the lower the P value, the higher the level of statistical significance).

In Table 11, the English column presents the average scores of learners who were taught and tested only in English for all four years of their schooling. The KEP column represents the mean percentage scores of learners taught in Kom, their mother tongue, for the first three years of their primary education but now being tested in English since they have returned to English-medium instruction.

An examination of Table 11 provides insight into (a) the status of reading skill development of each group after 4 years of primary education and (b) the differential impact of the first three years of instruction depending on the language in which reading was taught. First, the data suggest a very low level of performance, especially for those in the all-English program (a submersion model in the nomenclature of Thomas and Collier) who averaged barely above the level of random guessing. Second, the difference in performance between the two groups suggests that the children in the mother tongue program have developed some skills in reading but that the transition to reading in English is very incomplete. This may be because the process of transfer of literacy skills from the L1 to English requires more time, or because the children's knowledge of English is still weak, or both.

What do we learn about the two programs when we compare them by subsections of the assessment? First, the domain of highest performance for the KEP students was that of language structure – punctuation and grammar. A plausible explanation is that the KEP children have learned these features of language and language structure in their own language and can, therefore, readily apply these notions to English without a good grasp of the language.

Second, there was an interesting pattern in the results of reading comprehension which is less apparent in the data in Table 11. The test items in the section on reading comprehension were arranged from easiest to most difficult, from "superficial fact-finding" to "global comprehension." Not surprisingly, the performance of all students declined as the reading task became more difficult. At the same time, children from the KEP program demonstrated the largest advantage when the task was easiest – superficial fact-finding – and a smaller and statistically insignificant advantage when the task required global mastery of the meaning or intent of an entire text. This finding provides further support for the hypothesis that children from the KEP program have learned to read, but that limitations in their mastery of English constrain reading comprehension, especially on tasks requiring more global comprehension of texts.

Finally, the results on lexical knowledge are rather striking, as *both* groups achieved identical scores of 24.9% – a score comparable to that predicted by random guessing. The words selected for testing were judged important for comprehension of the text and were generally grade-level academic terms as opposed to everyday words. This result provides further support for the hypothesis – already advanced above – that the KEP group brings L1 reading skills to grade 4, but do not yet know enough English to apply or develop these skills. The group taught only in English, on the other hand, not only has not yet developed reading skills, but also is not much further ahead of the KEP group, if at all, in their mastery of English.

CONCLUSIONS

The data and analysis presented in this chapter point towards the following tentative and general conclusions about reading development in multilingual low-income countries.

- The norm for accuracy appears to have broader scope than just reading performance in Anglophone Northern countries and may, in fact, be generally universal (if we set aside, for the moment, issues of word length and orthographic complexity).
- When learners are taught to read in an L2/foreign language, Northern English-based norms for reading rate and comprehension are, at least in part, a function of language proficiency and thus are as difficult to attain as a high level proficiency in that language in multilingual contexts. This implies that a separate set of norms may be appropriate when instruction is available only in a second/foreign language.
- The evidence is strong that MLE programs sharply accelerate the acquisition of reading skills, though this advantage appears to be significantly reduced in early-exit versions of MLE when instruction shifts to L2.
- There is some evidence that lower levels of achievement in reading proficiency are due to reduced levels of applied practice in reading. This appears to apply regardless of the language of instruction or educational model employed.
- There is some evidence that the correlation between reading rate and comprehension may be less direct than supposed from research in developed countries.

In sum, the MLE data suggest that the dramatic lack of reading achievement widely observed in schools in multilingual low-income countries is not so much a function of going to school (or not) in such contexts as it is a function of a specific model of instruction – i.e. the lack of programs that use L1 for initial instruction including reading, writing, and mastery of other curricular content. The fact that reading achievement in MLE programs still trails that observed in the North suggests that the MLE strategy cannot, by itself, raise students to the highest potential levels of reading development. Skilled instruction and ample practice remain significant elements of reading skill development.

The extent to which reading achievement in MLE programs begins to approximate the norms proposed for Anglophone Northern countries suggests that these norms may have more universality than many of us have assumed with specific deficits – such as reading fluency (speed) – being a function of a very specific and addressable feature of the educational environment, i.e. actual practice reading.

Finally, the data on reading achievement presented in this chapter highlight the severe penalties imposed on learners being taught to read in a second or foreign language. These penalties are clearly reflected in the reading metrics reported for children educated in L2 submersion models, especially the lag in comprehension and the inconsistent relationship between reading accuracy and reading comprehension.

NOTES

[i] Early Grade Reading Assessment

[ii] Research Triangle Institute located in Raleigh, North Carolina

[iii] The measure of reading comprehension in grade 5 was not text or prose comprehension per se, but a broader assessment of language knowledge which included vocabulary knowledge, interpretation of figures of speech, solving logical problems, and ability to summarize the meaning of a text.

[iv] Careful readers will note that the percentages of decoders reported in Table 7 for the Traditional Model (L2 instruction) are markedly higher for grades 2 and 3 than those reported in Table 4. In Table 7, the percentages of decoders for each grade were estimated by performance on a written word recognition task. Since this task was presented using a multiple choice format, simple guessing may well account for the higher estimates seen in Table 7.

[v] In the field of multilingual education, early-exit programs are those using the child's L1 for a short initial period of 1-3 years, moving to the L2 as quickly as possible. In contrast, late-exit programs make greater use of the L1 as a medium of instruction, e.g. for 4-6 years, ultimately switching to the L2 but only after developing a strong educational foundation in the L1 AND a high level of proficiency in the L2.

REFERENCES

Abadzi, Helen (2010). *Reading fluency measurements in EFA FTI partner countries: Outcomes and improvement prospects*. Working Paper Series, the World Bank, Washington D.C.

Barr, Rebecca, Blachowicz, Camille L. Z., Katz, Claudia, & Kaufman, Barbara (2002). *Reading diagnosis for teachers: An instructional approach* (4th ed.) Boston, MA: Allyn and Bacon.

Cummins, Jim (1984). *Bilingualism and special education: Issues in assessment and pedagogy*. Clevedon: Multilingual Matters.

Hakuta, Kenji, Butler, Yuko G., & Witt, Daria (2000). *How long does it take English learners to attain proficiency?* University of California Linguistic Minority Research Institute Policy Report 2000-1.

Hasbrouck, Jan, & Tindal, Gerald (1992). Curriculum-based oral reading fluency norms for students in grades 2 through 5. *Teaching Exceptional Children, 24*, 41-44.

Ouane, Adama, & Glanz, Christine (Eds.) (2011). *Optimising learning, education and publishing in Africa: The language factor. A review and analysis of theory and practice in mother-tongue and bilingual education in sub-Saharan Africa*. Hamburg, Germany: UNESCO Institute for Lifelong Learning (UIL), the Association for the Development of Education in Africa (ADEA)/African Development Bank.

Thomas, Wayne, & Collier, Virginia (1997). *School effectiveness for language minority children*. (http://archive.austinisd.org/academics/curriculum/subjects/bilingual/docs/Dual_Collier_School_Eff ect_for_LMS.pdf)

Valencia, Sheila W., Smith, Antony T., Reece, Anne M., Min Li, Wixson, Karen K., & Newman, Heather (2010). Oral reading fluency assessment: Issues of construct, criterion, and consequential validity. *RRQ, 45*(3), 270-291.

Walter, Stephen (2007). *Preliminary report on education in Boyo Division*. Unpublished research report. Available from the author.

Walter, Stephen, & Chuo, Kain Godfrey (2011). *The Kom experimental mother tongue education project: Report for 2011*. Unpublished research report. Available from the authors.

Walter, Stephen, & Davis, Patricia (2005). *Eritrea national reading survey: September 2002.* Ministry of Education, Asmara, Eritrea. Dallas, TX: SIL International.

Walter, Stephen, & Dekker, Diane (2007). *The Lubuagan mother tongue education experiment (FLC): A report of comparative test results.* Unpublished research report. Available from the authors.

Walter, Stephen, & Trammell, Kristine (2008). *Results of the first rear of the Kom experimental education project.* Unpublished research report. Available from the authors.

Walter, Stephen, & Trammell, Kristine (2009). *The Kom MLE report for 2009.* Unpublished research report. Available from the authors.

Walter, Stephen, & Trammell, Kristine (2010). *The Kom experimental mother tongue education project: Report for 2010.* Unpublished research report. Available from the authors.

Stephen L. Walter
Language Development Department
Graduate Institute of Applied Linguistics, Dallas, USA

CAROL BENSON[i]

15. TOWARDS ADOPTING A MULTILINGUAL HABITUS IN EDUCATIONAL DEVELOPMENT

ABSTRACT

Ity fizarana ity dia mamakafaka ny voalaza ho *fahazarana mampiasa teny tokana* izay manenika ny fomba fampianarana sy fikarohana any amin'ny tany mahantra misy fimaroan-teny, na koa ny hevi-diso maromaro miompana amin'ny fiheverena raiki-tapisaka ny maha tokana ny fiteny sy kolotsaina manerana ny firenena midadasika iray – izay heverina fa hita taratra koa amin'ny rafi-mpampianarana nasionaly ao aminy. Ny fahazarana mampiasa teny tokana dia voaporofo amin'ny fironana mankany amin'ny fampifangaroana teny roa, ary koa amin'ny tsy mampitombina ny fahafehezana teny toy ny tera-tany, rehefa mampiasa ny teny faharoa na ireo tenim-pirenena vahiny. Ireo teoria na haitsikera asosok'ireo avy any amin'ny firenena tavaratra sy mpampiasa teny Anglisy dia mamaritra fa ireo lalam-pikarohana misy dia tsy azo ampiharina any amin'ny sehatra misy fimaroan-teny na amin'ny sehatra ibahanan'ny fampiasana teny hafa ankoatry ny teny Anglisy amin'ny fampianarana. Soa ihany fa efa misy ireo voambolana vaovao, sy rafim-pisainana ary fomba fikarohana, ka azo atao ny manangana sy mikolo *fahazarana mampiasa teny maro* izay mifanentana kokoa amin'ny toerana misy fampiasana teny maromaro amin'ny fanabeazana. Mihamitombo ireo asa fikarohana, misy avy amin'ny firenena tatsimo mpampiasa teny maro, izay mendrika omena hasina noho ny heriziky entiny izay miady tsara, manafaka ary mampandroso. (*Translated to Malagasy [mlg], a language of Madagascar, by Gil Dany Randriamasitiana and Elyette Randriamahenitsoa.*)

This chapter explores how educational approaches in low-income multilingual countries are pervaded by a *monolingual habitus*, or set of assumptions built on the fundamental myth of uniformity of language and culture. This habitus is evidenced in transitional bilingual approaches and unrealistic expectations for native-like proficiency in second or foreign languages. Northern biases have made research methodologies imperfectly suited to multilingual settings with dominant languages other than English. Fortunately, there are new terms, approaches and research that support a *multilingual habitus* more appropriate to linguistically diverse contexts of schooling and have great liberatory, transformative potential.

C. Benson and K. Kosonen (eds.), Language Issues in Comparative Education, 283–299.

INTRODUCTION

This chapter takes the position that educational research in multilingual contexts often fails to recognize multilingualism as a social and individual reality that requires appropriately designed approaches. I will demonstrate how a great deal of research in language education policy and practice, even in bi-/multilingual education, reflects a Northern[ii] and monolingual view of the world, a perspective which has been called a *monolingual habitus* (Gogolin, 2002). Language education and literacy research, e.g. research focusing on language and early literacy pedagogies and assessment methods, has long been dominated by an English native speaker perspective that is not fully applicable in most parts of the world. A monolingual habitus may cause us to conduct research that misses key aspects of multilingual contexts, such as the fact that many learners of dominant languages in both North and South are actually proficient speakers of non-dominant languages – a situation that Hélot (2007, 2008) calls *ignored bilingualism*. I argue that we as educational researchers can conduct stronger, more relevant research if we can adopt a multilingual perspective. Recent research from multilingual contexts gives us a way forward and demonstrates that it is possible to develop more liberatory, transformational education[iii] for those whose linguistic skills and experiences have long been ignored. Since multilingual contexts are the rule rather than the exception worldwide, a *multilingual habitus* is called for, requiring a paradigm shift in the field of bi-/multilingual education worldwide.

MONOLINGUAL HABITUS BUT MULTILINGUAL REALITY

The Monolingual Habitus Revealed

The notion of *habitus* is associated with the social theories of Bourdieu (1991), who defines *linguistic habitus* as a set of unquestioned dispositions toward languages in society. Bourdieu discusses the symbolic power of language in terms of a linguistic marketplace, defined as a human interactive space where even limited proficiency in a certain language or languages offers greater social capital than proficiency in others. Depending on the particular context, any one language may offer more or less capital; for example, proficiency in Wolof may give a multilingual Senegalese trader a great deal of social capital at a regional food market but much less at a university. The fact that people do not tend to question this status differential means that a certain linguistic habitus is in place.

In her criticism of European attitudes toward diversity, particularly in the reception of immigrant languages and cultures, Gogolin (2002) uses the term *monolingual habitus*, which she describes as a linguistic self-conception that can make us blind to multilingual, multicultural lifeways. One illustratration is the historic 'one nation, one language' approach in the formation of nation-states, which failed to recognize – worse, tried to erase – the natural linguistic and cultural diversity encompassed within state borders.[iv] When applied to education, a monolingual habitus causes us to view a learner as deficient if s/he does not speak the dominant language used for instruction, when we should recognize and make use of all of the linguistic, cultural and experiential resources that s/he brings with her to the classroom. A monolingual habitus would be seen by Ruiz (1984) as corresponding to a language-as-problem orientation, as opposed to a language-as-resource orientation. For generations of learners, as Hélot and Ó Laoire (2011) point out in Irish and other Northern contexts, the result of such a habitus has been cruel and abusive, when the slightest slip of one's home language has been met with aggression and derision at school, and has meant having a sign hung around one's neck or kneeling on one's knees for all to scorn.

A monolingual habitus can be found underlying terminology for language policy in society and in bi-/multilingual education. One example is the use of L1 and L2 for first and second languages, which in Northern contexts indicates that learners speak one language (*the* "mother tongue") at home – in other words, are monolingual speakers of one home language – and subsequently learn a second (dominant societal) language at school. The terms break down quickly when learners speak more than one language at home, when groups of learners enter school with different home languages or when the L1 of one group is the L2 of another. In Northern immigrant or regional minority contexts, L2 has the connotation of being the dominant language in society, so that in discussing "second language" learning and teaching, the assumption is that learners hear the language in the community and through the media if not in the home. But what if the so-called L2 is a language that is foreign to learners, and even to teachers and community members, in a setting where adults and even children may speak two or more local languages?

The Search for More Appropriate Terms

One partial solution has been to use terms we have discussed in the Introduction of this book, e.g. home or first language(s), along with making a distinction between *dominant* and *non-dominant languages* (*DLs* and *NDLs*) to indicate their relative status in society and in education. We are finding the term NDL useful for discussing the languages with which learners and their families are most familiar, particularly when these languages need special attention due to past and even present oppression. In multilingual societies, people are often proficient in more than one NDL, depending on the degree to which language communities interact, and according to economic or personal needs. Bi-/multilingualism in NDLs may occur in the family or in a child's immediate environment, which would necessitate pluralization of the definitions established by Skutnabb-Kangas (2000), as mentioned in the Introduction of this volume. It also means pluralizing our addition (Benson & Kosonen, 2012: 112), i.e. "languages that one speaks and understands competently enough to learn age-appropriate academic content," which may be important in contexts where some NDLs are more widely spoken than others.

An example of this situation comes from Mozambique, where speakers of Chope, an ethnolinguistic group that is relatively small in number and geographic distribution, are often compelled to learn Changana, a larger, cross-border language that is linguistically related on the Bantu continuum[v] (Chimbutane, 2011). More widely spoken languages, often known as *lingua francae*, may be linguistically similar to other NDLs, or they may be contact languages like creoles, and they do have potential as languages of instruction; see e.g. Brock-Utne's work (2006 and chapter 4 of this volume) on the potential of Kiswahili as a language of instruction in Tanzania. These languages would most closely correspond to the L2 label used in the North, as they are likely to be heard in domains outside the home. However, it is important to remember for educational purposes that the vast majority of NDL speakers entering school at age 6 or 7 are unlikely in either North or South to have developed L2 proficiency unless it is spoken at home, since they have not yet been exposed to domains in which these languages are widely used.

The NDL/DL distinction helps to remind us of the status differences between languages in society and in school, and to identify the types of languages in learners' repertoires, but what about the L2 problem? There is a great need in education to differentiate between an L2 that is widely heard and spoken in the learners' community or region and an L2 that may be second in numerical terms but is foreign for most learners, meaning that it is not used for normal communicative purposes. This distinction should be part of every educational decision, from curriculum standards (e.g. realistic expectations for each language, and the most appropriate languages on which to base initial literacy) to methodological approaches (e.g. communicative vs. special purposes strategies, along with the types of scaffolding[vi] and contextual support required if a language other than an L1 is used for teaching academic content), including teacher education (e.g. how teachers' own linguistic repertoires are built upon, in which languages they will be trained, and which methods they will learn to apply). The bi-/multilingual education literature sometimes makes the distinction when it comes to learners' linguistic repertoires, but we have yet to develop the terms and methodologies to deal appropriately with the distinction. This may have to do with the monolingual habitus prevailing in North and South, making it unpopular with education ministries to call an official language "foreign," along with the fact that generalizations are difficult – there are differences in people's outside exposure to DLs including *lingua francae* depending on factors like socioeconomic status, gender and rural/semi-urban/urban lifestyles. Language assessments for incoming learners should be a rule of thumb, since DL exposure varies by region, by community and even by individual. In recent work with teacher educators in Madagascar, I have proposed that we refine the term L2 to distinguish between $L2_{env}$ for a language to which learners are exposed in the environment outside school, vs. $L2_{sch}$ for a language to which learners are exposed only or main in school.[vii]

Regarding terms for bi-/multilingual education, recent years have seen some interaction and mutual calibration, both North-South and South-South. One example is the term *bilingual intercultural education*, which has called attention to the cultural as well as linguistic aspects of education for Indigenous learners, as mentioned in the Introduction to this volume. Recent work operationalizes the intercultural components, which were originally intended to give value to both non-dominant and dominant cultures but have now been recast in more liberatory terms to empower members of ND groups (see e.g. López, 2009). Another lesson that can be taken from many of these programs is that, at least in policy, bilingualism is for all: dominant groups are given opportunities to learn NDLs, which is also the intention of the educational language policy in South Africa (King & Benson, 2004; Alexander, 2003).

The term *mother tongue-based bilingual education*, particularly in Southern contexts, came into use because researchers at PRAESA[viii] at the University of Cape Town wanted to distinguish programs in African languages from elite bilingual programs in higher-income contexts. Elite bilingualism, where educated parents choose to put their children in programs using a foreign medium of instruction for cognitive enrichment, has similar methods but operates in a completely different context from efforts to make basic education accessible and equitable for all learners in low-income multilingual contexts. Thanks to colleagues working in Southeast Asia and beyond (see also websites and publications of UNESCO and others[ix]) most of us have now extended the term *bi-* to *multilingual education* (MTBMLE) in recognition of the fact that many education systems are dealing with more than two languages. In the Philippines, for example, the term MTBMLE has very recently become the foundation of the entire primary education system.[x] Another example is Ethiopia, where national policy calls for literacy and learning to take place in the learner's L1 for all eight years of primary schooling, with Amharic as national language and English as international language taught as subjects (Skutnabb-Kangas & Heugh, 2011). Problematization of the term "mother tongue" in other parts of the world has led many of us to prefer using L1 or "first language" while retaining the concept of basing education on the learner's first language, i.e. L1-based MLE.

Two European terms are worth mentioning here because the concepts they represent offer new directions for multilingual education. First, the Council of Europe (2006:4) refers to individual *plurilingualism* as a right and an aim of education: "All are entitled to develop a degree of communicative ability in a number of languages over their lifetime in accordance with their needs." The Council also provides a number of online tools to promote plurilingualism, including the Common European Framework of Reference for Languages which provides benchmarks allowing for self-assessment (Council of Europe, 2002). Even more applicable to multilingual countries with NDLs is the concept of the *multilingual curriculum* being developed in the Basque Country and other autonomous communities of Spain (e.g. Cenoz, 2009; Elorza & Muñoa, 2008). Despite the fact that not all learners speak the NDL at home, it is promoted through integrated plurilingual language planning, where competencies in three or four languages are taught using appropriate methodologies with realistic expectation levels and integrated into the entire school curriculum, maximizing the potential for cross-linguistic transfer (e.g. Bialystock et al., 2005). This type of language and literacy planning across the curriculum has potential applications in low-income multilingual countries, for it represents true multilingual thinking and is thoroughly consistent with current research on cross-linguistic transfer and on the role of identity in cognition.

MONOLINGUAL HABITUS BUT MULTILINGUAL REALITY
IN EDUCATIONAL DEVELOPMENT

Monolingualism: An Imperfect Fit

The focus on ex-colonial, international and/or other dominant languages is prevalent in educational planning and policy, where discussion of the "language barrier" appears to place the blame on learners who do not speak the language of the school at home. This represents backward planning, because in fact, the school is imperfectly designed for the learners. Instead of meeting learners where they are in their developmental processes, building on their languages, cultures, identities and experiences and motivating them to grow, the school imposes an unrealistic and rigid curriculum and approach on learners, preventing large numbers of them from succeeding. Is it conceivable that, for example, the 50% of Mozambican children who enroll but do not complete 7 years of primary schooling in Portuguese (2010 statistics, World Bank, 2011) are all mentally impaired? Are learners really the problem, or is the problem that a monolingual habitus has been imported along with Northern models of mass public education – which, incidentally, fail learners from non-dominant groups in Northern countries – and inappropriately applied to education in low-income multilingual contexts?

To illustrate the lack of appropriate planning, I make generalizations based on experience in Table 1 to illustrate the actual situation in many multilingual societies, juxtaposing stakeholders' skills with the typical expectations of an educational system. Even allowing for some local language use in lower primary, the general trend is to impose monolingualism on multilingual societies, disregarding the cognitive and linguistic experiences and development of learners who speak NDLs. My assumption for purposes of this illustration is that whether or not learners have access to literacy in their own languages when they begin school, the typical education system focuses on the teaching and learning of the dominant language (or the standard variety of the DL that is not necessarily accessible to learners) by grade 3 or 4. This means that most instruction and testing is done mainly or only in the DL by the third or fourth year of school. Even if learners are given opportunities to learn initial reading, writing and content in their own languages, they are not able to demonstrate what they know on formal assessments. According to bilingual education assessment research (Thomas & Collier, 2002; Heugh, 2011), early testing in the DL is not likely to yield accurate results about children's literacy skills, since they need time (along with cognitive and linguistic development in both/all languages) to transfer reading and writing competencies to the DL. Based on the limited opportunities children have for learning the DL outside school, Heugh (2011) calculates that they require between seven and nine years in school to develop the academic language (CALP per Cummins, 2000) needed to learn in and through the DL.

Similarly, whether teachers are from non-dominant or dominant groups, they can only gain access to formal training by passing entrance exams in the DL, and are trained and tested mainly or only in the DL. This means that if they are

Table 1. Actual competencies versus educational expectations

Stakeholders in multilingual societies	*Actual competencies*	*Typical educational expectations*
Learners from non-dominant ethnolinguistic groups	-Oral proficiency in one (or more) NDLs[xi] -Possible oral proficiency in LWC/lingua franca -In some cases,[xii] proficiency in non-standard (stigmatized) variety of DL	-Mono/bilingual DL(s)[xiii] or bilingual NDL-DL education -Focus on learning DL(s) and dominant culture(s) -Must demonstrate all content learning through DL(s) and pass exams in DL(s)
Teachers EITHER: from non-dominant ethnolinguistic groups OR: from dominant group(s)	-Oral proficiency in one (or more) NDLs -Likely oral and possibly written proficiency in LWC/ lingua franca -Variable oral and written proficiency in DL(s) -Oral and written proficiency in DL(s) only	ALL: -Must pass teacher's college entrance exam in DL(s)[xiv] -Trained through DL(s) -Must use curriculum and materials in DL(s) -May be placed outside home regions/languages/cultures
Adult family and community members from non-dominant ethnolinguistic groups	-Oral proficiency in one (or more) NDLs -Likely proficiency in widely spoken lingua franca -Possible DL skills (if access to formal education)	-Seen as incapable of making educational decisions[xv] -Want (or perceived to want) children to learn only DL(s)
Ministry of Education staff EITHER: from ND groups (succeeded in DL system) OR: from dominant group	-Likely to have LWC/lingua franca and DL proficiency (possibly also NDLs) -Formally educated in DL(s)	-Focus on DL(s) for all -Value elite/private DL(s) schools for own children -Policy and planning focus on DL(s)

supposed to be teaching through the NDL, at least at the lower levels of primary schooling, they are ill-equipped to do so, because they lack preparation in both the means (pedagogical and content-based vocabulary) and the methods (L1-based pedagogy, which is greatly different than L2 or foreign language pedagogy). The overwhelming message coming from professional development programs in DLs is to focus on the DL, not (as the research clearly indicates; see e.g. Walter, 2008) to base DL skills on a solid foundation in learners' home languages.

Regarding the stakeholders, adult family and community members may be asked to support schools by making repairs or contributing financially, but they are rarely asked to make curricular decisions, and there are both real (understanding-related) and perceived (status-related) barriers to communication if teachers do not use NDLs. In many contexts, families are rendered powerless to help their children with homework in the DLs, whereas even non-literate family members could help orally if children were working in the home language.

Finally, education officials, including policymakers and planners, are in their positions because they have gained access to the DL, and they tend to invest heavily in that language for their own children, even schooling them privately. When deciding how other people's children should be schooled in public programs, these officials often assume, reflecting a monolingual habitus, that parents only care about the DL – which is perceived as essential for securing future employment and improved social status. This assumption may or may not be true; for example, a survey conducted in the Western Cape province of South Africa (Plüddemann et al., 2004) gave parents a number of options from which to choose, and while it was true that they gave greater value to DLs than to their own NDLs, the majority chose approaches that made at least some use of the home language. Even where parents only want DLs, this is not because they feel they have a choice; they are clearly responding to the linguistic market (Bourdieu, 1991) and could be expected to react otherwise if their NDLs are recognized and valued (Benson, 2008).[xvi] In fact, pilots and experiments in MLE demonstrate to parents and policymakers the potential of NDL-based education, and can create demand, as is the case in Mozambique (Chimbutane & Benson, 2012).

Examining the mismatches illustrated in Table 1, we can only ask ourselves for whom the education system is designed. If only elite learners are exposed to the standard DLs outside school, yet the majority of the population (i.e. non-elite children) attend public schools, then should the schools not speak their languages and value their knowledge and experiences? And should they not maximize learners' bi- or multilingual competencies?

Recognizing and Counteracting the Monolingual Habitus

How can the monolingual habitus in our own work be recognized and counteracted? Most readers of this chapter will be researchers, teachers and people working in educational development in multilingual countries. The above discussion was meant to raise awareness of all of our unquestioned assumptions regarding language and education. While writing this chapter, I have been trying to become more aware of my own biases and learn from my multilingual colleagues as well as the multilingual contexts where we work. Tables 2 and 3 represent my efforts to identify possible indicators of a monolingual habitus in our work in education at each level, and to develop indicators of a multilingual habitus that could make our work more effective and appropriate.

Table 2. Possible indicators of habitus for basic levels of education

Education level	Monolingual habitus	Multilingual habitus
ADULT LITERACY[xvii]	-Reporting literacy data without specifying the language(s) -Providing literacy classes in a DL without considering learner proficiency ("That is what they want") -Evaluation of programs in terms of numbers of participants rather than what they are learning, or using overly simple standards e.g. "Can read own name and a simple sentence"	-Specifying the language(s) of literacy -Assessing proficiency and negotiating language(s) of literacy with participants -Developing critical literacy skills and empowerment -Assessing programs in terms of quality and usefulness of literacy competencies
EARLY CHILDHOOD	-Using early years to "introduce" DL to "bridge" to primary -Engaging in "The earlier, the better" rhetoric regarding DL -Limiting NDL to songs and "tokens" of home culture	-Building on children's knowledge and experiences -Developing strong pre-literacy and learning foundation in L1(s) and home culture(s) -Exposing learners to DL at developmentally appropriate levels
PRIMARY BASIC	-Using DL as medium of instruction without explicitly teaching it -If NDL/L1 is used, phasing out after 2-3 years before building strong foundation for literacy and skills transfer -Testing reading/writing only in DL (or only using DL competencies that are inappropriate for NDLs) -Expecting unrealistically high levels of DL proficiency -Focusing on accuracy in DL reading and writing -Code-switching unsystematically between DL and NDL -Failing to assess NDL/L1 proficiency or literacy -Assessing content knowledge only in DL -Aiming for monolingualism in DL	-Teaching initial literacy in NDL/L1 -Building strong literacy and learning foundation in NDL/L1 and home culture(s) -Using NDL/L1 as main medium of instruction for academic content, particularly in early grades and for new concepts -Teaching DL(s) as subject(s) at developmentally appropriate levels with appropriate methods and focus on meaning -Planning curriculum that systematically and holistically teaches language, literacy and content in all languages -Developing metalinguistic awareness -Assessing mainly in NDL or bilingually -Aiming for bi-/multilingualism based on NDL/L1

Table 3. Possible indicators of habitus for secondary and tertiary levels of education

Education level	Monolingual habitus	Multilingual habitus
SECONDARY	-Using only DL as medium of instruction -Code-switching unsystematically between DL and NDL -Using DL learning materials and textbooks -Testing only in DL	-Teaching bi-/multilingually using bi-/multilingual materials -Using DL materials as necessary, but scaffolding meaning and using methods appropriate to learners' needs -Valuing and developing metalinguistic awareness -Assessing in NDL or bilingually -Offering NDLs as subjects of study

TEACHER TRAINING	-Offering the entrance examination only in DL
	-Training only in DL even if teachers will use NDL/L1 as medium of instruction
	-Expecting teachers to teach through DL without assessing their DL proficiency
	-Failing to train in appropriate L1/L2/foreign language and literacy methods
	-Equating improved teacher qualifications with more study of and through DL.
		-Offering entrance examination in NDLs appropriate to the region (and/or bilingually)
		-Using the NDL as medium of training, at least part of the time
		-Developing pedagogical and technical vocabulary and structures in NDLs
		-Valuing and developing metalinguistic awareness
		-Training and giving opportunities to practice appropriate methods for:
		  • teaching initial and continuing literacy in NDLs
		  • teaching DL as second/foreign language
		  • teaching bi-/multilingually

TERTIARY	-Providing materials and instruction only in DL (or even an international DL)	-Offering entrance examination in NDLs (and/or bilingually) -Offering bi-/multilingual instruction and valuing metalinguistic awareness -Offering NDLs as subjects of study

In Tables 2 and 3 I have tried to show how unquestioned assumptions pervade our provision of educational services and our discussions of educational language issues. Overall, the indicators of a monolingual habitus have to do with a failure to make NDLs visible, to assess learners' or teachers' language- and literacy-related skills, or to design materials and methods appropriate to existing language resources. In contrast, the indicators of a multilingual habitus have to do with making the language(s) of teaching and learning explicit and developing appropriate methods, materials and assessments. Those of us who are educational consultants play an important role in connecting colleagues, staff of development agencies and education ministry officials with the resources they need to make decisions about their multilingual realities. If we fail to help them identify appropriate languages and approaches for adult literacy campaigns[xviii] or if we promote large-scale testing based on assumptions about early literacy that come from research on monolingual English speakers (I am referring to EGRA; see chapters by Schroeder and Walter in this volume), then we are doing our colleagues and ultimately the children of their countries a great disservice.

ADOPTING A MULTILINGUAL HABITUS IN POLICY AND RESEARCH

I believe that a monolingual habitus underlies much of what is wrong with current policies and development work in education, but that if we can learn to recognize and question this habitus, we can change it.

Those of us working in multilingual education have tried for years to find effective strategies to convince policymakers and practitioners of the tragedy of using languages of instruction that learners do not understand. One of the most useful strategies I have found is to discuss language myths by giving examples of countries other than the one in which I am working, leading workshop participants to apply lessons learned to their own contexts. This helps people discover the issues and consider their own solutions, which they are better placed than I am to create. I have learned a great deal from colleagues working in the field. For example, one of the most innovative quantitative strategies I have seen is that of Hovens (2002), who tested children in Niger using their L1s whether or not they had been taught bilingually. He found that the top performers were those taught bilingually and tested in the NDL, followed by those taught bilingually and tested in the DL (French in this case). Worst off were those taught and tested only in the DL, who were beaten out by those taught only in the DL but tested in the NDL. Hovens showed not only the benefits of testing in learners' best languages, but also the reality that cross-linguistic transfer happens in all directions. Policymakers could not help but see that the most efficient direction of transfer would be from the better known language to the lesser known one.

An innovative qualitative strategy I saw recently was that of Ajit Mohanty, who tired of presenting empirical results and began showing photos taken from the teacher's perspective of children's blank faces in DL-medium classrooms.[xviii] More recently, Chimbutane (2011) has used classroom discourse to illustrate the mind-numbing DL talk masquerading as "lessons," e.g. a grade 4 Portuguese lesson which, despite some interaction, failed to teach the names of three body parts.

Taking a look at educational policy, our research team working in Ethiopia identified an effect we called *washback* (Heugh et al., 2007; Benson et al., 2012). Also known as *backwash*, this concept from the testing literature refers to characteristics of summative (final) assessments that inadvertently influence how learners approach their studies. By analogy, we are referring to characteristics of the education system that inadvertently influence how multilingual education is practiced and perceived. In the case of Ethiopia, the theoretically sound national policy calling for L1-medium education for a full eight-year program of primary schooling is partially undermined by aspects of the rest of the system, including: secondary education taught through a foreign DL (in this case, English); an examination system almost completely in the DL for secondary and tertiary education, including the teacher's college entrance exam; and DL-medium pre-service and in-service teacher training programs. The exaggerated focus on the DL sends all the wrong messages to educators and stakeholders, causing pressure on the system to bring in English as a medium of instruction earlier and earlier in the system – despite solid evidence from national assessments at grades 4 and 8 that the regions with the highest performance are those investing in eight years of L1-medium schooling (Heugh et al., 2012). It is hoped that our warning regarding backwash will be heeded, as there are examples in other parts of the world where backwash has caused complete reversals of effective mother tongue-based schooling.

In the Maldives, for example, the once effective education system using the medium of Dhivehi, the language spoken as L1 by virtually the entire population, has been gradually dismantled in favor of English-medium instruction. The change to English, a foreign DL for most, has apparently been in reaction to low passing rates at the secondary level as assessed by Cambridge examinations (which were originally developed for native English speakers in the UK and bear little resemblance to the national curriculum). Needless to say, secondary passing rates have not improved, but primary failure rates have multiplied; meanwhile, stakeholders harbor unrealistically high aspirations for foreign DL proficiency (Benson, 2010).

Two important points about the state of educational language research need to be made here and in all of our work:

1. There is no research demonstrating that the use of a foreign DL as a medium of instruction is an effective way to teach proficiency in that language, particularly not in low-income contexts.
2. There is no research demonstrating that it is possible for a public school system to develop high proficiency in a DL among learners when that language is essentially foreign to both learners and their teachers.

Further, in the case of multilingual countries of the South, poverty and illness can make it difficult to attain even modest educational goals such as basic literacy and life skills competencies. These competencies are what mass public education and EFA are all about, after all: to improve people's opportunities to have healthy, productive lives.

As Tables 2 and 3 illustrate, adopting a multilingual habitus in educational policy and practice means giving value to existing linguistic and cultural resources, not ignoring them or trying to erase them. Bi-/multilingualism and interculturalism should be developed as part of a balanced educational approach. One inspiring model for this approach comes from the Ikastola education system in the Spanish Basque Country, which is implementing an *integrated language curriculum* that uses the NDL (Euskara) as the main language of teaching and learning while systematically teaching DL Spanish and one or two additional languages, English and/or French. Using what we know about cross-linguistic transfer, there is a set of competencies that can be learned in any language, oral and written competencies that are language-specific, and appropriate methods for teaching and assessment that aim for plurilingualism and pluriliteracies[xix] for all learners (Elorza & Muñoa 2008).

The South provides examples of materials and methods that would at least partially support a multilingual view of learning. One is the use of side-by-side bilingual learning materials, where the NDL is on one page and the DL on the facing page, illustrations are shared, and the content covers the same theme, either written in authentic language or based on translation. These materials provide vocabulary and concepts in both languages, allow family members to help learners with homework, support bilingual teaching methods like Preview-Review (alternating languages to activate prior learning and check for understanding), and promote linguistic comparison. Another idea, from promoters of multilingualism at PRAESA in Cape Town, South Africa,[xx] is to develop side-by-side bilingual tests, where test questions are the same on the NDL and DL sides, and learners can answer any one question in either language. Since the objective of the test is for learners to demonstrate knowledge of the subject, the language in which they demonstrate that knowledge is flexible. Side-by-side bilingual materials and tests could help teachers in both North and South move toward stronger, more additive approaches to bi-/multilingual education.

CONCLUSION

This chapter has challenged all of us to reconsider many of the assumptions made in educational development regarding language issues. If we can learn to recognize the monolingual habitus inherent in educational policies and practices, even bi- and multilingual ones, we have the potential to change the paradigm. This will lead to greater recognition of the linguistic and cultural resources that learners bring with them to the learning process, which will in turn lead to development of methods and materials that maximize those resources to promote not only communicative competence but also cognitive development. There are already some good examples of what is possible in both North and South.

Preparing learners for a healthy future, even a global one, should not in any context mean focusing on a single dominant language – it should mean developing the bi-/multilingual skills needed to have healthy, productive lives with meaningful interaction at the home and family, community, regional, national and global levels. If we meet the challenge of adopting a multilingual habitus, we will help learners develop these skills through educational approaches that are liberatory for all.

NOTES

[i] I am very grateful to Kimmo Kosonen, my very sharp co-editor, and to Dennis Malone, also a trusted colleague and friend, for their insightful and supportive comments and suggestions on earlier versions of this chapter.

[ii] With apologies for the geographically imprecise nature of the terms, I will use "North" and "South" to discuss high- and low-income countries, respectively.

[iii] The 2011 CIES conference theme of "Education which liberates" inspired me to consider the liberatory potential of adopting a multilingual rather than a monolingual habitus in education.

[iv] This approach can be traced to the roots of French nationalism, which are alive today according to Hélot (2008). The monolingual habitus also prevents people from noticing that the approach has failed overall; while certain languages are endangered (e.g. Basque in the French Basque Country), non-dominant identities (e.g. being Basque) persist and revitalization efforts continue.

[v] The Bantu language family is known as a continuum by linguistic scholars because of the relatively minor differences between neighboring languages, particularly in eastern and southern Africa. Prah (2008) among others argues that harmonization of major African languages would raise their status as international languages and as languages of instruction.

[vi] Scaffolding refers to providing contextual cues, gestures, hints, or terms that help learners bridge the gap between what they know and what they are trying to accomplish.

[vii] Interestingly, in Madagascar we have also found the need to refine the term L1, using $L1_{fam}$ to distinguish between the variety of Malagasy spoken at home with the family and $L1_{std}$ for the standard variety of Malagasy used in teaching and learning materials and the media.

[viii] PRAESA, Project for the Study of Alternative Education in Southern Africa, has long been a resource for multilingual educators under the leadership of Neville Alexander. The term was developed over the four years (2002-2005) during which PRAESA ran a Training of Trainers in Multilingual Education known as TOTSA (see Benson & Plüddemann 2010).

[ix] See e.g. this UNESCO site http://www.unesco.org/new/en/education/themes/strengthening-education-systems/languages-in-education/multilingual-education/, other SIL International links like http://www.sil.org/literacy/youtube_mle_videos.htm and the the newly-formed MLE network based in Washington DC http://www.mlenetwork.org/faq.

[x] See e.g. http://mlephil.wordpress.com/2012/03/08/deped-to-use-12-languages-for-june-classes/ regarding DepEd Order No. 16 calling for implementation of MTB-MLE in all public schools.

[xi] NDL in this broad context includes any language that is different from the DL, even "low" varieties of the DL itself, where they are significantly different in status and/or mutual intelligibility.

[xii] The example of Malagasy in Madagascar was mentioned above.

[xiii] In this broad context DLs may be plural, e.g. in contexts where bilingual education in DLs is offered without considering the NDL(s) of learners.

[xiv] Most countries use DLs to train teachers, even where they will be using NDLs to teach, e.g. in Ethiopia whose policy calls for 8 years of L1-medium education (Benson et al., 2012).

[xv] The bilingual education program in Cambodia is a notable exception, where Community School Management Committees made up of elders and parents recruit local teachers, give language- and culture-related input into the curriculum and monitor attendance (Benson & Kosonen, 2012).

[xvi] I am grateful to Dennis Malone for pointing out that parent perceptions are not innate but rather the result of long-term stigmatization of NDLs. In countless contexts parents were punished when they went to school for using their home languages, being made to kneel in the hot sun, having a sign hung around their necks, being struck or being subjected to other demeaning punishments.

[xvii] Here I am referring only to literacy programs, as I do not have enough experience with Adult Basic Education/Adult Learning and Education programs to comment.

[xviii] Professor Ajit Mohanty, powerpoint presentation on issues in multilingual education at the Building Peace conference, 8 April 2011, Istanbul, Turkey.

[xix] In this paper I have used the term literacy (singular) in the manner traditional to educational development, but more recent academic discussions are influenced by the New Literacy Studies (e.g. Street, 2003) that consider literacies to involve social contexts and modalities beyond simply reading and writing.

[xx] See e.g. http://www.praesa.org.za/projects/terminology-development.

REFERENCES

Alexander, Neville (June 2003). *Language education policy, national and sub-national identities in South Africa. Guide for the development of language education policies in Europe: From linguistic diversity to plurilingual education.* Reference study. Strasbourg, France: Council of Europe, Language Policy Division. (http://www.coe.int/t/dg4/linguistic/source/alexanderen.pdf)

Benson, Carol (2008). Language "choice" in education. PRAESA Occasional Papers No. 30. Cape Town: University of Cape Town.

Benson, Carol (November 2010). *Report of technical consultancy on language-in-education policy and curriculum development in the Maldives, September 2010.* Unpublished report prepared for the MoE and UNICEF in Male,' Maldives and Hifab International in Stockholm, Sweden.

Benson, Carol, Heugh, Kathleen, Bogale, Berhanu, & Gebre Yohannes, Mekonnen (2012). Multilingual education in Ethiopian primary schools. In Tove Skutnabb-Kangas & Kathleen Heugh (Eds.), *Multilingual education and sustainable diversity work. From periphery to centre* (pp. 32-61). London, UK: Routledge.

Benson, Carol, & Kosonen, Kimmo (2012). A critical comparison of language-in-education policy and practice in four Southeast Asian countries and Ethiopia. In Tove Skutnabb-Kangas & Kathleen Heugh (Eds.), *Multilingual education and sustainable diversity work. From periphery to centre* (pp. 111-137). London, UK: Routledge.

Benson, Carol, & Plüddemann, Peter (2010). Empowerment of bilingual education professionals: The training of trainers programme for educators in multilingual settings in southern Africa (ToTSA) 2002-2005. *International Journal of Bilingual Education and Bilingualism, 13*(3), 371-394.

Bialystok, Ellen, Luk, Gigi, & Kwan, Ernest (2005). Bilingualism, biliteracy, and learning to read: Interactions among languages and writing systems. *Scientific Studies of Reading, 9*, 43-61.

Bourdieu, Pierre (1991). *Language and symbolic power.* Cambridge, UK: Cambridge University Press.

Brock-Utne, Birgit (2006). Learning through a familiar language versus learning through a foreign language: A look into some secondary school classrooms in Tanzania. In Birgit Brock-Utne, Zubeida Desai, & Martha Qorro (Eds.), *Focus on fresh data on the language of instruction debate in Tanzania and South Africa* (pp. 19-41). Cape Town: African Minds.

Cenoz, Jasone (2009). *Towards multilingual education. Basque educational research from an international perspective.* Clevedon: Multilingual Matters.

Chimbutane, Feliciano (2011). *Rethinking bilingual education in postcolonial contexts.* Clevedon, UK: Multilingual Matters.

Chimbutane, Feliciano, & Benson, Carol (2012). Expanded spaces for Mozambican languages in primary education: Where bottom-up meets top-down. In Teresa McCarty & Nancy Hornberger (Eds.), *Globalization from the bottom up: Indigenous language planning and policy in globalizing spaces and places.* Special issue of the *International Multilingual Research Journal, 6*(1), 8-21.

Council of Europe. (2002). Common European Framework of Reference for Languages. (http://www.coe.int/t/dg4/linguistic/Cadre1_en.asp)

Council of Europe (Feb. 2006). Plurilingual education in Europe. 50 years of international cooperation. Strasbourg, France: Council of Europe, Language Policy Division.

(http://www.coe.int/t/dg4/linguistic/Source/PlurinlingalEducation_En.pdf)

Cummins, Jim (2000). Putting language proficiency in its place: Responding to critiques of the conversational/ academic language distinction. In Jasone Cenoz & Ulrike Jessner (Eds.), *English in Europe. The acquisition of a third language.* Clevedon: Multilingual Matters.

Cummins, Jim (2009). Fundamental psycholinguistic and sociological principles underlying educational successs for linguistic minority students. In Tove Skutnabb-Kangas, Robert Phillipson, Ajit Mohanty, & Minati Panda (Eds.), *Social justice through multilingual education* (pp. 19-35). Clevedon, UK: Multilingual Matters.

Elorza, Itziar, & Muñoa, Itziar (2008). Promoting the minority language through integrated plurilingual language planning: The case of the Ikastolas. *Language, Culture & Curriculum, 21*(1), 85-101.

Freire, Paulo (1970). *Pedagogy of the oppressed.* Trans. Myra Bergman Ramos. New York, NY: Herder and Herder.

Gogolin, Ingrid (2002). Linguistic and cultural diversity in Europe: A challenge for educational research and practice. ECER Keynote. *European Educational Research Journal, 1*(1), 123-138.

Hélot, Christine (2007). *Du bilinguisme en famille au plurilinguisme à l'école.* Paris: L'Harmattan.

Hélot, Christine (2008). Penser le bilinguisme autrement. In Christine Hélot, Britta Benert, Sabine Ehrhart, & Andrea Young (Eds.), *Penser le bilinguisme autrement* (pp. 9-27). Frankfurt am Main: Peter Lang.

Hélot, Christine, & Ó Laoire, Muiris (Eds.) (2011). *Language policy for the multilingual classroom. Pedagogy of the possible.* Clevedon, UK: Multilingual Matters.

Heugh, Kathleen (2011). Theory and practice – Language education models in Africa: Research, design, decision-making and outcomes. In Adama Ouane & Christine Glanz (Eds.), *Optimising learning, education and publishing in Africa: The language factor. A review and analysis of theory and practice in mother-tongue and bilingual education in sub-Saharan Africa* (pp. 103-156). Hamburg, Germany: UNESCO (UIL)/ADEA. (http://unesdoc.unesco.org/images/0021/002126/212602e.pdf)

Heugh, Kathleen, Benson, Carol, Bogale, Berhanu, & Gebre Yohannes, Mekonnen (2007). *Final report: Study on medium of instruction in primary schools in Ethiopia.* Research report commissioned by the Ministry of Education, Addis Ababa, September to December 2006.

Heugh, Kathleen, Benson, Carol, Bogale, Berhanu, & Gebre Yohannes, Mekonnen (2012). Implications for multilingual education: Student achievement in different models of education in Ethiopia. In Tove Skutnabb-Kangas & Kathleen Heugh (Eds.), *Multilingual education and sustainable diversity work. From periphery to centre* (pp. 239-262). London, UK: Routledge.

Hovens, Mart (2002). Bilingual education in West Africa: Does it work? *International Journal of Bilingual Education and Bilingualism, 5*(5), 249-266.

King, Kendall & Benson, Carol (2004). Spanish and indigenous language education in the Andes. In James Tollefson & Amy Tsui (Eds.), *Medium of instruction policies: Whose agenda? Which agenda?* (pp. 241-261). Mahwah, NJ: Lawrence Erlbaum Associates.

Kosonen, Kimmo (2010). Ethnolinguistic minorities and non-dominant languages in mainland Southeast Asian language-in-education policies. In MacLeans A. Geo-JaJa & Suzanne Majhanovich (Eds.), *Education, language, and economics: Growing national and global dilemmas* (pp. 73-88). Rotterdam: Sense Publishers.

López, Luis Enrique (2009). Reaching the unreached: Indigenous intercultural bilingual education in Latin America. Background paper prepared for the Education for All Global Monitoring Report 2010 *Reaching the marginalized.* Paris: UNESCO.
(http://unesdoc.unesco.org/images/0018/001866/186620e.pdf)

Plüddemann, Peter, Braam, Daryl, Broeder, Peter, Extra, Guus, & October, Michellé (2004). *Language policy implementation and language vitality in Western Cape primary schools.* PRAESA Occasional Papers no. 15. Cape Town, South Africa: PRAESA.
(http://web.uct.ac.za/depts/praesa/all%20andy%20pdf%20feb07mar11/Paper15a.pdf)

Prah, Kwesi K. (2008). Language, literacy and knowledge production in Africa. In Brian Street & Nancy Hornberger (Eds.), *Encyclopedia of language and education* (2nd ed.) Vol. 2: *Literacy* (pp. 29-39). New York: Springer.

Ruiz, Richard (1984). Orientations in language planning. *Journal of the National Association of Bilingual Education, 8*, 15-34.

Skutnabb-Kangas, Tove (2000). *Linguistic genocide in education – Or worldwide diversity and human rights?* Mahwah, NJ: Lawrence Erlbaum Associates.

Skutnabb-Kangas, Tove & Heugh, Kathleen (Eds.) (2012). *Multilingual education and sustainable diversity work. From periphery to centre.* London, UK: Routledge.

Street, Brian (2003). What's "new" in new literacy studies? Critical approaches to literacy in theory and practice. *Current Issues in Comparative Education, 5*(2), 77-91.

Thomas, Wayne, & Collier, Virginia (2002). *A national study of school effectiveness for language minority students' long-term academic achievement.* Santa Cruz, CA: Center for Research on Education, Diversity and Excellence. (http://crede.berkeley.edu/research/crede/research/llaa/1.1_final.html)

UNESCO (2003). *Education in a multilingual world.* UNESCO Education Position Paper. Paris: UNESCO. (http://unesdoc.unesco.org/images/0012/001297/129728e.pdf)

Walter, Stephen (2008). The language of instruction issue: Framing an empirical perspective. In Bernard Spolsky & Francis Hult (Eds.), *The handbook of educational linguistics* (pp. 129-146). Malden, MA: Blackwell.

World Bank (April 2011). *Project appraisal document. Report no. 60595-MZ.* Washington, DC: World Bank. (http://www-wds.worldbank.org/external/default/WDSContentServer/WDSP/IB/2011/04/11/000333037_20110411004759/Rendered/PDF/605950PAD0P1251OFFICIAL0USE0ONLY191.pdf)

Carol Benson
International Consultant in Educational Language Issues

CONTRIBUTOR BIOGRAPHIES

EDITORS

Carol Benson PhD is an experienced educator, researcher and consultant on educational language issues in multilingual societies. She has worked in formal (teacher training, curriculum development) and non-formal (literacy, gender equity) education in the Asia, Latin America and Africa regions, most recently in Cambodia and Madagascar. On leave from Stockholm University in Sweden, she continues to pursue interests in European regional and minority languages in education and is a believer in multilingualism for all. cbenson57@hotmail.com

Kimmo Kosonen PhD is Senior Consultant in multilingual education with SIL International as well as a lecturer and researcher at Payap University in Chiang Mai, Thailand. His research and publications focus on multilingual education policy and practice, non-formal education, language planning and the linguistic development of non-dominant languages in low-income countries. Originally from Finland, he has been living and working in Asia for about 15 years. kimmo_kosonen@sil.org

AUTHORS ACCORDING TO THE ORDER OF CHAPTERS

Jessica Ball MPH, PhD is a third generation Irish-English Canadian. She has worked on three continents at all levels of education from early childhood to post-graduate teaching certification for university professors. She has been instrumental in developing several innovative approaches to post-secondary education in Asia, Africa, and the Middle East. She is currently a professor in Child and Youth Care at the University of Victoria, Canada, where her research (www.ecdip.org) includes many collaborative studies on language issues involving Indigenous communities around the world. jball@uvic.ca

Onowa McIvor MA, PhD is Swampy Cree and Scottish-Canadian. She is the Director of Indigenous Education in the Faculty of Education at the University of Victoria, Canada. She was born and raised in Northern Saskatchewan and has been a grateful visitor on Coast and Straits Salish territories for over 15 years. Her current areas of research are Indigenous language revitalization and Indigenous education from ECCD and K-12 through post-secondary. omcivor@uvic.ca

Stephen Bahry EdD has been a second language educator in Canada, China and Central Asia. Currently he is a lecturer and visiting scholar at Ontario Institute for Studies in Education, University of Toronto, Canada. His dissertation focused on stakeholder perspectives on endangered non-dominant language and culture in education in China. His current work centers on educational attainment among linguistic minorities and on quality education that incorporates community perspectives, knowledge, culture and languages. s.bahry@utoronto.ca

Birgit Brock-Utne PhD is affiliated with the University of Oslo, Norway as a Professor in Education and Development. She is co-coordinator of the Language of Instruction in Tanzania and South Africa project (www.loitasa.org). She has been a visiting professor in Austria, Japan, New Zealand, Spain, Tanzania, and the USA, and has written, co-authored and co-edited many publications on peace studies, education, development and languages in Africa. birgitbuno@yahoo.no

Laura Menchaca Bishop MA is a PhD student in Sociocultural Anthropology at Cornell University. She has worked in a variety of educational contexts, from teaching English to refugees and immigrants at the International Rescue Committee to directing a teacher education program in the Dominican Republic. Her scholarly interests include critical approaches to education for social/political change; migration; Indigenous and feminist epistemologies; language policy/ bilingual education; and human rights. Lrm223@cornell.edu

Prema Kelley MA is a recent graduate from Teachers College, Columbia University, USA. She has taught at the elementary level in International schools in Beijing, China and Mexico City, Mexico. She currently teaches Spanish at Battery Park City School, New York, USA. She is dedicated to promoting dialogue between educational systems around the world and advocating for immigrant rights in the USA. pk2333@columbia.edu

Karla Giuliano Sarr MEd is a PhD candidate at the Center for International Education at the University of Massachusetts Amherst, USA. Her research interests include the implications of language issues, learning content for students and their communities, and the interplay between indigenous knowledge, globalization, and development. Previously Karla served as a Peace Corps Volunteer in Gabon and then worked at Africa Consultants International/Baobab Center in Senegal. ksarr@educ.umass.edu

Elizabeth Pearce holds an MEd in International Education Policy from Harvard University, USA, and is the Education Director for Save the Children in Bangladesh. Over the last 10 years, she has played a key role in the design, implementation and evaluation of multilingual education programs in Guatemala, Vietnam, the Philippines, Nepal and Bangladesh. She is co-author of CfBT Education Trust's guidelines *Closer to home: How schools in low- and middle-income countries respond to children's language needs* (2011). elizabeth.pearce@savethechildren.org

Meherun Nahar Shapna holds an MSS in Sociology from Dhaka University and an MEd from Asian University, Bangladesh. She is the Project Manager of Shishur

Khamatayan, Save the Children in Bangladesh's Multilingual Education program. Previously she worked for UNICEF's Hard to Reach project and for PROSHIKA, a large national NGO in Bangladesh. She began her career as a primary school teacher and soon became a passionate educational activist. meherun.nahar@savethechildren.org

Gowri Vijayakumar MEd is a PhD candidate in Sociology at the University of California Berkeley, USA, focusing broadly on gender, development, and globalization. Previously she worked for Save the Children as an Education Policy officer, contributing research to the policy report *Language and education: The missing link* (2009). As a research fellow with Save the Children in Bangladesh, she conducted research on a bilingual and bicultural preschool program for Adivasi children. gowri@berkeley.edu

Janella M. Johnson continues to work in the field of professional development for teachers at the Region VIII Equity Assistance Center at Metropolitan State University of Denver. In 2011 she completed her doctoral dissertation on cross-border professional development at the University of Arizona, Tucson, USA, and then worked as a coordinator for Project SEED (formerly CASS). Janelle was a teacher and teacher-educator in Guatemala for seven years. jjohn428@msudenver.edu

Rebecca Stone EdD is an international curriculum, training and literacy specialist. She has nine years of experience in creating and facilitating materials development, designing and delivering teacher training, and conducting research in Benin, Brazil, Cambodia, Egypt, Ethiopia, the Gambia, Mali, Niger, the Philippines, and Senegal. She specializes in participatory and active training design and implementation, early grade reading improvement, and mother tongue-based multilingual education in low resource contexts. rstone@air.org

Pauline Rea-Dickins PhD is Director of the Aga Khan University Institute of Educational Development, East Africa. She previously worked as Director of Research in the Graduate School of Education and Professor of Applied Linguistics in Education at the University of Bristol, UK. She is widely published in language program evaluation and language testing and assessment. Her most recent research project examined the dynamics of language in school achievement (www.bristol.ac.uk/spine). pauline.rea-dickins@aku.edu

Guoxing Yu PhD is Senior Lecturer and Coordinator of the Doctor of Education in Applied Linguistics at the University of Bristol, UK. His main research interests are language testing and assessment as well as school effectiveness in relation to language and literacy development. He has directed several funded research projects, and published in top journals of his field. Currently he is an Executive Editor of the journal *Assessment in Education*. guoxing.yu@bristol.ac.uk

Nuzzly Ruiz de Forsberg holds a PhD in International Education from Stockholm University, Sweden. She has worked for international organizations like the UN and EU on implementing and managing large-scale educational programs in Latin American and African countries. She has focused on human resource development of teachers and education managers in early childhood and primary education as well as in health education, HIV prevention, gender and special needs education. nuzzlyruiz@gmail.com

Alícia Borges Månsson holds an MA in International Education and has over a decade of experience working in development cooperation in coordination, management, preparation, implementation and evaluation of education and health projects in countries of Africa, Asia and Latin America. She has developed, coordinated and facilitated international training programs and seminars, and has undertaken research studies and assessments in educational reforms in Angola, Bolivia, Cape Verde, and Mozambique. alicia.bm@comhem.se

Kerry White received her MA in International Development Studies in 2012 at George Washington University's Elliott School of International Affairs, Washington DC, USA. Her capstone project was an evaluation of the impact of secondary school scholarships on young women in Malawi. She is currently a business development coordinator and member of the Latin America-Caribbean team at the Education Development Center. Kerry has lived in New York, Northern Ireland and China, and now calls Washington DC home. kerryewhite@gmail.com

Leila Schroeder MA is Senior Consultant in multilingual education and literacy with SIL International, based in Nairobi, Kenya. Prior to her twenty years of work in sub-Saharan African countries, she was a classroom teacher in the USA. She now develops language-specific reading curricula and materials to support first language literacy, oral second language instruction and literacy and early childhood language development, as well as training teachers and advising on orthography development for previously unwritten languages. leila_schroeder@sil.org

Stephen L. Walter PhD is Associate Professor of Language Development at the Graduate Institute of Applied Linguistics in Dallas, Texas, USA and Senior Consultant in literacy and education at SIL International. His research and publications focus primarily on multilingual education in low-income countries, most recently on MLE experiments in Cameroon, the Philippines, Thailand, and Vietnam with a focus on assessment and MLE program evaluation. His latest publications have appeared in the *International Review of Education* and the *Cambridge Handbook of Language Policy*. steve_walter@gial.edu

CPSIA information can be obtained
at www.ICGtesting.com
Printed in the USA
LVOW04s0116040916
502783LV00007B/16/P